```
<html>
<script

language=
```

JavaScript Essentials

About the Author...

Jason J. Manger is a U.K.-based
Internet consultant specializing
in Web-based solutions. He is
the author of four books and
two CD-ROMs.

JavaScript Essentials

Jason J. Manger

Osborne **McGraw-Hill**

Berkeley New York St. Louis San Francisco
Auckland Bogotá Hamburg London Madrid
Mexico City Milan Montreal New Delhi Panama City
Paris São Paulo Singapore Sydney
Tokyo Toronto

Osborne **McGraw-Hill**
2600 Tenth Street
Berkeley, California 94710
U.S.A.

For information on translations or book distributors outside the U.S.A., or to arrange bulk purchase discounts for sales promotions, premiums, or fundraisers, please contact Osborne/**McGraw-Hill** at the above address.

JavaScript Essentials

1234567890 DOC 99876

ISBN 0-07-882234-3

Publisher
Brandon A. Nordin

Acquisitions Editor
Megg Bonar

Project Editor
Mark Karmendy

Copy Editor
Marcia Baker

Proofreader
Pat Mannion

Computer Designer
Jani Beckwith

Series Design
Marcela V. Hancik

Illustrator
Lance Ravella

Quality Control Specialist
Joe Scuderi

Cover Design
Ted Mader Associates, Inc.

Contents at a Glance

Table of Contents

Foreword

Introduction to the Java Technologies

Java-related technologies have taken the Internet by storm, and deservedly so because they have brought the first executable content to the World Wide Web. *Executable content* is a phrase applied to HTML documents containing embedded programs that run *within* the hypertext document. Java was the first technology to bring such content to the Web allowing small Java programs, known as *applets*, to be embedded within a HyperText Mark-up Language (HTML) page. JavaScript arrived on the scene after Java had taken center stage, late in the fourth quarter of 1995, even though a prototype in the form of the scripting language LiveScript was already built into the Netscape Navigator 2.0 client. LiveScript was part of the Netscape LiveWire server product, and was intended as a scripting language to query information held on the server, as well as aiding in day-to-day administration tasks. Netscape abandoned the LiveScript name and started to collaborate with Sun Microsystems, developers of the Java programming language, on a new language, namely JavaScript.

JavaScript is the most important of many scripting languages currently in development. JavaScript, although available within a server-based product, is primarily a client-based technology and is built into the popular Netscape Navigator Web browser—the *de facto* Web client that, according to

Dataquest, is used by an estimated 84 percent of the World Wide Web (which itself now has an estimated 10 to 20 million Internet users).

"Scripting" Versus "Programming"

Many would argue that JavaScript is not a programming language at all, but rather a *scripting* language. Scripting and programming are closely related. Their concepts often overlap, although their purposes are quite different. Scripting is often seen as "cut-down programming"—tools for simple, repetitive tasks—although in fact these "scripts" form the backbone of many Internet-based solutions. Like Java, JavaScript programs are compiled into an internal representation—known as "byte-code"—which is then executed by interpreter software. Navigator 3.0 has a JavaScript interpreter built in as standard, allowing JavaScript source code to be parsed and executed.

The argument between "interpreted" and "compiled" languages is not the main distinguishing factor between Java and JavaScript. In reality there is no such thing as an interpreted or compiled language; nearly every programming language can be either compiled or interpreted, or both. Java programs undergo a process of manual compilation by the user into an architecture-neutral, byte-code format, which can be interpreted by a Java-aware Web browser such as Navigator, Hot Java, and now Microsoft's Internet Assistant. Java applets can therefore *migrate* anywhere on the Internet where the appropriate Web browser is installed, and all of the main operating-system platforms are now catered for. JavaScript is very similar in this respect because it too is compiled into a byte-code format before being executed by the browser, although users do not have to manually compile their code before it is executed; this is done automatically by Navigator, which interprets the literal code. JavaScript programs can migrate to any place a JavaScript-aware browser is installed, and the contents of the program will be executed.

JavaScript: Java "Lite"?

Java and JavaScript share very little, albeit for some similarities in language syntax and object creation. The description of JavaScript as Java "lite" is not accurate. Some of the standard Java objects and constructors have been shared with JavaScript, although Netscape really sees JavaScript as a foundation for building HTML applications that allow Java and HTML features to be more closely integrated with one another. Navigator 3.0 now has concrete facilities that allow JavaScript programs to communicate with Java applets running within the current application, allowing variables and functions defined within publicly defined Java classes to be referenced. This system, known as LiveConnect, is touched upon in Chapter 11.

For the HTML author JavaScript represents an excellent step forward to building HTML systems that *interact* with the user. Client-side integration is where JavaScript excels. It is not meant to be a full-scale programming language, such as Java and C++, but rather an extension to HTML that facilitates interaction with the underlying browser. With JavaScript, the standard HTML tags have been enhanced and have the ability to interact with JavaScript's objects and properties. Concepts such as "events" and "event-handlers" are gradually integrated into HTML, allowing it to be event-driven. Most important of all is the fact that JavaScript is *real* executable content—applications that are physically embedded within HTML documents, unlike Java applets that reside externally from the HTML document that invokes them.

Netscape's strength was in quickly realizing that Java had great potential to be highly popular, hence the rapid inclusion of a Java Virtual Machine (the software that interprets Java programs) into their *de facto* Web client Netscape Navigator 2.0. The integration of a Java Virtual Machine into Navigator 2.0 and 3.0 means that the majority of Web users is already running a Java-compatible system. At the time of writing, Netscape 2.0 and Atlas (Navigator 3.0) are the only commercial Web clients that fully support both JavaScript and Java. Sun's Hot Java was the first to support the Java language, and more companies are expected to license both technologies in the near future. Java has been licensed by Microsoft, IBM, and Oracle. JavaScript will probably follow this pattern now that Sun Microsystems and Netscape are co-developing the language as an open standard. Microsoft's Internet Explorer now supports JavaScript, albeit a few functions, and will be extended in later versions.

Netscape also realized that the Web development community, primarily the many thousands of HTML authors, required something more akin to "HTML programming"—effectively, a halfway house between HTML and Java. After all, Java itself provides very few facilities for an applet to communicate with the browser, something that JavaScript directly addresses, and that users need in their applications.

What Can I Actually Use JavaScript for?

All of the events generated by the Navigator browser, such as button-clicking and page-navigation, can be detected and acted upon by a JavaScript application. These events are important because they allow the program and browser to interface with each other more closely. For example, a JavaScript application can detect when a user leaves a page and can then invoke a suitable response. Selecting an item from a selection list, or submitting a form, can all be detected. JavaScript is also very good at handling housekeeping tasks such as form validation, string manipulation, and the generation of dynamic HTML. *Dynamic HTML* is the process of creating HTML content within a JavaScript application and is one of the most important facilities that the JavaScript language offers. Nearly all of the HTML applications that you eventually write will generate dynamic HTML in order to control the appearance of a hypertext document. An HTML/JavaScript application can control its own appearance according to pre-specified conditions that the author has laid down; for example, a Web site could change its appearance without its author having to daily re-alter all of the HTML tags.

Here are some of the other uses for the JavaScript language:

♦ Generating HTML *on the fly* from within a JavaScript program

♦ Validating fields in an HTML form prior to submitting them to a server

♦ Obtaining *local* user input to control JavaScript actions, and allowing the user to make choices to invoke various actions within the browser

♦ Showing properly windowed messages to the user, e.g. warnings and input-prompts, etc.

♦ Creating advanced navigational documents using frames and windows

♦ Detecting and interfacing with Java applets and Netscape plug-ins

JavaScript makes the once frowned upon phrase "HTML programming" more acceptable. We hope you find *JavaScript Essentials* of use in your work. Let me know how you get on.

Jason Manger

✉ wombat@spuddy.mew.co.uk

August 1996

Acknowledgments

I would like to acknowledge everyone at Osborne/McGraw-Hill for their hard work on this, my first U.S. book project. In particular I would like to thank Scott Rogers, for signing the contract, and Megg Bonar, my editor, for putting up with me. Thanks also to Mark Karmendy, Cynthia Douglas, Heidi Poulin, and Cindy Brown for all their valuable input.

At McGraw-Hill Europe my thanks to Fred Perkins and Maria Catt for coordinating this interdivisional project.

Introduction

Readership Details

JavaScript Essentials is aimed primarily at **HTML authors**. In many ways JavaScript can be thought of as an extension to HTML because it enhances the language with new facilities, such as objects and events. This is also a book for **Netscape Navigator users**. JavaScript is a client-based technology and is built into Navigator 2.0 and above. Novice programmers may also find JavaScript a stepping-stone to the more advanced Java programming language. Some exposure to HTML (HyperText Mark-up Language) is an essential prerequisite for using this book because JavaScript extends many of HTML's existing facilities. You cannot use JavaScript without some knowledge of HTML, and while *JavaScript Essentials* is not a guide to HTML itself, you will be exposed to a significant amount of HTML through using this book as various concepts and examples are introduced.

JavaScript Essentials is not structured as an "A-to-Z of JavaScript," but rather as a JavaScript/HTML primer. Each part of the HTML language (frames, forms, hyperlinks, etc.) is explained and then examined in greater detail to see how JavaScript can be applied to these individual areas. Each chapter contains detailed descriptions, tips, and examples. The emphasis in this book is on source code. Examining source code is by far the best way of learning the internals of any programming language, and a multitude of examples have been coded during the writing of this book for your benefit. Nevertheless, you can still expect to find rigorous descriptions and detailed explanations of each JavaScript concept.

Software Version Information

JavaScript works with both the 16-bit and 32-bit versions of Netscape Navigator version 2.0 and above. All of the JavaScript examples in this book have been tested with a range of Navigator versions including: **Navigator 2.01**, **Navigator 3.0 PR1**, **Navigator 3.0 PR2**, **Navigator beta 4**, **beta 5**, and **beta 6**, all of which were available at the time of writing. Needless to say, JavaScript has undergone many changes during these versions.

The majority of this book was written using **Netscape Navigator 3.0**. This is the minimum version we recommend that you use for your personal JavaScript development, although all currently documented features should also be forward-compatible with Navigator 4.0 (code-named "Galileo" at the time of writing). Many features of JavaScript running under Netscape Navigator 3.0 are not backwards-compatible with Navigator 2.0. Some of the new features found in **Netscape Navigator 3.0** include the following:

♦ New object-creation facilities, object constructors, and object prototyping

♦ Java/JavaScript interaction facilities

♦ Plug-in application detection and handling

♦ Window manipulation and focusing

♦ Image events and event-handlers

♦ Form-element types

♦ Data-type and object interrogation facilities

♦ Random number facilities

♦ Dynamic event-handler allocation

♦ Dynamic updating of buttons and selection objects

♦ Loading autonomous JavaScript programs from different URLs

What You Will Learn...

JavaScript Essentials is a practical guide to integrating JavaScript into your HTML documents, and for building "client-aware" applications. With *JavaScript Essentials* you can expect to learn how to:

♦ Program in the JavaScript language

♦ Develop interactive and dynamic HTML documents

♦ Integrate HTML constructs such as forms and hyperlinks with JavaScript programs

♦ Develop applications that use Navigator's latest facilities, such as frameset-documents

♦ Use JavaScript's cookie mechanism to create persistent objects, and use JavaScript to control plug-ins

♦ Interface Java and JavaScript programs with each other

Needless to say, through using this book you will also learn a significant amount of HTML, the *lingua franca* of the World Wide Web. Here is a quick overview of the book broken down by chapter: **Chapter 1** explains how to integrate JavaScript programs into HTML documents using the new <script> container tag. This chapter illustrates how it is possible to use the <script> container within the header and body sections of an HTML document, and discusses backwards-compatibility problems for other browsers and their solutions. **Chapter 2** examines JavaScript's integration with HTML hyperlinks and modifications to the <a href> tag. JavaScript's anchor and link objects are also explained in detail. Coverage of dynamic hyperlink and anchor creation is also discussed. **Chapter 3** is a guide to using JavaScript statements, including flow control and iteration statements such as for and while, and conditional statements, such as the if and ? statements. **Chapter 4** examines JavaScript's object model, and looks at JavaScript's diverse range of objects including internal objects, HTML-reflected objects, and navigator (browser) objects. **Chapter 5** is concerned with JavaScript's event-system. Events can be attached to HTML objects such as buttons, hyperlinks, frames, and time-outs, and each area is dealt with using a number of examples. **Chapter 6** examines how user-defined JavaScript objects can be created, and concentrates on Navigator 3.0's new constructors such as Array() and Object(). **Chapter 7** examines JavaScript's integration with HTML forms. Forms are the main mechanism for providing user input within a hypertext document, and JavaScript can be used for a variety of form validation and manipulation tasks. This chapter examines each form element (button, text-field, checkbox, etc.) and looks at how JavaScript reflects these elements into objects. **Chapter 8** discusses how windowed applications can be created, allowing multiple documents to be updated and manipulated. Window validation, opening, and closing are all discussed, as is Navigator's new opener property that makes parent-child window handling more straightforward. **Chapter 9** covers Netscape's new frameset-document features and examines how JavaScript applications can manipulate multiple-framed documents to create sophisticated navigational controls and multiple-document applications. Dynamic frame creation and variable scoping are also discussed in detail, and examples demonstrate each concept.

Chapter 10 looks at JavaScript's time-out events and how these can be used to create applications such as real-time clocks and other time-dependent applications. **Chapter 11** examines how Navigator 3.0 allows Java and JavaScript programs to communicate with one another, and introduces the new `document.applets` property for this purpose. **Chapter 12** looks at how JavaScript can be used to manipulate plug-in applications. Plug-ins are similar to "helper applications," although they run *within* the browser environment, rather like a Java applet. Many dozens of plug-ins now exist allowing HTML pages to deal with complex data-formats, including spreadsheets, word processing, and many other audio/visual files. Finally, **Chapter 13** examines Netscape's client-side cookie protocol and the JavaScript `document.cookie` property that facilitates the storing of information locally on disk.

A series of extensive appendixes have also been provided, including Questions & Answers, JavaScript resources on the Internet, JavaScript API and object property reference, mirror-site reference, ready-to-use JavaScript programs (for Netscape Navigator 3.0), URL reference, color code reference, plug-in guide, JavaScript error message reference, Internal GIF image reference, and much more besides.

Be on the look out for the Tip icon. Wherever you see it you can expect to find a quick recap, a tip, or just general advice on a JavaScript or Navigator concept.

What Software and Hardware Will I Need?

To develop programs in JavaScript you will need the following software:

♦ A copy of the **Netscape Navigator** Web browser, version **3.0** or above

♦ An **ASCII editor**, e.g. Windows 95 Notepad, to create your HTML/JavaScript applications

♦ For Internet connectivity, a 32-bit Winsock (TCP/IP software) and an account with an Internet service provider

This book is based upon the **Microsoft Windows 95** version of Netscape Navigator and all of the screen displays have been captured from this environment. The platform you run Navigator under is not critically important since JavaScript's features are essentially the same, irrespective of the underlying operating system that is being used. JavaScript programs are embedded within HTML documents and must be stored as "plain-text," i.e. in the ASCII format (a plain-text editor must be used to edit such files).

T IP: Windows 95 has a 32-bit TCP/IP stack built-in as standard, allowing you to use Netscape Navigator over the Internet to retrieve HTML documents, etc. Installation of this feature is not done by default during the Windows 95 setup, so you may want to read the next section and Appendix J about installing the Windows 95 Winsock. You can install such a Winsock after installing Navigator, although you will not be able to log on to the Internet without this *or* equivalent software, e.g. the Trumpet Winsock 32-bit TCP/IP stack (shareware) —see `http://www.trumpet.com.au` if you already have Internet connectivity.

Netscape Navigator 3.0 is a demanding application, although it will run very well on modest computers. However, memory and CPU power greatly aid the speed of the development process. It goes without saying that Pentium-powered machines will run JavaScript programs and Java applets with much greater response times. This book and all code examples were written and tested using a 486 DX 33-based PC with 4 megabytes of memory, and the speed was adequate. However, this machine specification should be considered the bare minimum; Windows 95 ideally requires 8 megabytes of memory to work effectively.

Installing the Windows 95 Winsock

In order to use Netscape Navigator with an Internet connection, your computer will need to *talk* a language called IP, or *Internet Protocol*. To achieve this you must install software known as a "TCP/IP stack"—TCP/IP being the fundamental protocol used by *all* computers connected to the global Internet network. Windows 95 arrives with a 32-bit TCP/IP stack as standard, and this can be installed if you require such connectivity. The 32-bit version of Netscape Navigator will not communicate with a 16-bit TCP/IP stack, so you must acquire a 32-bit replacement.

Installing Netscape Navigator 3.0

Navigator 3.0 arrives as a self-installing archive. Once downloaded you make a backup copy and then place the archive file in a unique directory location, e.g. `C:\TMP`, and then run the archive by entering its name on the command line within a DOS shell or, alternatively, by pressing the Windows 95 Start button and choosing Run, and then typing the name of the archive. You may want to make sure that you have placed this archive in a separate directory beforehand, however. The installation program will then decompress a number of files and they in turn will be installed in a directory of your choice, e.g. `\NETSCAPE3.0`.

TIP: It is possible to install multiple copies of Netscape Navigator on a single computer, although you must choose a unique directory location for each copy and remember to use the Netscape Options | Preferences menu to choose separate configuration files such as cache settings. You may want to ensure that only one bookmark file is used because this will be applicable to all versions of Navigator. Bookmark files are compatible across the family of Navigator browsers (it is not wise to run multiple Navigator versions while modifying bookmarks, however, because this has been known to cause corruption problems).

Near to the end of the installation process a new group folder for Navigator will be created, and a shortcut icon will be placed in your desktop in order to launch Navigator. You can then delete the files in the temporary directory that were used for the installation (the installation program will not do this automatically). You may want to back up the original Netscape archive just in case you accidentally delete one of Navigator's files, and therefore need to re-install the software from scratch.

Downloading Netscape Navigator   JavaScript is primarily a client-side technology, and is built into the Netscape Navigator browser. Navigator versions 2.0 and above support Java and JavaScript. At the time of writing, Navigator 3.0 is the most up-to-date version. Navigator resides primarily on Netscape's FTP server located at the URL,

```
ftp://ftp.netscape.com
```

although it is also available on many other mirror sites scattered across the Internet. Appendix C has a list of these. The directory in which the program resides is commonly called /pub. Look in the windows directory for the Microsoft Window's versions of the Netscape program. You can use any FTP client to download this file; indeed, you could also use the ftp:// URL in your current version of Navigator. Windows 95 also has a dedicated FTP client (FTP.EXE) that is installed along with the Dial-Up Networking module. You must have already installed the Microsoft 32-bit Winsock (TCP/IP stack) in order to use this facility. Netscape Navigator ships as a commercial product—see Netscape's home page on the Web at

```
http://home.netscape.com
```

for further details, although test versions are made freely available to users at no extra cost (for evaluation purposes). Please read the license details that

arrive with Navigator; you must agree to the license before using
the software.

Using Microsoft's FTP Client

If you have a 32-bit TCP/IP stack, such as the Windows 95 stack, you can use
the ftp.exe program to log in to a server to download Navigator. When
you invoke the ftp.exe program, use the open command along with the
name of the FTP site that you wish to contact; for example,
ftp.netscape.com. Alternatively, you can specify the name of the FTP
server's address directly after the ftp command on the DOS prompt. Once a
connection has been established the remote FTP server will ask you for a
username and then a *password* in order to gain access. Public FTP sites, or
anonymous FTP sites as they are commonly known, will accept the username
anonymous (and sometimes ftp) so that you can gain access to the server,
albeit limited access, to download publicly available files, such as Navigator.
Netscape's server contains a wealth of other information, of course. When
the server finally asks you for a password, simply enter your own Internet
e-mail address in the form user@host.

TIP: If you do not have an e-mail address just use a fictitious address
such as fred@host.com. Access to the server should then be granted. E-mail
is standard with most Internet providers, so if you haven't yet gotten an
Internet account go and subscribe now! Using Navigator without an Internet
connection is possible, although you will be severely limited in what you
can achieve in terms of accessing networked applications and documents,
etc. Without an Internet connection you need to acquire a null-WinSock
application (search the Net for the file MOZOCK.DLL; download it, and then
rename to WINSOCK.DLL. Finally, place it in Navigator's main directory).

You can now move to the appropriate directory and download Netscape, but
be sure to enable *binary* mode first. If you are using Navigator to download
files, binary mode will be invoked automatically. The binary command
should be used with command-driven FTP clients. Binary files are nontext
files, such as images and programs. After this comes the get command along
with the name of the file that you want to download. When the file has
been transferred to your computer the ftp> prompt will return. Now you
should just type **quit** to end your FTP session.

TIP: Each version of Netscape is stored in a different directory according to the platform that it runs under; for example, the Windows 95 version of Netscape resides in the `windows` subdirectory.

It can take approximately 45 minutes to download Navigator 3.0 using a V34/VFAST-type modem at a connection speed of 26-28 Kbps with continuous data transfer, depending on how busy the FTP server actually is. Mirror sites are more responsive if they are located nearer to your own Internet provider. Netscape's FTP server is generally busier in the morning between the hours of 9:00 A.M. and 12:00 P.M. PST (Pacific Standard Time), although in saying this it always seems to be busy these days!

As new versions of Navigator are released to the public new filenames are used to identify each new system. It is best to use Netscape's "mirror-site finder" to locate the most up-to-date version, which is located at the URL:

```
http://home.netscape.com/comprod/mirror/index.html
```

This page will ask you which country you are calling from, your platform details (computer type, and operating system, etc.) and the version of Navigator that you want to download. The nearest known FTP site will then be displayed, along with a hyperlink to the FTP server that has the file. Clicking on the appropriate link will download the file you require. Now it is time to make a cup of coffee, or two, and sit back and read the introduction to see what other delights await you in *JavaScript Essentials*; -)

Problems Accessing Netscape's FTP Server?

You are not alone. Netscape's Web and FTP servers can become *very* busy during peak hours. After all, it is one of the most popular Web sites situated on the entire Internet. For this reason you may have to keep reconnecting to their servers if their maximum user capacity has been reached. It makes sense, therefore, to contact a *mirror site* instead. Mirror sites are duplicate file systems that exist on computers all around the world. For example, a user in the United Kingdom would be silly to try and connect to one of Netscape's FTP servers when they can contact the main Netscape mirror in the UK at the FTP site `sunsite.doc.ic.ac.uk`. Since this site is geographically nearer, response times should be *much* faster.

T IP: Try the machines `ftp1` through `ftp20` as well (e.g. `ftp20.netscape.com`). These may give quicker response times. Mirror sites are usually always faster, remember.

After installing Netscape you should run the appropriate Netscape icon (the Windows 95 installation will create a new group window for you) and enter the Options | General Preferences menu to provide details such as your e-mail address and news/mail servers. If you intend to use Navigator for sending and receiving USENET news and/or e-mail messages, you must provide details of your news and e-mail servers.

Installing Netscape Navigator

As soon as you have downloaded a copy of Netscape, copy it to a temporary directory, e.g. `c:\tmp` (ensuring that this directory is empty—if not, create another) and then make a backup to a floppy disk. Then run the program by typing in the name of the file that you have previously downloaded; for example, the archive containing Netscape Navigator 3.0b4 is named `N3230B4M.EXE`, so you can either run a DOS shell and type this in, or press the Windows 95 Start button and type in the name, e.g. `\tmp\N3230B4M.EXE` in this example. Clearly, these names will have changed by the time you come to download Navigator for yourself (simply change accordingly).

The Navigator installation program will then be executed and the first dialog box you will see asks you to confirm the installation, as shown here:

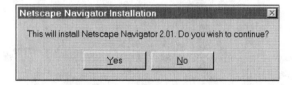

After clicking on Yes to continue, Netscape decompresses a number of files, and runs an Install Shield to install Navigator. Windows 95 now tracks all of the software programs installed under it, thus allowing fast de-installation at a later stage. After decompression, the first screen dialog box appears, as shown in the following illustration.

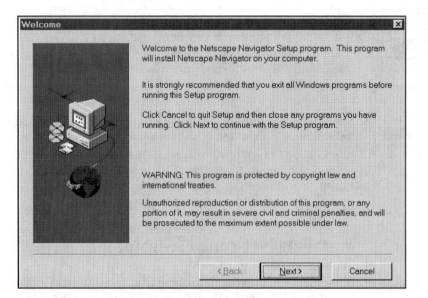

Click on the Next button to continue the installation. As you progress with the installation you are given the option of changing any settings that you have previously entered (until the actual file-copying process starts). You can of course cancel the installation using the Cancel button provided. After pressing the Next button the installation program needs to be told where you want to install this new version of Netscape, as shown here:

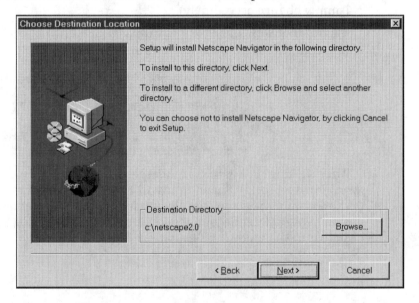

The previous directory location is shown on the screen, and you can accept this by pressing the Next button, in which case the old system will be overwritten, or you can choose Browse to select a new directory. For this example, you are going to install this version to a new directory called \netscape2.01 (you are installing Navigator 2.01 in this instance) so you select Browse and the following dialog box is displayed:

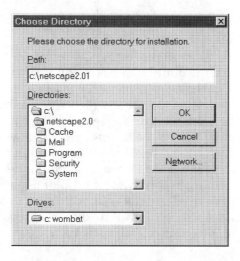

Rather than navigating your way through the list of directories in the lower window, you can quickly enter the name of the directory where you want to install Navigator using the field in the top portion of the window. In this example, type c:\netscape2.01. If the directory you have entered does not exist, the system will first ask you if it can create it. Finally, click on OK to save your choice and then click on the Next button to continue the installation process. Installation now involves copying across the decompressed files into the new directory that you previously selected, as shown here:

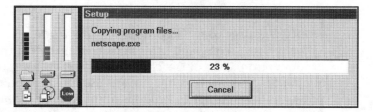

While the files are being copied, the installation program shows you a progress check. When the main percentage bar reaches 95%, the system will create a new folder (or window) for the Netscape program and icons for Navigator and for the README file that accompanies the program. The folders, when created, resemble the ones shown here:

The installation process is now complete. You can close the folder if you require, since the installation will have created an icon on the desktop to launch the new version of Navigator. Remember to delete all the files in the *temporary* directory from which you ran the installation program. You can do this from within a DOS shell using the DOS command `del c:\tmp\*.*`, where `c:\tmp` is the directory in which you ran the installation program. Finally, you will be asked whether or not you want to connect to the Netscape setup site to continue the configuration of the program. Connecting to this site at this point requires Internet access, and a properly configured TCP/IP stack. Choosing Yes to this will run the new version of Netscape where you will be shown a license agreement. Netscape will then attempt to connect you to its Web site at

```
http://home.netscape.com/home/setup.html
```

where you will be guided through the configuration details for Navigator. Depending on how your TCP/IP software is configured, Netscape will attempt to connect to an Internet service provider via your modem device. The Dial-up Networking module of Windows 95 will prompt you for such details automatically (when it is properly configured, that is). You can find more information on Windows 95's TCP/IP stack at the URL:

```
http://www.windows95.com
```

About the disk that Accompanies this Book
The disk that accompanies this book contains all of the source-code examples from each of the chapters (as well as from some appendixes). Supporting files, such as images, are also included on the disk. Each of the programs in *JavaScript Essentials* is numbered. This number corresponds to a file stored on the disk, for example Program 10-1 is the first program of Chapter Ten, and is stored as `10-1.htm` on the disk. More details on the disk, including an index, can be found in Appendix J.

Where Can I Go for More Help?

Well, you can try my home page at

`http://www.mcgraw-hill.co.uk/JJM/index.html`

or you are welcome to e-mail me at

`wombat@spuddy.mew.co.uk`

for a chat. Appendix C lists a number of useful Web- and Internet-based resources where you can obtain all kinds of information on JavaScript-related topics.

CHAPTER 1

Integrating JavaScript with HTML

One advantage of JavaScript is you can take an existing HTML document and make it JavaScript-compliant by making just a few small changes. In fact, no other software is required to use JavaScript because it is a language built into the Netscape Navigator browser. In this chapter you will learn how to:

♦ Use the `<script>` container to embed JavaScript programs within a Web page

♦ Hide JavaScript code from non-JavaScript browsers

♦ Deal with error messages and alert boxes

♦ Test your JavaScript programs within Navigator

The `<script>` and `<noscript>` Tags

Most JavaScript programs travel the Internet within the actual HTML documents requested by users. Whether or not an HTML document contains a JavaScript program cannot be determined until the document containing the program has been loaded into your browser. For Netscape to detect if such a program exists, a new HTML container tag called `<script>` has been introduced. Another container tag, `<noscript>`, has also been introduced to allow HTML authors to detect when JavaScript is *not* enabled, or available.

The `<script>..</script>` container tag is similar to the `<applet>..</applet>` container tag, which is used to load a Java applet (program) into the current hypertext page except with `<script>` the actual program code can be placed within the container tag; it doesn't *necessarily* have to arrive separately from the network.

TIP: Earlier versions of Netscape Navigator (i.e. version 2.0) didn't allow scripts to arrive from a server, although Navigator 3.0 fixes this problem with the `src` attribute, which allows the user to specify a URL where a particular script resides, as well as which script you want to load and run. See the syntax description later in this chapter for more information.

The `<noscript>..</noscript>` container tag was introduced with Navigator version beta 5. If you have JavaScript support disabled, which is quite possible using the Network/Languages preferences option in Navigator, or if a user's browser does not recognize the `<script>..</script>` container, the user will see any HTML text that is placed between the `<noscript>` and `</noscript>` tags. The whole issue of browser version support is a complex one. In reality, `<noscript>` is not really of any use to anyone with Netscape Navigator version 1.*x* because this version doesn't even recognize these particular tags. For example, Navigator 1.*x* will simply display all text within the `<noscript>..</noscript>` container since the tags will be ignored. However, Navigator 3.0 will not print the text within the tags because it can support JavaScript—unless support is temporarily disabled, as was mentioned earlier.

Where Can Scripts Appear Within an HTML Document?

Scripts can appear just about *anywhere* within an HTML document, but do not place HTML tags and JavaScript statements together indiscriminately. Remember to encapsulate JavaScript code within the HTML `<script>..</script>` container. The only exception is when JavaScript code is included in an event-handler. Event-handlers are discussed in Chapter 5; they allow browser-based events, such as button-clicks, form-submissions, page-loading, etc., to be intercepted and processed accordingly.

When Navigator encounters a `<script>` tag it *parses* the contents line by line until a `</script>` tag is reached. At this stage the JavaScript program is being checked for errors and is being compiled into a format ready for execution on your computer, much as Java is, although the programs are compiled *locally* within Netscape, in this instance. This also happens when a script is pulled from the network. If, at this stage, any errors are encountered, Navigator will display a series of alert boxes on the screen highlighting each error; you must acknowledge each dialogue shown to continue.

The main core of your JavaScript application should be placed within the `<head>..</head>` container of your documents because this is one of the first tags read into Navigator. In theory, a script can be placed anywhere within an HTML document, although most advisable is to place it before the `<body>..</body>` container, such as in the header so your JavaScript functions are loaded into memory as soon as the document is read into Navigator. Some authors like to place their script containers at the bottom of a program; the choice is really up to you. Function declarations are good candidates for placing in the header of a document, although "on-the-fly" scripts that generate HTML at specific parts of a document can be placed exactly as required.

The syntax for the Netscape-HTML `<script>` tag is as follows:

```
<script [language="JavaScript"]
        [src=URL]>
[JavaScript-statements...]
</script>
```

where `language` is optionally set to `"JavaScript"`. Note that the case is unimportant, as with all HTML tags, and `src` specifies a URL of a script you want to load from the network. If the `src` attribute is specified, the `[JavaScript-statements...]` part can be left empty because the script will be downloaded from the URL you have specified. When `src` is not used,

Netscape assumes the code for your program will be contained in between the <script> and </script> tags. JavaScript's statements are introduced later in Chapter 3.

Loading Local JavaScript Applications

To embed JavaScript code within an HTML document, simply use the <script> tag without the src attribute. For example, this HTML document displays a small greeting message on your screen when it is loaded:

```
<html>
<!--
   Program 1-1
-->
<head>
<script language="JavaScript">
alert("Welcome to the Mystic Megg home page!");
</script>
</head>
</html>
```

alert() is one of many JavaScript methods; in this case, it displays a windowed alert-style message on the screen—an exclamation mark icon is shown alongside the message. *Alert-style messages*, or *alerts*, are used to catch your attention; an OK button is provided, which must be pressed before you can continue. Free-standing code will be executed immediately, although you can define *functions* that contain a series of statements and that are only invoked when the function is referenced within the program. You will learn all about JavaScript functions later on in this book.

Loading Remote JavaScript Applications

Remote JavaScript applications are stored as separate files on a server. The src attribute specifies a URL that identifies the server and the location of the script you want to load. For example, you could load a script from a remote server using the following <script> tag:

```
<!--
   Program 1-2
-->
<script src="http://www.gold.net/users/ag17/welcome.js">
</script>
```

which specifies that the script named welcome.js will be downloaded from the host www.gold.net in the directory /users/ag17; then compiled and executed within Navigator. The <script> tag is a container tag, which must end with a `</script>` tag, even though no actual statements are included within the body of the script in this instance.

TIP: When using the `src` attribute in the `<script>` tag, you should name your scripts with the `.js` (for **Java**Script) extension because this filename extension is already supported (as a Multimedia Internet Mail Extension, or MIME, type) within Navigator. When you create the script externally, make certain the file is stored as a plain-text file, such as ASCII.

Server-side includes can also be used on some servers and could allow the incorporation of HTML/JavaScript code directly into a document. The availability of such facilities, however, depends upon the administrator—server-side includes tend to slow server performance and are disabled on this basis. For more information, see the URL:

`http://hoohoo.ncsa.uiuc.edu/docs/tutorials/includes.html`

which gives information for a variety of servers, including the popular NCSA and Netscape NetSite servers. The use of the `src` attribute can be useful for source-code secrecy, although since the code must be accessible from the server where it is stored, it may also be available for users to see by simply visiting the directory on the server where the script physically resides.

TIP: When pulling in code from a server using the `src` attribute, be sure to exclude the `<script>` and `</script>` tags, i.e. only place the literal JavaScript code within the file, and not any literal HTML tags.

The `language` attribute is always compulsory *unless* the `src` attribute is present. The `src` attribute is an optional part of the tag and, if specified, names a URL that loads a script. The URL can specify a local script that exists in the same directory as the current HTML file, for example,

```
<script src="myScript.js">
```

or can specify a script that is located on another Internet server, as shown earlier. Both the `src` and `language` attributes may be present together, although the `language` attribute can be omitted when the `src` attribute is not present (when the script is contained within the current HTML document).

Creating HTML "On The Fly"

By using multiple <script> container tags within the body of your
hypertext document, you can generate HTML *on the fly*. This is known as
dynamic HTML creation; it is useful for altering the structure and
appearance of your Web pages, according to external events, such as times,
dates, and user requirements. A Web site can alter its appearance on a daily
basis using this technique. Dynamic HTML creation is employed by a large
number of applications that are contained within this book.

Ensuring Backward Compatibility Using HTML Comments

The number of Web browsers continues to grow at an ever quickening pace,
which, in turn, makes the job of authoring compatible HTML pages for a
variety of browsers more difficult. All browsers will ignore tags they do not
recognize. For example, Navigator 1.2 will ignore the <script> and
<frameset> container tags because these tags were introduced with
Netscape Navigator version 2.0. Because <script> tags contain raw
JavaScript code and are not themselves contained within a tag, the text of
the program will be rendered onto the screen verbatim. To overcome this
problem, Navigator 2.0 and 3.0 allow the interpretation of JavaScript code
within an HTML comment container. HTML comments are container tags,
which start with <!--, and end with -->, and can span multiple lines. For
example, a single-lined HTML comment could resemble:

```
<!--Copyright (c) Joe Public 1996-->
```

whereas a comment spanning multiple lines could resemble:

```
<!--
 Copyright (c) Joe Public
  All Rights Reserved
-->
```

As many users have discovered, a significant problem with comments is they
can be "broken" internally by a JavaScript program, which uses character
combinations that resemble a closing comment tag.

For example, the ">" and "--" character sequences are both used within
JavaScript program code: the former issued as a greater-than operator
(and within HTML tags); and the latter used as a mathematical
decrement operator.

The use of such sequences within a program risks exposure of the JavaScript code within the `<script>..</script>` container, which is trying to hide from display.

Because the closing comment will actually occur *within* the JavaScript code portion, you must use a "`//`" in front of the "`-->`", where "`//`" is a JavaScript comment. In context with the earlier JavaScript program, which displayed a greeting message, this should now be modified, so it becomes:

```
<!--
  Program 1-3
-->
<script language="JavaScript">
<!--
  alert("Welcome to the Mystic Megg home page!");
//-->
</script>
<noscript>
<img src="welcome.gif" hspace=4>Welcome to the Mystic
Megg Home page on the Internet!
</noscript>
```

Note that the `<script>` and `</script>` tags should *not* be commented out. Non-Netscape browsers will now simply ignore the script. JavaScript aware versions of Navigator will still interpret the code because they will still recognize the `<script>` tag. This newly modified document is now *backward compatible* with other versions of Netscape Navigator; it ensures the JavaScript code is not placed literally within the browser, which would look rather strange.

T IP: Avoid placing comments inside each other because Navigator may get confused, and will issue an error. The placing of such elements within each other is termed "nesting," and only certain features can use this technique, most notably loops (iteration statements).

Also, notice how the `<noscript>..</noscript>` container has been used to display an image and a small greeting message instead of the `alert()` message—this alternative text will be shown when JavaScript has been disabled, or is not available.

Tips for Hiding JavaScript Code from Other Non-Netscape Browsers

Hiding JavaScript code from other Web browsers has always been a vexed area; this has caused many flame wars on the Net. Many, if not all, of the problems of "broken" comments are because a JavaScript program is using one of the character combinations found in the closing HTML comment tag (`-->`). The long-awaited `src` attribute of the `<script>` tag will solve these problems—other workarounds are possible in the meantime. Of course, some people may not want to use the `src` attribute. Many have suggested that this feature makes scripting more complicated because you must then worry about authoring HTML documents *and* source code files separately, rather than placing the script and HTML within a single file.

If possible, try to avoid using literal ">" characters within your JavaScript code because these characters may *break* a comment midway. The right-facing angle bracket (or *chevron*) is used in JavaScript as the greater-than operator; it is also used in HTML tags, which may eventually be dynamically written into the browser. Using the ">" as a greater-than operator can be overcome by inverting the operator. For example, instead of coding:

```
if (myVar1 > myVar2) {
   . . .
}
```

you could write:

```
if (myVar2 < myVar1) {
   . . .
}
```

Another method involves using a *hex-escape code*. Hex-escape codes take the form \x*nn* where *nn* represents a hexadecimal value of an ASCII character, for example, a ">"sign would be \x3e because 3e in hexadecimal is 62 in decimal, and ASCII 62 is a ">" sign. When you write some dynamic HTML, such as:

```
document.write("<hr>Welcome to my Page!<hr>");
```

you can, instead, write:

```
document.write("<hr\x3eWelcome to my Page!<hr\x3e");
```

JavaScript also provides an `unescape()` method, which accepts a hexadecimal argument, and then outputs the ASCII-equivalent character. You could also use code such as:

```
_lt = unescape("%3c");
_gt = unescape("%3e");
document.write(_lt+"hr"+_gt+"Welcome to my Page!"+_lt+"hr"+_gt);
```

which will remove *all* the chevrons from the source code. They will still appear within the HTML document correctly, so no effects will be lost. Removing both the "<" and ">" characters may be a little drastic because the ">" character is nearly always the culprit in such cases.

Some browsers also break a comment when they come in contact with two hyphens set side by side, for example as "--", mainly because this is also used with a closing HTML tag ("-->"). Because the "--" is also JavaScript's decrement operator, you can find alternatives for statements, such as:

```
myVar --;
```

and instead use

```
myVar -= 1;
```

which will achieve the same thing.

Using JavaScript Evaluation Within HTML Tag Attribute Values

Navigator 3.0 can now evaluate JavaScript expressions *within* HTML tag attribute values, allowing values to be constructed "on the fly" as a document is read into Navigator, rather than being hard-coded. The syntax:

```
&{expression};
```

is used for this type of inline evaluation, where expression is the JavaScript expression you want to be evaluated. For example, rather than coding an HTML <table> container tag with a fixed width, as:

```
<table width="100%">
```

you could instead write:

```
<table width="&{10 * 10};%">
```

By itself this tag does still not have much significance because the end result is a table with a width set equal to the size of the browser, i.e. at 100%. However, these inline evaluations can also reference JavaScript objects such as variables, so it would be possible for an element to be assigned a value based upon some previous calculation. For example, here is a table that receives its width value (50%) from a JavaScript variable, `tabWidth`:

```
<script>
<!--
  var tabWidth = 50;
//-->
</script>
<table border align="middle" width="&{ tabWidth };%">
<tr><td>Hello!</td></tr>
</table>
```

The use of this type of inline attribute evaluation is available only when assigning values to attributes, as with the `width` attribute in the previous example. Inline evaluation can be an extremely powerful tool since it allows HTML elements to be kept "variable," i.e. they are not hard-coded by the author. Attribute values can therefore be allocated on the basis of specific, predefined conditions. For example, here is a JavaScript program that allocates a new font face depending on the day of the week:

```
<!--
  Program 1-4
-->
<html>
<head>
<script language="JavaScript">
<!--
 var dateToday = new Date();
 var thisDay   = dateToday.getDay();
 var fonts     = new Array("Albertus Medium",
                           "Times",
                           "Helvetica",
                           "Courier",
                           "Albertus Extra Bold",
                           "Script",
                           "Times");
//-->
</script>
</head>
<body>
<font size="+1" face="&{ fonts[thisDay] };">
Here is some body text that has been allocated a dynamic font face
using the new <b>face</b> attribute of the <b>&lt;font&gt;</b> tag
(introduced in Netscape Navigator).</font>
</body>
</html>
```

The `face` attribute was introduced with Navigator 3.0 and allows a font face to be specified. You can see which fonts are supported by Navigator by selecting the Options menu and looking at the General Preferences/Fonts screen. In our program, the array `fonts` stores the names of seven fonts, one for each day of the week. The `<font>` tag uses the inline evaluation expression when assigning a value to the `face` attribute, so on a Sunday, for example, the font face "`Albertus Medium`" is selected—the JavaScript `getDay()` method returns 0 for Sunday, 1 for Monday, and so forth. By specifying the expression `fonts[thisDay]` within the inline evaluation, the value of `thisDay` indexes the `fonts` array and returns a font name as a string, which is then substituted as the value to the `<font face>` tag. Arrays and statements may not yet be known to you and are covered in detail within subsequent chapters.

Using `<noframes>` Containers for Backwards Compatibility Issues

One of the big problems for non-Navigator 2.0 and 3.0 users is providing a mechanism to tell them they need to upgrade to view JavaScript programs. Luckily, Navigator 1.1 and above all recognize the `<noframes>..</noframes>` container, which is used within frameset-documents to output some HTML text telling the user that they do not have a frames-compliant browser. By inserting some HTML-formatted text within the `<noframes>` container, you can deal with people using an earlier version of Navigator. For instance:

```
<!--
   Program 1-5
-->
<html>
<head>
<script language="JavaScript">
<!--
// ... whatever code ...
//-->
</script>
</head>
<noframes>
<hr>This document contains JavaScript facilities that can only
be used with Netscape Navigator 2.0 or 3.0. Please upgrade and
revisit us!<hr>
</noframes>
</html>
```

The previous code has a `<noframes>` tag that outputs a simple message whenever the user is accessing this page with Netscape version 1.*x*. Users are informed to upgrade to Netscape 2.0 or 3.0 and to revisit their site at a later date. People using Netscape 2.0 will not see this message, of course, because they have a frames-compatible browser and the tags will be ignored. Navigator also has a `navigator` object, which can test for a particular version of a browser being used, although the browser must support JavaScript to use this facility. Such tests are normally confined for different platforms of the Navigator browser *itself*.

TIP: Netscape 3.0 has a Disable JavaScript option in the Options/Network Preferences/Languages screen. This will make Navigator ignore every <script> tag it encounters within an HTML document.

Testing Your JavaScript Programs with Navigator

To test your JavaScript programs, simply load the HTML file containing the script into Navigator in one of the following ways:

♦ Use Navigator's File/Open option, and choose the file you want to load

♦ Use the Netscape `file:` URL to open a local file directly, follow these instructions:

To open a local file directly, simply enter a `file:` URL of the form:

♦ `file:///drive|/directory/filename`
♦ `file:/drive|/directory/filename`

both of which are equivalent. For example,

```
file:///c|/JS/Scripts/wombat.html
```

will load the HTML file named `wombat.html` from the directory `C:\JS\Scripts`. The "\" and "/" slashes can be used interchangeably as directory-level separators, although the `file:///drive|` part of the URL must be left intact (for each syntax). The HTML file will then be read into Navigator, and you will see the status bar message change to *Reading File...* as the file is loaded.

If any errors are detected, they will be shown on the screen within a small window in the top left-hand corner of the screen. Note the line number of the offending message in such instances, so you can quickly locate and correct the error. If the file you require exists within the *current* directory, simply click on the *Location:* field, type in the filename, and then press ENTER.

TIP: Any errors that exist with a JavaScript program will be shown via a dialogue box when the script is read into the Netscape browser. All errors cause program termination, that is, a *fatal* error. Note that JavaScript has no *warnings* as such. Nearly all errors will halt program execution at the point where the error occurred.

When you are satisfied with your JavaScript application, it can be uploaded to a Web server, using a suitable File Transfer Protocol (FTP) client. In theory, you should be able to test your application without uploading it to a Web server. Make certain to change all `file:` URLs to `http://` (networked documents) URLs, etc. Finally, because most JavaScript applications are embedded within HTML documents, no way currently exists to hide your source code from users who load up your application. The new `src` attribute of the `<script>` tag will allow scripts to exist separately from the HTML document that invokes them, and you may be able to configure your Web server to deny access to certain directories in which the source code for scripts is contained—although these features are server-dependent. All JavaScript programs are compiled internally by Navigator and a separate JavaScript compiler is now available as part of the Netscape LiveWire server product (see `http://home.netscape.com` for more details).

TIP: When testing and retesting programs, you must reload your document to see any new changes take effect. Navigator's caching of pages can sometimes cause problems because changes are not reflected when you view a modified document. To overcome this problem, instead of just clicking on the *Reload* button, first depress the SHIFT key and then click on the *Reload* button. This will reload everything, and will bypass the internal cache. By clicking on the *Location:* field and pressing ENTER on the URL, which actually loaded the current application, you can also achieve the same effect—although the SHIFT-clicking technique is more reliable.

Dealing with JavaScript Errors and Alert Messages

Navigator will issue an *alert message* whenever an error is encountered within a script. Scripts are read into memory before they are executed and parsed for errors. Examples of errors include syntax errors, where the format of a particular statement is incorrect. If JavaScript cannot find a file you have referenced or if it cannot find a variable you have referenced, an error will also be generated. When an error is detected, Netscape provides a small dialogue box with the following items of information:

♦   URL of the file in which the script is contained

♦   A description of the offending error

♦   The line number (approximate) where the error occurred

To clear an alert, simply press the OK button provided. Multiple alerts will be displayed if multiple errors occur. Netscape will then load the body of your hypertext document, although if an error has been trapped and you still try to use your application, it will function incorrectly until you eliminate the error. JavaScript's error message descriptions can be difficult to understand because they are often expressed in programming nomenclature. Once you become familiar with JavaScript's various error messages (see Appendix I), you will quickly learn how to find and correct such errors. Figure 1-1 illustrates a typical error message, which shows what happens when a "{" bracket is omitted in a function declaration. Here is the program that caused the error shown in the previous figure.

```
<!--
   Program 1-6
-->
<script language="JavaScript">
function AnError()
   // There is a { missing above ...
   alert("This function will generate an error");
}
</script>
```

By placing a "{" bracket after the AnError() function name, you can cure this error.

TIP: Alert boxes have the horrible habit of "stacking up" over one another when multiple errors are detected within a script. Recent versions of Navigator properly *tile* these alert messages, and you must close each box in the reverse-order of its appearance. This is not difficult because the boxes will overlay each other, and you can just keep clicking on each window's OK button until all the windows are removed.

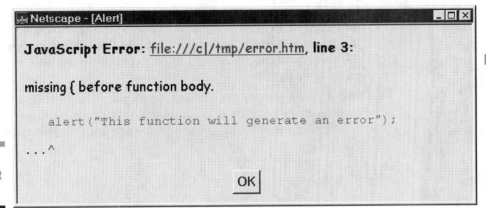

A typical
JavaScript alert
Figure 1-1.

NOTE: Moving the windows around is not advisable because the order will become confused. Windows must be shut down in the reverse order in which they first appeared.

Summary

♦ Place all JavaScript code within a `<script>..</script>` container. Do not indiscriminately mix HTML and JavaScript code. Use the `<noscript>..</noscript>` container to encapsulate HTML-formatted text that you wish to display when the user has disabled JavaScript, or when the user has a non-JavaScript aware browser.

♦ Place `<script>` tags anywhere within a document, either in the `<head>` or `<body>` part of a document. By incorporating scripts within the body, you can generate HTML text dynamically, straight into the document by using the `document.write()` function.

♦ Follow this procedure if an error occurs in your application and a JavaScript alert box appears. Read the message; then click on the OK button to close the window. If more than one window appears, you have multiple errors. Click on the OK button for each window until you return to Navigator. You cannot enter Navigator until all such windows have been closed.

♦ Make certain you enclose all code within an HTML comment container, for example, by using the "<!--" and "-->" tags, to ensure the code of a JavaScript program does not get rendered onto your screen. Navigator 3.0 and above can interpret the contents of such comments so the code will still be executed.

♦ Use the <noframes> container tag to place HTML code for non-JavaScript browsers. Navigator 1.*x* users can be shown a message telling them they need to use a JavaScript compliant browser to view your pages.

CHAPTER 2

Using Hyperlinks and Anchors with JavaScript

Hyperlinks are a cornerstone principal of the Web; they allow people to move from one document to another with the click of a mouse button. In HTML, a hyperlink is created using the `<a href=URL>..</a>` container tag, where `URL` is the address of the Web-resource where you want the destination for this link. This *destination* resource—a Web page, an image, or any other valid resource, such as a Gopher, News, or FTP server—is then loaded into Navigator. Note that tags are reflected as objects in JavaScript; every time a <a href> tag is scanned, Navigator treats that hyperlink as an *object*. Objects are accessed using their *properties*, for example, using the links property, which is discussed later in this chapter.

In this chapter you will learn how to:

♦ Create hyperlinks and anchors in HTML

♦ Use JavaScript to reference and to create hyperlinks and anchors

♦ Use different URLs with JavaScript to access different Internet resources

♦ Create hyperlinks and anchors in HTML

♦ Target anchors at frames within a frameset-document

♦ Use client-side imagemaps with JavaScript for advanced hyperlink navigation

JavaScript can access the hyperlinks and anchors you create using a series of standard properties, namely the links and anchors properties. In addition, JavaScript provides a series of methods that manipulate these values, allowing hyperlinks and anchors to be created *dynamically*, that is, without using raw HTML tags.

The links Property

When an HTML document is loaded into Navigator, each <a href> tag is scanned and its href (destination URL) attribute is placed into *the links property*. The links property is structured as an array and each hyperlink is stored in ascending order within this property. The complete syntax of the <a href> hyperlink tag is

```
<a href="URLtoLoad"
   [onClick="JavaScriptCmds"]
   [onMouseOver="JavaScriptCmds"]
   [target="frameName"]>LinkText
</a>
```

where URLtoLoad is a Uniform Resource Locator (URL) of a resource you want to load into Navigator, such as another HTML document. The onClick attribute is a JavaScript event-handler, which intercepts the user pressing the current hyperlink and allows a JavaScript command or function-call to be invoked. onMouseOver is another event-handler, which is invoked when the user moves over the hyperlink with the mouse pointer.

TIP: See more on the onMouseOver event, with code examples, in Chapter 5.

The target attribute is used within an HTML frameset-document. Frameset-documents are multiple regions of the Netscape browser that can contain separate documents. The frameName argument represents the name of a frame created using the Netscape-HTML <frame name=frameName> tag. See Chapter 9, for an in-depth discussion of frameset-documents and their integration into JavaScript programs. Consider the following hypertext document, which has three hyperlinks embedded within the <body> container:

2

```
<!--
  Program 2-1
-->
<html>
<head>
<script language="JavaScript">
<!--
var linkText = "";
function showLinks() {
  var item = 1;
  linkText = "LINK INDEX:\n" +
          "_____\n";
  for (n=0; n < document.links.length; n++) {
     linkText += item + ". " + document.links[n] + "\n";
     item ++;
  }
  alert(linkText);
}
//-->
</script>
<title>An introduction to the Web</title>
</head>
<body><basefont size=4>
<font size="+1">A</font>N <font size="+1">I</font>NTRODUCTION
<font size="+1">T</font>O <font size="+1">T</font>HE
<font size="+1">W</font>EB<hr>
The <a href="http://www.cern.ch">World-Wide Web</a> is that part
of the <a href="internet.htm">Internet</a> that deals solely in
hypertext documents. Hypertext is a way of providing multimedia
content within a document, with the added bonus of allowing links
known as <a href="hl.htm">hyperlinks</a> to other documents to be
created.<p>
```

```
<form><input type="button"
           value="Quick Link Index"
           onClick="showLinks()"></form>
</body>
</html>
```

The hyperlinks in the previous document are loaded into the `links` array; JavaScript can access them by referring to the appropriate array position. In the example, a button is placed at the bottom of the page using the JavaScript event-handler `onClick` to invoke the `showLinks()` function.

The `showLinks()` function builds up a list of the hyperlinks in the page by using a `for` loop to scan though the `links` array, creating a text string of each entry. The string is then displayed using the JavaScript `alert()` function. See Chapter 3 for more about JavaScript statements, such as the `for` loop construct. Notice the use of "\n" codes in the script. These signify where a line-feed (or line-break) is issued, thus breaking up the string into several lines, in this instance, one for each link entry. Figure 2-1 illustrates the previous example in action and shows the link-index generated by the program.

TIP: When you refer to a JavaScript property, such as `links`, precede the property with the object from which it is derived, that is, the `document` object, in this case. Refer to Appendix B for a list of properties and the objects to which they belong.

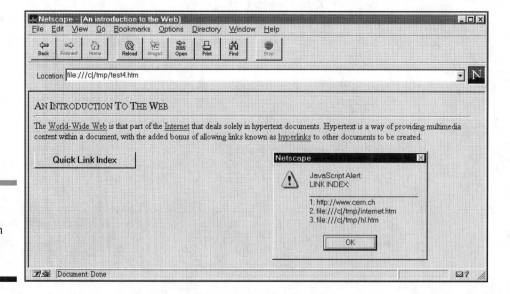

The current example as seen through Navigator

Figure 2-1.

The Anchors Property

Anchors are the targets for hyperlinks that refer to a specific part of a document—either stored locally or remotely—and are created using the `<a name=...>` tag. Anchors completely depend upon hyperlinks, although this is not true conversely.

The syntax for the `<a name>` hyperlink is

```
<a name="anchorName"
   [href="URLtoLoad"]>
AnchorText
</a>
```

2

Remotely stored anchors are referenced by a `<a href>` hyperlink tag as follows:

```
<a href="document.htm#anchorName">
linkText
</a>
```

where `anchorName` is the name of the anchor to reference, and `document` is the name of an HTML document in which the anchor exists. In this form of the `<a href>` tag, the anchor exists *outside* the current document; the file `document.htm` must be loaded first into Navigator, and then the anchor will be referenced accordingly.

NOTE: The hash (#) character is always a tell-tale sign that an anchor is being referenced. Navigator even has a `hash` property that simulates an `<a href="anchorName">` tag (more on this later in the section).

Anchors only function with hypertext documents and are defined with the `<a name=anchorName>..</a>` container. Anchors are particularly useful for creating indexes that allow a `<a href>` hyperlink to target a specific portion of text, either in the current document or in a remote (networked) document. Consider the remotely defined anchor referenced in the following hyperlink:

```
<a href="http://www.somehost.com/file1.htm#section6">Section 6</a>
```

This would define a hyperlink with the clickable text *"Section 6"*. When the user clicks on this link, the file named `file1.htm` is loaded into Navigator from the Web-server at the host `www.somehost.com` and the position of the document is moved to the anchor named as `section6`, that is, to the part of the file where a `<a name="section6">` tag is defined. Perhaps the section in question is structured as

```
<a name="section6">
<h2>SECTION 6 - THE SPUR-THIGHED TORTOISE</h2>
</a>
Welcome to section 6, which discusses the Spur-thighed Tortoise,
latin name ...
```

For local anchors, a `<a href>` tag of the form

```
<a href="#anchorName">
linkText
</a>
```

is used instead. Note the omission of any hypertext document to load in this instance. The currently loaded document is assumed to be the place in which the anchor is defined. Hyperlinks that do not specify an anchor using the # notation, simply load an entire document and leave the user at the beginning of the file—the default position.

Moving to an Anchor Using JavaScript

You can make Navigator jump to an anchor within a document by assigning the name of the anchor (as mentioned in the `<a name=...>` tag) to the `document.hash` property. For example, if you had an anchor defined within a document called `book.htm` as

```
<a name="chapter2">
CHAPTER 2 - INTRODUCTION TO HYPERLINKS<hr>
</a>
```

assigning the value `"chapter2"` to the `document.hash` property using the JavaScript statement

```
document.hash = "chapter2";
```

would make Navigator load the URL:

```
http://www.somehost.com/book.htm#chapter2
```

assuming the file `book.htm` resided in the root (top-level) directory of the Web server named as `www.somehost.com`, which would place you at that anchor within the document. If the anchor did not exist, you would be left at the top of the document.

Validating an Anchor

You can *validate* an anchor before it is referenced, although the procedure is not as straightforward as it may seem. The document.anchors property is an array of anchors defined within the current document, although individual elements cannot be accessed; such elements, when accessed, return a null value. Instead, you must name your anchors numerically, and in source-order, for example, <a name="0">, <a name="1"> and so forth, and then check the value of the document.anchors.length property to see if the anchor you have requested is less than or equal to this number. If not, the anchor does not exist, and you can issue a suitable error message. Consider the following JavaScript code:

2

```
<!--
   Program 2-2
-->
<html>
<head>
<script language="JavaScript">
<!--
function validateLink(theLink) {
 if (parseInt(theLink) > document.anchors.length)
    alert("Sorry, this anchor has not been defined");
else
    location.hash = theLink;
}
//-->
</script>
</head>
<body>
<form>
<input type="button"
       value="Chapter 1"
       onClick="validateLink('0')">
<input type="button"
       value="Chapter 2"
       onClick="validateLink('1')">
</form>
<a name="0">CHAPTER 1</a>
...
<a name="1">CHAPTER 2</a>
...
</body>
</html>
```

The main document body has been cut down in this example, although the anchors have been placed. When you click on a button, an `onClick` event invokes the `validateLink()` function and passes it the name of an anchor, such as `"0"` for the first anchor. The numeric value of this anchor (note the use of `parseInt()` for this) is then checked against the value of the link: if the link number is greater, an error message is generated; otherwise, the `hash` property is assigned the value of the link, and Navigator moves you to the appropriate `<a name>` entry within the document. In order to test this program ensure that there is a lot of space between the anchors, so that you can visibly notice the movement to the anchor. To test for a non-existent anchor, try renaming one of the `<a name>` tags, as well as renaming the argument to the `validateLink()` function. For example, renaming:

```
<a name="1">CHAPTER 2</a>
```

to:

```
<a name="3">CHAPTER 3</a>
```

and renaming the second button to:

```
<input type="button"
       value="Chapter 3"
       onClick="validateLink('3')">
```

will allow you to now see an alert message for the non-existent anchor.

Creating Hyperlinks with the `link()` Method

JavaScript provides the `link()` method for the creation of hyperlinks. This method has the syntax

```
linkText.link(URLName)
```

where `linkText` is a string object representing the text the user must click on to activate the hyperlink, and `URLName` is the URL of a resource to be loaded when the hyperlink is activated. JavaScript's `document.write()` method can be used to write links into the current hypertext document dynamically. For example, consider the following JavaScript function, which creates a hyperlink within the body of a hypertext document and blends it in with the remaining HTML tags:

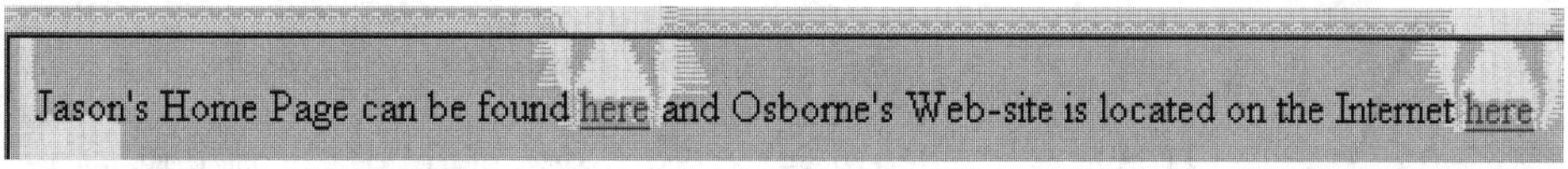

The two
hyperlinks
created in the
previous
example
Figure 2-2.

Jason's Home Page can be found <u>here</u> and Osborne's Web-site is located on the Internet <u>here</u>

2

```
<!--
  Program 2-3
-->
<html>
<body>
<basefont size=4>
Jason's Home Page can be found
<script language="JavaScript">
<!--
var linkText = "here";
var theUrl = "http://www.gold.net/users/ag17/index.htm";
document.write(linkText.link(theUrl));
//-->
</script>
and Osborne's Web-site is located on the Internet
<a href="http://www.osborne.com">here</a>
</body>
</html>
```

The `<script>` container can appear anywhere within an HTML document,
even in between portions of HTML-formatted text. The output of this
example is as shown in Figure 2-2. You would never have known the first
hyperlink was generated dynamically.

The use of dynamically-created hyperlinks is beneficial because you can
create links that change according to prespecified conditions, such as dates
and times. The following example creates a series of hyperlinks that depend
upon the current day of the week:

```
<!--
  Program 2-4
-->
<html>
<body>
<basefont size=4>
<img src="internal-gopher-menu"> Click
<script language="JavaScript">
<!--
var dateToday = new Date();
```

```
var day        = dateToday.getDay();
var linkText   = "here";
var aUrl= "";
if (day == 0) { aUrl="http://www.somehost.com/days/sunday.htm"; }
if (day == 1) { aUrl="http://www.somehost.com/days/monday.htm"; }
if (day == 2) { aUrl="http://www.somehost.com/days/tuesday.htm"; }
if (day == 3) { aUrl="http://www.somehost.com/days/wednesday.htm"; }
if (day == 4) { aUrl="http://www.somehost.com/days/thursday.htm"; }
if (day == 5) { aUrl="http://www.somehost.com/days/friday.htm"; }
if (day == 6) { aUrl="http://www.somehost.com/days/saturday.htm"; }
document.write(linkText.link(aUrl));
//-->
</script>
for today's news.<p>
</body>
</html>
```

In this example, a new `Date` object has been created and assigned to the variable `dateToday`. The `getDay()` method is applied to this value to extract a day number. The `getDay()` method returns `0` for Sunday, `1` for Monday, and so forth. This value is used in a series of `if` statements to select the URL you require for the hyperlink. The hyperlink is written out using the `document.write()` method. Again, notice how the script is embedded within the body of the document. You could place this entire script in a JavaScript function, and then call this from the script instead —just to separate the HTML from the JavaScript code, although the end-result is the same.

Creating Anchors with the `anchor()` Method

Just like the `link()` method, JavaScript also provides an `anchor()` method, which can be used to create anchors dynamically within a hypertext document. The syntax for this method is

```
anchText.anchor(anchName)
```

where `anchText` is the text to encapsulate in a `<a name>..</a>` container, and `anchName` is the name of the anchor. For instance, consider the following code extract:

```
var myAnchor = "The Spur-thighed Tortoise";
document.open();
document.writeln(myAnchor.anchor("section6"));
document.close();
```

This code would progmatically create an anchor which is the same as the following HTML

```
<a name="section6">The Spur-thighed Tortoise</a>
```

Using the `javascript:` URL with a `<a href>` Hyperlink

The `javsacript:` URL allows a JavaScript statement, or expression, to be evaluated. Using this URL within a `<a href>` hyperlink is possible to invoke JavaScript functions or statements and to launch hyperlinks progmatically. Consider the following script:

```
<!--
  Program 2-5
-->
<html>
<head>
<script language="JavaScript">
<!--
  function myFunction() {
    alert("Hello World!");
  }
//-->
</script>
</head>
<body>
<a href="javascript:myFunction()">Click me</a>
</body>
</html>
```

Notice how the `href` attribute launches a JavaScript function in this case. Another way of invoking a function is to use the alternative method

```
<a href="#" onClick="myFunction()">Another way</a>
```

which replaces the `href` attribute with a hash (#) and uses an `onClick` event-attribute to launch the function. Both methods are equivalent within Navigator. You needn't just invoke a JavaScript function; you could actually load a resource *and* invoke a function at the same time, for example, using the HTML:

```
<a href="file.htm" onClick="myFunction()">Click me</a>
```

which will load the document named `file.htm` when the link is clicked upon and, at the same time, will launch the user-defined function `myFunction()`. The uses for this type of link are numerous. For example, you could load two frames at once—one dynamically, and one from an external file—or combinations of both, perhaps. The following script creates a frameset-document with two horizontal frames of equal size. The upper frame (`topFrame`) simply loads an external networked file, while the bottom frame is updated dynamically.

```
<!--
   Program 2-6
-->
<html>
<head>
<script language="JavaScript">
<!--
function myFunc() {
  parent.frames[1].document.open();
  parent.frames[1].document.write("This is some " +
                    "automatically " +
                    "loaded frame-text.");
  parent.frames[1].document.close();
}
var topFrame = "<a href='http://www.osborne.com' " +
                "onClick='parent.myFunc()'>Click me</a>";
var botFrame = "";   // Empty to start with
//-->
</script>
</head>
<frameset rows="50%,*">
<frame src="javascript:parent.topFrame">
<frame src="javascript:parent.botFrame">
</frameset>
</html>
```

Make certain to use the `open()` and `close()` methods because the upper frame's contents may not be rendered otherwise. If you need to load a local file from your hard disk, use a local file URL of the form: `file:///driveLetter%7c/directory/filename`. Or write the concatenated expression `"<base href="+location+">"` into the same frame where the `<a href>` hyperlink is placed—where `location` represents the JavaScript `location` object—or the URL of the frame. Note that Navigator will lose track of a file if either method is not employed. For example, here is the same script, but it uses the `<base href>` tag. Notice the URL prefix has now been removed from the file:

```
<!--
  Program 2-7
-->
<html>
<head>
<script language="JavaScript">
<!--
function myFunc() {
  parent.frames[1].document.open();
  parent.frames[1].document.write("This is some newly "+
                  "loaded frame-text.");
  parent.frames[1].document.close();
}
var topFrame = "<base href="+location+">" +
               "<a href='file.htm' " +
               "onClick='parent.myFunc()'>Click me</a>";
var botFrame = "";
//-->
</script>
</head>
<frameset rows="50%,*">
<frame src="javascript:parent.topFrame">
<frame src="javascript:parent.botFrame">
</frameset>
</html>
```

See Chapter 9 for more information on frameset-documents.

Manipulating `link` Properties Using the Document Object

A number of other `document` objects relate to hyperlinks and can be changed within a JavaScript program. These include the hyperlink colors used by Navigator, such as `linkColor` and `vlinkColor`. All of these properties can be set at any time simply by assigning them a value. Values in this case include Netscape color-code verbs, for example, `Black`, or RGB (`#RRGGBB`) triplets specified in the hexadecimal (`0-FF`) format, where `RR` is Red, `GG` is Green, and `BB` is Blue. Appendix G has more information on color codes.

The `aLinkColor` property describes the active link color property. *Active links* are hyperlinks that have been clicked on while the mouse button is held down over the link. The color is reset to `linkColor` after the mouse button is released. The `linkColor` attribute is the default color for a hyperlink (blue is the default color within Navigator). `vlinkColor` represents a *visited link,* a hyperlink clicked on before, in either the current or a past Navigator session, which is stored in the NETSCAPE.HST file. For example, you could change the color of every hyperlink in a page using the single JavaScript statement

```
document.linkColor = "Yellow";
```

where `Yellow` is the color code for the RGB triplet `"#FFFF00"`, that is, 100% red, 100% green, and 0% blue. The equivalent statement would be

```
document.linkColor = "#FFFF00";
```

Note that the former is only Netscape 2.*x* and 3.*x* compatible. Both encoding schemes work in Netscape 2.*x*, but color-code verbs are not backwards-compatible with Netscape 1.*x*. The ability to change hyperlink colors allows a site to change its appearance without altering dozens, perhaps hundreds, of HTML files. Consider the following JavaScript/HTML document, which changes the active hyperlink color according to the day of the week:

```
<!--
   Program 2-8
-->
<html>
<head>
<script language="JavaScript">
<!--
function changeLinkColors() {
  var dateToday = new Date();
  var dayToday  = dateToday.getDay();
  var linkText  = "here";
  var theUrl    = "";
  if (dayToday == 0) { document.linkColor = "Yellow" } // Sun
  if (dayToday == 1) { document.linkColor = "Aqua"   } // Mon
  if (dayToday == 2) { document.linkColor = "White"  } // Tue
  if (dayToday == 3) { document.linkColor = "Red"    } // Wed
  if (dayToday == 4) { document.linkColor = "Blue"   } // Thu
  if (dayToday == 5) { document.linkColor = "Green"  } // Fri
  if (dayToday == 6) { document.linkColor = "Black"  } // Sat
}
changeLinkColors();
//-->
```

```
</script>
</head>
<body>
<basefont size=4>
If it is a Sunday, <a href="this.htm">this</a> link will be
colored <font color="Yellow">Yellow</font>.
</body>
</html>
```

The principal is essentially the same as the previous example, which changed the hyperlink name but, in this case, a different value is assigned to the `document.linkColor` property. Note both the use of the new `<font color=...>` tag, which is also new to Navigator 2.0, and how the `changeLinkColors()` function is called automatically, that is, you have *no* choice as to whether or not the function is called; the colors are set automatically.

2

Using Hyperlinks with Client-Side Imagemaps

An *imagemap* is an image that is broken into a series of regions, known as *hot-spots*, each of which can be associated with a different URL. Until Netscape 2.0, imagemaps were a server-side feature, although client-side imagemaps are now possible through the use of the new HTML `<map>..</map>` container. The syntax of the `<map>` tag is as follows:

```
<map name="mapName">
<area shape="poly" | "rect" | "circle" coords="coordList,.."
      href="fileOrUrl">
</map>
```

Each of the `<area>` tags identifies a hot-spot within the image, which when clicked upon, will launch (via the `href` attribute) a unique URL. By using the `javascript:` URL, you can launch a JavaScript expression, or function-call. Hot-spots are based upon an `x,y` pixel addressing scheme (starting at `00,00` for the top-left corner of an image).

Polygons (`poly`) are shapes with multiple sides, such as triangles, and are widely used for complex shapes, for example, a country and its borders. More simple-shaped regions can be specified with the `rect` (rectangle) and `circle` (circular) attributes. Rectangular coordinates are based upon the upper-left and bottom-right pixels of the rectangle, whereas circles are measured from the middle of the circle to the outer circumference. The format of each coordinate is important; for example, here is a simple polygon definition:

```
<map name="myMap">
<area shape="poly" coords="2,1 109,1 194,1 4,191 2,1"
      href="http://www.somehost.com/somefile1.htm">
</map>
```

Notice how polygons are just start- and end-points, essentially groups of lines that form to make an enclosed region. Rectangles are by far the simplest shapes because you only need to know two coordinates—the upper-left x,y and the lower-right x,y coordinate. For example:

```
<map name="myMap">
<area shape="rect" coords="146,145 247,228"
      href="http://www.somehost.com/somefile2.htm">
</map>
```

If possible, try to make the starting and ending coordinates match, so an enclosed region is made, as in the previous example. Circles take the form:

```
<map name="myMap">
<area shape="circle" coords="248,82 196,66"
      href="http://www.somehost.com/somefile3.htm">
</map>
```

where the outer circle is the first set of coordinates. You need the help of software to arrive at the pixel coordinates because the process can be complex. You can either:

♦ Use a dedicated imagemap editor, such as mapedit (see Appendix C for the location of this software) to create all regions and generate a map-file, which you can then incorporate into your JavaScript application; or

♦ Use an image-editor that shows pixel-coordinates, such as the Windows 95 Paint program, etc. You must convert the image to a GIF or JPEG format afterwards. Shareware tools to this include Lview and GifEdit.

To associate an image with a <map> specification, the <img src> tag has been modified to accept a usemap attribute. The older ismap attribute is kept, but it is for use with server-side imagemap systems. For example, you could have the HTML tag

```
<img src="fileOrUrl" usemap="#mapName">
```

where mapName is the name mentioned in the name attribute of the previous <map> tag. Here is the entire application. As you can see, the more detailed a hot-spot becomes, the larger the number of coordinates required. You can cut the number of coordinates for polygons by using rectangles instead; the rectangles can even be placed within the image to show you exactly where to click.

```
<!--
  Program 2-9
-->
<html>
<head>
<title>MCGRAW-HILL: EUROPE SALES & MARKETING TEAM</title>
<script language="JavaScript">
<!--
var mapFrame =
  "<base href=" + location + ">" +
  "<body bgcolor='Black' background='back1.gif' text='White'>" +
  "<map name='europe'>" +
  "<area shape='poly' coords='51,8 63,10 61,19 77,21 68,36 " +
  "95,70 103,73 107,80 101,85 101,91 98,93 88,98 80,97 61,102 " +
  "66,105 63,105 52,103 49,106 45,107 42,107 53,96 55,92 59,91 " +
  "47,90 46,86 46,83 29,84 16,93 1,87 2,77 10,67 6,61 9,51 " +
  "17,54 23,44 36,43 44,44 41,42 43,36 30,37 34,20 34,12 41,5 " +
  "47,5 51,6' href='javascript:parent.UnitedK()'>" +
  "<area shape='poly' coords='149,154 144,156 151,160 146,163 " +
  "146,168 152,172 166,170 172,172 175,177 183,185 184,191 " +
  "191,195 196,198 198,202 203,206 206,205 208,207 211,211 " +
  "216,212 216,218 215,223 205,224 198,225 188,228 183,236 " +
  "221,235 223,231 229,230 233,224 234,218 234,216 231,214 " +
  "235,213 239,213 243,209 240,201 231,198 228,198 228,194 " +
  "218,191 214,193 208,187 207,180 206,175 199,167 198,160 " +
  "203,159 203,150 185,140 175,142 168,148 164,154 161,150 " +
  "154,151 151,154' href='javascript:parent.Italy()'>" +
  "<area shape='poly' coords='164,47 164,55 166,62 159,63 " +
  "152,63 151,77 150,82 146,85 144,92 146,98 146,99 142,103 " +
  "141,107 145,109 147,114 142,116 149,118 156,119 156,123 " +
  "155,130 158,135 164,136 170,137 179,136 184,136 186,138 " +
  "193,138 196,135 198,128 197,118 192,113 188,107 188,103 " +
  "194,101 198,100 205,97 211,94 215,89 212,82 209,78 " +
  "204,75 204,66 206,59 205,55 201,54 190,56 184,57 183,58 " +
  "181,58 178,56 171,51 170,48 163,48' " +
  "href='javascript:parent.Netherlands()'>" +
  "<area shape='poly' coords='141,65 139,73 134,74 135,69 " +
  "132,68 125,76 125,85 126,88 122,90 118,91 114,92 125,95 " +
  "126,101 133,105 136,109 141,110 137,104 142,98 142,93 " +
  "142,82 149,77 149,66 139,65' " +
  "href='javascript:parent.Netherlands()'>" +
  "<area shape='poly' coords='174,22 177,31 179,34 177,37 " +
```

```
"174,39 169,44 171,47 161,45 161,37 161,34 161,30 165,30 " +
"169,28 172,25 176,20' " +
"href='javascript:parent.Netherlands()'>" +
"<area shape='poly' coords='108,95 103,97 103,109 100,109 " +
"89,111 88,116 80,115 74,111 73,111 73,118 65,120 56,118 " +
"52,121 50,126 55,136 57,137 58,138 63,142 71,143 73,148 " +
"75,150 75,157 75,163 74,170 74,175 76,180 91,186 102,186 " +
"108,189 119,191 122,183 126,178 127,178 137,181 141,181 " +
"150,177 153,173 141,169 142,158 140,155 147,150 147,139 " +
"159,138 151,133 152,122 138,118 138,111 131,111 128,107 " +
"123,104 122,98 115,96 109,95 107,95' " +
"href='javascript:parent.France()'>" +
"<area shape='poly' coords='287,0 258,21 255,33 248,49 " +
"240,46 230,46 219,52 212,57 211,59 209,59 208,72 216,82 " +
"219,92  198,103 191,106 203,122 198,136 194,141 207,149 " +
"220,148 230,153 246,157 252,153 259,153 264,152 264,158 " +
"276,171 277,174 276,182 281,193 296,194 299,196 300,197 " +
"311,192 312,195 323,198 330,199 339,199 346,200 345,0 " +
"285,0 286,0' href='javascript:parent.EEurope()'>" +
"<area shape='default' href='javascript:parent.Default()'>" +
"</map>" +
"<basefont size=5>" +
"<img align='right' hspace=10 border=1 src='europe.gif' " +
"usemap='#europe'><br>" +
"<img align='left' src='compass.gif'> McGRAW-HILL " +
"EUROPE: SALES & MARKETING<p><br clear='left'>" +
"<basefont size=3>" +
"<dl><dd><img width=11 src='bullet.gif'> Please click on " +
"a country using your mouse.<p>" +
"<dd><img width=11 src='bullet.gif'> A list of " +
"representatives for " +
"this region will then be shown in the lower window.</dl><br>";

function Germany() {
    parent.frames[1].location.hash="int";
}
function Netherlands() {
  parent.frames[1].location.hash="nether";
}
function France() {
    parent.frames[1].location.hash="int";
}
function UnitedK() {
    parent.frames[1].location.hash="uk";
}
```

```
  function Spain() {
     parent.frames[1].location.hash="int";
  }
  function Italy() {
     parent.frames[1].location.hash="int";
  }
  function EEurope() {
     parent.frames[1].location.hash="int";
  }
  function Default() {
     parent.frames[1].location.hash="top";
 }
//-->
</script>
</head>
<frameset rows="40%,*">
<frame src="javascript:parent.mapFrame">
<frame src="europe2.htm">
</frameset>
</html>
```

Figure 2-3 illustrates the popular `mapedit` program in action with the `europe.gif` image file used in this example. `mapedit` writes a `.map` file to disk after you have allocated all your image coordinates. You can then read this file into an ASCII editor and incorporate it into your JavaScript program.

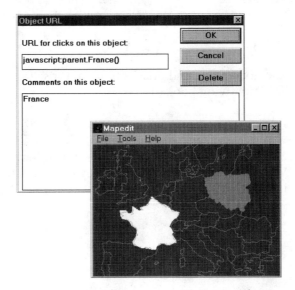

The mapedit
program in
action with
the europe.gif
image file
Figure 2-3.

As you move the mouse cursor over a particular country, the Navigator status-bar shows the function that will be invoked. Notice the `<area shape='default'>` tag. A shape named `default` will deal with occurrences of mouse-clicks on undefined regions within the imagemap. In this case, such a click will invoke the `Default()` function, which will assign the value "top" to the `hash` property. An `<a name='top'>` tag is defined at the top of the `europe2.htm` file, which moves you to the beginning of the document.

The file loaded into the lower frame, `europe2.htm`, is an HTML-formatted file with a series of `<a name>` tags, which can be addressed by the various functions shown in the previous script using the `loction.hash` property. In this way, you can be moved to a specific portion of the document depending on the country on which you click. For example, this entry was extracted from the file for the United Kingdom. The `<a name="uk">` tag identifies this entry:

```
<a name="uk">
<font size="+1">U</font>NITED
<font size="+1">K</font>INGDOM &
<font size="+1">R</font>EPUBLIC OF
<font size="+1">I</font>RELAND<br>
<img src="line.gif" width="60%" height=2><br>
</a>
<dl>
<dt><img src="bullet.gif" width=10> 
<font size="+1">F</font>RED <font size="+1">P</font>ERKINS
<dd><img src="rb.gif" width=10> Group Vice President,
Europe<br>
</dl>
```

The documents and images that comprise this example can be found on the accompanying book disk.

Summary

Hyperlinks allow movement to resources located on the World Wide Web, irrespective of distance. They are a core document-navigation feature in HTML.

♦ A *hyperlink* is created using an HTML `<a href>` tag; it allows a Web-based resource, such as a hypertext page, etc., to be loaded into Navigator. An *anchor* is a target for a hyperlink and can only exist within an HTML document. Anchors are placed at strategic points so hyperlinks can quickly move you to these portions of the document.

♦ Every `<a href>` hyperlink tag is reflected into the JavaScript `links[]` array, just as `<a name>` anchors are reflected into the `anchors[]` array.

♦ Anchor and links can be created by using HTML tags or "dynamically" by using the equivalent JavaScript methods: `anchor()` and `link()`.

2

The `hash` property of the `location` object can be used to move to a named anchor, that is, a `<a name>` tag defined within a particular window, thus simulating a `<a href>` hyperlink tag. The `hash` property can also be used to *validate* an anchor before its selection.

♦ Client-side imagemaps can be used with the `javascript:` URL to invoke a JavaScript function or expression. By specifying a JavaScript-based URL in the `href` attribute of an `<area>` tag, you can invoke an action depending on the `x,y` coordinate selected. Use a map editor, such as `mapedit`, to create the imagemap coordinates; then incorporate them into your JavaScript or HTML portion of the document.

CHAPTER 3

Using JavaScript Statements

The JavaScript language is compact and supplies the developer with around a dozen statements. Statements are the building-blocks of a JavaScript application, which provide a range of facilities, from placing annotations in programs to testing complex conditional expressions. Statements are combined with a variety of other JavaScript facilities, such as variables, objects, and properties to bring together a working application. This chapter provides a quick overview of each statement in the JavaScript language. In particular, you will learn how to:

♦ Use JavaScript's statements in your Web-applications

♦ Properly structure your JavaScript programs

♦ Use iterative and conditional statements to control your application

♦ Create user-defined functions

JavaScript Statements

JavaScript programs can be made up of *code-blocks* or single statements. Code-blocks are groups of statements that are enclosed in { and } brackets. Each statement, if it occupies a single line, can have a delimiting semi-colon (;) to indicate the statement has terminated, as examples in this chapter will illustrate. Each statement has a syntax associated with it. This syntax shows you which values are acceptable to use within the statement, and tells you which, if any, are compulsory or optional. In this chapter, a value expressed as [value] is optional within the statement; otherwise, it must be supplied.

T IP: JavaScript is a case-sensitive language. Ensure that all statements and function names are quoted correctly. If they are not quoted correctly, a compile-time error will occur.

Comment and Annotation Statements

Syntax:

```
// commentText
/* commentText */
```

Comments are user-created annotations that can be placed anywhere within a JavaScript program. Their purpose is purely documentary, although they can be used to remove areas of a program during testing (without physically removing the actual code in the process). Comments normally display author and copyright information and explain the workings of a program; they are actively encouraged. JavaScript supports two types of comments, namely: // and /* commentText */ , the former used for single-line comments and the latter used for multiple-line comments, where commentText represents the text of the comment. For example:

```
/*
This is a JavaScript comment spanning three lines
*/
```

```
// This is a JavaScript comment occupying one line
```

Looping and Iteration Statements

JavaScript has a number of statements for achieving *iteration,* that is, repeating a series of statements (or *looping,* to use the more familiar programming term). This section covers the `for` loop, `for..in` loop, `while` loop, and the `break` and `continue` statements.

The for loop
Syntax:

```
for ([initial-expression;] [condition;] [update-expression]) {
    Statement(s)...
}
```

3

The `for` statement allows statement iteration to be implemented in JavaScript. It is one of the three looping statements in the JavaScript language; the others are `while` and `for..in`. The `for` statement can be used to iterate either single or multiple statements. If multiple statements (a *code block*) are to be iterated, the { and } brackets must encapsulate all of the statements. A single statement can simply be placed by itself without any bracketing. All three parameters to the `for` statement are optional and are used to control the execution of the loop. If all parameters are used, a semicolon (;) must separate each part, as specified in the earlier syntax description.

To start the loop, an `initial-expression` statement is commonly used to initialize a numeric counter-variable that is used to track the loop's progress; `condition` is used to set the scope of the loop, principally the condition under which the statements in the loop are executed, and is also optional. If omitted this evaluates to a true condition. The `condition` is evaluated upon every iteration of the loop. Control passes to the next JavaScript statement when the loop's condition is eventually met. Last is the `update-expression`, which is primarily used to update the loop-counter. Updating the loop-counter will control the lifetime of the loop because the `condition` part of the loop is normally dependent upon the update-expression.

TIP: The `continue` statement (discussed later in this section) can be used to jump directly to the `update-expression` within the current loop, bypassing any later statements within the loop body.

For example, a loop could write some HTML-formatted text into the
Navigator window using the JavaScript writeln() method as follows:

```
<!--
   Program 3-1
-->
<html>
<head>
<script language="JavaScript">
<!--
function testLoop() {
   var String1 = '<hr align="center" width=';
   document.open();
   for (var size = 5; size <= 100; size+=5)
      document.writeln(String1 + size + '%">');
   document.close();
}
//-->
</script>
</head>
<body>
<form>
<input type="button"
       value="Test the loop"
       onClick="testLoop()">
</form>
</body>
</html>
```

In the preceding example, the program writes a series of HTML horizontal
rule tags (<hr>) that increase in size from 5% to 100% in increments of 5
(size+=5) making a total of exactly 20 iterations. The variable String1
stores the HTML tag and is updated within the loop to include a new width
value via the variable size. The end result of each iteration is a new
String1 value that contains a series of <hr> tags that increase in width.
When the variable size reaches 100 the loop exits. Because only one
statement is included in the loop, code-block bracketing is not required.
The body of the HTML document contains a button that invokes the
testLoop() function. The function statement is discussed later in this
section. onClick is a JavaScript event-handler, so this button invokes the
JavaScript function named testLoop when it is clicked on by the user.
JavaScript event attributes, such as onClick, are discussed in more detail
in Chapter 5.

The `for..in` loop

Syntax:

```
for (index in objectName) {
    statements
}
```

Another variation of the `for` loop is the `for..in` loop, which is used to loop over the properties within an object, identified by the variable `objectName`. The index-variable, `index`, stores the current value that has been returned.

TIP: A property is a value that belongs to an object. Many JavaScript objects have a series of properties whose values can be accessed and changed; for example, the window in which you view all HTML documents is itself an object, named in JavaScript, not surprisingly, as `window`. Another example is the `document` object, whose properties are all the tags in your HTML document, such as hyperlinks, anchors, and forms.

3

Here is a simple script that displays each of the properties of the JavaScript `document` and `window` objects:

```
<!--
  Program 3-2
-->
<html>
<head>
<script language="JavaScript">
<!--
function showResults(obj, name) {
  document.writeln("<table cellpadding=5 border=1>" +
                   "<tr><td align=middle>" +
                   "<b><font size=-1>" +
                   name +
                   "</font></b></td></tr>");
  for (i in obj) {
      document.writeln("<td><font size=-1>" +
                       i +
                       "</font></td>");
      document.writeln("</table><p>");
```

```
    }
}
showResults(document, "document");
showResults(window, "window");
//-->
</script>
</head>
</html>
```

The user-defined function `showResults()` is run automatically in this
script because it is called without intervention from the user. Notice how the
`for..in` statement loops over the properties in an object and how the
results are then placed into an HTML table structure displayed within the
browser. The user-defined function `showResults()` accepts two arguments:
First, the required object and, second, a descriptive string used as a title
within the HTML table, which is finally output for that object. Figure 3-1
illustrates the output from this script.

T **IP:**   Apart from using standard JavaScript objects, you can create your
own objects and then incorporate these into `for..in` loops.

Chapter 4 discusses this topic in more detail.

The output
from the
`showResults()`
function seen
through
Navigator
Figure 3-1.

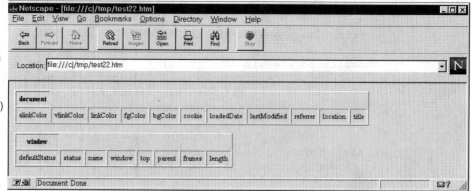

The `while` Loop

Syntax:

```
while (loopCondition) {
      statements
}
```

The `while` statement is the third looping construct in the JavaScript language; the others are the `for` loop and `for..in` statements, respectively. With this form of loop you can execute one or more JavaScript `statements` *while* a particular condition (`loopCondition`) is set. If a code-block is executed within the body of the loop, the code segment must be bracketed using { and }.

Consider the script below, for example, which uses a `while` loop to implement a simple multiplication table. The table required is submitted to the `TimesTable()` function. The `while` loop iterates 12 times, and the value of the variable `thisLoop` is less than or equal to 12. The table is finally output with some simple HTML-formatting tags using the standard JavaScript function `write()`. The `prompt()` method provides a way of obtaining keyboard input from the user; it is provided to allow the input of a number for the choice of table to be generated:

3

```
<!--
   Program 3-3
-->
<html>
<head>
<script language="JavaScript">
<!--
function TimesTable(number) {
  var thisLoop = 1;
  document.writeln("Times Table for: <b>" +
                   number + "</b><hr><pre>");
  while (thisLoop <= 12) {
        document.writeln(thisLoop + " x " +
        number + " = " + (thisLoop * number));
        thisLoop++;
  }
  document.writeln("</pre>");
}
TimesTable(prompt("Enter a number",10));
```

```
//-->
</script>
</head>
</html>
```

Another way of writing this program with a `for` loop instead of the `while` statement could be:

```
for (var thisLoop=1; thisLoop <= 12; thisLoop++)
    ...
}
```

The variable `thisLoop` takes the values 1 through 12 in this example.

Breaking Out of a Loop—*break*
Syntax:

```
break;
```

The `break` statement is used to break out of a loop, such as a `for` or `while` loop, terminating it at the point the statement is reached, and then passing control to the next statement immediately after the loop. For example, consider the following JavaScript program:

```
<!--
  Program 3-4
-->
<html>
<script language="JavaScript">
<!--
function loopTest() {
    var index = 1;
    while (index <= 12) {
          if (index == 6)
              break;
          index++;
    }
    // The break statement brings us here.
}
loopTest();
//-->
</script>
</html>
```

In this example, the variable `index` is first initialized to 1 and a `while` loop is set to iterate while the value of the `index` variable is less than or equal to 12 (`index <= 12`). However, the `if` statement checks to see if `index` equals 6 (`index == 6`); if it does, the `break` statement terminates the `while` loop at this point. The end result is the `while` loop will always terminate after six loop-iterations; as a result the `index` variable will never reach 12. When the `break` statement is reached control will pass to the next statement outside of the scope of the current loop, as indicated by the comment in the script. The variable `index` is incremented (`++`) to ensure it increases in size by one upon each loop iteration. Unlike the `for` statement, the `while` statement must take any loop-condition variables in the body of the loop.

Continuing a Loop—`continue`
Syntax:

```
continue;
```

The `continue` statement is used to terminate the execution of a block of statements that exist within a `for`, `for..in`, or `while` loop, continuing execution of the loop at the next iteration. In contrast to the `break` statement, which exits the loop, `continue` does not terminate the loop. In a `while` loop a `continue` statement makes the loop restart, jumping back to the condition of the loop, while in a `for` loop (and `for..in` loop) it jumps to the `update-expression`.

Creating a User-Defined Function
Syntax:

```
function functionName(arguments, ...) {
        statements
}
```

A *function* is a block of one or more JavaScript `statements` that performs a specific task and then, optionally, returns a value. Functions and procedures are the same in JavaScript: *Procedures* are blocks of code that are executed, and their results displayed, and functions are blocks of code that perform some processing and return a specific value. The `{` and `}` brackets define the *scope* of the function, that is, the statements that make up the body of the function. Functions can also accept *arguments*—values passed to the function, which may be taken from values stored or created elsewhere in your application, such as from a JavaScript object property or from direct user-input. Multiple function arguments are separated by a comma (,) as shown in the previous syntax description.

NOTE: Functions cannot be *nested* inside each other.

When a function is encountered by Navigator, it is read into memory. The function is not executed until explicitly referenced in a *function-call*. A function-call resembles:

```
functionName(parameters, ...)
```

where functionName is the name of the function, and parameters is a list of one or more arguments (values) passed to the function.

TIP: Placing your JavaScript programs in the <head>..</head> container of your hypertext document is advisable. This will ensure that any functions are read into memory as soon as the document is loaded into Navigator. Try to avoid issuing statements *outside* the scope of a function. Try to use one of JavaScript's event-handling attributes instead (see Chapter 5), or allow the user to invoke the function using a form-button, for example, an <input type=button> tag.

If a function needs to return a specific value, the (optional) return statement should be used with the value, or expression, you want to return. For example, this function creates a horizontal rule of a specified height and width without the need to use raw HTML tags:

```
<!--
   Program 3-5
-->
<html>
<head>
<script language="JavaScript">
<!--
function hr(w, h) {
   // Draw a horizontal rule. Note: do not use open() or
   // close() since we do not want to open a new document.
   document.writeln("<hr align=left width=" +
                    w + "height=" + h + ">");
```

```
}
//-->
</script>
</head>
<body>
<h3>
JavaScript Essentials <script>hr("75%","4")</script>
</h3>
</body>
</html>
```

The preceding `hr()` function accepts two string arguments, w and h, which represent the width and height values to pass to a <hr width=w height=h> tag. For example, if this function is now placed within a complete HTML document, the `hr()` function could be called whenever a horizontal rule is needed:

3

```
<!--
  Program 3-6
-->
<html>
<head>
<script language="JavaScript">
<!--
function hr(w, h) {
   document.open();
   document.write("<hr align=left width=" +
                  w + "height=" + h +">");
   document.close();
}
//-->
</script>
</head>
<body>
<h3>
JavaScript Essentials <script>hr("75%","4")</script>
</h3>
</body>
</html>
```

T IP: When embedding scripts within the *body* of an HTML document, remember to comment-out code. Navigator, as with most Web browsers, does not like nested comments, so avoid if possible. One set of comments is enough to hide your JavaScript code. See Chapter 1 for more details on comments.

The alignment of the horizontal-rule has been hard-coded as `"left"` in the example, although you could easily modify this to allow the alignment to pass as an argument. Remember, the `<script>` tag must encapsulate any function calls within the body of an HTML document, and the functions themselves must also be encapsulated in this way because they are JavaScript code, not HTML.

TIP: Functions are useful for writing routines that can be reused in your applications.

Returning Values from a Function—`return`
Syntax:

```
return value;
return ( value );
```

The `return` statement is used within a `function` statement to return a specific value. The bracketed syntax is optional and is normally used when returning an expression, rather than a single value. Use of the `return` statement is optional within JavaScript functions because not all functions have to return a specific value.

For example, you could have the function `calcYears()` that returns the number of hours in a certain number of years; you would specify the latter as the function-argument `years`.

```
function calcYears(years) {
    hoursinYear = 24 * 365;
    return(hoursinYear);
}
```

The function-call `calcYears(1)` would return `8760`. You can also return an expression; for example:

```
return(hoursinYear * 60);
```

would return the number of minutes in that particular year.

TIP: If you ever need to leave a function at a specific point, without using any complex `if` statements, simply issue a `return` statement by itself. You will be returned to the statement immediately following the statement that invoked the function.

Returning a single value is commonplace, although a `return` statement could also return an array value (a multidimensional variable), for example:

```
function returnArray() {
  var myArray = new Object();
  myArray[1] = "JavaScript";
  myArray[2] = "Java";
  return(myArray);
}
```

3

Accessing Function Arguments Using the `arguments[]` Array

New to Navigator 3.0 is the `arguments` array. The `arguments` array contains a list of parameters that are passed to the current function, so `arguments[0]`, for example, would be the first argument, and so forth. The total number of arguments is stored in the `arguments.length` property. So, for a function definition such as:

```
function showData("europe") {
    ...
}
```

the parameter `"europe"`—a string object in this instance—would be stored in the array `arguments[0]`. Here is a small code extract that prints all the arguments passed to a function:

```
function showArgs() {
    argList = "";
    for (var n=0; n <= arguments.length; n++) {
        argList += n + ". " + arguments[n] + "\n";
    }
    alert(argList);
}
```

For example, here is a larger example that incorporates the `showArgs()` function. Notice how the function is called with only two parameters, and how the program stores the `null` value for the empty parameter. The `showArgs()` function builds up a string of arguments, and then displays these using the `alert()` method:

```
<!--
  Program 3-7
-->
<html>
<script>
<!--
function showArgs(a, b, c) {
   var argList = "";
   for (var n=0; n <= arguments.length; n++) {
       argList += n + ". " + arguments[n] + "\n";
   }
   alert(argList);
}
showArgs("java", "script")
//-->
</script>
</html>
```

Conditional Statements—`if...else`

Syntax:

```
if (condition) {
   statements1
} [ else { statements2 } ]
```

The `if...else` statement is a conditional statement that allows one or more JavaScript statements to be executed, depending on a user-defined condition. The `condition` part of the `if` statement is an expression, which, when held true, executes the JavaScript statements in the code-block `statements1`. A code-block must be enclosed in { and } brackets; single statements do not require this, however. The optional `else` part of the `if` statement allows the code-block identified by `statements2` to be executed if the main `if` statement `condition` is false, for example, when the condition is not met. It is also possible to *nest* `if` statements inside each other. For example:

```
<!--
  Program 3-8
-->
<html>
<head>
<script language="JavaScript">
<!--
```

```
today    = new Date();
minutes = today.getMinutes();
if (minutes >=0 && minutes <= 30)
    document.write("<body text=White bgcolor=Blue>");
else
    document.write("<body text=White bgcolor=Black>");
//-->
</script>
This is the body of the document.<p>
</body>
</html>
```

The *?* Statement

JavaScript also supports a conditional testing statement of the form:

```
? (expression) trueStatements : falseStatements
```

where `expression` is a JavaScript expression that evaluates to `true` or `false`, and where `trueStatements` and `falseStatements` are one or more JavaScript statements that are invoked depending on the outcome of the expression: `trueStatements` for a true expression, and `falseStatements` for a false expression, respectively. You can think of this statement as a shorthand `if..else`. For example, the following script could alter the background color of a document based upon the number of seconds in the current time:

```
<!--
  Program 3-9
-->
<html>
<head>
<script language="JavaScript">
<!--
  var today     = new Date();
  var secs      = today.getSeconds();
  var backColor = (secs >=0 && secs <=30) ?
                   "Blue" : "Black";
  document.write("<body text=White bgcolor=" +
                   backColor +
                   ">");
//-->
</script>
</head>
The body of our text goes in here.<p>
</body>
</html>
```

The value "Blue" is placed in the variable backColor if the variable minutes is between 0 and 30, for example, in the case of a true outcome for the (secs >=0 && secs <=30) expression. Otherwise, the value "Black" is used (the false outcome). The variable backColor is then concatenated into a string that specifies the background color within an HTML <body> tag, which is then written into the browser and interpreted by Navigator accordingly.

The following example uses the ? statement to execute a JavaScript statement, rather than assigning a value to a variable, as with the previous program:

```
<!--
  Program 3-10
-->
<html>
<head>
<script language="JavaScript">
<!--
  var today = new Date();
  var secs  = today.getSeconds();
  (secs >=0 && secs <=30) ?
      document.write("<body text=White bgcolor=Blue>") :
      document.write("<body text=White bgcolor=Black>");
//--
</script>
</head>
The body of our text goes in here.<p>
</body>
</html>
```

simply invokes a document.write() method based upon the value of the secs variable, thus allowing JavaScript statements to be executed directly.

Nested ? Statements

You can also *nest* ? statements inside one another to incorporate more test conditions. For example, consider the following script, which is an extension of the previous example, and which checks for more values. Rather than using multiple ? statements, all of the testing has been combined into a single JavaScript statement:

```
<!--
  Program 3-11
-->
<html>
<head>
```

```
<script language="JavaScript">
<!--
  var today = new Date();
  var secs  = today.getSeconds();
  (secs >=0 && secs <=30) ?
        document.write("<body text=white bgcolor=Blue>") :
            (secs >=31 && secs <=50) ?
                    document.write("<body text=White bgcolor=Black>") :
                    document.write("<body text=White bgcolor=Beige>");
//-->
</script>
</head>
The body of our text goes in here.<p>
</body>
</html>
```

3

The script first tests to see if the value of the secs variable is between 0 and 30, and if it is the background color is changed to Blue. If the value of secs is greater than 30 the script does another check to see if the value is between 31 and 50. If this expression yields a true outcome, the background color is changed to Black, otherwise it is changed to Beige. As you can see, the false expression part has been replaced with a nested ? statement.

TIP: The ? statement executes quickly within JavaScript, and is a better replacement for the if...else statement in many cases. Use it whenever possible, especially when assigning values to variables that depend on a prespecified condition.

Creating Variables

Variable creation can be achieved by using the var statement or by directly assigning a value to a variable using the assignment operator (=).

The **var** Statement
Syntax:

```
var variableName [= value|expression]
```

The var statement creates a new variable identified by the name variableName. The *scope* of the newly created variable will either be local or global, depending on where the variable is created. The programmer may assign a literal value or an expression to the variable that has been created.

In fact, you can omit the var statement completely when creating a new variable, although, in this instance, you must assign a value to the variable.

For example, in the following script, the variable myVar is defined twice with two separate values: one within the scope of the testFunction() function, and one outside of the function. To see the values of both variables, two alert() methods have been used. Notice the inclusion of the this statement (described at the end of this section), which refers to the object myVar that is defined within the *current* function:

```
<!--
  Program 3-12
-->
<html>
<head>
<script language="JavaScript">
<!--
var myVar = "Outside";
function testFunction() {
  var myVar = "Inside";
  alert("this.myVar: " + this.myVar);
  alert("myVar: " + myVar);
}
testFunction();
//-->
</script>
</head>
</html>
```

When the preceding document is loaded into Navigator, the first alert-box displays the value "Outside", while the second alert-box displays the value "Inside", as expected. If the this statement is omitted from the second alert-statement, however, you will find two "Inside" values are shown. This is because the scope of the current function overrides any variables defined outside of function-body; therefore, you see the *local* value of the variable myVar. The this statement cannot be used outside of a function-call.

The *scope* of variables created with var (and by direct assignment) depends on the whereabouts of the statement. If var is used outside of a function the variable will be accessible to the entire application, although variables created *within* functions are only available for use within that function, that is, they are *local* to the function, rather than *global*. For example:

```
<!--
  Program 3-13
-->
<html>
<head>
<script language="JavaScript">
<!--
function TestFunction() {
  var localVar = "Hello";
}
alert(localVar);
//-->
</script>
</head>
</html>
```

would result in the error "`localVar is not defined`" because `localVar`
has been referenced outside the scope of the function `TestFunction()` in
which the variable was originally defined.

3

Referring to the Current Variable—*this*
Syntax:

`this[.property]`

`this` is not so much a statement as an internal property. The value of `this`
contains the current 'object' and can have standard properties such as
`name`, `length,` and `value` applied accordingly. The `this` statement cannot
be used outside the scope of a function or function-call reference. When
the `property` argument is omitted, the current object is passed literally;
however, you must apply a valid property to the object in order to yield
a result.

The `this` statement is also useful when 'disambiguating' an object by
binding it within the scope of the current object and for making your code
more compact.

T IP: The `this` statement *cannot* be used outside the scope of a JavaScript
function or function-call.

For example, you could call a user-defined function from within an
`OnChange` event-handler using `this` to pass the current value of the object:

```
<!--
  Program 3-14
-->
<html>
<head>
<script language="JavaScript">
<!--
function sendData(arg) {
  alert("The " + arg.name +
        " field has changed.");
}
//-->
</script>
</head>
<body>
<form>
<table>
<tr>
 <td>Name:</td>
 <td><input name="persname" type="text"
            onChange="sendData(this)"></td>
</tr>
<tr>
  <td>E-mail:</td>
  <td><input name="email" type="text"></td>
</tr>
</table>
</form>
</body>
</html>
```

When the user changes the contents of the persname field (and that field loses focus), the sendData() function is called with the argument this. The value of this at this stage is the actual <input> tag itself. You must now apply a property to the value to extract the information you require. In this example, the name property has been extracted. You could have passed the argument this.name, of course. To see the contents of the text-field, you could use this.value. Without the this statement the sendData() function must be altered as follows:

```
function sendData(arg) {
  alert("The " +
        document.forms[0].persname.name +
        " variable has changed.");
}
```

which now refers to the name of the text-field `persname` directly, and is slightly more long-winded because you have to form an object-hierarchy to get to the field you require. This expression would be further extended if you need to refer to a specific window.

Here is another example using the `form` property (this refers to the current `form` object) to display all of the form elements defined within that form:

```
<!--
  Program 3-15
-->
<html>
<head>
<script language="JavaScript">
<!--
function seeElem(f)  {
  var elementList = "";
  for (var num=0; num < f.elements.length; num++) {
      elementList += num +
                    ". " +
                    f.elements[num] +
                    "\n";
  }
  alert(elementList);
}
//-->
</script>
</head>
<body>
<form>
<table>
<tr>
 <td>Name:</td>
 <td><input name="persname"
           type="text">
</tr>
<tr>
   <td>E-mail:</td>
   <td><input name="email"
           type="text"></td>
</tr>
</table>
<input type="button"
      value="See elements"
      onClick="seeElem(this.form)">
</form>
</body>
</html>
```

3

This script loops through the `elements` array and extracts each form element, adding it to a string, which is then formatted and displayed to the user using an `alert()` box. Notice how the entire form object has been passed to the `seeElem()` function.

Specifying an Object—`with`

Syntax:

```
with (objectName) {
    statements
}
```

The `with` statement makes the object identified by `objectName` the default object for the JavaScript statements in the code-block `statements`. The use of `with` is a convenience because it can cut down the amount of code you must write. For example, use the `with` statement using the JavaScript `Math` object as follows:

```
with (Math) {
    document.writeln(PI);
}
```

which allows you to eliminate using the `Math` prefix when you refer to `Math` object constants such as `PI`. Or, you could use the `with` statement with the `document` object:

```
with (parent.frames[1].document) {
    writeln("Some <b>HTML-formatted</b> text");
    write("<hr>");
}
```

which saves prefixing the `writeln()` methods with the target document. In this case, this is a frameset-document. Chapter 9 presents an in-depth look at Navigator's frameset-document capabilities.

Summary

Statements are used to build structure into a JavaScript application; they control the testing of conditions and iterative processing.

♦ JavaScript's looping statements allow statements to be executed iteratively. They include the `for` loop for general statement iteration, `for..in` for looping over object properties, and `while` for allowing a series of statements to be executed while a specific condition holds true.

Use the `break` statement to break out of a loop, and `continue` to restart an iteration from the current point of execution.

♦ JavaScript's conditional statements include the `if..else` and `?` statements; the latter is a shorthand notation for the former `if..else` statement. Conditional statements build *choice* into your JavaScript applications and allow the flow of control within a program to be determined, perhaps on progmatic conditions, or even user-input from an HTML-form, etc.

♦ Variables are created using the JavaScript `var` statement; they can optionally be assigned a value. Or, you can omit the `var` and assign a variable directly. The latter method is normally used when overwriting the contents of a variable; the former method is used when first creating a variable.

♦ User-defined functions are created using the JavaScript `function` statement. Functions allow JavaScript statements to be grouped together, and then executed as and when required. Functions can be passed arguments, which can then be used accordingly. In order to call a function, the name of the function is specified, along with any arguments, using the syntax `functionName(argList)`, where `argList` is a comma-separated list of arguments. Likewise, a function without any arguments is called using an empty argument list, for example, `functionName()`. Functions may return one or more values if a `return` statement is specified (this is optional). JavaScript also supplies the `arguments[]` array which is a reflection of each argument that has been passed to the current function. Any missing parameters are stored as `null` values.

3

♦ Code annotations are created using JavaScript's comment mechanisms. Two forms of comment are provided: the single-line comment `//` and the multiple-lined container comment `/* */`. Remember that HTML `<!--` and `-->` comment container tags are not valid *within* the JavaScript `<script>..</script>` container.

When referring to an object, the `with` statement can be used to specify a group of statements that manipulate the *same* object. This technique is a shorthand notation that saves the programmer from prefixing a property with the name of an object.

CHAPTER 4

JavaScript's Objects, Methods, and Properties

The JavaScript language is based upon an object-oriented data model, and objects operate at a number of different levels. HTML documents, or rather, the tags of which they are comprised, are *reflected* as a series of objects that can be accessed and manipulated by a JavaScript application. JavaScript also has a number of internal objects, some of which represent primitive data-types, such as strings.

There are also generic object-types that can be used for the creation of structures, such as arrays, etc. In this chapter you will learn

♦ What object *methods* and *properties* are

♦ How the JavaScript object hierarchy is structured

♦ Which objects are created automatically and which are not

♦ How to manipulate internal objects such as Strings and Dates

The JavaScript Object Model

Think in terms of objects for all of your future HTML-authoring and programming with JavaScript. Much of the HTML language Navigator understands has been modified to include additional attributes, which make JavaScript more object-based. While JavaScript is not a fully-fledged object-orientated language like Java, for example, it does share many object-oriented characteristics. The main object families in Navigator fall into three groups, namely:

♦ Navigator objects

♦ Internal or built-in objects

♦ HTML-reflected objects

Navigator objects are *browser-dependent* objects such as the window, location, and history details. Internal objects include primitive types, such as Strings, mathematical constants, and internal formats, such as Dates. HTML-reflected objects relate to the HTML tags that make up the current document; they include items such as hyperlinks and forms.

Object Methods

Objects have *methods* associated with them that allow objects to be manipulated and interrogated and, in some cases, allow object values to be changed. For example, a string of text is treated as a string object in JavaScript and could be converted to lowercase using the `toLowerCase()` method. You can also write your own object methods using JavaScript.

TIP: When using a object method, be sure to prefix it with the name of the object to which it belongs, for example, `document.write()`, rather than `write()` by itself; the latter will result in an error. The syntax descriptions of each object shown later in this chapter will show you which syntax to use. Some methods do not require prefixing, which occurs when you deal with the top-level `window` object.

Object Properties

Another term used in context to an object-driven environment is a *property*. A property is a value that belongs to an object. All of the standard JavaScript objects have such properties, for example, the `document` object has a property called `bgColor`, which is a reflection of the `<body>` tag's `bgcolor` attribute—the background color, in this instance. Properties are referred to by placing a period (`.`) after the object name, followed by the required name of the property. The properties available to an object depend on the object being referenced. User-defined objects can also be allocated properties.

TIP: Some properties are termed *read-only* because they cannot be changed by having a new value assigned to them. In such cases, you can only access, that is, read values, from these properties. Properties that *can* be changed include the document colors, for example, `document.bgColor` and the current URL, for example, `window.location`, etc. These latter properties are known as *read/write* properties.

4

Navigator Objects

Navigator supports a wide range of different objects types. *HTML-objects* are objects that reflect the values of HTML tags, such as anchors, hyperlinks, and form objects, such as text-fields and radio-boxes. The "top-level" objects, or *Navigator objects,* are those reflected from the browsers environment, for example, the window, location, and history objects, etc. Some Navigator objects are created "automatically," as documented in the following table:

Object Name	Description
`window`	The top-level object in the JavaScript object hierarchy. A frameset-document also has its own window object.
`document`	The document object contains properties that relate to the current HTML document, such as the name of each form, the document's colors, etc. Most of the HTML tags are reflected through document properties in JavaScript.
`location`	An object that contains properties relating to the current document's location, for example, URL.
`navigator`	Details about the current version of Navigator.

Object Name	Description
history	The history object contains details of all URLs the user has visited in the current Navigator session. Navigator's Go menu contains details of the URLs visited in the current session and is a reflection of the history property.

Each of the objects shown in the table will now be discussed in more detail.

The `window` Object

The `window` object refers to the main Navigator window, which is the top-level object in JavaScript, mainly because every document must exist within a window. Because Navigator version 2.0 and above support multiple windows in the form of a frameset-document—created using the `<frameset>` container tag—the window to which you are referring becomes ambiguous. You must, therefore, use the `parent` object, along with the `frames` property, to refer to the window you need to reference. Frames and windows are one and the same thing in JavaScript. For example, `parent.frames[0]` refers to the first frame within the Navigator browser. A window is always assumed to exist, although autonomous windows can also be opened and referenced using the `window.open()` method, as detailed in Chapter 8.

To use a `window` object's methods and properties, use any of the following syntaxes:

♦   `window.propertyName`

♦   `window.methodName(parameters)`

♦   `self.propertyName`

♦   `self.methodName(parameters)`

♦   `top.propertyName`

♦   `top.methodName(parameters)`

♦   `parent.propertyName`

♦   `parent.methodName(parameters)`

♦   `windowVar.propertyName`

♦   `windowVar.methodName(parameters)`

♦   `propertyName`

♦   `methodName(parameters)`

where `windowVar` is a variable that refers to a `window` object, as shown earlier in the first syntax description. The `self` property is a synonym that refers to the "current" window (within a frameset-document), whereas the synonym `top` refers to the top-level Navigator window, and is analogous to self when referring to the current window. The `parent` property can also be mentioned because frame objects and `window` objects are treated identically.

NOTE: The `parent` and `top` properties refer to different things. Both can be used instead of a frame name, depending on *where* the frame resides. The `parent` property refers to the *current* frameset-document; `top` refers to the top-most window that may contain either a frame or a *nested* frame. Nested frames are covered in greater detail within Chapter 9 and may require specific use of the `top` property.

Properties

The `window` object has the following properties:

♦ `defaultStatus`—a reflection of the default text-message displayed within the Navigator status bar at the bottom of the screen

♦ `frames`—an array of frames within a `<frameset>` document

♦ `length`—the number of frames in the current `<frameset>` document

♦ `name`—a reflection of the current window title as set in the `windowName` argument passed to the `open()` method (see syntax)

♦ `parent`—a synonym referring both to a `windowName` argument and a frame within a `<frameset>` document. Remember, frame objects are the same as window objects.

♦ `self`—a synonym referring to the current window

♦ `status`—a transient message in Navigator's status bar

♦ `top`—a synonym referring to the *main* Navigator window

♦ `window`—a synonym referring to the current window

Methods

The `alert()` method can be used to display a text-message; `close()` closes a window; `confirm()` allows yes/no choices to be entered (and returns a boolean `true`/`false` value); `open()` opens a new window; `prompt()` prompts the user for input; `setTimeout()` attaches a time-out event to a window; and `clearTimeout()` clears a time-out event set with `setTimeOut()`.

4

Event-Handlers

A window object does not have an event-handler until a document is actually loaded into it. Documents have `onLoad` and `onUnLoad` event-handling attributes, as do `<frameset>` documents, defined in the `<body>` container.

Examples

To create a window measuring 400 × 400 pixels and load it with the home page of Osborne's Web-site, this JavaScript statement could be used:

```
myWin = open("http://www.osborne.com",
             "myWindow",
             "width=400,height=400");
```

To close the window, you would use:

```
myWin.close();
```

This statement could also be used from a script in any other window to shut down the window "`myWin`".

TIP: See Chapter 8, which discusses JavaScript's `open()`, `close()`, `focus()`, and `blur()` methods, for more about manipulating `window` objects.

The document Object

The `document` object is a reflection of the entire hypertext document or, rather, the `<body>..</body>` part of the document. Documents are nested within windows inside the Navigator browser, that is, the document is bound to a window. All of the HTML objects within a hypertext document (discussed later) are properties of the `document` object because they reside within the document itself. For example, the first form within a document can be referred to in JavaScript as `document.forms[0]`, while the first form within the second frame could be referred to as `parent.frames[0].document.forms[0]`, and so forth.

The `document` object is useful because it provides methods that allow dynamic-HTML to be written into the Navigator browser. A document is created in HTML through the use of the `<body>..<.body>` tag. Unless such a container is used, many of the properties of this object will be unavailable, although you can set many of the properties by assigning values directly to them.

Syntax:

```
<body background="bgImageOrUrl"
      bgcolor="backgroundColor"
      text="foregroundColor"
      link="unfollowedLinkColor"
      alink="activatedLinkColor"
      vlink="followedLinkColor"
      [onLoad="handlerText"]
      [onUnload="handlerText"]>
</body>
```

Where `bgImageOrUrl` specifies a bitmap image used to tile the Navigator background and can be stored in the GIF or JPEG format. *Tile* is used to refer to a bitmap file that is replicated across the entire screen, thus tiling the window. The colors of a document's elements (text colors, background colors, and hyperlinks) are chosen using the `alink`, `bgcolor`, `link`, `text`, and `vlink` attributes, all of which can be expressed as any of the following:

♦ Red-Green-Blue triplets of the form `"#RRGGBB"` or `"RRGGBB"`, where `RR` is Red, `GG` is Green, and `BB` is Blue, and each triplet is specified in the hexadecimal notation ranging from `0-FF` where FF is the highest color intensity; for example, `"0000FF"` is Blue.

♦ A color verb string, for example, `"Blue"` (Note: Netscape 2.0 and above only). Appendix G contains a list of color-codes supported by Navigator.

4

To use the `document` object's properties and methods, use the following syntax:

♦ `document.propertyName`

♦ `document.methodName(parameters)`

Properties

The `document` object has an extensive range of properties, mainly because it must reflect each HTML tag within the current document:

♦ `alinkColor`—reflects the `<body>` tag's `alink` attribute

♦ `anchors`—an array that reflects all the anchors within the document

♦ `bgColor`—reflects the `<body>` tag's `bgcolor` (background color) attribute

♦ `cookie`—specifies a cookie (a small piece of information saved to disk)

♦ `fgColor`—reflects the `<body>` tag's `text` attribute

- ◆ `forms`—an array that contains each `<form>` in the current document
- ◆ `images`—an array of images in the current document, for example, `<img>` tags, and is new to Navigator 3.0
- ◆ `lastModified`—reflects the date at which the current document was last modified
- ◆ `linkColor`—reflects the `link` (default hyperlink color) attribute
- ◆ `links`—an array that reflects each hyperlink in the current document
- ◆ `location`—reflects the URL of the current document
- ◆ `referrer`—reflects the URL of the document that passed control to the current document (or the *calling* document)
- ◆ `title`—reflects the contents of the `<title>..</title>` container
- ◆ `vlinkColor`—reflects the `<body>` tag's `vlink` (visited link color) attribute

Visited links (URLs) are stored in the `NETSCAPE.HST` file.

Methods

The `clear()` method can be used to clear the current document. Note that this method does not function properly in Navigator, but a successive `open()` and `close()` will clear the window. To write information into the browser, the `write()` and `writeln()` methods have been supplied. These methods write HTML-formatted strings of text into the browser, meaning you can create any HTML document dynamically, including complete JavaScript applications.

TIP: One of the most consistent mistakes with JavaScript involves trying to write data into the browser screen on an *ad hoc* basis. Writing data into a window over another document is inadvisable because the effects can sometimes crash Navigator. Instead, a *stream* of data should be written into the window. To do this, start with a `document.open()`, and then use as many `document.write()` statements as you need. End this with a `document.close()` to send the data into the browser. If you want to append data into a window, omit the `open()` and `close()` methods; make certain you are targeting the correct window.

Event-Handlers

The `onLoad` and `onUnLoad` event-handling attributes can be used in `<body>` and `<frame>` tags.

Examples

To write HTML-formatted text into the browser, you can use the `document.writeln()` function. For example, you could create an image-tag dynamically—showing the image—by using the JavaScript statements:

```
document.open();
document.writeln("<img src='myimage.gif'>");
document.close();
```

You could even create a complete JavaScript application dynamically. For instance:

```
document.open();
document.writeln("<script language='JavaScript'>" +
          "alert('Hello World!')" +
          "</script>");
document.close();
```

To invoke a Java applet, simply create an `<applet>` tag dynamically, for example:

```
document.open();
document.writeln("<applet code=myApplet.class " +
          "codebase=classes width=100 height=50>" +
          "</applet>");
document.close();
```

Notice how some strings have been concatenated (joined) together in the previous example using the + operator. Use this technique whenever lines of code become too long to fit within your editing program, or simply to break up complex strings into more manageable chunks.

The `location` Object

This object is a reflection of the current document's location, with respect to its *Uniform Resource Locator*(URL). The URL is a mechanism closely tied to the entire concept of the World Wide Web, and *all* documents, whether local or networked, have a unique URL. A URL is an address of a resource on the World Wide Web and many different URLs are supported by Navigator, allowing it to interface to a variety of Internet-based services such as Gopher servers, News (USENET) servers, File Transfer Protocol (FTP) servers, mail servers, as well as HyperText Transfer Protocol (HTTP) servers, or

4

Web-servers, as they are more commonly known. Manipulation of the `location` object allows a document's URL to be altered. Location objects are associated with the current `window` object, into which a document is loaded. Documents do not contain URL information; this a browser-related feature.

Syntax:

```
[windowRef.]location.propertyName
```

where `windowRef` is an optional variable that defines a specific window you want to access (see details in the later section on the `window` object). The `windowRef` variable can also refer to a frame within a frameset-document by using the `parent` property, a synonym used when referring to multiple `window` objects. The `location` object is a property of the `window` object; if you need to reference a `location` object without specifying a particular window, the current window is assumed. If you specify a particular window or frame using the syntax:

```
windowRef.location.propertyName
```

the location of the specified window will be used.

T IP: Confusing the `location` object with the location *property* of the `document` object is easy. The value of `document.location` cannot be changed, although the location properties of a window can be changed; for example, by using a JavaScript expression of the form:
`window.location.property`. The value of `document.location` is set to the value of `window.location` when a document is initially loaded because documents exist within windows (remember the object-hierarchy). This can be changed at a later stage, however, by assigning a new URL value.

Properties

The `location` object has the following properties:

♦   `hash`—specifies the anchor name in the URL, if it exists

♦   `host`—specifies the `hostname:port` portion of the current URL

♦   `hostname`—specifies the host and domain name (or numeric IP address) of the current host's URL

♦   `href`—specifies the complete URL of the current document

♦   `pathname`—specifies the URL-path portion of the URL, for example, after the hostname

♦ `port`—specifies the communications port the server uses

♦ `protocol`—specifies the beginning of the URL, including the colon, for example, `http:`

♦ `target`—a reflection of the `target` attribute in the `<a href>` tag

Methods

No methods are defined for the `location` object.

Event-Handlers

No event-handlers are associated with the `location` object.

Examples

To set the URL of the *current* window to a new URL use the following statement:

```
self.location = "http://www.osborne.com";
```

which in this case loads Osborne's Web site into the current window. You could omit the "`self.`" entirely, in fact, since a window object would be assumed by JavaScript.

4

To load a new URL into a specific frame of a frameset-document, the statement:

```
parent.frames[0].location = "http://www.osborne.com";
```

could be used, where `parent.frames[0]` refers to the first frame within the current `<frameset>` document in this instance—see Chapter 9.

The `history` Object

The `history` object is a list of URLs visited in the present session, and that are contained within Navigator's *Go* menu. History objects are associated with the current document. A number of history-based methods allow different URLs to be loaded into Navigator, and for navigation back and forth between URLs loaded previously.

Syntax:

♦ `history.propertyName`

♦ `history.methodName(parameters)`

Properties

The `length` property contains the number of entries in the `history` object.

Methods

The `back()` method allows the previous URL to be loaded into Navigator, while the `forward()` method performs the inverse function. The `go()` method can also be used with a `history` object.

Event-Handlers

No event-handlers are defined for the `history` object.

Examples

To see the previously loaded document, use

```
history.go(-1);
```

which is the same as saying

```
history.back();
```

If you need to target a specific window, or frame, the `parent` property can be used. For example:

```
parent.frames[0].history.back();
```

moves to the previous document loaded into the first frame within a `<frameset>` document.

If you have multiple navigator windows open, you can use an expression such as:

```
window1.frames[0].history.forward();
```

which will move forward one document within the first frame of the first window, where `window1` is a variable that defines the `window` using the `open()` method. See Chapter 8 for more information on window manipulation within JavaScript.

The `navigator` Object

The `navigator` object contains details of the current version of the Netscape Navigator browser. This object can be used to determine version information, details of plug-ins, and MIME types.

Syntax:

```
navigator.propertyName
```

Properties

The navigator object has the following properties:

- ♦ `appCodeName`—the code name of the browser
- ♦ `appName`—the name of the browser
- ♦ `appVersion`—specifies version information for the Navigator
- ♦ `userAgent`—specifies the user-agent header; `plugins`—an array of plug-ins installed on the system (new to Navigator 3.0)
- ♦ `mimeTypes`—an array of MIME-types supported (new to Navigator 3.0)

The `length` property of the `plugins` and `mimeTypes` arrays will yield the size of each structure, that is, the number of plug-ins and MIME-types supported, depending on what you have actually installed.

Methods

No methods are defined for the `navigator` object.

Event-Handlers

No event-handlers are associated with the `navigator` object.

Internal Objects

4

Internal objects are not related to the browser or to the currently loaded HTML document; instead, they are related to objects that can be manipulated internally by the developer. Such objects include primitive types, such as strings, and more complex objects, such as dates. The following table illustrates the internal, or *built-in* objects that Navigator supports.

Those entries marked with a ✔ denote an object constructor introduced with Netscape Atlas, Navigator 3.0.

Object Name	Description
Array ✔	Array structure
Date	Internal date and time manipulation
Math	Mathematical object and properties

Object Name	Description
`Object` ✔	Generic object type
`String` ✔	Text string object

Each of the internal objects in this table will now be discussed.

Array Objects

Arrays are multidimensional objects that are referenced using a numeric index variable. Many of the HTML-reflected objects within JavaScript are structured as arrays because they can contain multiple values. How many of these objects require HTML applications is left up to the user; no limits are imposed by Navigator, although resources are finite in relation to your system's memory resources. Examples of array-structured objects in Navigator include hyperlinks, anchors, forms, and frames. More details on these can be found in the next section. Arrays can be created in one of three ways (the final two are new to Netscape Atlas):

♦ Use a user-defined function such as the `makeArray()` function described in Appendix D to assign multiple values to an object

♦ Use the `Array()` constructor to create the array

♦ Use the `Object()` constructor to create the array

The two final techniques differ between Navigator versions (2.*x* and Atlas). For more details on object manipulation and variable creation, including sections on the `Array()`, `Object()`, and `makeArray()` techniques, see Chapter 6.

Array objects have no methods or properties associated with them.

The `Date` Object

The `Date` object is borrowed from Java and contains both date and time information. A selection of date-manipulation methods is supplied by JavaScript to extract various parts of this object. Dates can be altered dynamically, for example, to add and subtract values from date-formatted variables to produce new dates. A date object is created using the syntax:

```
dateObj = new Date(parameters)
```

Where `dateObj` is a variable into which the new `Date` object will be stored. The `parameters` argument can include the following values:

♦ An empty parameter list, for instance, `Date()`, which simply extracts the current date and time

♦ A string representing the date and time of the form: "Month day, year time," for example, `"March 1, 1996 12:00:00"` (Note: Time is in 24-hour format)

♦ A set of values for the year, month, day, hour, minute, and seconds. For instance, the string: `"96,3,1,12,30,0"` is the same as the 1st of March 1996 12:30 P.M.

♦ A set of integer values for only the year, month, and day, for example, `"96, 3, 1"` is the same as 1 March 1996. The time-elements in the new object will all be set to zero if they are not specified.

Properties
The `Date` object has no properties.

Methods
Date objects can use any of the following JavaScript methods: `getDate()`, `getDay()`, `getHours()`, `getMinutes()`, `getMonth()`, `getSeconds()`, `getTime()`, `getTimeZoneoffset()`, `getYear()`, `Date.parse()`, `setDate()`, `setHours()`, `setMinutes()`, `setMonth()`, `setSeconds()`, `setTime()`, `setYear()`, `toGMTString()`, `toLocaleString()`, and `Date.UTC()`. Appendix B documents each method.

4

Event-Handlers
Event-handlers are not used with internal objects.

Examples
A new `Date` object could be created using today's (local) date and time using the JavaScript statement:

```
todayDate = new Date();
```

where `Date()` is the date-constructor that creates a new `Date` object. Likewise, a `Date` object can be created with a different date by passing the necessary parameters to the object, for example:

```
// 8th August 1996 12:00:00
theDate = new Date(96,8,8,12,00,0);
```

A more extensive example is an HTML/JavaScript application that prints a simple header containing the date and time at the top of an HTML document:

```
<!--
  Program 4-1
-->
<html>
<head>
<script language="JavaScript">
<!--
function showHeader() {
  var theDate = new Date();
  document.writeln("<table cellpadding=5 width=100% border=0>" +
                   "<tr><td width=95% bgcolor=gray align=left>" +
                   "<font color=White>Date: " + theDate +
                   "</font></td></tr></table><p>");
}
showHeader();
//-->
</script>
</head>
</html>
```

Here is another HTML/JavaScript application that uses the Date() method to extract the current hour, and uses it to change the background pattern of the current HTML document, by using Netscape's background attribute within the HTML <body> tag:

```
<!--
  Program 4-2
-->
<html>
<script language="JavaScript">
<!--
  theTime = new Date();
  theHour = theTime.getHours();
  if (theHour < 18) // < 6pm local time
    document.writeln("<body background='day.gif' text='White'>");
  else
    document.writeln("<body background='night.gif' text='White'>");
//-->
</script>
This is the text of the body...
</body>
</html>
```

Notice how the script is used to create the first <body> tag. The final </body> tag is output literally within the document, which is valid because all the necessary HTML tags are output in the correct order. Using similar code, you can load different backgrounds, according to a certain day or hour, or you can alter your page layout (including images) according to the same criteria. For instance, in the previous example, the image file `night.gif` is used as a background when it is greater than 6 P.M., otherwise, the graphic `day.gif` is used instead. Both files are assumed to exist in the same directory as the HTML file that references them. You can, of course, refer to any image stored on the Internet using a URL of the form

```
http://hostname/imagefile-path
```

where `hostname` is the name of an Internet host where the image resides, and `imagefile-path` is the pathname to a file stored in the GIF or JPEG format—the formats Navigator can use for inline images. Without the use of a CGI-script, the use of dates to determine a background image would have been impossible in earlier versions of HTML. JavaScript clearly does away with the need for a CGI script in this instance.

The `Math` Object

The `Math` object is built into the Navigator browser and contains properties and methods used for manipulating numerical values. Common mathematical constants are also contained within the `Math` object.

4

Syntax:

```
Math.propertyName
Math.methodName(parameters)
```

Properties
The `Math` objects properties are mathematical constants, namely:

♦ E

♦ LN2

♦ LN10

♦ LOG2E

♦ LOG10E

♦ PI

♦ SQRT1_2

♦ SQRT2

Methods
A number of mathematical functions are provided. Please refer to Appendix B, where each is explained in more detail.

- abs()
- acos()
- asin()
- atan()
- ceil()
- cos()
- exp()
- floor()
- log()
- max()
- min()
- pow()
- random()
- round()
- sin()
- sqrt()
- tan()

Event-handlers

Not applicable to internal objects.

Examples

To access a mathematical constant, simply prefix its name onto the Math object, for example:

```
var piVar = Math.PI;
```

would place the value of the constant *pi* into the variable piVar.

To use a Math method, such as abs(), use the required method with any arguments, for instance:

```
myValue = -8.68;
var absVal = Math.abs(value);
```

stores the value 8.68 into the variable myValue and stores 8.68 into the variable absVal; thus, it makes the number positive.

TIP: Remember each of the `Math` methods discussed in this section is documented in Appendix B. Remember also to prefix all `Math` methods with `'Math.'` before using them.

Generic Objects

JavaScript has borrowed Java's `Object()` object-constructor, which can be used to create a *generic* object. This object, when created, has no specific type. The type of the object is allocated later. For example, to create an array quickly, you could use the statements:

```
var myObject = new Object();
myObject[1] = "Value 1";
myObject[2] = "Value 2";
```

See Chapter 6 for further examples of Navigator 3.0's new `Object()` and `Array()` constructor functions.

4

String Objects

A *string* is a sequence of characters joined together and enclosed in double (") or single (') quotes; for instance, `"wombat"` is a string object containing six characters. To manipulate string objects, use the general syntax:

♦   `stringName.propertyName`
♦   `stringName.methodName(parameters)`

where `stringName` is the name of a string object or string variable (both are the same). Strings can be created in three different ways, namely:

♦   Use the `var` statement to create the string and optionally assign it a value

♦   Use an assignment operator (=) with a variable name to create the string and optionally assign a value

♦   Use the `String()` constructor to create a string—a feature new to Navigator 3.0

See Chapter 6 for further examples of Navigator's `String` objects.

Properties

The `length` property contains the length of the string, for example, the expression `"Netscape".length` yields the value 8, because, in this instance, eight characters exist in the string `"Netscape"`.

Methods

The following string manipulation methods are supported. Please refer to Appendix B for a description of each of these JavaScript `String` methods.

- `big()`
- `blink()`
- `bold()`
- `charAt()`
- `fixed()`
- `fontcolor()`
- `fontsize()`
- `indexOf()`
- `italics()`
- `lastIndexOf()`
- `link()`
- `small()`
- `strike()`
- `sub()`
- `substring()`
- `sup()`
- `toLowerCase()`
- `toUpperCase()`

Event-Handlers

String objects are built into Navigator and do not have event-handlers.

Examples

Based upon the creation of the following string, using any the following JavaScript statements:

```
var test = "This is a String";
test = "This is a String";
```

```
var test = String("This is a String");
test = String("This is a String");
```

the following table illustrates the values returned by a number of string methods upon the `test` string variable in our example.

Statement	Result	Notes / Return Values

test.fontsize(6)	`<font size=6>`
	`This is a string`
	`</font>`
		The string is encapsulated with a `<font>` container to make the text larger or smaller. No return value is forthcoming; the effect is seen when using a `document.write()` with the string as an argument.

test.length	16	The length of the string is returned.
test.toUpperCase()	THIS IS A STRING	The string value is returned, in uppercase.
test.toLowerCase()	this is a string	The string value result is returned, in lowercase.
test.italics()	This is a String	The string is encapsulated with a `<i>` container tag to make the text italicized. No return value is forthcoming; the effect is seen when using a `document.write()` method with the string as an argument.

4

HTML-Reflected Objects

The tags that make up an HTML-document are reflected into a series of objects in JavaScript. Each such object is organized hierarchically; the parent of all objects is the Navigator browser or `window` object, itself. This hierarchy resembles that shown in Figure 4-1.

JavaScript objects have *descendants*, for example, a hyperlink is an object and is descended from the `document` object. Descendents are also known as *properties* in JavaScript. For instance, a hyperlink is known as a property of the `document` object, and the property name is called `links` under

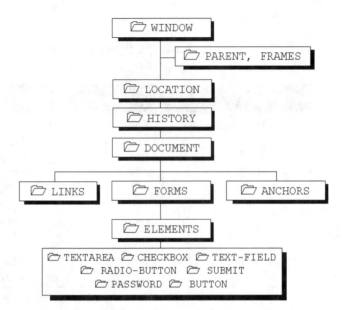

The JavaScript
HTML-object
hierarchy
Figure 4-1.

JavaScript. The distinction between objects and properties can be difficult to differentiate. For example, a hyperlink is an object and it is also a property of the document object, whose property *name* is links. You will learn all about the various properties of specific JavaScript objects later in this book. Consider the following HTML document stored at the hypothetical URL http://www.somehost.com/document.htm:

```
<!--
  Program 4-3
-->
<html>
<head>
<title>A sample document</title>
</head>
<body bgcolor="White">
<form>
<input type="checkbox" checked name="cb1">Item 1
</form>
</body>
</html>
```

When this document is loaded into Navigator, a number of HTML objects will be created automatically, such as a document object with the following properties:

```
document.title="A sample document"
document.bgColor="White"
document.href="http://www.somehost.com/document.htm"
document.forms[0].cb1.defaultChecked=true
```

As you can see, the `<title>` tag is reflected into the `document.title` property, and the document's background color, as set in the `<body>` tag, is reflected into the `document.bgColor` property. The checkbox defined within the form will be reflected as `document.myForms[0].cb1`. `defaultChecked` is a JavaScript property that belongs to a checkbox object and stores a `true` or `false` value, depending on whether or not the `checked` attribute is specified (this attribute, when specified, checks the box by default).

Because documents can have multiple objects, such as hyperlinks or forms, embedded within them, many of JavaScript's objects are structured as *arrays*. Arrays are variables that can hold multiple values and are accessed by specifying an "index" number that references a particular array element. For example, `forms[0]` is the first form within the current document. If another `<form>..</form>` container was defined later in the current HTML document, this could be accessed as `document.forms[1]`.

4

NOTE: Array index numbers start at zero in JavaScript. See Chapter 6 for more on JavaScript's array features.

In the context of our example, the top-level object is `window` because a window must exist for the document to be loaded into. The existence of the `window` object is automatically implied in JavaScript; you need not mention it; for example, `document.forms[0]` and `window.document.forms[0]` refer to the same thing, namely the first form within the current HTML document. If you need to refer to a form in another window, that is, a frame, simply create an expression of the form:

```
parent.frames[n].document.forms[n].
```

where "n" identifies the array-elements you require.

TIP: Remember the object-hierarchy when you access various properties. This will save you frustration when you build your applications, some of which may have many different forms, frames, and links contained within them.

The remainder of this section covers each of the HTML-objects built into the Navigator browser. Appendix B documents the various object methods and properties supported by each HTML-object. The following sections discuss each object and show its properties, event-handlers, and syntax, and include a description and source-code example, if relevant. These objects are used in the later chapters of the book where more complex applications are created. Navigator supports the following objects, as shown in the following table. Entries with a ✔ are objects that have arrays associated with them (the name of the array is given in brackets).

Object Name	Description
anchor (anchors array)✔	Array of `<a name>` tags in the current document
button	A hypertext button created with `<input type=button>`
checkbox	A checkbox created with `<input type=checkbox>`
elements✔	All of the elements within a `<form>` container
form (forms array) ✔	An array of HTML `<form>` container objects
frames (frames array) ✔	A frameset-document object (window)
hidden	A hidden text field created with `<input type=hidden>`
images (images array) ✔	An array of images, that is, `<img>` tags in the current document
link ✔	An array of hyperlinks in the current document
navigator	Version and client information object
password	An `<input type=password>` field
radio	A radio box created with `<input type=radio>`
reset	A reset button created with `<input type=reset>`
select (options array)✔	A `<select>` objects `<option>` elements

Object Name	Description
`submit`	A submit button created with `<input type=submit>`
`text`	A text-field created with `<input type=text>`
`textarea`	A textarea field created with a `<textarea>` container

Entries that have an array associated with them are *multidimensional* objects. Some HTML tags can specify more than one selection-option, for example, a `select` object, which is a reflection of an HTML `<select>` tag. Consider the following `<select>` tag that has two selectable options:

```
<form>
<select name="womenInMyLife">
<option>Maria
<option>Megg
</select>
</form>
```

4

A `<select>` object is an object in its own right, although in order to access items *within* the object (here, the `<option>` tag), an array is provided, in this case, the `options` array. The `options` array is a list of values that are reflections of each `<option>` tag in a `<select>` container. In essence, there are two objects: One that allows you to refer to the select object as a whole (to find out how many options actually exist within it), and a second, which allows you to refer to individual elements within the object. When you come across two such entries in the future, you will know the object in question uses an array to refer to multiple elements that may be contained within it. A caveat exists to what has previously been explained, which depends on the object's *parent*: An HTML `<a name>..</a>` (anchor) tag is an object that has an `anchor`'s array associated with it, and yet this tag occurs by itself. What is happening here? The answer is an `anchor` object's *parent* is the `document` object, and documents can have multiple anchors defined within them. Windows can also have multiple documents associated with them by using the `<frameset>` container.

Think hierarchically and this will become clearer. The remainder of this chapter is devoted to each of the HTML-reflected objects found within Navigator. Each entry contains a syntax description, an overview, and a list of methods and properties applicable to that object.

Anchor Object (and `anchors` Array)

An *anchor* is an item of text that is the target of an `<a href>` hyperlink tag, and is a property of the document object. As well as anchor objects, JavaScript also reflects all `<a name>` tags into the `anchors` array. Anchors are targets for `<a href>` hyperlinks and are mainly used to index the contents of hypertext documents, thus allowing rapid movement to a particular region of a file by clicking on a hyperlink that references a given anchor.

Syntax:

```
<a [href=locationOrURL]
   [name="anchorName"]
   [target="windowName"]>
   anchorText
</a>
```

The value of `locationOrURL` specifies a destination anchor or Uniform Resource Locator (URL). When this attribute is used, this anchor object is also reflected as a link object. The `name="anchorName"` specifies the name of the anchor that will be the target for a hypertext link within the current HTML document. The `target="windowName"` specifies a window (or a synonym such as `_self`) into which the link is loaded and can only be used when the `href` attribute is used. The `anchorText` value specifies the actual text to display at the anchor and is optional; for example, you could structure the tag as `<a name="myAnchor"></a>`.

TIP: An anchor can also be created using the JavaScript `anchor()` method. See Appendix B for a syntax description. Also see Chapter 2 for more information on both links and anchors.

The `anchors` Array

A JavaScript program can refer to an anchor within the current hypertext document by using the `anchors` array. The `anchors` array contains an entry for each `<a name>` tag in the current document, although each anchor must use the `name` attribute for this to function correctly. If a document contains a named anchor, defined with the JavaScript statement:

```
<a name="s1">Section1</a>
```

this anchor will then be reflected in Navigator as `document.anchors[0]`, noting that array positions start at zero in JavaScript. To get to this anchor from a hyperlink, the user will have had to click on a tag that resembled `<a href="#s1">...</a>`. The anchors array can be referred to as follows:

♦ `document.anchors[i]`

♦ `document.anchors.length`

where `i` is a numeric value representing the anchor required. By using the `length` property, the number of anchors in a document can be ascertained, although individual elements will always return a null value. This means you cannot access individual anchor names by referring to an array element, like hyperlink. Hopefully, this will be provided in a later version of Navigator. See Chapter 2 for more examples of more complex anchor-manipulation examples using JavaScript.

Properties
The `anchors` object itself has no properties, although the `anchors` array has a `length` property that returns the number of anchor elements. The `anchors` array is a read-only structure.

Methods
No methods exist for the `anchors` object. A string object can use the `anchor()` method to create an anchor dynamically, however.

4

Event-handlers
No event-handlers exist for the `anchors` object.

Examples
To count the number of anchors with a document, simply use the code:

```
<script language="JavaScript">
<!--
  alert("There are " + document.anchors.length +
        " anchors in the current document.");
//-->
</script>
```

Button Object

A *button* (see the following example) is a clickable region of the screen that can invoke a JavaScript statement using the `onClick` event-attribute. Buttons are properties of the form object, and must be enclosed in an HTML `<form>..</form>` container.

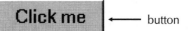 ←—— button

Syntax:

```
<input type="button"
       name="buttonName"
       value="buttonText"
       [onClick="handlerText"]>
```

where `name` specifies the name for the new button object, and is reflected into the `name` property. The `value` attribute specifies text display on the buttons face, which is reflected into the `value` property. A button's properties and methods can be called in the following way:

♦ `buttonName.propertyName`

♦ `buttonName.methodName(parameters)`

♦ `formName.elements[i].propertyName`

♦ `formName.elements[i].methodName(parameters)`

where `buttonName` is the value of the `name` attribute, `formName` is either the value of the `name` attribute of a form object or an element that exists within the `forms` array. For example, `forms[0]` is for the first form, and `i` is an index variable used to access a particular array element, a button element, in this case.

Properties
The `name` and `value` properties are a reflection of the `<input>` tag's `name` and `value` attributes for the button. Accessing these values could be useful to show a list of buttons active within the current document, and then display these for the user. The `type` property of a button object will always be set to `"button"`.

Methods
The `click()` method can be used with button objects. See Appendix B for more information on `click()`, although be aware that this feature was unreliable in Navigator 2.0 and the beta versions of Atlas (Navigator 3.0).

Event-Handlers
The `onClick` event-handler allows a JavaScript statement, or function-call, to be attached to a button object, which invokes that statement or function.

Examples

A simple button to display the current date and time could be structured using an `onClick` event-attribute with an `alert()` method and the `Date()` constructor, as follows:

```
<form>
<input type="button"
        value="Date and Time"
        onClick='alert(Date())'>
</form>
```

See Chapter 7, where treatment of form-based HTML objects is discussed in greater detail.

Checkbox Object

A checkbox is a on/off toggle switch. Checkboxes are properties of the form object, and must be enclosed in a `<form>..</form>` container. The following illustrates a simple checkbox:

      ☐ Checkbox 1

      ☑ Checkbox 2

      ☐ Checkbox 3

4

Syntax:

```
<input name="checkboxName"
        type="checkbox"
        value="checkboxValue"
        [checked]
        [onClick="handlerText"]>textToDisplay
```

where `name` is the name of this checkbox object and is reflected in the `name` property, and `value` is the value returned to a server when the checkbox is checked (that is, it is active) and when the form is submitted. The optional `checked` attribute specifies that the checkbox is displayed as checked by default, and the `defaultChecked` property will be set to `true` (this is a boolean property) when this attribute is specified. The `checked` property can be used to check when the checkbox is checked by the user; this also uses a boolean value. The text for the checkbox option is specified as the value `textToDisplay`.

A checkbox can be accessed in any of the following ways:

♦ `checkboxName.propertyName`

♦ `checkboxName.methodName(parameters)`

♦ `formName.elements[i].propertyName`

♦ `formName.elements[i].methodName(parameters)`

where `checkboxName` is the value of the `name` attribute of the checkbox object, and `formName` is the name of a form in which the checkbox exists. For example, `forms[0]` would be for the first form, or `forms['myForm']` for a `<form>` tag that uses the `name` attribute set as `"myForm"` (`<form name="myForm">`). The variable `i` represents the item required from the `elements` array, should you want to use this alternative property to access a particular checkbox.

Properties
`checked` will be set to true if the checkbox is activated; `defaultChecked` is true if the `checked` attribute is used within a `<input>` tag, for example, `<input checked type=checkbox>`. The `name` reflects the `name` attribute in the `<input name=... type=checkbox>` form of the tag, while `value` reflects the `value` attribute of the tag. The `type` property of a checkbox object will always be set to `"checkbox"`.

Methods
The `click()` method can be used with a checkbox object although, currently, the `click()` method does not function properly within Navigator.

Event-Handlers
Only one event-handler is provided, namely, `onClick`. See Chapter 5 or the examples for more details.

The `elements` Array

The `elements` array is an array containing every item with an HTML form, such as checkboxes, radio-buttons, text objects, etc., in source order. This array can be used as an alternative way of gaining access to individual form-elements within JavaScript, providing a way to reference form objects programatically without using the `name` attribute of an object. The `elements` array is a property of the `forms` object, and must, therefore, be preceded by the name of the form from which you need to access an element, as shown in the following syntax description.

The syntax is

♦   `formName.elements[i]`
♦   `formName.elements.length`

where `formName` is either the name of a form or an element in the `forms` array, for example, `forms[1]`, or the value of a `<form>` tag's `name` attribute, and `i` is a numeric variable that indexes the elements array. The `length` property contains the number of elements within the `<form>..</form>` container being accessed. The `elements` array is a read-only structure; therefore, values cannot be assigned into an object dynamically.

Properties

Only one property is defined, namely `length`, which is a reflection of the number of elements within the form being referenced; for example,

`document.forms[0].elements.length`

would contain the number of elements within the first form of the current document.

Examples

To see all of the elements within a form, simply use the `showElements()` function below that scans through the `elements` array of a specific form (passed as argument `f`), and then builds a string that contains the name of each element. A sample form has been included to demonstrate the output. The `formElements` string is finally displayed within the browser using an `alert()` box, as shown in Figure 4-2.

```
<!--
  Program 4-4
-->
<html>
<head>
<script language="JavaScript">
<!--
function showElements(f) {
  var formElements = "";
  for (var n=0; n < f.elements.length; n++) {
      // Build a string containing each element:
      formElements += n + ":" + f.elements[n] + "\n";
  }
```

4

```
        alert("The elements in the form '" +
                f.name +
                "' are:\n\n" +
                formElements);
}
//-->
</script>
</head>
<body>
<form name="ExampleForm">
<table border=0>
<tr>
 <td>
  <input name="cb1" type="checkbox" checked>Option 1<br>
  <input name="cb2" type="checkbox">Option 2
 </td>
</tr>
<tr>
<td>Name:</td>
<td><input type="text" size=45 name="fullname"></td>
</tr>
<tr>
 <td>Address:</td>
 <td><textarea name="ta"></textarea></td>
</tr>
<tr>
 <td>
  <input type="button"
          value="See elements"
          onClick="showElements(this.form)">
 </td>
</tr>
</form>
</table>
</body>
</html>
```

Notice how the showElements() function is called with the argument
this.form, which refers to the *current* form. If this were omitted, you would
have to refer to the form within the showElements() function as
document.forms[n].elements[n], which is more long-winded.

The form Object (and forms Array)

A *form* is an area of a hypertext document created using the
<form>..</form> container, which allows user-input to take place. A
number of tags only work within forms, such as text-fields and textures,

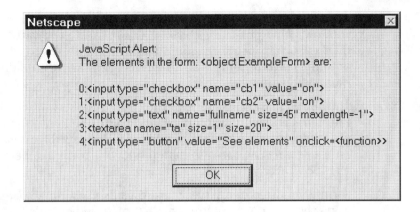

checkboxes, radio-buttons, and selection-lists—all of which are separate JavaScript objects in their own right. JavaScript allows form-processing to happen locally by accessing a forms field to extract values, although it is also possible to submit data to a remote Web server. Figure 4-3 illustrates an example form made up of some objects including a text-field, textarea, some radio-buttons, checkboxes, and a selection object.

Syntax:

```
<form name="formName"
      target="windowName"
      action="serverURL"
      method="get" | "post"
      enctype="encodingType"
      [onSubmit="handlerText"]>
</form>
```

where name is a string specifying the name of the form (this can be used instead of using the `forms[i]` method of referring to a form). The `target` attribute specifies the window in which all form-responses should go, and

4

A form and miscellaneous form-objects as rendered by Navigator (with annotations)
Figure 4-3.

requires a window or frame to exist with the name specified. The special window-name _blank, _parent, _self, and _top can also be used to load the feedback from a form-submission to be directed to a new (blank) window or to the current frame. See Chapter 9 for more information on frameset-documents.

The action attribute specifies the URL of the server, which will receive the form-data, when submitted, and specify a Common Gateway Interface (CGI) script such as a Perl program or a Netscape LiveWire application on the server. You can also mail results of a form to a person using the mailto: URL.

Forms submitted to a server require a *submission method*, and this is specified using the method attribute. The GET method appends the form-data to the end of the action attributes URL, whereas the POST sends form information as one long stream of data, allowing a script or program to read from the stream (known as the *standard input stream*) to extract the information that has been sent. This method also sets an environmental variable called QUERY_STRING on the server, providing another (perhaps slightly easier) way of extracting the data.

The enctype attribute specifies a Multimedia Internet Mail Extensions (MIME) type for the data being sent. The default is application/x-www-form-urlencoded, although file-uploads are now possible in Navigator using the new multipart/form-data MIME type. The encoding property contains the information you provide here.

To specify an object or property, use any of the following techniques:

♦   formName.propertyName

♦   formName.methodName(parameters)

♦   forms[i].propertyName

♦   forms[i].methodName(parameters)

where formName is the reflection of the name attribute of the form object, and i is an integer variable used to access a particular element of the forms array, that is, a particular <form> defined within the current document.

Using the forms Array

Any form within the current hypertext document can be referred to using the forms array. Accessing the forms array is simply a matter of specifying the forms array and an index number for the form you require; for example, forms[0] is the first <form> container within the current document.

- `document.forms[index]`
- `document.forms.length`
- `document.forms['name']`

where i is an integer representing the form required. You can also assign a form-expression to a variable and use this instead. For example:

```
var myForm = document.forms[1];
```

You can then refer to a form element, for instance, a text-field defined with the HTML such as:

```
<form>
<input type=text name=myField size=30>
...
</form>
```

using the variable `myForm`. For example, you could assign the contents of the preceding text field, named `myField`, into a new variable called `result` using the JavaScript statement:

4

```
var result = myForm.myField.value;
```

The number of forms in a document can be found simply by using the `length` property, for example, `document.forms.length`. The `forms` array is a read-only structure.

Properties
The form object has six properties, most of which are reflections of the values passed to the `<form>` tag, for example:

- `action`—a reflection of the `action` attribute
- `elements`—an array reflecting all of the elements within a form
- `encoding`—a reflection of the `enctype` attribute
- `length`—the number of elements within a form
- `method`—a reflection of the `method` attribute
- `target`—a reflection of the `target` attribute

The `forms` array has only one property, namely `length`, the number of forms within the complete hypertext document (not to be confused with `document.forms[i]`, which refers to a *specific* form).

Methods

The submit() method can be used to submit a form progmatically, from within a JavaScript program, rather than using an <input type=submit> tag, which most forms have (forms that send data to a server, that is).

Event-Handlers

The onSubmit event-attribute can be used to intercept the submission of a form, either when the form is submitted by a person using an <input type=submit> tag placed within the scope of the <form> container, or when a JavaScript submit() method tries to submit the form.

Examples

This sample form sends e-mail to a person via a textarea field:

```
<form method="POST"
      action="mailto:someperson@somewhere.com"
      enctype="text/plain">
<input type="submit" value="Send mail">
<textarea name="email" rows=4 cols=60>
</textarea>
</form>
```

The `frame` Object (`frames` Array)

Navigator 2.0 and 3.0 support a new feature known as *frameset-documents*. Frameset-documents are multiple windows within a screen that can contain separate HTML documents, each with its own unique URLs. You can navigate in each frame independently of all the others. To work with frameset-documents, the frames array allows separate frame documents to be referenced from within a JavaScript program. Chapter 9 presents an in-depth coverage of the <frameset> container, which explains how it can be used to build complex document navigation techniques into an HTML application. The frame object is a property of the window object, and frames array is a property of both the frame and window objects.

A frameset-document replaces the normal <body>..</body> tag and has the syntax:

```
<frameset rows="rowHeightList,...[%]"
          cols="columnWidthList"
          [onLoad="handlerText"]
          [onUnload="handlerText"]>
          <frame src="locationOrURL"
                 name="frameName"
                 scrolling="yes|no"
```

```
            noresize>
</frameset>
```

where `rows` and `cols` are comma-separated lists of values, which specify the dimensions of the frame. A percent sign (`%`) can be used to specify the size of a frame *relative* to the Navigator window, or pixel measurements (the default) can be specified, in which case the percentage sign is omitted. For example:

```
<frameset rows="50%,50%">
...
</frameset>
```

specifies two horizontal frames of equal size within the browser. The `<frame>` tag defines the individual frames within the document and contains the `src` attribute that specifies a file, or URL of a networked HTML document, to load into the frame. The `name` attribute names the frame and can be used to reference a frame without the `frames` array (to be discussed). To access the properties of a frames object, you can use any of the following addressing techniques:

- `parent.frameName.propertyName`
- `parent.frames[i].propertyName`
- `window.propertyName`
- `self.propertyName`
- `parent.propertyName`

4

The `frames` Array

Individual frames can be accessed by using the `frames` array and the `parent` property. For example, if you had two frames defined in HTML as:

```
<frameset rows="50%,50%">
<frame name="top" src="file1.html">
<frame name="bot" src="file2.html">
</frameset>
```

you could reference the first frame using the expression `parent.frames[0]`, and reference the second as `parent.frames[1]`, hence, the syntax:

- `frameRef.frames[i]`
- `frameRef.frames.length`

- `windowRef.frames[i]`
- `windowRef.frames.length`

To obtain the number of frames within a frameset-document, the `length` property can be used. All elements in the `frames` array are read-only values.

Properties

The `frame` object has the following six properties:

- `frames`—an array reflecting all of the frames in a window
- `name`—a reflection of the `name` attribute of the `<frame>` tag
- `length`—the number of child frames within a parent frame

A number of synonyms can also be used:

- `parent`—a synonym for the window or frame containing the *current* frameset-document
- `self`—a synonym for the current frame
- `window`—another synonym for the current frame

The `frames` array has one property, `length`, which returns the number of child frames within a parent frame.

Methods

The `clearTimeout()` and `setTimeout()` methods can be used with frameset-documents.

Event-handlers

The `onLoad` and `onUnLoad` event-handlers are valid in the `<frameset>` tag.

Examples

This frameset-document example automatically creates two frame objects, referred to in JavaScript as `frames[0]` and `frames[1]`, or `frames["f1"]`, and `frames["f2"]`, respectively:

```
<frameset rows="50%,*">
<frame name="f1" src="http://www.osborne.com">
<frame name="f2" src="http://www.books.mcgraw-hill.com">
</frameset>
```

See Chapter 9 for an in-depth treatment of frameset-documents.

Hidden Object

A *hidden* object is a text-field that does not display when viewed through Navigator. Hidden fields are useful for storing values in structures other than JavaScript variables, although they exist only during the lifetime of the currently loaded document. Form fields can also be set by JavaScript dynamically, opening up new possibilities for data manipulation between the client and server. Hidden fields are properties of the `form` object and must be encapsulated within a `<form>..</form>` container.

Syntax:

```
<input type="hidden"
       [name="hiddenName"]
       [value="textValue"]>
```

where `name` is the name of field, and is optional (instead, you can use the `forms[i].fieldName` or the `form.elements[i]` arrays to access such values). The value of the text-field is reflected in the `value` field, which you must specify when you assign values to the field. This attribute also allows a default value to be placed in the field. To use the properties of a hidden object, any of these syntaxes can be used:

4

- ◆ `fieldName.propertyName`
- ◆ `formName.elements[i].propertyName`

where `fieldName` is the name of the hidden field, as set by the `name` attribute of the `name` attribute of the `<input>` tag, and `formName` is the name of the form in which the hidden field is defined.

Properties
A hidden object has the following properties:

- ◆ `name`—a reflection of the `<input>` tag's name attribute
- ◆ `value`—a reflection of the `<input>` tag's `value` attribute
- ◆ `type`—a reflection of the `type` attribute, for example, `"hidden"`

Methods
The hidden object has no methods.

Event-Handlers
The hidden object has no associated event-handlers because it is hidden.

Examples

A simple hidden field could take the form:

```
<form name="hiddenField">
<input name="hidField1" type="hidden" size=30 value="page 1">
</form>
```

that defines a hidden field called `hidField1`, which is 30 characters in width and has the default value "`age1`". You could update this field with a statement such as:

```
document.hiddenField.hidField1.value = "page 2";
```

The `image` Object (and `images` Array)

Navigator 3.0 now reflects all images into "image objects," and provides an `images` array that can be used to refer to any image defined with an <img> tag. In particular, images can now be updated dynamically by modifying their `src` property.

Syntax:

```
<img src="fileOrUrl"
    [alt="altText"]
    [lowsrc=fileorUrl"]
    [width=w]
    [height=h]
    [border=b]
    [vspace=v]
    [hpsace=h]
    onAbort="statement|function()"
    onError="statement|function()"
    onLoad="statement|function()">
```

where `src` is a filename or URL of the image you want to display, and must refer to an image in the GIF or JPEG formats; and `alt` is some alternative text displayed when: (i) the image is being loaded, and (ii) images are disabled by the user. The `lowsrc` attribute was introduced with Navigator 1.1. It allows a low-resolution image with the same dimensions as the image specified in the `src` attribute to be displayed beforehand, thus building up the image in two stages. Many sites use this to display a monochrome version of the image first, and then a color version, simply for the visual effect. A simple two-frame animation could also be achieved using this technique. The `width` and `height` attributes specify the dimensions of the image in pixels, whereas `border` specifies the width of a border around the image, again, in pixel measurements. Finally, the vspace and hspace attributes specify the vertical and horizontal "gap" that surround the image, thus allowing the image to have space allocated around it. Unfortunately, you cannot specify left or right "horizontal space," or top or bottom "vertical space;" the gap will surround all sides of the image in such cases.

To access the properties of an image object, use the syntax:

♦   document.images[i].propertyName

where i is an numeric index specifying the image you require—the first image in a document being document.images[0]. The images array is a property of the document object; make certain to prefix the array name with "document" when you refer to an image. The <img> tag does not recognize the name attribute, so it is not yet possible to say "document.imageName".

Properties

All of the image objects properties are reflections of the <img> tags attributes, albeit for the complete property. All properties are read-only, apart from the src and lowsrc attributes, which can be dynamically changed.

4

- ♦ src—a reflection of the <img> tag's src attribute
- ♦ lowsrc—a reflection of the <img> tag's lowsrc attribute
- ♦ height—a reflection of the <img> tag's height attribute
- ♦ width—a reflection of the <img> tag's width attribute
- ♦ border—a reflection of the <img> tag's border attribute
- ♦ vspace—a reflection of the <img> tag's vspace attribute
- ♦ hspace—a reflection of the <img> tag's hspace attribute
- ♦ complete—a boolean property that indicates whether or not the image was successfully loaded by Navigator (true = image loaded; false = image not loaded)
- ♦ type—images will have the string "image" stored in this property

Note that image-loading has changed significantly in Navigator 3.0. The border-area of an image is now shown prior to loading and the alt attribute value will be shown within the border just before an image is loaded to give you an indication of what will appear. An image can be changed dynamically by assigning a new URL to the src or lowsrc attribute. This works best when the newly assigned image is of the same size as the original; different sized images will be scaled to fit within the area of the first image. When altering lowsrc dynamically, do so *before* setting the src property because this is the normal image-loading order for low- and high-resolution images (in fact the term "low resolution" is not really applicable because, if required, you can use images of the same resolution).

Methods

The `image` object has no associated methods.

Event-Handlers

Image objects have three new event-handling attributes that can be specified in the `<img>` tag:

♦ `onAbort`—Image-loading abort condition, that is, the user presses ESC, *Stop*, or clicks on another hyperlink when this image is being loaded.

♦ `onError`—Event is triggered when an image-loading error occurs, that is, the image cannot be found at the specified URL, or the server supplying the image is not responding.

♦ `onLoad`—Event is triggered when an image is loaded. Animated images, such as GIF89a files, will trigger this event multiple times, as each animation sequence is loaded.

Examples

This simple script allows you to update an image by pressing a form-button:

```
<!--
  Program 4-5
-->
<html>
<body bgcolor="White">
<img src="europe.gif" alt="Europe">
<hr noshade>
<form>
<input type="button"
       value="See UK"
       onClick="document.images[0].src='uk.gif'">
</form>
</body>
</html>
```

If the image `europe.gif` was a view of Europe and the image `uk.gif` was a picture of the United Kingdom, you could provide a "zoom" function to allow the detail of specific countries to be viewed. This technique is useful because you need not bother with frame or window manipulation to redisplay an image. In the program, the value "uk.gif" is assigned to the `src` attribute of the first image, thus updating it accordingly.

Consider using the `alt` attribute for all images you reference with `<img src>` because the loading of images has changed in Navigator 3.0. "Alternative text" now allows you to see which image is appearing prior to the image actually loading (useful if a document has many images). Small images, such as bullets, etc., do not need an `alt` attribute, and Navigator may not even display such text if the image-display area is too small to accommodate it.

JavaScript's ability to update images on the fly can be useful for animation effects. Consider the following application that animates a small GIF image:

```
<!--
  Program 4-6
-->
<html>
<head>
<script language="JavaScript">
<!--
  var alternate = 0;
  function animIcon() {
    if (parent.alternate == 0) {
      parent.f1.document.images[0].src = "rb.gif";
      parent.alternate = 1;
    }
    else {
      parent.f1.document.images[0].src = "yb.gif";
      parent.alternate = 0;
    }
    setTimeout("parent.animIcon()", 1000);
  }
//-->
</script>
</head>
<frameset rows="10%,*">
<frame name="f1" src="frame1.htm">
<frame name="f2" src="frame2.htm">
</frameset>
</html>
```

4

In this example the document has been structured as two row-based frames. The files `rb.gif` and `yb.gif` are a small red and yellow ball, stored as GIF images. The `animIcon()` function uses the `images` array to update both images within the first frame (named as "f1" in the example). The document `frame1.htm` must have an `<img src>` defined so that the image can be referenced and then updated, and could resemble the following:

```
<html>
<body>
<img src="yb.gif" hspace=4>This is an animating image.
</body>
</html>
```

The file `frame2.htm` has no significance, and can contain any HTML that you require. This application uses JavaScript's time-out mechanism to repetitively update the image every second. Chapter 10 has more information on JavaScript's time-out events. The example and images can be found on the accompanying book disk.

The `link` Object (`links` Array)

A *link* (hyperlink) *object* is a clickable piece of text that defines a hyperlink to another Web-resource, commonly, another hypertext page. Clicking on the link then loads that document into the current window. Hyperlinks need not always load HTML files; they can load images and just about any other file. You can also change the URL type in order to load other resources, e.g. `ftp://` for an FTP server, or `news://` for a news (USENET) server, etc. Figure 4-4 illustrates a typical hyperlink, and shows how the status bar shows the current link address, i.e. URL for that link.

Syntax:

```
<a href=locationOrURL
    [name="anchorName"]
    [target="windowName"]
    [onClick="handlerText"]
    [onMouseOver="handlerText"]>
    linkText
</a>
```

where `href` represents a filename or URL to load, for example, `"file1.html"` for a file that exists in the current directory, or `"http://host/file"` for a networked document. Other URLs are also

A typical
hyperlink and
Navigator
status-bar
message
Figure 4-4.

Jason's Home Page

http://www.gold.net/users/ag17/index.htm

valid, including `ftp:`, `gopher:`, `news:` and `javascript:`. See Appendix E for a list of URL prefixes that work in Navigator. The `name` attribute names the hyperlink, making it into an `anchor` object. The `target` attribute is used with frameset-documents to load the document mentioned in `href` into a particular frame within the current frameset-document. `linkText` is the text placed within the link, which can be clicked upon by the user to activate the link. To access a property of a `link` object, use the syntax:

```
document.links[i].propertyName
```

where `i` is an integer value that references the link within the `links` array.

The `links` Array

Hyperlinks can be referenced within a JavaScript program by accessing the `links` array structure; for example, a document with two `<a href>` tags will be reflected into JavaScript as `document.links[0]`, and `document.links[1]`, respectively. The syntax for accessing the `links` array is

♦ `document.links[i]`

♦ `document.links.length`

4

where `i` indexes the link required, and `length` returns the number of hyperlinks within the current document. Link objects are read-only objects, so you cannot dynamically allocate a hyperlink into the array.

Properties

The `link` object has the following properties defined:

♦ `hash`—specifies the anchor name in the URL if it exists

♦ `host`—specifies the `hostname:port` portion of the current URL

♦ `hostname`—specifies the host and domain name (or numeric IP address) of the current host's URL

♦ `href`—specifies the complete URL of the current document

♦ `pathname`—specifies the URL-path portion of the URL, for example, after the hostname

♦ `port`—specifies the communications port the server uses

♦ `protocol`—specifies the beginning of the URL including the colon, for example, `http:`

♦ `target`—a reflection of the `target` attribute in the `<a href>` tag

The links array has one property, namely length, which is a reflection of the number of links within a document.

Methods
No methods are defined for the link object.

Event-Handlers
onClick and onMouseOver can be used in <a href> tags. See Chapter 5 for more information on these event-handling attributes.

Examples
A link that displays a status-bar message while the user is hovering over the link can be coded as follows:

```
<a href="links.htm"
   onMouseOver="window.status='Click for the latest sites!';
             return true">
New sites
</a>
```

See Chapter 2 for more examples of JavaScript with hyperlinks and anchors.

Password Object

A *password* object is a text-field whose contents are kept secret by replacing all characters entered into the field with an asterisk character (*). Note that the value of the field is stored normally. Take care not to expose this if this type of field is used for security reasons. Password objects are properties of the form object and must be encapsulated within a <form>..</form> container. The following illustrates a password object as seen through Navigator:

Syntax:

The syntax of the password-field is as for a text-field, except the type attribute is changed to "hidden". Text-fields default to "text" in any event.

```
<input type="password"
       name="passwordName"
       size=integer
       [value="textValue"]>
```

where the `name` attribute allocates a name for the password-field, and whose value is also reflected into the `name` property for this element. The `size` attribute specifies the size (in characters) of the field, and the `value` field is used to assign a default value to the password-field. This value is reflected in the `value` property of this object. To use a password-field's properties and methods, use the syntax:

- `passName.propertyName`
- `passName.methodName(parameters)`
- `formName.elements[i].propertyName`
- `formName.elements[i].methodName(parameters)`

where `passName` is the value of the `name` attribute of a password-field object, and `formName` is either the value of the `name` attribute of the form object or an element in the `forms` array, for example, `forms[0]`. The `i` variable is used to index an array position of the element that you require.

Properties

The following properties are available to a `password` object:

- `defaultValue`—the default value as mentioned in the `value` attribute
- `name`—a reflection of the `<input>` tag's `name` attribute
- `value`—a reflection of the *current* value of the password object's field
- `type`—all password objects have the string `"password"` stored in this property, which is a reflection of the `type` attribute of the current `<input>` tag

Methods

The `focus()` method can be used to give focus to a password field; `blur()` can be used to remove this focus. The `select()` method can be used to select the data within a field and should be used in conjunction with the `focus()` method.

Event-Handlers

No event-handlers are associated with the `password` object.

The `radio` Object

A `radio` object represents a radio button defined within an HTML form. Radio buttons offer multiple-choice selections to the user, only one of which can be selected (the opposite of a checkbox). The `radio` object is a property

4

of the `form` object and must, therefore, be contained within a `<form>..</form>` container. The following illustration shows three radio-button objects as rendered through Navigator:

⦿ Radio button 1
○ Radio button 2
○ Radio button 3

Syntax:

```
<input type="radio"
       name="radioName"
       value="buttonValue"
       [checked]
       [onClick="handlerText"]>textToDisplay
```

where `name` names the radio button. Note that radio buttons must be given the *same* name, that is, the same `name` attribute. The `value` attribute names a value, which is returned to the server when this form is submitted and defaults to the value `"on"`. The `checked` attribute allows a radio button to appear selected by default (only the first item is set if multiple `checked` attributes are mentioned). The `defaultChecked` property of this object (to be discussed later) will be `true` if this attribute is specified. The `onClick` attribute allows the association of an event-handler with the radio button, so when it is clicked on, a JavaScript function or statement can be invoked. Each radio button should have some text to describe that selection; `textToDisplay` is used for this purpose. To access a radio button's methods and properties, use the syntax:

♦ `radioName[i].propertyName`

♦ `radioName[i].methodName(parameters)`

♦ `formName.elements[i].propertyName`

♦ `formName.elements[i].methodName(parameters)`

where `radioName` is the value of the `name` attribute of the radio object you require, and `formName` is either the value of the `name` attribute of a form-object or an element in the `forms` array. The element's array can be used to access radio boxes because they are also form elements. For example, you could refer to the first radio box named `rad1` in the first form of the current document with the JavaScript expression: `document.forms[0].radioName[0]`.

Properties

The following properties are contained within the `radio` object:

♦ `checked`—a boolean value, `true` or `false`, depending on whether or not a radio-button is selected

♦ `defaultChecked`—reflects the `checked` attribute of the `<input type="radio">` tag, another boolean value

♦ `length`—represents the number of radio buttons within a radio object

♦ `name`—a reflection of the `name` attribute in the `<input>` tag

♦ `value`—a reflection of the `value` attribute of the `<input>` tag

♦ `type`—a reflection of the `type` attribute, for example, `"radio"`

Methods

The `click()` method can be used to select a radio button, although this may have no effect under Navigator versions that run in Windows.

Event-Handlers

The `onClick` event-handler can be used to activate a JavaScript statement when a radio button is clicked on by the user.

4

Examples

A simple radio-button object could be created with the HTML:

```
<form name="buttons">
<input type="radio" name="radBut" checked>Yes
<input type="radio" name="radBut">No
</form>
```

The first radio-button could be referred to as `document.buttons.elements[0]` or as `document.buttons.radBut[1]`.

NOTE: Radio buttons that are accessed using the name of the radio button (as in the `name` attribute of the radio-button object) are returned in *reverse* order. Chapter 7 examines a number of JavaScript programs that can be used to access radio-button values.

The `reset` Object

A `reset` object is a button within an HTML form that resets every field to its default value (such default values are specified using the `value` attribute).

Syntax:

```
<input type="reset"
       name="resetName"
       value="buttonText"
       [onClick="handlerText"]>
```

where `name` specifies the name of the reset object, and is reflected in the `name` property of the reset object, and where `value` allocates some text to place on the button's face, and is reflected in the property of the same name or `value`. To access a reset object's methods and properties, use the syntax:

♦   `resetName.propertyName`

♦   `resetName.methodName(parameters)`

♦   `formName.elements[i].propertyName`

♦   `formName.elements[i].methodName(parameters)`

where `resetName` is the name of a reset object, as specified in the `name` attribute of the object; and where `formName` is the name of the form in which the reset object exists, and can be specified using the `forms` array, or by quoting the name of the form, as set in the `<form>` tag's `name` attribute.

Properties

The `name` property is a reflection of the `<input name=...>` attribute. The `value` property is a reflection of the `<input value=...>` attribute. The `type` property is a reflection of the `type` attribute and, in the case of a reset object, will be set to `"reset"`.

Methods

The `click()` method can be used with a reset object, although its use is not recommended since this feature has not worked in earlier versions of Navigator.

Event-Handlers

The `onClick` event attribute can be used with a reset object.

The `select` Object (and `options` Array)

A *select* object represents a series of selectable values placed within a pull-down menu. This object is a reflection of an HTML `<select>` tag, and is a property of the `form` object. The options within a select object are reflected into the `options` array. Select objects are properties of the form object, whereas the options array is a property of the select object itself.

Syntax:

```
<select name="selectName"
        [size="integer"]
        [multiple]
        [onBlur="handlerText"]
        [onChange="handlerText"]
        [onFocus="handlerText"]>
        <option value="optionValue" [selected]>textToDisplay
</select>
```

where `name` is the name of the select object, and is reflected in the `name` property, and where `size` represents the number of options when the select object is first displayed. The `multiple` attribute specifies the object is not displayed as a pull-down selection list, but, instead, that all objects are shown as one large list (therefore occupying more space). Select objects that use `size` or `multiple` are similar in that multiple items can be selected.

A `<select>..</select>` container is useless without `<option>` tags. These tags specify each value that can be selected by the user; as many options as are required can be specified. The `value` attribute of the `<option>` tag represents the value sent to a server when the form in which this select object is submitted (see the `submit` object), and is also reflected in a property of the same name. A default option can be specified using the `selected` attribute, which causes the specified option to appear by default when the selection-list first appears. This default value is also reflected into the JavaScript property named `defaultSelected`. Each selection-option must also have some descriptive text (`textToDisplay`) with it to inform users about the option that they are selecting. These values are reflected in the `value` property accordingly. To use a select object's properties and methods, use the general syntax:

4

♦ `selectName.propertyName`

♦ `selectName.methodName(parameters)`

♦ `formName.elements[i].propertyName`

♦ `formName.elements[i].methodName(parameters)`

where `selectName` is the name of the select object, as specified in the `<select name=...>` part of the tag, and where `formName` is the name of the form in which the select object exists (for example, `forms[0]`); or by specifying the `name` attribute assigned to a `<form name=...>` tag.

The individual options within a select object can be accessed using the `options` or `elements` array, using the syntax:

♦ `selectName.options[i].propertyName`

♦ `formName.elements[i].options[index1].propertyName`

where `selectName` is the `name` attribute of a `<select>` tag, and `formName` is the name of the form required, that is, the form in which the select object exists.

The `options` Array

The `<option>` tag values within a select object can be accessed using the `options` array. If a `<select>` tag named `browser` contains two options, these are reflected in JavaScript as `browser.options[0]`, and `browser.options[1]`, respectively.

The `options` array also has a `length` property that contains the number of `<option>`s in that select object. For example, `browser.options.length` would contain the value 2 in context to the previous example.

Properties
The select object has the following properties:

♦ `length`—contains the number of `<option>`s in a `<select>` container

♦ `name`—reflects the `name` attribute

♦ `options`—reflects the value of each `<option>` tag, i.e. the text specified after the `<option>` tag in this case

♦ `selectedIndex`—contains the index of the selected option (or in the case of multiple selected objects, the first selected option)

♦ `type`—set to `"select-one"` for single selection-objects; set to `"select-multiple"` for multiple selection-objects (those that use the `multiple` or `size` attribute)

The options array has the following properties:

♦ `defaultSelected`—reflects the `selected` attribute of the `<option>` tag

♦ `index`—contains the index number of an option, that is, the array position

♦ `length`—contains the number of options in a select object

♦ `selected`—selected option (this allows you to select an option)

♦ `selectedIndex`—contains the index of the selected option. Selection options start at position zero in JavaScript because the `options` array also starts at position zero

♦ `text`—reflects the text that follows an `<option>` tag

♦ `value`—reflects the `value` attribute

Methods

The `blur()` and `focus()` methods can be used with select objects.

Event-Handlers

The `onBlur`, `onChange`, and `onFocus` event-handling attributes can be specified.

Examples

The following `select` object contains three options. By clicking on the supplied form-button, the `showSelected()` function displays the user's current selections in the form of the currently selected option, via the text property, and the option-number, via the `selectedIndex` property. The `selectedIndex()` function accepts a single parameter, namely, the name of a form. This value is passed from the `onClick` event-handler as the value `this.form`, where `this.form` refers to the current form. In the script, the `selNum` variable extracts the value of the `selectedIndex` property from the `select` object and is used in the `selText` variable to index the `options` array to extract the actual option selected by the user.

4

```
<!--
  Program 4-7
-->
<html>
<head>
<script language="JavaScript">
<!--
 function showSelected(f) {
  var selNum  = f.planets.selectedIndex;
  var selText = f.planets.options[selNum].text
  alert("Selection option selected: " + selNum + "\n" +
        "Selection option text: " + selText);
 }
//-->
</script>
</head>
<body>
<form name="mySelection">
Where <i>do</i> the Aliens exist?
<select name="planets">
<option>Mars
<option selected>Mercury
<option>Earth (McGraw-Hill?)
</select>
```

```
<p>
<input type="button"
       value="See selection"
       onClick="showSelected(this.form)">
</form>
</body>
</html>
```

The `submit` Object

A `submit` object is a button on an HTML form, which causes the current form to be submitted to a server specified in the `<form>` tag's `action` attribute. The submit object is a property of the `form` object; it is normally the last field found within a form, although it can be mentioned anywhere within the scope of the `<form>` container. Forms are submitted to a server program for further processing; for example, the form contents could be saved into a database.

Syntax:

```
<input type="submit"
       name="submitName"
       value="buttonText"
       [onClick="handlerText"]>
```

where `name` is the name of the submit object and is reflected in this property's `name` property, and `value` is a string that represents the text displayed on the face of the button, and is reflected in the submit object's `value` property. To use this object's methods and properties, use the following syntaxes:

♦   `submitName.propertyName`

♦   `submitName.methodName(parameters)`

♦   `formName.elements[i].propertyName`

♦   `formName.elements[i].methodName(parameters)`

where `submitName` is the value of the `name` attribute of the submit object, and `formName` is the value of the `name` attribute of a form object within the current document, or, an element in the `forms` array, for example, `forms[0]` for the first form within the current document.

Properties

The `name` property is a reflection of the submit object's `name` attribute, and `value` reflects the submit object's `value` attribute. The `type` property is a reflection of the `type` attribute, for example, `"submit"`.

Method

The `click()` method can be used with a submit object, although its use is not recommended since this feature has not worked in earlier versions of Navigator.

Event-Handlers

Only one event-handler is defined, namely `onClick`, which detects the pressing of the submit object's button.

The `text` Object

A *text* object is a text field defined with the `<input type="text">`, and allows alphanumeric data-input. The text object is a property of the `form` object and must be encapsulated within a `<form>..</form>` container. Text objects are read-write structures; they can be updated dynamically from within a JavaScript program. The following illustrates a typical text object:

```
This is a text field
```

4

Syntax:

```
<input [type="text"]
       name=textName"
       value="textValue"
       size=integer
       [onBlur="handlerText"]
       [onChange="handlerText"]
       [onFocus="handlerText"]
       [onSelect="handlerText"]>
```

where `name` specifies the name of the text object, and is reflected in the `name` property of the text object, and where `value` specifies the text within the field. Again, this is reflected in the `value` property of the text object, as well as into the `defaultValue` property. The `size` attribute dictates the size of the field, in characters. `<input type>` tags default to `"text"` if the `type` attribute is omitted. To access a text object's methods and properties, use the syntax:

◆   `textName.propertyName`

◆   `textName.methodName(parameters)`

◆   `formName.elements[i].propertyName`

♦   `formName.elements[i].methodName(parameters)`

where `textName` represents the `name` attribute of the text object, and `formName` is the name of the form in which this text object exists, such as `forms[0]`.

Properties

The `defaultValue` reflects the `value` attribute (default value of the field when the form is rendered); `value` reflects the *current* value of the text object; and `name` reflects the `name` attribute of the text object. The `type` property is a reflection of the `type` attribute, for example, `"text"` (which will also be allocated when the `type` attribute is omitted).

Methods

Three methods can be used with this object, namely: `focus()`, `blur()` and `select()`.

Event-Handlers

Four event-handlers work with text-field objects, namely: `onBlur`, `onChange`, `onFocus` and `onSelect`.

Examples

The following example uses an `onFocus` event so, when the user moves into the field named `fullname`, the current text within that field is highlighted (selected) using the JavaScript `select()` method. In this instance, the `this` property refers to the current field.

```
<form>
Name: <input type="text"
              name="fullname"
              value="Joe Public"
              size=35
              onFocus="this.select()">
</form>
```

The `textarea` Object

A `textarea` object is a reflection of a textarea field within an HTML form. *Textareas* are properties of the form object and must be enclosed within a `<form>..</form>` container. Use this type of field for creating multiple lined input areas for free-form plain-text. The following shows a typical textarea object as rendered by Navigator:

```
This is a textarea
```

Syntax:

```
<textarea name="textareaName"
          rows="integer"
          cols="integer"
          [onBlur="handlerText"]
          [onChange="handlerText"]
          [onFocus="handlerText"]
          [onSelect="handlerText"]>
          [textToDisplay]
          [wrap="hard | soft"]
</textarea>
```

where `name` is the name of the textarea object, and is reflected in the textarea's `name` property (to be described later). The `rows` and `cols` attributes specify the size of the textarea field; both units are specified as characters. The `textToDisplay` value is some optional (default) text to place in the textarea field when it first appears—the `defaultValue` property reflects this value. The `wrap` attribute specifies how text is *wrapped* when text entered into the field passes the maximum number of columns: a soft-wrap breaks up the text so it fits within the box; a hard-wrap simply ignores line breaks and places the text as one long line. To access a textarea's methods and properties, use the general syntax:

♦ `textareaName.propertyName`

♦ `textareaName.methodName(parameters)`

♦ `formName.elements[i].propertyName`

♦ `formName.elements[i].methodName(parameters)`

where `textareaName` is the `name` attribute of the textarea object, and `formName` is the name of the form on which the textarea is defined as `forms[i]`.

Textareas can be updated dynamically by assigning them a value; for example: `document.forms[0].myArea.value = "New Value"` assigns the string-value `"New Value"` into the textarea named with the `<textarea>` name attribute as `myArea`.

4

T **IP:** If you need to break up lines within a textarea, the newline character can be used, although this differs according to each platform. Under windows, the `\r\n` codes should be used (return, and newline codes). Macintosh and Unix-based systems need to use just a single `\n`; for example: `document.forms[0].myArea.value = "Hello\r\nThere"` places the strings "Hello" and "There" on separate lines because a line-break occurs in-between both words. By using the `navigator` object, you can test with which browser the user is viewing your pages and, depending on this value, make your program use the line-break code required. This will make your application compatible across multiple software platforms.

Properties

Textarea objects can access all of the following properties:

♦ `defaultValue`—reflects the `<textarea>` value attribute, that is, the text placed in between the `<textarea>..</textarea>` tags

♦ `name`—reflects the `<textarea>` name attribute

♦ `value`—reflects the *current* value of the textarea object, that is, the text within the field

♦ `type`—set to `"textarea"` for a textarea object

Methods

The `focus()` method can be used to give focus to a textarea object, so the cursor is placed within that object; `blur()` can be used to move focus away from the textarea object. The `select()` method can also be used to select, or *highlight*, the information within the textarea when the textarea is given focus.

Event-Handlers

Four event-handling attributes can be used with a textarea: The `onBlur` attribute detects when focus moves away from the textarea; `onChange` detects when the textarea's contents have changed; `onFocus` detects when the user selects the textarea field; and `onSelect` detects when the text within the field is highlighted.

Examples

The following example illustrates two fields: first, an ordinary text-field and, second, a textarea field. Whenever the contents of the textarea change, the user-defined function `taChange()` is invoked. This results in a message that tells the user the field has altered:

```
<!--
  Program 4-8
-->
<html>
<head>
<script language="JavaScript">
<!--
function taChange() {
  alert("The textarea field has changed.");
}
//-->
</script>
</head>
<body>
<form>
Enter some text:
<input type="text" size=35 name="sometext"><p>
Enter some more text:<br>
<textarea name="tarea"
          rows=5
          cols=40
          onChange="taChange()">
</textarea>
</form>
</body>
</html>
```

4

For Navigator to know the textarea field has changed, you must reselect the field, that is, give it focus, at which point the onChange event-handler will then be activated.

Summary

JavaScript supports a wide range of objects that can be manipulated by the programmer. JavaScript's object model has the potential to confuse because of the many different categories of objects that exist. Understanding the different "types" of JavaScript objects, and how these objects acquire values, is a fundamental prerequisite for any JavaScript developer.

♦ Each of the tags within an HTML document becomes an "object" in JavaScript. Each object is referred to by a unique name—for example, a <form> container becomes a "form object"—and each form within a document is reflected as an element in the forms array, where forms[0] is the first form in the *current* document. Some HTML tags can contain multiple values internally, such as a <select> container, which may have many <option>s associated with it. In this case, the object will have an additional array that contains the additional values; for example, an HTML `<select>` container tag is known as a "selection object." Select objects do not contain values, as such, but `<option>` tags do; therefore, an `options` array is provided for this purpose.

♦ Objects fall into three classes: (i) HTML reflected objects; (ii) Internal objects; and (iii) Navigator objects. HTML "reflected" objects mirror each of the tags that make up the current document, such as the various forms, links, anchors, etc. Internal objects are items such as strings and dates; they are unrelated to the current hypertext document. Navigator objects are browser-specific objects, such as the `location`, `history`, and `window` objects; they relate specifically to the Navigator browser itself.

♦ All of JavaScript's objects are associated with a series of properties and methods. Object *properties* are values that belong to an object, some of which are termed *read-only*, in that they cannot be assigned values; others are termed *read-write,* meaning they can be altered. An example of a read-write property is the browser background color (`document.bgColor`); an example of a read-only property is `Math.PI`, a mathematical constant. A *method* is similar to a function and allows an object to be manipulated. For example, a `window` object has an `open()` and `close()` method that opens and closes a browser window.

♦ Many objects are created automatically by Navigator, such as the `window` and `document` objects. All documents must exist within a window, so a `window` object is created by default; it is always *assumed* to exist. Window objects also have a number of *synonyms* that can be used, including `top`, `self`, and `parent`, which refer to the top window, current window, and a frame, respectively. Frames (or "frameset-documents," as they are more commonly known) are treated as `window` objects under JavaScript and use the `parent` property in order to access a particular frame.

♦ Some HTML tags can have an event-attribute associated with them. For example, an HTML `<a href>` tag can specify an `onClick` or `onMouseOver` event attribute that invokes a specific JavaScript expression, such as a function-call, when the link is clicked, or when the user is "hovering" over a hyperlink.

♦ Navigator 3.0 has added a new type property to all form elements, which reflects the *type* of that element. If the tag for such an element has a `type` attribute, it is reflected into the type property for that object. Some elements not have such a type, however, such as textareas and selection-lists, in which case a name is automatically allocated, for example, `textarea` (textarea field), `select-one` (single item selection-list), and `select-multiple` (for a multiple selection-list).

♦ Images are also treated as "objects" in Navigator 3.0, and have properties associated with them, for example, `src`, which is a reflection of the `src` attribute of the `<img>` tag.

4

CHAPTER 5

Using JavaScript's Event System

This chapter examines JavaScript's event-driven capabilities. The *event system* is a series of event types that JavaScript can intercept. By "catching" an event, it is possible to make JavaScript more interactive; for example, the user could click a button and this could be associated with a JavaScript function that performs a specific task, i.e., opens a window or alters some text in a form-field, etc.

The JavaScript Event System

JavaScript has extended the HTML dialect by introducing a number of new event attributes. These new attributes work in conjunction with HTML tags such as hyperlinks and form elements. One of JavaScript's main methods of obtaining user-input is by using an HTML form, and the objects within forms are well supported by JavaScript's new event-driven capabilities. *Forms* are containers for items such as text-fields, text-areas, selection-lists, and buttons, all of which can now have events "attached" to them. Attaching an event to a form element allows a greater degree of interaction to take place. Events are organized into a number of different categories, namely:

Document events:

♦ Document loading and unloading

Hyperlinks:

♦ Link invocation, that is, a link is clicked on

Form events:

♦ Click events: buttons, radio buttons, checkboxes, submit and reset buttons

♦ Focus, blur, and Change events: text-fields, text-areas, and selection-lists

♦ Select events: text-fields, and text-areas

Image events:

♦ Image events: image-loading, image-loading error, and image-load abort.

Mouse events:

♦ Hyperlink activation, and de-activation (moving on and off a hyperlink)

Document events include document-loading and unloading actions, while hyperlink events detect the activation of a link. Form events are the most numerous in JavaScript because they apply to a variety of HTML form-container tags. Image events are new to Navigator 3.0 and allow image-loading and error events to be detected. Images are now "objects" in their own right and have their own properties; for example, `document.images[0].src` is a reflection of the `src` (URL) attribute in the first `<img src>` of the current document. Navigator's new image-event attributes are discussed later.

Event-handlers are bound to an HTML tag for a specific object; for example, an image-event would be specified within a `<img>` tag, whereas a hyperlink-event would be specified within a `<a href>` tag, etc. In order to deal with the interception of an event, the author must also write an *event-handler* function. Event-handlers can be complete JavaScript functions, or just groups of one or more JavaScript statements separated by semicolons (`;`). The following table lists each event-handler and its invocation method—the middle column shows the actual event-handler tag-attribute that should be used within the HTML tag you require.

TIP: HTML is a case-insensitive language, so an event-handler specified as "`onClick`" is the same as "`onclick`." You can use whichever format you require—the former method has been used in this book to aid readability.

Event Name	Event-attribute	Event occurs when...
Blur event	onBlur	Removes input focus from form element
Change event	onChange	Changes value of text, textarea, or select element
Click event	onClick	Clicks on form element or link
Focus event	onFocus	Gives a form element input focus
Load event	onLoad	A document is loaded
MouseOver event	onMouseOver	Mouse pointer moves onto a hyperlink
MouseOut event	onMouseOut	Mouse pointer moves away from a hyperlink
Select event	onSelect	Selects form element's input field
Submit event	onSubmit	Submits a form
Unload event	onUnLoad	The current document is unloaded, that is, a new document is loaded into Navigator

5

TIP: Event-handler attributes can also be combined. For example, the `onClick` and `onMouseOver` attributes could be mentioned in a single HTML tag to provide event-handlers for both event-types. For example, an object that displays some text while the user is over a hyperlink could invoke a JavaScript function when finally clicked (see later examples). This facility is only possible with tags that support multiple events, however—these details are documented in the following sections.

Losing Field Focus—`onBlur`

The `onBlur` event-attribute works with the following HTML tags:

♦   `<input type="..." onBlur="expr|function()">`

♦   `<textarea onBlur="expr|function()">..</textarea>`

♦   `<select onBlur="expr|function()">..<option>..</select>`

This attribute specifies a JavaScript statement (or function) to execute when a field in an HTML form loses its *focus,* that is, as soon as the user *leaves* the field with the `onBlur` attribute—this can be done either by clicking on another field within the current form, by clicking on another form, or just by trying to leave the current field to move to another, that is, using the TAB key or clicking on the field using the mouse. `onBlur` is particularly useful for field validation functions with forms. Consider the following HTML document and script that validates a person's age:

```
<!--
  Program 5-1
-->
<html>
<head>
<script language="JavaScript">
<!--
function checkAge(age) {
  if (age == "") // Empty field?
    age = 0;
  if (age <= 18) {
    document.forms[0].age.value = "";     // Reset age
    alert("Your age must be greater than 18");
    document.forms[0].age.focus();        // Refocus field
  }
}
//-->
</script>
</head>
```

```
<body>
<basefont size=4>
<form>
<table border=0>
<tr><td>Age</td><td><input name="age" size=5
                      onBlur="checkAge(this.value)"></td><tr>
<tr><td>Name</td><td><input name="name" size=25></td><tr>
</table>
</form>
</body>
</html>
```

With the preceding script, the function `checkAge()` is called when the user leaves the field named `age`, that is, when the field `age` loses its focus. Pressing the TAB key or clicking the mouse on the *Address* field or elsewhere in the document will trigger the event. The `checkAge()` function checks the age argument to see if it is less than or equal to 18. If this is the case, a warning is issued using the `alert()` method and the field is reset to a null (empty) value. When a value greater than 18 has been entered into the `age` field, the user will be allowed to move freely between any other fields that exist within the same form.

TIP: When passing values to a JavaScript function, you can make your code more compact by calling the function, using the expression `function(this.value)`, where `function` is your function and `this` refers to the current field value. The `value` property stores the *literal* value of that field. This is by far the easiest, and most compact, way of passing values to an external function. The alternative is not to pass any values but, instead, to refer to the field directly within the function being called, for example, `document.forms[0].age.value`, etc., which is longer to code.

5

When a field loses focus—that is, it *blurs*—focus normally passes to another field the user is trying to select, although this need not be the case. Focus can be lost simply by clicking elsewhere in the browser or by pressing a forms *Submit* button—see `onSubmit`.

NOTE: Pressing the ENTER key within a field has no effect on movement.

As a further example, consider the following script that uses the `onBlur` event-attribute to detect when the field named `f1` loses its focus. Unless the word `"wombat"` is entered into the first field, the second field cannot gain focus, that is, you cannot select it:

```
<!--
  Program 5-2
-->
<html>
<head>
<script language="JavaScript">
<!--
function checkField(formName)  {
  if (formName.f1.value != "wombat") {
     document.forms[0].f1.focus();
     document.forms[0].f1.select();
  }
}
//-->
</script>
</head>
<body>
<form>
<pre>
Field1 <input name="f1" onBlur="checkField(this.form)"><br>
Field2 <input name="f2">
</pre>
</form>
</body>
</html>
```

The field `f2` remains unselectable, both through use of the mouse and the TAB key, until the first field is populated with the string `"wombat"`. The user-defined `checkField()` function is invoked by the `onBlur` event and uses an `if` statement to test the value of field `f1`. If the field does not contain the value required, the `focus()` method is used to place focus back on the first field, and the `select()` method selects the contents of the field ready for a new value to be typed.

Changing Field and Selection Values—`onChange`

The `onChange` event-attribute can be used with the following HTML tags:

♦   `<select onChange="expr|function()">..<option>..</select>`

♦   `<input type=text onChange="expr|function()">`

♦   `<textarea onChange="expr|function()">...</textarea>`

The onChange attribute specifies a JavaScript expression to execute when a field in an HTML form loses its focus *and* the value within the field has changed. It is similar to onBlur, with the addition of the check to see if the contents of the field have altered since this field was last visited. The onChange field must lose *focus* to be activated, that is, you must move to another field within an HTML form after changing the value of the field.

TIP: Because onChange events are triggered when the field loses focus, it is necessary to have more than one field defined for the first field to lose focus, that is, for the field to lose focus to the next field. An HTML form with a single field clearly cannot lose focus to another field because it doesn't exist (hence, the event cannot be triggered). In the case of a selection-list, the onChange event is triggered immediately after a new selection is made.

Here is a small example of a selection-object that uses an onChange event to detect when a different option is chosen by the user:

```
<!--
  Program 5-3
-->
<html>
<head>
<script language="JavaScript">
<!--
function selectChange() {
    selIdx = document.forms[0].marsupials.selectedIndex;
    newSel = document.forms[0].marsupials.options[selIdx].text;
    alert("Selection has changed to: " + newSel);
}
//-->
</script>
</head>
<body>
<basefont size=4>
<form>
Please choose a marsupial:
<select name="marsupials" onChange="selectChange()">
<option>Kangaroo
<option>Wombat
<option>Koala
</select>
</form>
</body>
</html>
```

5

The preceding script has a single selection object called `marsupials` with three choices. The choices are stored within the `<option>` tags. The user-defined JavaScript function `selectChange()` is called whenever a different option is selected. This program makes use of the `options` property array to access the `<option>` tag values, and the `selectedIndex` property that returns the option currently selected by the user. More on these properties can be found in Chapter 7. You may want to pass the `this` property to the `selectChange()` function to make your code more compact. See Chapter 3 for more details on the `this` statement.

Catching Button Clicks and Link Activations—`onClick`

The `onClick` attribute can be used with the following HTML tags:

- `<a href=URL onClick="expr|function()">...</a>`
- `<input type="checkbox" onClick="expr|function()">`
- `<input type="radio" onClick="expr|function()">`
- `<input type="reset" onClick="expr|function()">`
- `<input type="submit" onClick="expr|function()">`
- `<input type="button" onClick="expr|function()">`

`onClick` specifies the JavaScript code to execute when an object such as a hyperlink, reset button, or checkbox is clicked upon by the user. In the case of checkboxes and radio buttons an `onClick` event is generated when an item is checked, or enabled. The simplest way of using `onClick` is with a button created using the `<input type="button">` tag within a `<form>..</form>` container.

Consider the following code that uses some form buttons with an `onClick` event:

```
<!--
  Program 5-4
-->
<html>
<head>
<script language="JavaScript">
<!--
function whatsnew() {
  alert("You clicked: What's New");
}
function catalog() {
```

```
    alert("You clicked: Search Catalog");
}
//-->
</script>
</head>
<body>
<form>
<input type="button" value="What's New"
       onClick="whatsnew()"> 
<input type="button" value="Search Catalog"
       onClick="catalog()">
</form>
</body>
</html>
```

When the user clicks on a button, the appropriate JavaScript function is called—either `whatsnew()` or `catalog()`, depending on the button clicked. The JavaScript `alert()` method has been used to display a simple message when a button is activated.

This example uses checkboxes with an `onClick` event-handler within an HTML form:

```
<!--
  Program 5-5
-->
<html>
<head>
<script language="JavaScript">
<!--
function checkb1() { alert("You clicked on checkbox 1"); }
function checkb2() { alert("You clicked on checkbox 2"); }
function checkb3() { alert("You clicked on checkbox 3"); }
//-->
</script>
</head>
<body>
<form>
<input type="checkbox" onClick="checkb1()">Wombat<br>
<input type="checkbox" onClick="checkb2()">Koala<br>
<input type="checkbox" onClick="checkb3()">Kangaroo
</form>
</body>
</html>
```

The `onClick` attribute detects when a checkbox is both activated and deactivated. To test for checkboxes that are *activated* only, you must use the checked property that contains the value on if a checkbox (or radio button) is checked. This modified example shows you how:

```
<!--
  Program 5-6
-->
<html>
<head>
<script language="JavaScript">
<!--
function cb1(f) {
  if (f.checked) {
     alert("Checkbox 1 is checked");
  }
}
function cb2(f) {
  if (f.checked) {
     alert("Checkbox 2 is checked");
  }
}
//-->
</script>
</head>
<body>
<form name="checkForm">
<input type="checkbox" checked name="c1"
       onClick="cb1(this.form.c1)">Item 1<br>
<input type="checkbox" name="c2"
       onClick="cb2(this.form.c2)">Item 2
</form>
</body>
</html>
```

Notice how the two functions in the onClick event-attribute now pass an argument, namely the checkbox of the current form (c1 or c2), where form is the form property of the current form object, that is, of the current <form> container. The value of this.form.c1 or this.form.c2 argument is then passed to the appropriate function, either cb1() or cb2() the whereupon the checked property of the checkbox argument passed to the function through the "f" argument is examined. The checked property returns a boolean value—true for a checked box, and false for an unchecked box.

In the example, you will have noticed the first checkbox has a checked attribute specified. This means this particular checkbox will be enabled by default when the document is initially loaded. JavaScript provides the defaultChecked property for this purpose, which returns a true value if the `checked` attribute of an `<input type="checkbox">` is specified. In context to the preceding example, the value of the `defaultSelected` property would be `true`.

TIP: Specifying the `checked` attribute—to make a checkbox selected by default—will not invoke a JavaScript function that uses the `onClick` event-handler. `onClick` literally means *"on click,"* that is, when the user physically clicks the object.

Confirming Hyperlink Activation with `<a href>`

Navigator 3.0 has altered the `onClick` event-attribute so it can now return a `true` or `false` value, which in turn controls whether or not the URL or JavaScript statement in the `href` part of the link should be activated. For example, consider the following script that uses the JavaScript `confirm()` method to ask the user if he or she wants to load the selected hyperlink; `confirm()` returns either a `true` or `false` value, depending on whether the user clicked on OK or CANCEL:

```
<a href="http://www.gold.net/users/ag17/index.htm"
   onClick="return confirm('This page requires Navigator 3.0.')">
Essential Internet Home Page
</a>
```

The use of such confirmations is highly beneficial because without prior warning—through some explanatory text—no way exists to tell the user what requirements a particular page has, in terms of browser capabilities, etc. Placing such a message *before* invoking a page to save any further delays makes sense. Even though methods such as `confirm()` return boolean values, an explicit `return` statement is still required.

Catching the Field Focus—`onFocus`

The `onFocus` event-attribute works with the following HTML tags:

♦   `<input type="text" onFocus="expr|function()">`

♦   `<select onFocus="expr|function()">...</select>`

♦   `<textarea onFocus="expr|function()">...</textarea>`

`onFocus`, as the name suggests, allows an event to be associated with a field that is given *focus*. In Netscape, a form-field obtains focus either when the user clicks on the field with a mouse, or when he or she uses the TAB key to move into the field.

5

NOTE: Selecting information within the field is a selection event, not a focus event.

Document Loading Events—`onLoad`

The `onLoad` event-attribute can be used within the following HTML tags:

◆ `<body onLoad="expr|function()">...</body>`

◆ `<frameset>..<frame onLoad="expr|function()">..</frameset>`

The `onLoad` attribute can be placed in the HTML `<body>` container to invoke a JavaScript function when Navigator has *finished* loading the current document. The event occurs when Navigator has completed loading the text of an HTML document into the current window, or within the current *frameset-document*. A frameset-document is one in which the window is broken into separate regions, each of which can be loaded with a separate document (or URL). Please see Chapter 9 for more information on frames.

TIP: The `onLoad` event isn't of much use for writing text into documents because the event is triggered *after* a document has been loaded. However, the event is useful for triggering a function, etc., after a document has been *fully* loaded into the Navigator browser. Some JavaScript-based Web sites set a global variable using an `onLoad` event to ensure the whole document has been loaded before calling any JavaScript functions that are defined within the document. This is done in case an error occurs when trying to call a function that has not been loaded; for example, the user has pressed the ESC key and interrupted the loading of the document.

Refer to the later section on the `onUnLoad`, which allows an event to be associated with the unloading of a document or frameset-document.

Catching Mouse Events— `onMouseOver` and on `MouseOut`

The `onMouseOver` attribute allows a JavaScript expression to be invoked when the mouse cursor is positioned over an active hyperlink. Inversely, `onMouseOut` (introduced in Navigator 3.0) triggers an event when the mouse cursor moves away from a hyperlink.

- ◆ `<a href="..." onMouseOver="expr|function()">..</a>`
- ◆ `<a href="..." onMouseOut="expr|function()">..</a>`

`onMouseOver` allows a JavaScript statement, such as a function-call, to be activated when the user is positioned over an active hyperlink that specifies the `onMouseOver` attribute. `onMouseOver` events are useful for altering status-bar messages and text-fields, and they are particularly useful for allowing JavaScript events to be triggered when a user is contemplating whether or not to select a particular hyperlink. The `<a href>..</a>` container can encapsulate images and the display-area of a Java applet via the `<applet>` container, so the target need not always be a simple, text-based link.

`onMouseOut` allows a JavaScript statement to be invoked when the mouse cursor moves away from a hyperlink, and is useful when the need arises to cancel a specific task. For example, the user, while positioned over a hyperlink, could activate an `onMouseOver` event that starts an animation. When the user moves away from the link, an `onMouseOut` event could then halt the animation. Prior to the introduction of the `onMouseOut` event, this would not have been possible, since there was no method of detecting when the user actually left a hyperlink (in Navigator version 2.0).

Consider the following `onMouseOver` example, which updates a text-area field depending on a thumbnail image over which the user is positioned. The images are encapsulated in a series of `<a href>` container tags, therefore making the entire image into a hyperlink. The variables `book1txt`, `book2text`, `book3txt`, and `book4txt` contain HTML-formatted text that describes each book mentioned. Later in the application, a series of `<a href>` hyperlinks makes use of the `onMouseOver` event to execute a JavaScript statement to update the text-area field with one of these variables:

5

```
<!--
  Program 5-7
-->
<html>
<head>
<script language="JavaScript">
<!--
  function clearField() {
    document.forms[0].book_text.value =
    "Book details will appear here<p>.";
  }
  var book1txt =
    "Title  : ESSENTIAL JAVA*:\r\n" +
    "Author : Jason Manger\r\n" +
    "ISBN   : 0-07-709292-9\r\n\r\n" +
```

```
            "A book on two of the newest technologies to hit the Web, " +
            "the Java and JavaScript programming languages. A guide " +
            "for novices and experts alike.";
         var book2txt =
            "Title  : NETSCAPE NAVIGATOR:\r\n" +
            "Author : Jason Manger\r\n" +
            "ISBN   : 0-07-709190-6\r\n\r\n" +
            "An in-depth guide to the de facto Web-browser, Netscape " +
            "Navigator. This book also covers HTML to level 3.0, and " +
            "includes details of Navigator's news and mail " +
            "facilities, as well as much more besides.";
         var book3txt =
            "Title  : HITCH HIKING THRU CYBERSPACE: WITH NETSCAPE" +
            "NAVIGATOR\r\n" +
            "Author : Jason Manger\r\n" +
            "ISBN   : 0-07-709786-6\r\n\r\n" +
            "A CD-ROM that comes in two parts. Part I arrives with a " +
            "copy of Netscape Navigator and includes a hypertexted " +
            "version of Jason's books: WWW Mosaic and More, Netscape " +
            "Navigator and The Essential Internet Information Guide. " +
            "Part II contains everything except the Navigator " +
            "software. No less than 10 top tools are included, " +
            "including Netmanage Chameleon TCP/IP software for " +
            "Internet access. ";
         var book4txt =
            "Title  : THE WORLD-WIDE WEB, MOSAIC AND MORE\r\n" +
            "Author : Jason Manger\r\n" +
            "ISBN   : 0-07-705170-6\r\n\r\n" +
            "A guide to the popular Mosaic browser and detailed " +
            "information on CGI (Common Gateway Interface) scripting, " +
            "all in one book. CGI allows HTML to interface to a back " +
            "end database, providing interactivity within a hypertext " +
            "document.";
//-->
</script>
</head>
<body bgcolor="Silver" link="Yellow" text="White"
      onLoad="clearField()">
<img align="left" src="mgh5.gif" hspace=12 border=0>
<basefont size=4>
<img width=13 src="rb.gif"> Please move your mouse over a
book cover to see details for that particular book.<p>
<center>
<table cellspacing=20 border=0>
<tr valign="bottom" align="middle">
<td>
<a href="essjava.htm"
```

```
onMouseOver = "document.forms[0].book_text.value = book1txt">
<img border=1 src="essjav1.gif">
</a>
</td>
<td>
<a href="netnav.htm"
onMouseOver = "document.forms[0].book_text.value = book2txt">
<img border=1 src="netnav.gif">
</a>
</td>
<td>
<a href="hhcs.htm"
onMouseOver = "document.forms[0].book_text.value = book3txt">
<img border=1 src="hhcs.gif">
</a>
</td>
<td>
<a href="www.htm"
onMouseOver = "document.forms[0].book_text.value = book4txt">
<img border=1 src="swwwm&m.gif">
</a>
</td>
</tr>
</table>
</center>
<center>
<form>
<textarea rows=8 cols=70 name="book_text" wrap="soft">
</textarea>
</form>
</center>
<img src="logo.gif" align="right">
</body>
</html>
```

5

This example could be altered to invoke just about any JavaScript-related event, including color manipulation, and even frameset-document updating.

The onMouseOut event can be useful in starting and stopping specific tasks. For example, here is an application that displays a simple image-animation (by manipulating JavaScript's images[] array) while the user is hovering over a hyperlink. An onMouseOver event starts the animation, while an onMouseOut event stops the animation when the user moves away from the link. Remember that links need not be textual. The <a href> is a container tag, and can therefore encapsulate other elements, such as images, i.e. via the <img src> tag:

```
<!--
  Program 5-8
-->
<html>
<head>
<script language="JavaScript">
<!--
 var alternate = 0;
 var timerId;
 var images = new Array("yb.gif", "rb.gif");      // Image URLs
 function startAnimation() {
    alternate = (alternate == 0) ? 1 : 0;          // Alternate images
    document.images[0].src = images[alternate];    // Update image
    timerId = setTimeout("startAnimation()", 1000); // 1 second update
 }
//-->
</script>
</head>
<body>
<img border=0 hspace=5 width=10 src="rb.gif">Hover over
<a href="#" onMouseOver="startAnimation()"
            onMouseOut="clearTimeout(timerId)">
this</a> link to start the animation.<p>
</body>
</html>
```

In the previous script, the image named as "rb.gif" is first displayed on the
screen, next to a hyperlink. The function startAnimation() simply
alternates the display of two images using the src property of an image
object that is held in the images array. The value of the variable alternate
is either 0 or 1, and is used to index the images array in order to perform
the animation. A time-out event is used to implement the continual
image-update process. The array() constructor creates a new array object,
which in this example has two elements, both of which are names of images
that are assumed to exist in the same directory as the script. As you try out
the example, the animation will become smoother as the images are cached
to disk by Navigator. Move on and off the hyperlink to see the effect. Of
course, this program can be extended to perform just about any task, other
than an animation. Notice how the clearTimeout() method is called in
the onMouseOut event-attribute, thus stopping the animation. JavaScript's
time-out events are covered in Chapter 10.

Field Selection Events—onSelect

The onSelect event attribute can be used with the following HTML tags:

♦   `<input type="text" onSelect="expr|function()">`

♦   `<textarea onSelect="expr|function()">...</textarea>`

This event-attribute triggers an event when the text in a field is *selected* by the user. Selection in this case is not simply clicking on a field, but rather selection of the text *within* the field by highlighting the text using the mouse or keyboard.

Form Submissions—`onSubmit`

The `onSubmit` event-attribute can be used with form-containers only:

♦   `<form onSubmit="expr|function()">...</form>`

`onSubmit` intercepts the pressing of an `<input type="submit">` button, which all forms that send data to a remote Web server must have.

All of JavaScript's functionality happens within the "client," such as Navigator, and it is not always necessary to submit form-values to a server if the intention is only to carry out some *local* processing of the data. If used in conjunction with a boolean function—that is, a function that returns `true` or `false`—form-submission can be halted, which is useful for form-validation purposes. Without JavaScript, a form can only be validated on the server via a Common Gateway Interface (CGI) script. We can avoid server-side form-validation by ensuring that a form is validated within the client. Consider the following HTML/JavaScript example, which uses an HTML form with the `onSubmit` attribute to validate a text-area field so it is not left empty by the user:

5

```
<!--
  Program 5-9
-->
<html>
<head>
<script language="JavaScript">
<!--
function validateForm(f) {
  if (f.value == "") {
    alert("Please enter some text into the " +
          "feedback field");
    return false;
  }
  else {
    // Ok, let the form submit the data:
    return true;
  }
```

```
//-->
</script>
</head>
<body>
<pre>
<form name="myForm"
      method="post"
      action="http://www.somehost.com/cgi-bin/process_form.pl"
      onSubmit="validateForm(myForm.feedback)">
Full Name: <input type="text" size=30 name="persons_name"><br>
Feedback : <textarea name="feedback" rows=5
cols=50></textarea><p>
<input type="submit" value="Send Data">
</form>
</pre>
</body>
</html>
```

In the preceding example, an `onSubmit` event-handler has been used to stop the current form from being submitted to a Web server until the text-area field (named `feedback`) has been submitted. Notice the use of JavaScript `return` statements to return the appropriate `true` or `false` values: `true` to allow submission of the form; `false` to deny submission of the form.

In order that an HTML form can submit data to a remote Web server, you must learn some CGI-scripting skills. CGI is a ubiquitous standard that allows an HTML form to link into a gateway script running on a Web server. A variety of languages can be used to implement CGI solutions, although Practical Extraction and Report Language, or Perl, C, and the Unix shells currently seem the most popular. In the preceding example, the `action` attribute of the <form> tag specifies the name of the script that will take the data from the form and process it. *Processing* is a loose term that could mean storing the form-data in to a database, validating the contents of the form, etc. The value of a forms `method` attribute specifies a *transmission method* for that form, and `"post"` is a transmission method whereby the data from the form is sent in one large continuous chunk, and is received on the standard-input stream by the script on the server that is specified in the `action` attribute. The script in the example is named `process_form.pl` (a Perl script in this instance) and could resemble the following:

```
#! /usr/bin/perl
require "cgi-lib.pl";
&ReadParse;
open(F,">>feedback.htm");
theName = $in{'persons_name'};
theFeedback = $in{'feedback'};
```

```
print F "<hr>Feedback from <b>$theName</b>.<hr>";
print F "<dl><dd>$theFeedback</dl>";
close(F);
```

This simple Perl script uses a library known as `cgi-bin.pl` and is widely available on the Internet to extract form-field data into an array (called `$in` in this case). So, for example, the form-field named `persons_name` is reflected in the Perl program as `$in{'persons_name'}`. The script then writes the information that it receives from the form into the file `feedback.htm`. In fact, it appends data to the file, using the ">>" notation, which you probably know from DOS and Unix, so the file can *grow* over time as more entries are added. The file is also written out with some basic HTML-formatting so it can be read into a browser such as Navigator. More information on the Perl scripting language can be found at `http://www.perl.com`, and via Netscape in USENETs `comp.lang.perl` newsgroup.

TIP: Client-side JavaScript cannot be used for CGI-based solutions because all processing is happening within the client and, in any event, JavaScript does not have the stream-reading and data-manipulation facilities of a scripting language such as Perl. However, Netscape's LiveWire software includes a server-side JavaScript module, which includes NSAPI database-access routines for CGI-type solutions. Hardened programmers may want to look at the Java class sources for the NSAPI/Java integration routines—what bliss ;-)

5

A CGI based solution, such as the Perl script above, is currently the only way of storing data from an HTML-form on to a remote server. JavaScript has no client-side facilities for storing data to disk, mainly because of security concerns. You can e-mail form-data to a server, using the `mailto:` URL.

Writing an E-Mail Interface Using JavaScript

The `mailto:` URL offers some interesting possibilities to the JavaScript developer. If you look at the syntax for the `<form>` tag, you will see an `action` attribute exists, which specifies the URL that handles the "submission" of the form. By using an `onSubmit` event-handler to intercept such a submission, you can dynamically alter the `action` attribute through use of the `form` object's `action` property. This property is a reflection of this attribute.

The `mailto:` URL allows an e-mail message to be sent to a mail-server for delivery to a recipient via the Internet. For example, if you typed:

```
mailto:wombat@spuddy.mew.co.uk
```

into Navigator's *Location* field, you could send me a message; Navigator will provide a window for you to enter your message, etc. You can also mimic this interface by using JavaScript. Consider the following application:

```
<!--
  Program 5-10
-->
<html>
<head>
<title>JavaScript E-mail-form interface</title>
<script language="JavaScript">
<!--
  function sendMail() {
    if (document.forms[0].recipient.value == "") {
      alert("No recipient has been specified!");
      return false;
    }
    if (document.forms[0].message.value == "") {
      alert("No message has been entered!");
      return false;
    }
    if (document.forms[0].subject.value == "") {
      document.forms[0].subject.value = "No subject";
      return false;
    }
    // Construct a mailto: URL with all the details:
    document.forms[0].action = "mailto:" +
                   document.forms[0].recipient.value +
                   "?subject=" +
                   document.forms[0].subject.value;
    return true;
  }
//-->
</script>
</head>
<body>
<basefont size=3>
<h2>E-mail form<hr></h2>
Please enter a recipient, optional subject, and the body of
your message,
and then press the <b>send mail</b> button.<p>
<form method="post" enctype="text/plain">
<table border=0>
<tr>
<td align="right"><b>To:</b></td>
<td><input type="text" name="recipient" size=60>
</td>
```

```
</tr>
<tr>
<td align="right"><b>Subject:</b></td>
<td><input type="text" name="subject" size=60></td>
</tr>
<tr valign="top">
<td align="right"><img border=0 hspace=3
    src="internal-gophertext"></td>
<td><textarea name="message" rows=4 cols=60></textarea></td>
</tr>
</table>
<hr>
<input type="submit" value="Send mail" onClick="sendMail()">
</form>
</body>
</html>
```

This application creates a number of form-fields to allow the user to specify a recipient, subject, and message-body for an e-mail message. The button of the form allows transmission of the details to the mail-server specified in Navigator's Options/ Preferences menu. Before this happens, though, control is passed to the `sendMail()` function. The `sendMail()` function checks to see that a recipient and message have been entered (if not, it warns the user and returns a `false` value, thus halting the transmission). If all is correct, it modifies the `action` property of the form to construct a `mailto:` URL, which incorporates all the details entered by the user. When a function is called using `onSubmit`, the boolean value returned by the function controls the user's ability to submit the form—a `true` value submits the form; a `false` value halts the submission. The `mailto:` URL used in this application has the syntax:

```
mailto:recipient?subject=subjectLine
```

where `?subject=` allows an optional subject-line to be sent, a feature not widely publicized. The `submit()` method is then called and submits the form as normal. `-submit()` mimics the selection of an `<input type="submit">` button. Notice the form did not have an `action` property to begin with; this has been allocated later by the `sendMail()` function.

NOTE: Be sure to watch the status bar to see the status of the e-mail message as it is sent. It is unwise to place a message saying the message has been successfully sent because your mail-server may be temporarily unavailable, busy, etc. Figure 5-1 shows the application in action.

When the message shown in Figure 5-1 finally arrived in my in-box it resembled the following:

```
From: Jason <wombat@spuddy.mew.co.uk>
X-Mailer: Mozilla 3.0b3 (Win95; I)
MIME-Version: 1.0
To: wombat@spuddy.mew.co.uk
Subject: Eureka!!!
Content-type: text/plain
Content-Disposition: inline; form-data

recipient=ag17@cityscape.co.uk
subject=Eureka!!!
message=This is a form submitted by Navigator, using JavaScript.
```

where "Jason" is the name entered in Navigator's Options/Mail and News Preferences screen, as is the From: line value. The To: line was specified from the program, as was the Subject: line. The Content-type: line is set to the value of the enctype attribute in the <form> tag; Content-Disposition is added automatically by Navigator. The next three lines are the actual body of the e-mail message, and represent the form-fields of the same name.

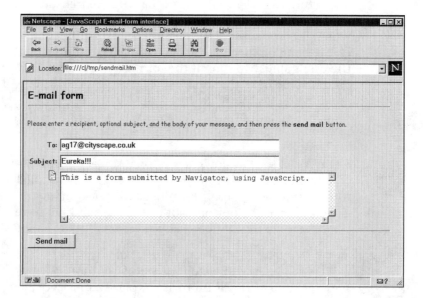

The e-mail interface as seen through Navigator

Figure 5-1.

Document Unloading Events—onUnLoad

The onUnLoad event-attribute can be used with the following HTML tags:

♦   <body>...</body>
♦   <frameset>...</frameset>

This attribute works in the opposite way to onLoad, described previously, in that a JavaScript function or statement can be invoked when the user *leaves* the current document. This event-attribute also works with frameset-documents (see Chapter 9).

Navigator 3.0's New Image Events

Navigator 3.0 introduced a series of new "image events" associated with an image object. An *image object* is an inline image placed within a hypertext document using the HTML <img src=URL> tag. Both GIF and JPEG formatted files are recognized by Navigator as inline images ("inline" being the term used for images rendered within a Web page).

Event Attribute	Event Triggered When...
onAbort	The user clicks on a link or presses Stop or ESC when the current image is being loaded.
onError	An error occurs when loading the image, that is, the image does not exist, or the image is corrupted, or the server providing the image hangs, i.e. crashes or dies, etc.
onLoad	The image is loaded into the page. Animated GIF images (GIF89a formatted files) will throw an onLoad event every time the image repeats from the first animation-frame.

5

For example, an onLoad event-attribute could be used to invoke a JavaScript function that shows how many loops an animated GIF image has displayed:

```
<!--
  Program 5-11
-->
```

```html
<html>
<head>
<script language="JavaScript">
<!--
  var count = 0;
  function updateCounter() {
     count ++;
     document.myForm.loops.value = count;
  }
//-->
</script>
</head>
<body>
<img src="drag89.gif" onLoad="updateCounter()"><p>
<form name="myForm">
Image loops: <input type="text" name="loops">
</form>
</body>
</html>
```

When the image `drag89.gif` is loaded, an `onLoad` event triggers the `updateCounter()` function, which, in turn, increments a numeric counter variable, and then also updates a text-field to show the user how many loops have passed. A loop occurs when all of the image-frames within the GIF file have been shown. As the image animates, the text-field will be updated. Individual frame-updates cannot be detected, however.

T IP: GIF89a images, or "animated GIFs" as they are more commonly known, can be created very easily using the Alchemy Mindworks *GIF Convertor* package. Appendix C contains the address of their page where you can download a shareware version of the package. Search for "GIF89" using a search-engine and you will find many dozens of freeware images that can be used in your pages. The disk that accompanies this book also has some examples that you can use in your Web pages.

More information on Navigator's new image objects can be found in Chapter 4. The `drag89.gif` image can also be found on the disk. The reader should be aware that image events were still bug-prone in the late beta versions of Navigator 3.0. (For example, it was impossible to refer to the `images` array when more than one `<img src>` tag was placed in a document, without crashing Navigator.) Hopefully, improvements will be made in the final release of Navigator 3.0N.

Dynamically Allocating an Event-Handler

Navigator 3.0 now allows event-handler functions to be allocated to elements dynamically. For example, a button can be created without an onClick event-handler, but can be allocated dynamically; i.e. by assigning the onClick handler, it can be allocated at a later stage. Event-handlers that already exist for a given object can also be reset so a new JavaScript function or statement is associated with that object.

Consider the following example, which displays a button and allows users to attach an event of their choice to the button using an appropriate hyperlink. In this case, the button is allocated an onClick event, which invokes a JavaScript function to load a file into the current document (this is done by assigning the name of a file to the location property of the current window). The button is created without an event-handler, so an appropriate selection must be made before the button can be activated:

```
<!--
   Program 5-12
-->
<html>
<head>
<script language="JavaScript">
<!--
  function button1() {
    location = "1.htm";
  }
  function button2() {
    location = "2.htm";
  }
  function button3() {
    location = "3.htm";
  }
//--
</script>
</head>
<body>
<form>
<input name="but1" type="button"
       value="Go!">
</form><p>
<img src="internal-gopher-menu">
<a href="#" onClick="document.forms[0].but1.onclick=button1">
Make button load 1st file
</a><br>
<img src="internal-gopher-menu">
<a href="#" onClick="document.forms[0].but1.onclick=button2">
Make button load 2nd file
```

5

```
</a><br>
<img src="internal-gopher-menu">
<a href="#" onClick="document.forms[0].but1.onclick=button3">
Make button load 3rd file
</a>
</body>
</html>
```

Notice how the event-handler is "attached" to the button `but1`, using a statement within an `onClick` attribute of the form:

```
onClick="document.forms[0].but1.onclick=button3"
```

where `document.forms[0].but1` is the button to which a new event-handler should be allocated.

NOTE: The name of the event-handler function must be specified without brackets, for example, `button3` instead of `button3()`, because the former is a function-reference, and the latter is a function-call. The goal here is not to call the function but, instead, to reference it, or *associate* it with an event for that button.

You may also have noticed the event attributes have been specified in lowercase, for example, `onclick` rather than `onClick`. This *is* a requirement because while HTML is case-insensitive, JavaScript is not. In fact, you may consider using the lowercase version throughout all of your JavaScript applications.

Event-handlers for other HTML-objects can also be added, just as long as the event-handler is valid for that object. If it isn't, the event would simply not be allocated. For example, if you stated the following in context to our previous example:

```
document.forms[0].but1.onload=button3
```

the event will be ignored because an `onLoad` event is not valid for a button object in JavaScript. You can also allocate multiple event-handling attributes to an object (when they are valid) simply by specifying them one after another as individual JavaScript statements. You could also place them within a function and then call this function instead.

Summary

Events are one of the main additions to the Netscape-HTML dialect and are the main foundation for incorporating interactive capabilities into Web pages.

♦ Event attributes are added to HTML tags to detect both system and user-initiated events. User-initiated events include hyperlink and button clicks, whereas system-initiated events include the loading of images and documents. Some events overlap in that they can be both user- and system-initiated; for example, document loading and unloading can be handled by a program (by altering the `window.location` property, or by the user entering a new URL into Navigator's *Location:* field).

♦ Some event attributes can be combined; for example, `onClick` and `onMouseOver` are valid for hyperlinks created with a `<a href>` tag, although not all HTML tags allow such combinations. The earlier syntax descriptions of each event-handling attribute will show you all possible valid combinations.

♦ An event-handler can now be "reset" by allocating a different JavaScript function (or statement, etc.) to the event-handler in question. This is a feature new to Navigator 3.0, and it allows events to be allocated to tags dynamically. You can even add events to tags that didn't have an event associated with them. Be sure to specify the function you are assigning to the event-handler *without* any brackets (for example, `myfunc()` becomes `myfunc`) and specify the event-handling attribute in lowercase (for example, `onClick` becomes `onclick`). This is the *only* time you must worry about quoting event-handlers in lowercase.

5

CHAPTER 6

Manipulating
User-Defined Objects
and Variables

Variables are repositories for values that exist during the
lifetime of a JavaScript application. Over the course of
writing a JavaScript application, you will make use of
variables to store values and to make calculations. Besides
the "standard" objects found in the JavaScript language, you
are also allowed to create your own user-defined objects
and properties. In this chapter, you will learn how to:

- Create and manipulate user-defined JavaScript variables
- Create and manipulate user-defined JavaScript objects
- Use JavaScript's new `Array()` and `Object()` constructors

JavaScript variables can store a variety of values, including

- **Strings:** groups of characters joined together
- **Numeric values:** *integers* and *real* numbers
- **Boolean values:** *true* and *false* values
- **Arrays:** multidimensional variables
- **Dates:** the current date and time

The Lifetime of a JavaScript Variable

The lifetime of user-defined variables is confined to the window in which they are created, and depend on *where* your variables are actually defined. Remember that since JavaScript programs are embedded within HTML documents, loading a new document into Navigator will remove any variables you have previously created. This is also true for other items of code, such as function definitions. Solutions to this problem include:

- Creating variables within a top-level frameset-document
- Using client-side cookies

Frameset-documents are covered in more detail in Chapter 9. They allow the browser screen to be broken up into a series of different regions, known as *frames*. The concept here is to define a frameset-document with all the variables and functions you require in the top-level document, and then use the `window` object's `parent` or the `top` properties to access these from the other frames in your application. In this way, you can load new documents and still change the contents of a frame without losing any previously created variables. Hidden fields also allow you to store values temporarily within an application (see Chapter 7), while "cookies" allow small items of information to be stored locally, on disk. Navigator uses the `cookies.txt` file to store such information. By setting the value of a cookie, and then examining it at a later stage, you can access the values you require—a sort of nonvolatile memory. The only disadvantage with the cookie technique is the number of cookies may grow very large if you need to manipulate a large quantity of variables. Also, cookies can only store *simple* values such as text strings, not complex values like arrays and objects (although arrays can be simulated, and objects-expressions stored as strings can be evaluated using the `eval()` method). See Chapter 13 for more details on creating and manipulating cookies.

Naming and Creating User-Defined Variables

Variable creation is loosely implemented in the JavaScript language. For example, it is unnecessary to state the *type* of a variable when it is first created, and variables can be defined with or without values; variables can even be *coerced* to a different data-type at a later stage. Variable names must start with either an alphabetic character (`a-z` or `A-Z`) or an underscored character (`"_"`), after which the remainder can contain a combination of letters, numbers, and underscores. For example, the following variable names are valid in JavaScript:

♦ `cookieName`

♦ `_frameName`

♦ `Days_In_Year`

Remember, JavaScript variables are case-sensitive, so referring to a variable called "cookieName" as "cookiename" will return an error saying the variable is not defined.

A user-defined variable is created in one of two ways:

♦ Using the `var` statement with the assignment operator (`=`)

♦ Using an assignment operator (`=`) to create a variable directly

The `var` statement can be used both to create and initialize a variable with a given value. The assignment operator (`=`) is used to store the value and is optional for variables created without an initial value. For example:

```
var daysInYear = 365;
```

would create a numeric variable called `daysInYear` that contains the numeric value `365`. The variable would exist within the scope of the current window. If you create this variable within the top-level frameset-document, you could refer to this variable as `top.daysInYear`, and you could safely reload a new document into the current window without losing the variable.

JavaScript allows you to overwrite variables at a later stage, even with a different data-type, for example:

```
daysInYear = "365";
```

6

which now stores the string value of `"365"` into the `daysInYear` variable, overwriting the previous contents, and *coercing* the variable to a string object in this instance. You can also create a variable without using the `var` statement, for example:

```
personsAge = 30;
```

although in this instance, whether or not the variable `personsAge` is a newly created variable is unclear. You could have already created this elsewhere in the application and you could now be overwriting it with a new value. For clarity, you should create all new variables using the `var` statement. Some versions of Navigator have been known to crash when referring to variables that have not been `var`'ed beforehand.

Variables can also exist in an empty-state, for example:

```
var tempVar;
```

creates a variable called `tempVar` that has no data-type and, therefore, has no initial value. This type of declaration is known as a "null variable."

TIP: A variable that has no value is termed a *null* variable. The JavaScript term `null` can be applied to such variables to see if they are currently undefined, for example:

```
var nullVar;
alert(nullVar == null);
```

will display a "`true`" value because the variable `nullVar` does not yet contain a value. Do not confuse null with empty, however. A string object with the value "" is *not* null; it is empty.

The actual type of the variable (string, number, etc.) can be set as and when you need to use the variable. In contrast to languages, such as C, where the type of a variable must be set before using it, JavaScript is much more flexible. Remember that you cannot refer to a variable *until* it has been created. If you need to create a variable *on the fly* within a statement simply prefix it with `var`. For example:

```
for (var initVal=0; initVal <= document.links.length; initVal++) {
    ...
}
```

creates and initializes the variable `initVal` for use as a counter in a `for` (loop) statement.

TIP: A single `var` statement can also assign *multiple* values to variables, for example, using a JavaScript statement of the form:

```
var name="Jason",
    email="wombat@spuddy.mew.co.uk";
```

JavaScript allows you to break lines that end with a comma (`,`) so you can place each variable on a separate line, if this improves readability.

Creating String Objects

A *string* is a collection of characters enclosed in single (`'`) or double quotes (`"`); for example, `"JavaScript"` is a string value, as is `"42"`. Strings are treated as *objects* in JavaScript; in fact, strings are the most common object you will encounter, and the JavaScript developer is provided with a wide range of standard string-manipulation functions. In order to create a string object, you can use any of the following techniques:

♦ Assigning a value using the `String()` constructor

♦ Using the `var` statement and the assignment operator to assign a value to a string

♦ Omitting the `var` statement and assigning a value directly to a string variable

The second and third methods are the most common, given that the `String()` constructor didn't appear within the language until Navigator 3.0.

6

TIP: The term "constructor" is borrowed from Java and refers to an object "method" that has the same name as the object concerned. A "method" is analogous to a function in the JavaScript language. For example, `Array()` is a constructor that creates an array-object, and `String()` is a constructor that creates a string object. `Array()` is not a standard JavaScript method as such but, instead, allows an instance of an object with this type to be created. You must use the `new` statement to create such objects, as the following describes.

The simplest, and most common, way of creating a string object is to use a statement such as:

```
var bookName = "JavaScript Essentials";
```

which places the string `"JavaScript Essentials"` into the string variable `bookName`. The `bookName` variable is now treated as a "string object" and can use any of the standard JavaScript string methods, for example, `substring()`, etc. Or the `var` statement can be omitted to leave a statement of the form:

```
bookName = "JavaScript Essentials";
```

and it is also possible under Atlas to use the new `String()` constructor with the `new` statement to create a string. The `String()` constructor is new to Netscape Atlas. In fact, an object called "String" doesn't even exist within JavaScript—mainly because strings are created arbitrarily as and when the user needs them. Consider the following statement that uses the `String()` constructor:

```
var bookName = new String();
```

which creates an empty string object called `bookName`. At this stage the value of `bookName` is `" "` —that is, an empty string— and the value of the property `bookName.length` is `0`.

The `String()` constructor also accepts a string as an argument, thus allowing a value to be assigned to the new string object. For example:

```
var bookName = new String("JavaScript Essentials");
```

A string object can also contain a number of special embedded codes that control formatting, as documented in the following table:

Code	Code Description
\n	The new-line character
\r	Carriage-return code
\f	Form-feed code
\x*nn*	The ASCII representation of the hexadecimal code *nn*
\b	The BACKSPACE (DEL) key

TIP: Formatting codes can be used in any string, although the interpretation of the code will depend on the method you are using to parse the string. For example, the new-line code `'\r\n'` will be interpreted properly within `<textarea>` containers and JavaScript methods such as `alert()`, but *not* within HTML-formatted text— for example, within a text-string placed in a JavaScript `document.write()` method.

So, for example, the JavaScript statement:

```
alert("JavaScript\nEssentials");
```

would display the words `"JavaScript"` and `"Essentials"` on two separate lines within an alert-box because the new-line code has been included.

When using string objects, be sure to use the same type of quote to encapsulate the string, For example, the statement:

```
myString = "This is an invalid string';
```

is invalid since different kinds of quotation marks have been used to create the string. An error will be issued when this line is eventually parsed.

String objects have only one property, namely `length`, which contains the number of characters in the string object. JavaScript's string-processing methods are documented in their entirety within Appendix B, although a summary can be seen in the following table. String methods are organized into two main categories:

♦   HTML-formatting
♦   String-manipulation

The formatting methods are used when strings are used with methods— such as `document.write()`— that send data to the Web browser; these are marked with a ✔ in the table. The string-manipulation methods are used to examine and alter the internal contents of a string object.

6

Method	Description
`anchor()`	Creates a named anchor out of a string, that is, a `<a name>` tag

Method	Description
big() ✔	Encapsulates the string in a `<big>..</big>` container making it appear larger
blink() ✔	Encapsulates the string in a `<blink>..</blink>` container making it blink
bold() ✔	Encapsulates the string in a `<b>..</b>` container making the text bold
charAt()	Returns the position of a specific character in a string
fixed() ✔	Encapsulates the string in a `<tt>..</tt>` monospace font tag
fontcolor() ✔	Encapsulates the string in a `<font color=colorCode>..</font>` tag making the text a different color when viewed
fontsize() ✔	Encapsulates the string in a `<font size=fontSize>..</font>` container making the text either larger or smaller
indexOf()	Returns the first position of a character based on a starting position
italics() ✔	Encapsulates the string in a `<i>..</i>` container tag making the text appear italicized
lastIndexOf()	Returns the last position of a character based on a starting position
link()	Turns a text string into a `<a href>..</a>` hyperlink
small() ✔	Encapsulates the string in a `<small>..</small>` container making the text appear smaller
strike() ✔	Encapsulates the string in a `<strike>..</strike>` container tag making the text appear as struck out (platform dependent)
sub() ✔	Encapsulates the string in a `<sub>..</sub>` tag making the text appear as subscript
substring()	Returns a portion (substring) of a text string
sup() ✔	Encapsulates the string in a `<sup>..</sup>` container tag making the text appear as superscript
toLowerCase()	Converts a string to lowercase
toUpperCase()	Converts a string to UPPERCASE

Numeric Variables

Numeric values can either be *integers* (whole numbers) or *floating-point* numbers (values with fractional part). For example, the values 0, -3, and 68 are all integers, whereas 8.68 and 2.71828 are floating-point, or *real* numbers as they are sometimes called. Numeric values can be manipulated using operators such as *, /, +, -, ++, --, and +=, and by using JavaScript's `Math` object.

The JavaScript `Math` object contains mathematical methods and stores various mathematical constants, such as `PI` (for the value of *pi*). Appendix B has more details of such properties.

Boolean Variables

Boolean, or logical, variables, can only hold the literal values `true` and `false`, and are used for logical expressions, for example:

```
resultOk = true;
```

stores a `true` value into the variable `resultOk`. To test if this variable is `true`, a statement of the following form can be used.

```
if (resultOk) {
    alert("resultOk is true");
} else {
    alert("resultOk is false");
}
```

NOTE: The "{' and '}" braces are optional here because only one statement in the body of the `if` and `else` statement is being used.

6

You could also use the equality operator to check for a `true` value, that is, `resultOk == true`, although the operator is superfluous. The former method is more compact and more widely used with logical variables. The `!` operator can be used to test for values that are not true; for example, `!resultOk` would return the value `true` if `resultOk` is `false`, and the value `false` if `!resultOK` was true.

TIP: The numeric values 1 and 0 can also be used in place of `true` and `false` because these evaluate to the same value; for example, `1 == true`, and `0 == false`.

Array Variables

Array variables are an ordered set of values associated with a single variable. In fact, many of the standard object-properties in JavaScript are structured as arrays, such as links and anchors. With JavaScript, an array is referenced using the expression:

```
arrayname[index]
```

where `arrayname` is the name of the array and `index` is a numeric variable that specifies a "position," or an "element" within the array. For example, `arrayname[0]` is the first element in the array. Note that array positions start at zero in JavaScript. The actual elements within an array can be of any data-type; for example, strings, booleans, and arrays can also contain elements of different data-types. JavaScript provides three methods of creating an array, namely:

♦   The `Array()` constructor

♦   The `Object()` constructor

♦   Using a preprogrammed function (a user-defined constructor)

The `Array()` constructor creates an array object and optionally assigns values to the elements within the array. Elements can also be added dynamically as, and when, required by assigning values to individual elements of the array. It is also possible to "miss out" an element and assign values in a nonsequential manner. The `Array()` constructor must be used with the `new` statement to create a new instance of an array object; for example, the code:

```
var anArray = new Array();
anArray[0] = "http://www.osborne.com";
anArray[1] = "http://www.mcgraw-hill.co.uk";
```

creates an array called `anArray` that contains two elements, both of which are string objects. Arrays start at position zero (0) when using the `Array()` constructor, and the `length` property is automatically provided. In this example, the value of the expression `anArray.length` will, therefore, be 2.

Array elements can also be placed into the array by mentioning them directly in the constructor itself, for example:

```
var anArray = new Array("http://www.osborne.com",
                        "http://www.mcgraw-hill.co.uk");
```

which is equivalent to the previous example, albeit more compact. As mentioned, you could also create a *dense* array (an array in which all elements have a value) containing multiple data-types, for example:

```
var anArray = new Array(true, "8.68", Date(), 68);
```

that places a boolean value in `anArrray[0]`, the string `"8.68"` in `anArray[1]`, a Date object (the value of which will be the current date and time) into `anArray[2]`, and the numeric value `68` into `anArray[3]`.

The size of an array and, hence, the value of the `length` property, created with the `Array()` constructor, is dependent on the `index` value used to address a specific element. For instance:

```
var anArray = new Array();
anArray[50] = "This is array element 51";
```

specifies that array element `51` is set to the string value `"This is array element 51"`, hence, the value of `anArray.length` is now `51`, noting arrays start at position `0`.

Another way of assigning the length of an array is to specify the number of elements in the `Array()` constructor; for example:

```
myArray = new Array(10);
```

creates an array with `11` elements (numbered `0` to `11`). The value of the `length` property cannot be set explicitly, because length is a *read-only* property. Another way of assigning `11` to the `length` property would be to have:

```
myArray = new Array();
myArray[10] = 0;
```

or to assign `11` elements into an array manually. For example:

```
myArray = new Array(0,0,0,0,0,0,0,0,0,0,0);
```

6

Another way to create an array is to write your own `Array()` constructor function. Consider the following JavaScript function, called `makeArray()`. `makeArray()` works by using a `for` statement to create as many array elements as are specified in the `arraySize` argument that is passed to the function:

```
function makeArray(arraySize) {
   this.length = arraySize;
   for (var x = 0; x <= arraySize; x++) {
      this[x] = 0;
   }
   return this;
}
```

This function uses the JavaScript `this` statement. In this case, the statement refers to the current function, so if we stated:

```
browser = new makeArray(3);
```

the `makeArray()` function would create three array variables, namely: `browser[0]`, `browser[1]`, and `browser[2]` respectively, each of which is set to the value zero. When `makeArray()` is invoked with a `new` statement, the variable assigned to the value returned by the `makeArray()` function, which is `browser` here, is reflected in the value of the `this` statement. The size of the array is assigned to `browser.length`; then a series of browser elements is created: `browser[0]` to `browser[arraySize]`. Finally, the `browser` object is returned from the function. Arrays and objects are one and the same in JavaScript.

Now, values can be assigned to our array using the following assignment statements. In this hypothetical example, this is version-description for a number of Netscape browsers, all stored as strings. For example:

```
browser[0] = "Netscape Atlas";
browser[1] = "Netscape 2.01";
browser[2] = "Netscape 2.0";
```

Once again, the array element starts at zero (0), because this was specified in the `makeArray()` function. The `makeArray()` function has now been superseded by `Array()`, although the former is still widely used, and is compatible with future versions of Navigator.

Adding an element is easy when you know the index of the array position. Unfortunately, no way exists to ascertain this unless you examine the `length` property of the array, so sometimes you must use code, such as:

```
nextElement = myArray.length;
myArray[nextElement] = "Some value";
```

Of course, you could write a JavaScript function to this, and pass it the name of the array and the value you want to assign. For example:

```
function add(arrayName, value) {
  var nextElement = arrayName.length;
  arrayName[nextElement] = value;
}
```

Here is a working program that creates an array with three elements, adds one new element, and then prints its value on the screen:

```
<!--
  Program 6-1
-->
<html>
<head>
<script language="JavaScript">
<!--
  var x = new Array();
  function add(arrayName, value) {
    var nextElement = arrayName.length;
    arrayName[nextElement] = value;
  }
  x[0] = "1";
  x[1] = "2";
  x[2] = "3";
  add(x, "new value!");
  alert("The new value is: " + x[3]);
//-->
</script>
</head>
</html>
```

Navigator 3.0 also introduced the new `Object()` constructor, which can also be used to create a "generic object," such as an array. As mentioned, objects and arrays are treated the same, although the `Object()` and `Array()` constructors work differently. Multiple array elements cannot be passed to the `Object()` constructor so, for example:

```
var myObj = new Object("value 1", "value 2");
```

would not work. Furthermore, arrays created with the `Object()` constructor do not have a `length` property: You must either traverse the array with a

6

`for` loop and count the elements progmatically, or you can hard-code the length in the first array-element and then access this. This is not much use for an array whose contents may change dynamically, perhaps even beyond your control, so stick to using `Array()` in such cases. Arrays created with `Object()` also start at position zero (0). To create an array using `Object()` use code such as:

```
var thisArray = new Object();
thisArray[0] = 2; // This is the length of the array
thisArray[1] = "http://www.cityscape.co.uk";
thisArray[2] = "http://www.dircon.co.uk";
```

To access the size of the array in this example use `thisArray[0]`. The value of `thisArray.length` will be `null`, that is, undefined.

Here is a more extensive JavaScript program that uses array objects to store a number of JavaScript objects, and then prints their properties. The `makeArray()` function has been used in this example, although the `Array()` constructor could have been used:

```
<!--
  Program 6-2
-->
<html>
<head>
<script language="JavaScript">
<!--
  function MakeArray(n) {
    this.length = n;
    for (var x = 0; x <= n; x++)
            this[x] = 0;
    return this;
  }
  function writeData() {
    var counter;
    var JavaObjs = new MakeArray(4);
    var objName  = new MakeArray(4);
    // Actual object references:
    JavaObjs[0] = window;
    JavaObjs[1] = document;
    JavaObjs[2] = history;
    JavaObjs[3] = Math;
    // The names of the objects (strings):
    objName[0] = "window";
    objName[1] = "document";
    objName[2] = "history";
    objName[3] = "Math";
```

```
            document.write("<table cellpadding=4 border=1>");
            for (counter = 0; counter <= 3; counter++) {
                document.write("<tr><td align=middle><b>" +
                                    objName[counter] + "</b></td>");
                for (i in JavaObjs[counter]) {
                    document.write("<td align=middle>" + i +
                                        "</td>");
                }
                document.write("</tr>");
            }
            document.write("</table>");
        }
        //-->
        </script>
        </head>
        <body onLoad="writeData()">
        </body>
        </html>
```

The previous script prints the properties of four common JavaScript objects that every hypertext document automatically inherits. The results are written into an HTML table for readability. Figure 6-1 illustrates the output from the script.

Here is another application that implements a simple color-selection system. Rather than storing a list of color-code verbs (such as "Silver", etc.) into the program, and then allowing the user to pick a color, this system does something more ambitious: It allows the user to enter a RGB value into a series of fields, and then to change the background color accordingly. First, a way of converting decimal numbers into their hexadecimal equivalent must be found. The function DecToHex() has

6

The output from the example as seen through Navigator
Figure 6-1.

window	length	frames	parent	top	self	window	name	status	defaultStatus		
document	title	location	referrer	lastModified	loadedDate	cookie	bgColor	fgColor	linkColor	vlinkColor	alinkColor
history	length	current	previous	next							
Math	E	LOG2E	LOG10E	LN2	LN10	PI	SQRT2	SQRT1_2			

been included in this script (see Appendix B) in which arrays are used to store a hexadecimal conversion table:

```
<!--
  Program 6-3
-->
<html>
<head>
<script language="JavaScript">
<!--
  var r=0, g=0, b=0, rgb=0, inc=0, cnt=0, cnt2=0;
  var part1 = "", part2 = "";
  function makeArray(n) {
    this.length = n;
    // Create the array, starting at position 1 in this
    // instance, although it could be 0 just as long as
    // you alter the hexTable definition to start at 0
    for (var x=1; x <=n; x++) {
        this[x] = 0;
    }
    return(this);
  }
  hexTable = makeArray(16);
  // Col:Row
  hexTable[1]  = "00:00";
  hexTable[2]  = "10:01";
  hexTable[3]  = "20:02";
  hexTable[4]  = "30:03";
  hexTable[5]  = "40:04";
  hexTable[6]  = "50:05";
  hexTable[7]  = "60:06";
  hexTable[8]  = "70:07";
  hexTable[9]  = "80:08";
  hexTable[10] = "90:09";
  hexTable[11] = "A0:0A";
  hexTable[12] = "B0:0B";
  hexTable[13] = "C0:0C";
  hexTable[14] = "D0:0D";
  hexTable[15] = "E0:0E";
  hexTable[16] = "F0:0F";

  function seeColors() {
    // Validate the form input:
    ok = true;
    if (document.forms[0].red.value > 255)   { ok=false }
    if (document.forms[0].green.value > 255) { ok=false }
    if (document.forms[0].blue.value > 255)  { ok=false }
    if (!ok) {
```

```
            document.forms[0].rgbval.value = "";
            alert("Error: value greater than 255 detected.");
        }
        else {
            r = DecToHex(document.forms[0].red.value);
            g = DecToHex(document.forms[0].green.value);
            b = DecToHex(document.forms[0].blue.value);
            rgb = r + g + b;
            document.bgColor = "#" + rgb;
            document.forms[0].rgbval.value = "#" + rgb
        }
    }

    function DecToHex(decval) {
      inc = 0;
      cnt = 1;
      while ((inc += 16) <= decval) {
          cnt ++;
      }
      inc  = inc - 16;
      cnt2 = Math.abs(decval - inc) + 1;
      part1 = hexTable[cnt].substring(0,2);
      part2 = hexTable[cnt2].substring(3,5);
      // Trim off any trailing and leading 0's
      if (part1.substring(2,1) == "0") {
         part1 = part1.substring(0,1);
      }
      if (part2.substring(0,1) == "0") {
         part2 = part2.substring(2,1);
      }
      return(part1+part2);
    }
//-->
</script>
</head>
<body>
<tt>
<basefont size=4>
<form>
BACKGROUND (HEX) <input name="rgbval" size=8>  
R: <input name="red"   size=5 value=00> 
G: <input name="green" size=5 value=00> 
B: <input name="blue"  size=5 value=00><p>
<input type="button"
       value="See Results"
       onClick="seeColors()"></p>
</form>
</tt>
```

6

```
</body>
</html>
```

You could easily extend this program to change the color of a specific frame within a frameset-document, as well, and you could alter other colors, such as the foreground or hyperlink colors. In this example, the form-fields red, green, and blue allow input of a decimal value in the range 0-255 (0-FF in hexadecimal). When you enter a number and click the *See Results* button, the seeColors() function is invoked, which carries out the conversions, updates the document.bgColor property, and changes the screen color. Using arrays it is also possible to create a "client-side" database that allows simple searches. The "database" in this case could be stored as an array. Consider the following application that does just this:

```
<!--
  Program 6-4
-->
<html>
<head>
<title>Book Search</title>
<script language="JavaScript">
<!--
var bookNames  = new Array();
var bookUrls   = new Array()
var bookType   = new Array()
var tabDef1    = "<table cellpadding=3 width='100%' " +
                 "border=1>";
var tabDef2    = "</table><br>End of listing.<p>";
var emptyFrame = "<body></body>";

// The book database:
bookNames[0] = "The Essential Internet Information Guide, " +
               "Jason J Manger";
bookNames[1] = "Netscape Navigator, Jason J Manger";
bookNames[2] = "WWW, Mosaic and More, Jason J Manger";
bookUrls[0]  = "http://www.gold.net/users/ag17/eiig.htm";
bookUrls[1]  = "http://www.gold.net/users/ag17/netnav.htm";
bookUrls[2]  = "http://www.gold.net/users/ag17/wwwm&m.htm";
bookType[0]  = "CD";
bookType[1]  = "book";
bookType[2]  = "book";

function search() {
 var hits = 0;
 var emptTab = "";
 var tmp = parent.frames[0].document.forms[0].searchfor.value;
 var searchfor = tmp.toLowerCase();
```

```
        for (var n=0; n < parent.bookNames.length; n++) {
            if (bookNames[n].toLowerCase().indexOf(searchfor) != -1) {
                hits ++;
                // Construct a table row. I am assuming that the
                // book.gif and cd.gif images are in the X:\JS\
                // directory:
                emptTab += "<tr><td width='1%'>" +
                            "<img border=0 width=30 " +
                            "src='file:///c%7c/js/" +
                            parent.bookType[n] +
                            ".gif'></a></td>" +
                            "<td><a href='" +
                            parent.bookUrls[n] +
                            "'>" +
                            parent.bookNames[n] +
                            "</a></td></tr>";
            }
        }

        // Show results:
        if (hits == 0) {
            // No hits:
            alert("No books matching '" +
                    searchfor +
                    "' were located.");
        }
        else {
            // Show the results as a table:
            parent.frames[1].document.open();
            parent.frames[1].document.write("<font size='+2'>" +
                                "Search Results<hr></font>");
            parent.frames[1].document.write("There were <b>" +
                                hits +
                                "</b> matches for " +
                                "the string '" +
                                searchfor +
                                "'.<br>");
            parent.frames[1].document.write(parent.tabDef1 +
                                emptTab +
                                parent.tabDef2);
            parent.frames[1].document.close();
        }
    }
//-->
</script>
</head>
<frameset rows="50%,*">
<frame src="search.htm">
```

6

```
<frame src="javascript:parent.emptyFrame">
</frameset>
</html>
```

This application, above, allows you to search a book database. The database is stored in a series of arrays which define the name of the book, the product category (book or CD), and a URL that points to an HTML page that has more information on the book, etc. (These are stored on my own personal home page.) The user enters a search string into a text field (named searchfor). By using a `for` loop to scan through the bookNames array we can then see if this string exists in one of the book titles. The JavaScript indexOf() method is invaluable for this purpose. indexOf() returns the position at which some text, specified by the user, exists within a particular string object. The string object in this case is the current element in the bookNames array, and the string we are searching for is stored in the searchfor variable. The statement:

```
if (bookNames[n].toLowerCase().indexOf(searchfor) != -1)
```

therefore allows us to see if the search-string exists within the current title, and hence if it exists in the book database. indexOf() returns the value -1 if the string cannot be located; hence we can ascertain whether or not a book title has been found within the current database entry. The entire application is stored as a frameset-document in which the results of the search are displayed in the lower frame—all user input is carried out in the upper frame. Notice how the `javascript:` URL has been used to load an empty frame by setting the frames src attribute to the value of a JavaScript string variable. As entries are located all of the details from the various arrays are placed in a string, emptTab, which is finally used to display an HTML table containing all of the results. A variable, hits, tracks the number of entries that have been found, and if zero, the user is informed that no matches have been made.

The application also displays a series of GIF images to denote the type of product that has been located—either a book or CD-ROM in this instance (note that the application expects to find these images in the X:\JS directory, where X: is your hard-disk drive letter, e.g. C:\JS for the C drive).

The file search.htm that is read into the first frame contains an HTML form and a text field to allow the user to enter a search-string, and is structured as follows:

```
<html>
<head>
<script language="JavaScript">
```

```
<!--
  function checkField() {
    if (document.forms[0].searchfor.value == "") {
      // An empty field has been submitted:
      alert("Please enter a search string.");
    }
  }
//-->
</script>
<body>
<font size="+2">Book Search<hr></font>
Please enter a search string.<p>
<form>
<input name="searchfor" type="text" value="">
<input type="button"
       onClick="checkField(); parent.search()"
       value="Search">
</form>
</body>
</html>
```

More information on frameset-documents can be found in Chapter 9, including the use of the `javascript:` URL to populate frame contents, as well as information on the JavaScript `parent` property.

String and Number Conversions

This section discusses how differently typed variables are handled internally by JavaScript. *Concatenation* is the joining of strings together, although in JavaScript numeric values that are concatenated with strings are themselves converted into string objects to yield a result. This concept is best explained with a series of examples. Consider the case where the following JavaScript variables were declared:

6

```
var Days = "334";
var DaysInDec = 31;
```

which declares two variables: a string object `Days` that contains the string `"334"` and the numeric variable `DaysInDec` that stores the value 31. Now issue the statement:

```
DaysNow = Days + DaysInDec;
```

The value of the `DaysNow` variable would be set to `"33431"` and *not* the value of the numeric expression 334 + 31. JavaScript knows string concatenation is being performed because the `Days` variable is a string object. Therefore, it converts the variable `DaysInDec`—initially a numerically typed variable—into a string object because the left-hand operand, variable `Days`, is a string. The end-result is that the right-hand operand, `DaysInDec`, has been physically "joined," or concatenated, onto the first variable. The same outcome would also happen with the JavaScript statement:

```
DaysNow = DaysInDec + Days;
```

If you actually want to add the values together, in the *numeric* sense, you should begin with the value of `Days` numerically typed. In the context of our example the JavaScript statement:

```
MyValue = DaysInDec + parseInt(Days);
```

would yield the numeric value `365` because the `parseInt()` method changes the type of the `Days` variable to a number. Because JavaScript will automatically coerce a number into a string when concatenating, even the nonsensical statement:

```
tempVal = 365 + "JavaScript";
```

will yield a result—the string `"365JavaScript"` in this case. The `"+"` operator is a special case in JavaScript because it is used both with string objects and with numerical variables. When using different operators, such as the subtraction operator `"-"`, the results become more meaningful. For example, the JavaScript statement:

```
tempVal = 365 - "10";
```

would yield the numeric value `355` because the left-hand operand (`365`) is numeric, and the value `"10"` (a string) would be converted to a number—the opposite behavior for concatenated objects that use the `"+"` operator.

TIP: You can safely carry out numeric functions on "stringified" numbers, that is, numbers stored within strings, whenever the left-hand operand is a number.

In JavaScript the `"-"` operator does not deconcatenate strings. For example, the statement:

```
tempVal = "365" - "10";
```

would also yield a *numeric* result (the value 355 again, in this case).

TIP: In order to carry out numeric calculations on strings— that is, on strings that contain numbers— simply use the `parseInt()` method on the string to convert it to a number beforehand, as shown previously.

If you need to ascertain the data-type of a particular variable, the `typeof()` operator can be used.

You can convert a numeric value to a string by prepending an empty string on to the numeric variable, for example.

```
numericValue  = 100;                 // Numeric: 100
numericString = "" + numericValue;   // String: "100"
```

A much better solution, however, would be to use the JavaScript `String()` constructor, for instance, with the statement:

```
numericString = String(numericValue);
```

The `String()` constructor is used to create a string object, which was covered previously.

Using JavaScript Expressions

Expressions are combinations of variables, operators, and methods that evaluate to a single value. You have already seen examples of expressions that use JavaScript's assignment operator (=) in previous sections. This section briefly looks at JavaScript's operators and how these are used to form expressions and to assign values to variables.

6

Conditional Expressions—The **?** Statement

Conditional expressions include comparisons against the value of certain JavaScript and user-defined variables. JavaScript has an evaluation statement called ? whose syntax is:

```
? (condition) statements1 : statements2
```

where `condition` is an expression you want to evaluate, `statements1` is the JavaScript statements executed when the `condition` is `true`, and statements2 is the statement executed when the condition is `false`. You can also assign values to variables using this statement. For example, consider the following statement that assigns a string to a variable depending on a numeric expression:

```
timeType = (hour >= 12) ? "PM" : "AM"
```

This statement will assign the string value `"PM"` to the variable `timeType` when the variable `hour` is greater than or equal to `12`; otherwise `timeType` is set to `"AM"`. The timeType variable is assigned to the value returned by the ? statement in this example, although the assignment is optional. For instance, the assignment could be done away with and `statements1` and `statements2` parts replaced with function-calls or another statement. The ? statement is really a shorthand version of the `if .. else` statement, which in context to the previous example would resemble:

```
if (hour >= 12)
   timeType = "PM";
else
   timeType = "AM";
```

Assignment Operators

Assignment expressions use operators to assign values to variables. The operators in JavaScript include those shown in the following table:

Operator	Description
=	Direct assignment to left-hand operand
+=	Add and assign result to left-hand operand
+	Add and assign result to left-hand operand
++	Add and assign result to left-hand operand
-=	Subtract and assign result to left-hand operand
-	Subtract and assign result to left-hand operand
--	Subtract and assign result to left-hand operand
*	Multiply and assign result to left-hand operand
*=	Multiply and assign result to left-hand operand
/	Divide and assign result to left-hand operand
/=	Divide and assign result to left-hand operand

Each of these assignment operators assigns values to a left-hand operand based upon the value of the right-hand operand. The basic assignment operator (=) assigns the value of the right-hand operand to its left-hand operand, for example:

```
myVal = 68;
```

makes variable `myVal` take the numeric value `68`, while:

```
myVal = myVal * 10;
```

increases the value of the variable `myVal` 10 times. Many of JavaScript's assignment operators are shorthand operators; thus, in the previous case, this statement could have been used:

```
myVal *= 10;
```

to increase the value of the variable `myVal` by 10 times. All of the other JavaScript operators work in a similar way. Remember, strings use the "+" operator for concatenation, so an expression such as:

```
var myVar = "Hello";
myVar += "!";
```

will join a "!" character onto the string `"Hello"`.

Comparison Operators

JavaScript's comparison operators are identical to those found in other programming languages, such as C. They include the following:

Operator	Performs
==	Equality (equal to)
!=	Inequality (not equal to)
!	Logical inequality
>=	Greater than or equal to
<=	Less than or equal to
>	Greater than
<	Less than

6

Notice how the equality operator is == as opposed to a single equals sign (a single equals sign is the assignment operator in JavaScript). The inequality operator is != in JavaScript, as in the C programming language (mainly because the logical *not* operator in JavaScript is the single exclamation mark). Used within a JavaScript while loop, the following JavaScript code implements a simple times-table program:

```
<!--
  Program 6-5
-->
<html>
<head>
<script language="JavaScript">
<!--
var stopLoop = false;
var counter = 1;
while (!stopLoop) {
      document.writeln(counter + " x 10 = " +
      (counter * 10) +
      "<br>");
      counter ++;
      stopLoop = (counter > 12) ? true : false;
}
//-->
</script>
</head>
<body>
</body>
</html>
```

The variable stopLoop is initially set to false, and the while loop keeps running while stopLoop is not true, for example, !stopLoop. When stopLoop is set to true (after 12 iterations of the loop, in this case) the loop terminates and the program exits. The statement:

```
stopLoop = (counter > 12) ? true : false;
```

translates to: "If the variable counter is greater than 12, set variable stopLoop to true; otherwise, set variable stopLoop to false" and is a shorthand notation for the longer version of the if statement:

```
if (counter > 12)
   stopLoop = true;

else
   stopLoop = false;
```

Logical Operators

JavaScript's logical operators are && (logical *and*) and || (logical *or*) respectively. They are used with boolean values. For example, if the assignment statements were:

```
age1 = true;
age2 = false;
age3 = true;
```

the JavaScript expression

```
age1 || or age2
```

would yield a `true` value because the expression uses the logical *or* operator, and only one of the values in the or-expression must yield `true` to return a `true` value. The and operator (`&&`) requires all values in the expression to yield `true` for a `true` value to be returned, thus the expression:

```
age1 && age2
```

would yield a `false` result in this context because the boolean variable `age2` is set to `false`. You can mix values by bracketing-off the appropriate parts, for example:

```
if ((age1 && age2) || age3) {
    function1();
}
else {
    function2();
}
```

translates to "Invoke the `function1()` function if age1 and age2 are both true, or if just age3 is true, otherwise execute the `function2()` function." In context to the original variable settings, the function `function1()` would be invoked because the value of variable age3 is `true` and satisfies the end condition in the `if` statement.

String Operators

The string operators in JavaScript are + and +=, which can be used to join strings together. In the statements:

```
var part1 = "Java";
var part2 = "Script";
```

6

then the JavaScript statement:

```
var part3 = part1 + part2;
```

would place the string value `"JavaScript"` into the string variable `part3`. A number of methods are supported that manipulate strings—Appendix B contains details of each JavaScript method. String concatenation has been discussed earlier in this chapter.

Creating and Manipulating User-Defined Objects

The JavaScript language adheres to an object-based model, in which an *object* is a construct with *properties* that are JavaScript variables. Each object can have a number of *methods* associated with it. An object's properties are accessed with JavaScript using the notation:

```
object.property
```

where `object` is the name of the JavaScript object, including both user-defined and standard Navigator objects, and `property` is the name of the property to access. A period (`.`) must separate the property from the object. Properties are created by assigning them to a specific object; for example, an object could be created called `browser`, which tracks details of Web browser systems. To do this, a new function called `browser()` must be created; then these details can be passed to it as a series of arguments:

```
function browser(name, platform) {
  this.name = name;
  this.platform = platform;
}
```

The `this` statement is used in JavaScript to refer to the *current* object. Within the scope of a function-body the value of `this` refers to the current function, hence, `this.name` is really a shorthand notation for `browser.name`, and `this.platform` is shorthand for `browser.platform`. The `browser()` function shown above simply defines the structure for a browser-object and assigns initial values to the `name` and `platform` *properties*. At this stage, the `browser()` function is now treated as a "browser object."

A function by itself will not create an instance of an object, however. The statement that actually creates such an object is called `new`, and is used as follows:

```
atlas = new browser("Netscape Atlas", "Windows 95")
```

where `atlas` is the name of a new `browser` object. In this instance, the
name property will be *"Netscape Atlas"* and the `platform` property will be set
to *"Windows 95"* accordingly. To refer to these properties, such as the
`platform` property, use the JavaScript expression of the form:

```
atlas.platform
```

which in the context of this example would yield the value `"Windows 95"`.
Objects can also store properties that are themselves separate objects. For
example, if a `person` object were defined with the JavaScript function:

```
function person(name) {
  this.person = name;
}
```

new `person` objects (named `pers1` and `pers2`) could be created using the
statements:

```
pers1 = new person("Jason");
pers2 = new person("Maria");
```

Extending this example, a new object called `emailAddress`, which
associated an e-mail address with a `person` object, would be defined
as follows:

```
function emailAddress(name, address) {
  this.name = name;
  this.address = address;
}
```

6

and two new `emailAddress` objects were created as follows:

```
e1 = new emailAddress(pers1, "jason@somewhere.com");
e2 = new emailAddress(pers2, "maria@sometime.com");
```

the e-mail address for the person *Jason* could be ascertained, using
the notation:

```
e1.name.person;
```

where `e1` is an `emailAddress` object and `name` is the name property of the
object. Name objects are taken from `person` objects; by adding a `person`
object to the end of the expression, the person's name is returned. You could

even create an entirely new JavaScript function to display all of a person's details, as illustrated in the following with the showDetails function:

```
function showDetails() {
  var persDet = "Name: " + this.name.person + "\n" +
                "E-mail: " + this.address;
  document.write(persDet);
}
```

By altering the function definition for emailAddress to include a reference to the showDetails function as follows:

```
function emailAddress(name, address) {
  this.name = name;
  this.address = address;
  this.showDetails = showDetails;
}
```

you can now call the showDetails function using the statement:

```
e1.showDetails();
```

Because variable e1 is associated with an emailAddress object (see previous example) that itself refers to a person object via the variable pers1, the following information can be retrieved:

```
Name: Jason
E-mail: jason@somewhere.com
```

Here is an extended example that constructs an "object database" and allows the user to search for a particular person and to be shown that person's details:

```
<!--
  Program 6-6
-->
<html>
<head>
<script>
<!--
 // Create the 'object database' and arrays:
 var pers1 = new person("Jason");
 var pers2 = new person("Maria");
 var addresses = new Array();
 addresses[0] = 2;
 addresses[1] = new emailAddress(pers1,
```

```
                         new Array(2, "jason@somewhere.com",
                                      "wombat@spuddy.mew.co.uk"));
      addresses[2] = new emailAddress(pers2,
                         new Array(1, "maria@sometime.com"));
      function person(name) {
        this.person = name;
      }
      function emailAddress(name, address) {
        this.name = name;
        this.address = address;
      }
      function showAddresses(thisPerson) {
        var eMailAddr = "";
        var found     = false;
        for (var i=1; i <= addresses[0]; i++) {
           if (addresses[i].name.person.toLowerCase() ==
                             thisPerson.toLowerCase()) {
             found = true;
             eMailAddr += addresses[i].name.person + ":\n";
             for (var n=1; n <= addresses[i].address[0]; n++) {
                 eMailAddr += n + ". " +
                                  addresses[i].address[n] + "\n"
             }
           }
        }
        (!found) ? alert("That person cannot be found.") :
                 alert(eMailAddr);
      }
      //-->
      </script>
      </head>
      <body onLoad="showAddresses(prompt('Please enter a name',''))">
      </body>
      </html>
```

6

The program starts by creating some `person` objects, which are assigned into the variables `pers1` and `pers2`, and have only one property, `name`, which, in this case, is the name of the person. An array of e-mail address objects is then created. It is beneficial to store objects within arrays since they can be searched progmatically using a JavaScript `for` statement. An `Array()` constructor is used to create the `addresses` array, which is then assigned three values. Remember that the `Array()` constructor has no `length` property associated with it, so you must "hard-code" the number of elements within the first array slot. This has been done with the statements:

```
var addresses = new Array();
addresses[0] = 2;
```

To allocate a person multiple e-mail addresses, an `emailAddress` object is passed an `Array()` constructor argument containing the valid addresses for this particular person. For instance, user "Jason" has two such addresses, which are passed to the `emailAddress` function as:

```
addresses[1] = new emailAddress(pers1,
                new Array(2, "jason@somewhere.com",
                             "wombat@spuddy.mew.co.uk"));
```

The actual searching for a user is carried out using the `showAddresses()` function, which uses a `for` loop that scans through the `addresses` array previously created. For example:

```
for (var i=1; i <= addresses[0]; i++) {
    ...
}
```

where `addresses[0]` contains the length of the array, as a hard-coded value (2 in the example because two users are defined—you can alter accordingly). Later on in the example is an HTML `<body>` tag that uses an `onLoad` event-attribute to prompt the user to enter a name—the JavaScript `prompt()` method is used to get the user's input, which is then passed to the `showAddresses()` function. The `showAddresses()` function accepts a single parameter, `thisPerson`, that contains the person for which the user is searching. Use an `if` statement of the form:

```
if (addresses[i].name.person.toLowerCase() ==
    thisPerson.toLowerCase()) {
    ...
}
```

where `addresses[i].name.person.toLowerCase()` contains the lowercase entry for the current person in the `addresses[]` array. When comparing values taken from user-input with hard-coded values, it is best to convert everything to lowercase so the search works irrespective of what is entered. You wouldn't want the search to fail just because someone entered `"jason"` instead of `"Jason"`. The `toLowerCase()` method is used for the conversion process in this instance. If a match against the current array element is found, the text-variable `eMailAddr` is set to the name of the current person who has been located (`addresses[i].name.person`). Another `for` loop then scans through the `address` property of the `emailAddress` object. This is structured as an array because the `Array()` constructor was used to assign values into this particular object property, so each e-mail address for the current person can be picked out. For example:

```
for (var n=1; n <= addresses[i].address[0]; n++) {
    eMailAddr += n + ". " +
    addresses[i].address[n] + "\n";
}
```

Notice how the `eMailAddr` variable is modified by appending each array element onto it. Each e-mail address is also numbered. The boolean `found` variable is then checked to see if any matches have been located. This variable is set to `false` initially, and only becomes `true` when a match is made. A ? statement is used to test the value and output an appropriate `alert()` method, for instance:

```
(!found) ? alert("That person cannot be found.") :
           alert(eMailAddr);
```

where `!found` means the `found` variable is `false` (`!` is the logical *not* operator), in which case the user is told no matches have been found; otherwise, the value of the `eMailAddr` variable is displayed instead.

Adding a New Property to an Object

You can add a new property to an existing object simply by assigning the property to the object, for example:

```
function person(Aname) {
  this.name = Aname;
}
joe = new person("Joe Public");
```

would create a new `person` object called `joe` that has only one property, `name`. You could now assign a new property, `age`, to this specific object using the JavaScript statement:

6

```
joe.age = 30;
```

All other `person` objects will remain unaffected; such objects will not have an `age` property, so accessing it will result in an `"undefined"` value being generated. The `undefined` value can be detected using the `typeof()` operator, to be discussed later, or by using the `propertyExist()` function presented in the following section.

Deleting Objects and Properties

Assigning a `null` value to an object will effectively delete the object; then you cannot reference it from that point onward. An object property can be nullified in the same way. You may want to use the `propertyExist()` function for such purposes, as the following details.

Testing for Object and Property Existence

You can validate a property by testing its value against the special JavaScript value `"undefined"`, which is returned instead of a property value when that property does not exist. By writing a small JavaScript function, this condition can be tested, for example, with the `propertyExist()` function:

```
function propertyExist(objProp) {
  var testProp = "" + objProp;
  if (testProp == "undefined")
    return false;
  else
    return true;
}
```

This function returns `true` if the property passed to it exists; otherwise it returns `false`. The first statement in the function coerces, or changes, the data-type of the object into a string, so the string `"undefined"` can be checked against it. The prepending of an empty string (`""`) onto the `objProp` argument allows the conversion of the object into a string to allow the comparison. This function could be used in a program that needs a particular property to exist before invoking another JavaScript statement:

```
if (propertyExist(maria.email)) {
   location = "mailto:maria@somewhere.com";
}
```

In this case, the `location` property of the current window will not invoke the `mailto:` URL with the person `maria@somewhere.com` unless the `email` property of the `maria` object exists. In Navigator, the `mailto:` URL invokes the e-mail interface for sending text-messages across the Internet. Notice how the object and property are passed literally, and not as a string. Here is a larger example that makes the `propertyExist()` function return a `false` value:

```
<!--
  Program 6-7
-->
<script language="JavaScript">
<!--
```

```
function propertyExist(objProp) {
  var testProp = "" + objProp;
  if (testProp == "undefined")
     return false;
  else
     return true;
}
function email(personsName, personsAddress) {
  this.name    = personsName;
  this.address = personsAddress;
}
pers1 = new email("Jason", "jason@somewhere.com");
pers2 = new email("Maria");
alert(propertyExist(pers2.address));
//-->
</script>
```

In this instance the object `pers2` exists, but the `address` property has not been assigned a value. A `false` value is, therefore, returned for this property. You can check if a complete *object* exists simply by testing for a `true` condition, for example, in context to the earlier examples:

```
if (pers1) {
   // The object 'pers1' exists
   ...
}
else {
   // The object 'pers1' does not exist
   ...
}
```

Using the `typeof` Operator

6

The `typeof()` operator is new to Navigator 3.0 and allows the type of a variable or object to be ascertained. For instance:

```
typeof("Hello World");
```

would return the string `"string"`. The `typeof()` operator can be used to great effect when checking to see that various objects exist; it can be used in place of the earlier functions, if required. If you use `typeof()` with an object property, the type of that particular property is returned, for example, `"string"`, etc. The following table illustrates the values returned by `typeof()`.

typeof() Return Value	Example	Description
`"function"`	`typeof(parseInt)`	The argument is a function, either a standard JavaScript function, or a user-defined function.
`"boolean"`	`typeof(true)`	The argument is a boolean value, such as `true` or `false`.
`"number"`	`typeof(8.68)`	The argument is a number.
`"object"`	`typeof(document)`	The argument is a standard JavaScript object, or a user-defined object.
`"string"`	`typeof("wombat")`	The argument is a string object.
`"undefined"`	`typeof(undefVar)`	The argument is undefined (assuming `undefVar` is a variable or object that has not yet been created).

NOTE: The `"undefined"` value is returned both for null variables and for objects that do not yet exist. Also note that the null value is, in fact, an object within its own right, so `typeof(null)` will return the string `"object"`.

Adding New Constructor Methods to an Object

All JavaScript objects now have a `prototype` property that allows an object to be "extended" in that new constructors for the object can be created. For example, you could create your own string manipulation methods, as shown in the following example. This program defines a function, `countChars()`, which counts the number of occurrences of a specified character (passed to the function as argument "c"). A string object called `sentence` is created, which contains a sample sentence, and the new `prototype` property is assigned to the `String` object as follows:

```
String.prototype.count = countChars;
```

where `count` is the new object property that will become the new constructor (rather like a function call) for a string object. The expression is assigned the value `countChars`, which, in this case, is a reference to the countChars() function defined within the document. The effect of this statement means the count() constructor can now be applied to any string object.

```
<!--
   Program 6-8
-->
<html>
<head>
<script language="JavaScript">
<!--
function countChars(c) {
   var hits=0;
   for (var counter=0; counter <= this.length; counter++) {
       // The value of 'this' will take the value
       // of the string that has been specified
       // in the statement invoking this function
       aChar = this.toLowerCase().substring(counter,counter+1)
       if (aChar == c)
           hits ++;
   }
   return(hits);
}
var sentence =
       new String("The quick brown wombat jumped over " +
                  "the lazy dog.");
 String.prototype.count = countChars;
 var numChar = sentence.count("a");
 alert("There are " + numChar + " occurences.");
//-->
</script>
</head>
</html>
```

In the example, the numChar variable is assigned the value of the expression sentence.count("a"). The prototype definition for count() states the countChars() function should be referenced; hence, this function is applied to the string object sentence, which then returns the number of occurrences. The function itself is very simple: It uses a for loop to scan through the string object—this value is held in the special value this—extracting each character of the string using the substring() method. All characters are converted to lowercase so all characters are considered—"a" is not the same as "A" in JavaScript, since unlike HTML, JavaScript is a case-sensitive language.

Remember that constructor functions are not called directly, but are instead referenced using the prototype property of the object in question. You

6

refer to the name after the `prototype` property to invoke the function you have defined. This allows you to specify a constructor by appending it to an object, which is much more compact. Expressions such as `string.toLowerCase()` are common in JavaScript; object prototypes allow you to create your own constructors to perform object-manipulation.

Without the use of an object prototype, the value of the string would have to be passed to the `countChars()` function, rewriting it as:

```
function countChars(aString, c) {
  var hits=0;
  for (var counter=0; counter <= this.length; counter++) {
     thisChar =
         aString.toLowerCase().substring(counter,counter+1)
     if (thisChar == c)
         hits ++;
  }
  return(hits);
}
```

This doesn't look too different from the original function. Only the `this` statement has been replaced with the name of a string-argument. With this modified function, the following expression could not be formed now:

```
numChars = sentence.count("a");
```

where `sentence` is the string object to be examined. Instead you would have to say:

```
numChars = count(sentence, "a");
```

so the constructor is not applied *to* the string object. Object prototypes allow your code to become more "object-based" by applying constructors to objects, rather than calling a function with the parameter you need to process. At the end of the day, you can choose whichever method you like.

Summary

Variables are repositories for temporary values that exist during the lifetime of a JavaScript application. Variables are said to have a *scope* that specifies where that variables value can be examined. Global variables are variables defined outside of a `function` declaration; local variables exist *within* JavaScript functions.

♦ Variables are created using the `var` statement; they can optionally be assigned a value. The `var` statement can be omitted when assigning a variable a value using the JavaScript assignment (=) operator.

♦ JavaScript supports a variety of variable types, including strings, boolean (`true`/`false`) values, and numbers. Items such as strings are represented internally as "objects" in their own right, e.g. string objects, which also have their own constructor, for example, `String()`.

♦ User defined objects are created using the `new` statement in combination with a constructor function that assigns *properties* to the object. A property is a value that belongs to an object; it is accessed by specifying the object name followed by a period (`.`), and then the property name; for example, `person1.address` specifies that you wish to access the `address` property of the object named as `person1`. Navigator's built-in objects are accessed in exactly the same way; for example, `document.bgcolor` is the background color of the current HTML document—a reflection of the `<body>` tags `bgcolor` attribute.

♦ Netscape Atlas has introduced the `Object()` and `Array()` constructors for creating new objects. `Array()` creates an array and provides a `length` property equal to the number of array elements. `Object()` does not have such a property, so you must hard-code the number of elements into the array at the first element position. `Array()` can be assigned elements within the constructor; `Object()` cannot. Arrays and objects are the same thing in JavaScript (try the expression `javascript:Object() == Array()` for proof).

♦ Use the `typeof()` operator to determine the data-type of an object, or variable, or to determine whether or not a particular object actually exists.

6

CHAPTER 7

Using JavaScript with HTML Forms

Forms provide the only means, outside JavaScript, of allowing data entry into an application. The HTML `<form>` container can be used with a number of tags that provide interactivity, and JavaScript reflects these tags as objects within your application to allow further manipulation.

An Introduction to HTML Forms and JavaScript

The JavaScript language has extended many of the existing form-elements, mainly to allow specification of event-handlers. By clicking a button or choosing an item from a selection list, you can now generate events that can be intercepted and processed accordingly in JavaScript. This chapter examines how JavaScript can be used to interface with form-elements, such as text-fields, checkboxes, radio buttons, and selection lists, as well as how such items can be dynamically updated and further manipulated using JavaScript.

In this chapter you will learn

♦ How JavaScript references forms within HTML

♦ How to access and manipulate form-elements, such as radio buttons and selection lists

♦ How to add event-handlers to form-elements

♦ How to use JavaScript-enhanced forms for data-validation purposes

The `<form>` Container

The `<form>..</form>` container is a repository for form-elements such as text-fields, text-areas, radio buttons, selection lists, and checkboxes. Forms allow you to enter input, and then store it for further processing. Before the introduction of JavaScript, forms were the only method of obtaining input from the user within an HTML document. JavaScript has provided the `prompt()` method for ad-hoc input, although forms remain the only way of embedding an input-capability directly into a page. The HTML `<form>` tag under JavaScript has the following syntax:

```
<form name = "formName"
      [method = "POST|GET"]
      [action = "URL"]
      [enctype = "type"]
      [onSubmit = "function()|expression"]
form tag elements
</form>
```

where `name` specifies a name for the form; `enctype` specifies an encoding-type for the submitted form-data (this is specified as a MIME type); `method` is a form-transmittal method; `action` represents a URL of a CGI script that receives the form-data; and `onSubmit` is a JavaScript event-handler that allows interception of a `<input type="submit">` tag.

The CGI versus JavaScript Debate

Prior to Navigator 2.0 and JavaScript, an HTML form could only send its data to a CGI—a standard for exchanging data between an HTML document and a remote server—script running on a remote server. CGI is a widely used standard, and is ubiquitous in the vast majority of interactive Web sites. Central to the concept of CGI is the "CGI script," a program or script written in a language of your choice, which accepts data submitted from an HTML form. Just what the CGI script does with the data depends upon the script. Form-data is sent in an encoded format from the client, so most scripts process this into a more manageable form, perhaps storing it on the server in a *flat-file* (a file with no rigid internal structure) or within a structured database. CGI-based solutions have been used for many purposes, such as guest-books, HTML/e-mail forms, and even for playing games.

With JavaScript, form-processing, such as validation, can be handled locally on the client and, in many cases, without the need for a server entity. The `method` and `action` attributes are mainly of use to developers who are programming a CGI script, which will accept the form data and process it further. JavaScript is limited in its storage capabilities—"cookies" currently offer the only way of storing data to disk locally (see Chapter 13), although the server-side JavaScript module in Netscape's LiveWire product does have a database capability. With JavaScript, the emphasis is on manipulating form-data locally. One of the main problems with forms is validation, and JavaScript has a big role to play here. Without performing form-validation locally, the server must take on this task. Server-side validation is complex because each field within a form must be vetted, and then, if any errors are found, a suitable response must be sent back to the client. This can be a horrendous task to perform, especially if there are multiple errors to correct. Using JavaScript to validate a form before submitting it to a server makes good sense. This both saves time and helps alleviate network-traffic. Once a validated from has been submitted, the server is assured the data it has accepted is correct and complete. Validation is discussed later in this chapter.

Form-Elements

The body of a `<form>` container can contain any of the following HTML form-element tags, as illustrated in the following table.

7

Description	HTML Tag Element
Checkbox	`<input type="checkbox">`
Form submit button	`<input type="submit">`
Hidden field	`<input type="hidden">`
Push button	`<input type="button">`

Description	HTML Tag Element
Radio-box	`<input type="radio">`
Selection list	`<select></select>`
Text-field	`<input type="text">`
Text-area field	`<textarea></textarea>`

Each of these form-elements is represented in JavaScript as a series of `form` object properties, and each is dealt with later in the chapter.

How JavaScript Deals with Forms

Every `<form>..</form>` container read into Navigator is reflected in JavaScript as a *form object*. This means each such form will have an entry in the JavaScript `forms` array; for example, `forms[0]` is the first form within the current HTML document. Likewise, each element within a form, such as a radio button, selection list, or a text-field, is also represented as an object. To access and manipulate such objects, you must adopt a hierarchical view of your HTML document. Consider the following HTML document, which contains two forms and numerous other form-elements:

```
<!--
  Program 7-1
-->
<html>
<head>
<title>Some sample forms</title>
</head>
<body>
<basefont size=4>
<tt>
<form name="form1">
Your name <input type="text" size=30 name="fullname"><p>
Please check all CD-ROMS you have seen:
<dl>
<dd><input value="eisk" type="checkbox" name="cd1">Essential
Starter Kit<br>
<dd><input value="hhcs" type="checkbox" name="cd2">Hitch-hiking
Cyberspace<br>
</dl>
</form>
<form>
<textarea name="comments" rows=5 cols=50>
Please enter some comments here
```

```
</textarea><p>
Which books have you read
<select name="books">
<option>Essential Java*
<option selected>Netscape Navigator
<option>WWW Mosaic and More
<option>Essential Internet Guide
</select><p>
</form>
</tt>
</body>
</html>
```

In Navigator, this form would resemble one shown in Figure 7-1. As you can see, some options have already been selected, or populated, with data.

As this document is loaded, JavaScript will reflect each form-element as a series of objects. For example, the two <form> containers can now be accessed as document.forms[0] and document.forms[1], respectively. Notice how the first form uses a name attribute; you can refer to this form using the JavaScript expression document.forms["form1"]. Note that this type of reference is not possible with the second form in the example because it does not use a name attribute. Now that the first form has been named in this way, you can completely do away with using the forms array; just use form1 instead, for example, document.form1. You can use whichever method you like, depending on the attributes you have used to define the form.

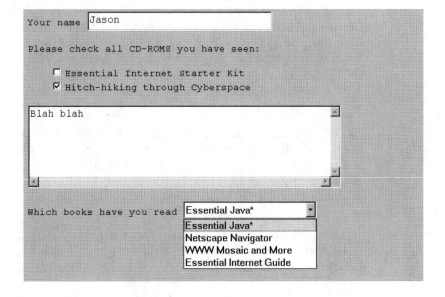

The form as rendered by Navigator

Figure 7-1.

7

The first text-field in the first form will be represented in JavaScript as `document.forms[0].fullname` (or `document.form1.fullname`, etc.) and the actual text within the field can be accessed by specifying the `value` attribute, for example, `document.forms[0].fullname.value`—which is `"Jason"` from Figure 7-1. You could also update this text dynamically because text-field objects are *read-write* structures.

Next are two checkboxes, named `cd1` and `cd2`. These are reflected into JavaScript as the values `document.forms[0].cd1` and `document.forms[0].cd2`, respectively. By using the `checked` property of a checkbox object, you can detect which box is currently selected. For example, the value of the JavaScript expression `document.forms[0].cd1` is `true`, in relation to our example and Figure 7-1, because the checkbox named `cd2` is currently selected. Because a `value` attribute was used with each checkbox, the value for each option can also be retrieved, in this case, by using the `value` property of the checkbox object— using the JavaScript expression `document.forms[0].cd2.value`—which yields the value `"hhcs"`. The use of `value` attributes is optional within a checkbox, although some applications may need to associate a value with a radio-box so that further processing can take place. Later examples in this chapter will give you more insight.

In some cases, you may not have allocated a `name` attribute to an object. How would you access an element, such as a checkbox, in this case? You would use the `elements[i]` array, which is a list of all the objects within a form, in source order. In context to the example, the value of the JavaScript expression `document.forms[0].elements[2].value` is `"hhcs"`. Element numbers start at zero in JavaScript, so you are looking at the third element in this case. The third element in `forms[0]`, the first form, is the second checkbox, which is the same as `document.forms[0].cd2.value`. As you can see JavaScript provides many ways to achieve the same thing. The `elements` array can be used to scan through all of the elements in array *progmatically*, that is, using a JavaScript `for` statement. Note that this technique would be impossible using the `forms` array because every form-element would need to be named independently.

TIP: Name all your HTML elements using the `name` attribute. You can use the `elements` array to access the elements within a form, even if an element does not use a `name` attribute, although the former method is by far the most convenient.

The next part of the HTML file defines a new form. This does not have a `name` attribute so you must refer to it as `forms[1]` from within your JavaScript application. You could assign the value of `forms[1]` to a variable and use that, which many be easier, especially if a form exists within another window. The first element in the second form is a text-area object. In JavaScript, the value held within this field would be accessed as `document.forms[1].comments.value`, where `comments` is the name of the text-area object, as named in the `name` attribute of the `<textarea>` tag. Again, if this tag did not use a `name` attribute, the `elements` array can be used—the value `"Blah blah"` would be returned in context to the example.

Finally, there is a `select` object, defined with an HTML `<select>` container tag; it is named `books`. Objects such as these represent the most tricky to manipulate in JavaScript because they contain multiple values. Armed with the HTML-object properties shown in Chapter 4, however, you can see a `select` object has a `selectedIndex` property, which tells you which `<option>` tag has been selected. There is also an `options` array, which reflects every `<option>` in the `<select>` container. Select objects also have a `text` property that reflects the text after the `<option>` tag. To see which option is selected, you could use the expression

```
document.forms[1].books.options.selectedIndex
```

where the value `0` will be returned because the first item in the example is selected (selection list indexes start at zero in JavaScript). To find out *what* the first example is—that is, what text is next to the `<option>` tag—look at the following, rather hideous, expression:

```
document.forms[1].books.options[document.forms[1].books.options.selectedIndex].text
```

By leaving out the portion in-between the `options[]` array, you have the smaller, although incomplete, sub-expression.

```
document.forms[1].books.options[].text
```

Now the `options` array must be indexed. In particular, an expression that returns the `selectedIndex` property of the `options` array must be specified. To do this, a way must be traced down the object-hierarchy to get to this value; hence, the long expression. Luckily, you can simplify such expressions by breaking up the statement—in an *inside-out* manner—to form just two JavaScript statements: The first stores the selected-item; the second specifies the actual array element required by using the previously stored value. For example:

```
itemSelected = document.forms[1].books.options.selectedIndex;
itemText = document.forms[1].books.options[itemSelected].text;
```

7

The variable `itemText` now holds the required `<option>` text,
`"Essential Java*"` in context to Figure 7-1. Further explanations of these
individual form-elements will be discussed throughout the remainder of this
chapter.

Referring to Form-Fields Using JavaScript

Two accepted ways exist to access form-fields from within a JavaScript
program, namely

♦   Refer to the "fully-qualified" name of the field from within a JavaScript
    function

♦   Pass the form-field value directly to the function using the `"this.form"`
    notation

A "fully-qualified" field-name uses the object-hierarchy to refer to the field,
starting from the top-level window, or frameset parent, and working down
to the `document` object; and then the appropriate `forms` and field-element
name. For example, the following application accesses a form by using a
"fully-qualified" reference to the required form-field.

```
<!--
  Program 7-2
-->
<html>
<head>
<script language="JavaScript">
<!--
  function getData() {
    alert("You entered: " +
          document.forms[0].myField.value);
  }
//-->
</script>
</head>
<body>
<form>
<input name="myField" type="text" size=45><br>
<input type="button"
       value="Click"
       onClick="getData()">
</form>
</body>
</html>
```

In this case, an `onClick` event-handler within a button invokes the `getData()` function, which displays the text entered into the text-field. Note that to access the text-field, the complete name of the form-field has been specified. The current window is always assumed in JavaScript, so it is unnecessary to give a window name prefix to the `document` object, *unless* the form exists within a separate (autonomous) window, or within a frameset-document (a multiple-celled document).

The more compact way to refer to a form-field is to use the `this` statement, as follows:

```
<!--
  Program 7-3
-->
<html>
<head>
<script language="JavaScript">
<!--
  function getData(val) {
    alert("You entered: " + val);
  }
//-->
</script>
</head>
<body>
<form>
<input name="myField" type="text" size=45><br>
<input type="button"
       value="Click"
       onClick="getData(this.form.myField.value)">
</form>
</body>
</html>
```

The JavaScript expression `this.form` refers to the current form object. By prefixing the name of the field followed by the `value` property, you can send the value of a field directly to the function `getData()`. Notice how `getData()` also accepts an argument, `val`, which is the literal value of the text-field. You must use the `value` property of a form-element to access its literal value. Some scripts just pass the value `this.form` to a function, and then refer to the field required by adding the name of the field and the `value` property accordingly. All of these methods are valid; make certain you are aware how they exist. The golden rule of field-referencing is to remember the object-hierarchy when you refer to forms that may exist within autonomous windows or separate frames (see Chapters 8 and 9 for information on these respective subjects).

7

Manipulating Form-Elements with JavaScript

This section provides further examination of how form-elements can be manipulated by JavaScript. Each form-element will be considered, and examples will illustrate how JavaScript can be used to manipulate and enhance each element.

Checkboxes

Checkboxes are created with an `<input type="checkbox">` tag; they allow you to select multiple options in an on/off style manner. In JavaScript, a checkbox is reflected in two different objects

◆ The `elements` array

◆ An array named after the radio button's `name` attribute

Consider the following HTML and JavaScript program, which displays two checkboxes and then allows you to see their properties by using an `alert()` box:

```
<!--
  Program 7-4
-->
<html>
<head>
<script language="JavaScript">
<!--
function showValues() {
  alert("CHECKBOX 1:\n" +
        "value  : " + document.forms[0].cb1.value + "\n" +
        "name   : " + document.forms[0].cb1.name + "\n" +
        "checked: " + document.forms[0].cb1.checked + "\n" +
        "CHECKBOX 2:\n\n" +
        "value  : " + document.forms[0].cb2.value + "\n" +
        "name   : " + document.forms[0].cb2.name + "\n" +
        "checked: " + document.forms[0].cb2.checked);
}
//-->
</script>
</head>
<body>
<form>
Which payment method?<br>
<input type="checkbox"
       name="cb1"
       value="VS">Visa<br>
<input type="checkbox"
```

```
        name="cb2"
        value="MC" checked>Mastercard<p>
<input type="button"
        value="See values"
        onClick="showValues()">
</form>
</body>
</html>
```

The `checked` property contains a boolean value, which will be `true` when a checkbox is selected, and `false` at all other times. The `checked` attribute signifies a default checkbox, that is, a checkbox that is active when the form is first displayed—a property called `defaultChecked` will be set `true` when this checkbox is enabled. Default checkboxes are set using the `checked` attribute within the `<input>` tag. You can also reference a checkbox by using the JavaScript `elements` array; for example, here is a slightly modified example of the previous document that uses the `elements` array:

```
<!--
  Program 7-5
-->
<html>
<head>
<script language="JavaScript">
<!--
function showValues() {
  alert("CHECKBOX 1:\n" +
      "value  : "+document.forms[0].elements[0].value + "\n" +
      "name   : "+document.forms[0].elements[0].name + "\n" +
      "checked: "+ document.forms[0].elements[0].checked + "\n" +
      "CHECKBOX 2:\n\n" +
      "value  : "+document.forms[0].elements[1].value + "\n" +
      "name   : "+document.forms[0].elements[1].name + "\n" +
      "checked: "+document.forms[0].elements[1].checked);
}
//-->
</script>
</head>
<body>
<form>
Which payment method?<br>
<input type="checkbox"
        name="cb1"
        value="VS">Visa<br>
<input type="checkbox"
        name="cb2"
        value="MC">Mastercard<p>
```

7

```
<input type="button"
       value="See values"
       onClick="showValues()">
</form>
</body>
</html>
```

In this example, the first two form-elements are the checkboxes. Make certain you use the `elements` array to ensure the correct form-elements are being referenced.

TIP: Checkboxes can be updated "dynamically" by assigning a `true` or `false` value to the `checked` property of the checkbox—either through the `elements` array or through the checkbox name. For example, in context to the previous example, you could have either

```
document.forms[0].elements[1].checked = true;
```

or

```
document.forms[0].cb2.checked = true;
```

which, in this case, would select the second checkbox (the "Mastercard" option).

If you use the `elements` array when you refer to checkboxes, you can place these checkboxes within their *own* `<form>` to make referencing each box easier. You could even name the form containing the checkboxes using the `name` attribute and refer to these directly instead of using the `forms` array property.

Hidden Fields

Hidden fields are text-fields that do not appear within the browser and, therefore , you cannot select them. Such fields can be used to store values during the lifetime of an application. To create a hidden field, an `<input type="hidden">` tag should be used. The field value can be accessed through JavaScript by

♦   Referring to the field using the `elements[]` array
♦   Referring to the value of the field's `name` attribute, as set in the `<input>` tag

Password Fields

Password fields are text-fields whose content is masked with a series of asterisks (*); they can be used to shield the display of sensitive information. The literal value of the field, as accessed through the `value` attribute of the field, will *not* be hidden, however. Password fields are created with an `<input type="password">` tag, and are accessed by

♦ Referring to the field using the `elements[]` array

♦ Referring to the value of the field's `name` attribute, as set in the `<input>` tag

Radio buttons

Radio buttons are created with an `<input type="radio">` tag; they allow you to select *one* of a group of options.

NOTE: When you name a series of radio button objects, *each* button must have the *same* name; that is, each radio button must have the same `name` attribute value. In JavaScript, a radio button is reflected in two different objects

♦ the `elements` array
♦ an array named after the radio button's `name` attribute

To see how radio buttons are handled using JavaScript, consider the following script, which implements a radio button system for selecting a simple yes/no response:

```
<!--
  Program 7-6
-->
<html>
<head>
<script language="JavaScript">
<!--
function seeValues() {
  alert("Radio button 1 is: " +
        document.forms[0].elements[0].checked + "\n" +
        "Radio button 2 is: " +
        document.forms[0].elements[1].checked);
}
//-->
</script>
```

7

```
</head>
<body>
<form>
<input name="yesno"
       type="radio"
       checked>Yes<br>
<input name="yesno"
       type="radio">No<p>
<input type="button"
       value="Click me"
       onClick="seeValues()">
</form>
</body>
</html>
```

When the button in the example is clicked upon, the `seeValues()` function displays the current state of each button by using the `checked` property of each radio button. The `elements` array was used to access each radio button in this instance.

Even though radio buttons must all have the same `name` attribute value, the `elements` array is not the only way to access such values. Each radio button object is stored in an array so, in the previous program, `yesno` is an array of radio buttons, for example, `yesno[0]` and `yesno[1]` respectively.

Consider the following application that uses a series of radio buttons to allow you to invoke a search-engine. The document is structured as a frameset-document; the search-engine's home-page is loaded in the lower frame; the choice of engine loaded in the lower frame depends upon the selection in the upper frame:

```
<!--
  Program 7-7
-->
<html>
<head>
<script language="JavaScript">
<!--
var topFrame =
    "<basefont size=3>" +
    "Which site shall I load in the lower frame?<br>" +
    "<form>" +
    "<input name='radioBut' type='radio' " +
    "value='http://www.infoseek.com' checked>InfoSeek<br>" +
    "<input name='radioBut' type='radio' " +
    "value='http://altavista.digital.com'>Alta Vista<br>" +
    "<input name='radioBut' type='radio' " +
```

```
         "value='http://www.yahoo.com'>Yahoo!<p>" +
         "<input type='button' value='Go!' " +
         "      onClick='parent.loadUrl(this.form)'>" +
         "</form>";

var botFrame = "";

function loadUrl(f) {
   for (var n=0; n < f.radioBut.length; n++) {
      if (f.radioBut[n].checked) {
         parent.frames[1].location = f.radioBut[n].value;
         break;
      }
   }
}
//-->
</script>
</head>
<frameset rows="50%,50%">
  <frame src="javascript:parent.topFrame">
  <frame src="javascript:parent.botFrame">
</frameset>
</html>
```

The function `loadUrl()` takes a radio button object as an argument. This argument is passed to the function through the form-button, which invokes the `loadUrl()` function, that is,

```
<input type="button" value="Go!"
       onClick="parent.loadUrl(this.form)">
```

The value of `this.form` is the current form, and is substituted for the "f" argument within the function:

```
function loadUrl(f) {
   for (var n=0; n < f.radioBut.length; n++) {
      if (f.radioBut[n].checked) {
         parent.frames[1].location = f.radioBut[n].value;
         break;
      }
   }
}
```

7

A `for` loop then works its way through each radio button. If the current radio button element is selected, the boolean `checked` property will be set to `true`; hence, `f.radioBut[n].checked` will also be `true`. Now you know which radio button is selected, and you can extract the `value` property to see what is held in the `<input>` tag's `value` attribute. In this case, each `value` attribute stores the URL of a search engine. This value is assigned to the lower frame's `location` property and the search engine is then loaded accordingly. The loop is exited here because the selected item has been found (and only one item *can* be selected). See Chapter 9 for more information on frames and the loading of URLs.

The `loadUrl()` function could have been rewritten to use the `elements` array instead. The function would now need to take the form:

```
function loadUrl(f, start, end) {
  for (var n=start; n <= end; n++) {
      if (f.elements[n].checked) {
          parent.frames[1].location = f.elements[n].value;
          break;
      }
  }
}
```

Notice the addition of the new `start` and `end` arguments, which represent the starting and ending elements to be examined, that is, the first radio button element number and the last radio button element number. Remember the `elements` array contains *all* the elements within a form—not just radio buttons. For this reason, you must tell the function the element index number, i.e. an array position, at which to begin and to end. In context to the main program, you would invoke this new function with the call:

```
<input type="button" value="Go!"
       onClick="parent.loadUrl(this.form,0,2)">
```

which makes the `loadUrl()` function start with element 0, the first radio button, and end at element 2, the third radio button. Elements 0, 1, and 2 are the first three elements in the form—in fact, they are the *only* elements within the form. You may want to add or to insert other form elements later, in which case the element numbers must be adjusted.

NOTE: The current form object is passed to the function, rather than the radio button object; the radio button objects are retrieved from the `elements` array.

In addition to the `checked` and `value` properties, the `defaultChecked` property can also be used to determine if a default radio button default is selected. Default radio buttons use the `checked` attribute; for example:

```
<form>
How do you wish to pay?<br>
<input value="visa"
        name="payment"
        type="radio">Visa<br>
<input value="ax"
        name="payment"
        type="radio"
        checked>American Express<br>
<input value="mc"
        name="payment"
        type="radio">Mastercard<br>
</form>
```

denotes the middle radio button is enabled when the buttons first appear. In this case, the `defaultChecked` property of this radio button will be set to `true`. Note that a radio button also can be both `checked` and `defaultChecked` at the same time.

TIP: Radio buttons can be set dynamically by assigning a `true` or `false` value to the checkbox. In context to the previous example:

```
document.forms[0].elements[0] = true;
```

would select the first checkbox (the "Visa" option).

Reset Buttons

A *reset button,* as the name suggests, resets the current form so each element is allocated its original default value. Default values are allocated to form-elements on a tag-by-tag basis. For example, checkboxes use the `checked` keyword, while text-fields use a `value` attribute to specify some default text. A reset button takes the general form

```
<input type="reset" value="Reset the form">
```

Because the `<input type="reset">` tag produces a button, you must use the `value` attribute to allocate some text to the face of the button.

Selection Lists

Selection lists allow for either single or multiple selections from a list of options. The `<select>` container tag is used to house the list; each list-option is mentioned next to a `<option>` tag within the list; you can

7

specify as many options as you require. The options of a selection list are reflected into the `options` array; all options start at array-position `0` and continue upwards. JavaScript provides the `selected` property (a boolean property), which returns `true` if a specific option is selected, and `false` otherwise. The `<option>` tag also accepts a `selected` attribute that selects an option by default. The JavaScript `defaultChecked` property will return `true` when such an option is selected, and `false` otherwise. The `selectedIndex` property returns the numeric value of a selection-option you have chosen, while the `text` property returns the text specified after the `<option>` tag.

Lists can also be presented in numerous ways. If a `<select>` tag specifies a `multiple` attribute, the complete list is displayed and you can select multiple options. Your JavaScript application that processes each list must do so according to the structure of the list. The `<select>` tag also accepts a `size=n` attribute that specifies the number of list options to display. Note the following rules for processing lists:

♦   When using a `<select multiple>` list, all `<option>`s are completely displayed and you can select *multiple* options. Your JavaScript program, which processes this form of selection list, must loop through the `options` array and check the `selected` property of each. If a `true` value is returned, you know that option has been selected. Continue the loop until all options have been processed. The `length` property of the `options` array will contain the number of elements in the selection list; for example, a form named as `myForm` would use `myForm.options.length` to ascertain the number of options in a selection list. Note that the `selectedIndex` property is of *no* use with multiple selection lists. Use the `text` property to gain access to each `<option>`'s text-part.

 NOTE: The `selectedIndex` property will be set to `-1` if no options have been selected. Do not try to access `options[-1]` or an error will occur: Catch the condition first and warn the user, or take other appropriate action. Use the CTRL key with each mouse click when selecting multiple items. This will also toggle options on and off.

When using a `<select>` tag by itself, the default list appearance will be single. Note that you can only select a *single* option from the list. Use the `selectedIndex` property to gain access to the option, and the `text` property to gain access to the `<option>`'s text-part. If no `selected` attributes are specified for any of the options, the list defaults to the first option (`0`); a value of `-1` is not returned for this type of list.

♦ When using `<select size=n>`, the first "n" options will be displayed in the selection list, although multiple options still *cannot* be chosen. Use the `selectedIndex` and `text` properties, as before. If no `selected` attributes are specified for any of the options, the list defaults to the first option (0); a value of -1 is not returned for this type of list.

Single Selection ("Pop-Up") Lists   The simplest form of selection list uses a `<select>` tag and as many `<option>` tags as are required. This mode of selection list allows a single selection. The entire list of options will "pop-up" when you click on the selection list. Shown below is the list in its default (left) and its "pop-up" (right) states. Some prefer the phrase "drop-down" instead of "pop-up," although this is inaccurate because not all selection lists drop downwards. The direction of the list depends upon the space left at the bottom of the screen. Some lists appear in an upwards direction because not enough space exists below the `<select>` tag to display all options. Navigator also supplies a scroll bar within the selection list when the number of options specified becomes large.

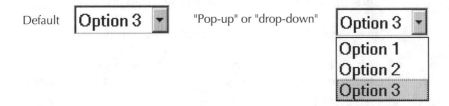

The list alternates between its "pop-up" and single option display as you click on the list and select an option. For example, consider the following selection list:

```
<!--
  Program 7-8
-->
<html>
<body>
<form>
<select>
<option>Option 1
<option>Option 2
<option selected>Option 3
</select>
</form>
</body>
</html>
```

7

which provides three options. Only a single option is displayed when the list first appears, although because a `selected` attribute has been specified for the third `<option>`, this item will be displayed by default. To access the other list options, a small button is provided by the side of the list; when you click this button, it displays the other options; then you can select one. Or you can click on the current option, and the list will also appear.

The `<select>` object in this example has no name; therefore, it can only be accessed through the `elements` array. The `elements` array is an array of form-objects in source-order, and is bound to each form in an HTML document. In this instance, the value of `document.forms[0].elements[0]` is the selection list. This form has not been named either, so the `forms` array has been used to reference the selection list. There is only one form, so `forms[0]` would refer to this.

To retrieve the value from the first `<option>` tag, you will need to refer to the `document.forms[0].elements[0].options[0]` property. But using this expression is not enough because the `text` property must be used to retrieve the text placed after the `<option>` tag. To retrieve the text in the first option, you would need to use the expression:

```
document.forms[0].elements[0].options[0].text
```

which in the example contains the value `"Option 1"`. This seems complex because none of the HTML tags have been named. If you restructure the HTML as:

```
<!--
  Program 7-9
-->
<html>
<body>
<form name="f1">
<select name="selObj1">
<option>Option 1
<option>Option 2
<option selected>Option 3
</select>
</form>
</body>
</html>
```

you could use the alternative expression:

```
document.f1.selObj1.options[0].text
```

to retrieve the value of the first selection item, that is, the first <option> item.

You must use the selectedIndex property to retrieve the item selected. This property contains the index number of the <option> tag currently selected, and should be used to index the options[] array. In the example, in relation to the "pop-up" or "drop-down" selection list shown previously, where the third option is selected, the expression:

```
document.forms[0].elements[0].selectedIndex
```

would return the value 2. Array values start at zero (0) in JavaScript, so 2 is the third element in this instance. Remember the selectedIndex property must be applied to a selection object and, in this instance, elements[0] refers to the <select> container because it is the only form-element that exists. If you used the HTML example with the name tags intact, this expression could be safely changed to:

```
document.f1.selObj1.selectedIndex
```

which is much easier than constantly referring to array index-numbers. If you could store the value of this expression into a JavaScript variable, you could pass it to the options array and extract the option selected using the text property, for example, using a JavaScript statement such as:

```
var selIx = document.f1.selObj1.selectedIndex;
```

This line is not valid HTML, so it must be placed within a <script> container. The following example is of a script and selection list in a single document, which allows you to see which option has been selected:

```
<!--
  Program 7-10
-->
<html>
<head>
<script language="JavaScript">
<!--
function showItem() {
  var selIx   = document.f1.selObj1.selectedIndex;
  var optText = document.f1.selObj1.options[selIx].text;
  alert("Item selected: " + optText);
}
//-->
</script>
</head>
```

7

```
<body>
<form name="f1">
<select name="selObj1">
<option>Option 1
<option>Option 2
<option selected>Option 3
</select><p>
<input type="button"
       value="See value"
       onClick="showItem()">
</form>
</body>
</html>
```

Notice the variable `optText` that uses the `selIx` variable to index the `options` array to extract the value currently selected. A form-button (`<input type="button">`) uses an `onClick` event-handler to invoke the `showItem()` function, which in turn displays the selected option. The option itself is displayed though the use of an `alert()` method, which is passed the `optText` variable as an argument.

Note that you can omit the `options` array entirely from your applications because a selection object is itself an array, so the `options` array is superfluous. For example, in the case of the HTML tag:

```
<select name="selObj1">
```

you can now access each option as `selObj1[0]`, `selObj1[1]` and `selObj1[2]`, including all the properties of these objects, for example, `selObj1[0].selected`, `selObj1[0].text`, etc.

This technique cannot be used, however, when the selection object is not named with a `name` attribute. The JavaScript expression `document.f1.elements[0].text` would not yield the value of the first option within a selection list because the value of `elements[0]` actually refers to the selection list "object" in its *entirety*, rather than to an individual element within that list. When a selection list is named, this problem is overcome; you can then shorten your code by completely omitting the `options` array.

All options that you select are stored as boolean (true/false) values in the selected property so, in the case of the third `<option>` tag, when selected, the value of the JavaScript expression:

```
document.f1.selObj1.selected
```

is `true`, as is the expression:

```
document.f1.selObj1.options[2].selected
```

although, as you now know, the "options[2]" part is superfluous and can be removed (because the selection-object has been named). You could, therefore, code the showItem() function differently by scanning through the options array to see which selected property was set to true.

Consider the slightly modified example of the previous script, which does this, and which does require use of the selectedIndex property:

```
<!--
  Program 7-11
-->
<html>
<head>
<script language="JavaScript">
<!--
function showItem() {
  var optText = "";
  for (var i=0; i < document.f1.selObj1.length; i++) {
      if (document.f1.selObj1[i].selected) {
          optText = document.f1.selObj1[i].text;
          break;
      }
  }
  alert("Item selected: " + optText);
}
//-->
</script>
<head>
<body>
<form name="f1">
<select name="selObj1">
<option>Option 1
<option>Option 2
<option selected>Option 3
</select><p>
<input type="button"
       value="See value"
       onClick="showItem()">
</form>
</body>
</html>
```

This script uses a for statement to iterate as many times as there are options in the <select> container. The value of document.f1.selObj1.length contains the number of options (three, in this case) so the loop will iterate three times. The variable "i" is used as a counter to index the selection-list object, and is incremented upon every iteration. On the first iteration, you are checking the value:

```
document.f1.selObj1[0].selected
```

which, if `true`, stores the value of the `text` property of the current option into the variable `optText`. A `break` statement (see Chapter 3) then exits the loop at this point, and the `alert()` method displays the selected item. This method is longer than using `selectedIndex`; in fact, you are duplicating what `selectedIndex` already does.

The most compact notation to access a selected-items `text` property would be to use the final version of the `showItem()` function, as shown in the following example:

```
<script language="JavaScript">
<!--
function showItem(f) {
  alert("Selected item: " +
        f.selObj1[f.selObj1.selectedIndex].text);
}
//-->
</script>
```

and pass the value of `this.form` in the function-call, which invokes `showItem()`. For example:

```
<form>
<input type="button"
       value="See value"
       onClick="showItem(this.form)">
</form>
```

In this instance, `showItem()` is called as `showItem(document.form1)`, and because the selection-object is named, you can index it directly as an array, passing the value of the objects `selectedIndex` property (which is required in this instance) as an array index value. In this example, you don't need to name the form because the value of `this.form` still refers to the current name of the form, whether or not it is named.

Multiple Selection Lists

Multiple selection lists eliminate the need for a "pop-up" list by showing the entire list-options, shown here.

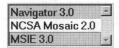

Such lists also facilitate *multiple* item selections, which are made by clicking on entries while you hold down the CTRL key. The `multiple` attribute must be specified in the `<select>` tag for this type of list; the `selected` attribute can also be specified within as many `<option>`s as you require. Below is a multiple section list (right-hand list) in comparison to a single selection list (left-hand list).

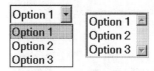

Another "feature" of multiple selection lists is none of the options can be selected, a valid outcome for many applications. This presents the need for some further validation because accessing the `options` array, when no options are selected, will result in a fatal error. Note that the `selectedIndex` property is useless in a multiple selection list because it will only return the *first* option selected; it will *not* return any other options selected. You must check the `checked` property against each element of the `options` array with this form of selection list. For example, here is a multiple selection list with three items:

```
<!--
   Program 7-12
-->
<html>
<body>
<form name="form1">
Which browsers have you used?<br>
<select multiple name="objSel1">
<option selected>Navigator 3.0
<option>NCSA Mosaic 2.0
<option>MSIE 3.0
</select>
</body>
</html>
```

The code required to access multiple items is similar to that shown in the previous section for single item selection lists, except you must scan the entire array and extract more than one item. Consider the following script, which will process a multiple selection list:

7

```
<!--
  Program 7-13
-->
<html>
<head>
<script language="JavaScript">
<!--
function showItem(selField) {
  var optText = "";
  var counter = 1;
  for (var i=0; i < selField.length; i++) {
      if (selField[i].selected) {
          optText += counter +
                     ". " +
                     selField[i].text +
                     "\n";
          counter ++;
      }
  }
  if (counter==1)
     alert("No items have been selected.");
  else
     alert("Items selected:\n" + optText);
}
//-->
</script>
</head>
<body bgcolor="White">
<form name="form1">
Which Web-browsers have you used?<br>
<select name="selObj1" multiple>
<option>Navigator 3.0
<option>NCSA Mosaic 2.0
<option>MSIE 3.0
</select>
<p>
<input type="button"
       value="See value"
       onClick="showItem(this.form.selObj1)">
</form>
</body>
</html>
```

This application presents the selection list and, when the form-button is clicked, the showItem() function is invoked. This function is then passed (supplied as an argument) to the current selection-object as an argument (this.form.selObj1). When getItem() starts, it starts a loop that iterates through each element in the options array. The value of selObj.length contains the number of <options>s in the selection list. Because the selection list has been named, it can be indexed directly. The for loop, therefore, looks at each option's selected property, and if it is true, concatenates this to the string object, called optText. A counter variable is also maintained that will be used to number each of the options selected. When the loop finishes, an alert() method displays the options selected. A test has also been placed to check whether or not any options have been selected so an appropriate message can be displayed.

TIP: The defaultSelected property is another boolean value that can be used in your applications. This property is set to true when you specify the selected attribute of an <option> tag, and when you select the option (or leave it selected), which allows you to see if a default option has been left selected.

The final form of multiple-list is the <select size=n> selection list. This list doesn't actually allow multiple selections but, instead, allows multiple items to be *seen* at any one time. You can use the code as for the single selection list in the previous section, which uses the selectedIndex property.

Some multiple selection lists do not allow you to move through the list. This occurs when the number of options in the list is small, and when the list can fit within the page without the need for scroll bars to display further options. It is still possible to provide an "up/down" navigation system with such a list, however, as the following application demonstrates. This program presents a multiple selection list, and then displays two images, which show an up- and down-arrow, respectively. Both images are hyperlinks with an associated onClick event-attribute (if you do not like the images, you can change these to buttons). Clicking on the up-arrow invokes the up() function; clicking on the down-arrow invokes the down() function:

```
<!--
  Program 7-14
-->
<html>
<head>
<script language="JavaScript">
<!--
var num = 0;
function up() {
  var num = document.forms[0].selOpts.selectedIndex;
  if (num != 0) {
```

7

```
        document.forms[0].selOpts[num].selected   = false;
        document.forms[0].selOpts[num-1].selected = true;
    }
}
function down() {
    var num = document.forms[0].selOpts.selectedIndex;
    if (num != (document.forms[0].selOpts.length - 1)) {
        document.forms[0].selOpts[num].selected   = false;
        document.forms[0].selOpts[num+1].selected = true;
    }
}
//-->
</script>
</head>
<body>
<center>
<table border=0>
<tr>
<form>
<td colspan=2>
<select multiple name="selOpts">
<option selected>Egypt
<option>South America
<option>Instanbul
<option>The Gallapogas Islands
<option>Indonesia
<option>Malasia
<option>South Africa
<option>Portugal
<option>Spain
<option>The United Kingdom
</select>
</td>
<td>
<tr>
<td align="left">
  <a href="#"
     onClick="up()"
     onMouseOver="window.status='Up'; return true">
  <img border=0 src="up.gif"></a>
</td>
<td align="right">
  <a href="#"
     onClick="down()"
     onMouseOver="window.status='Down'; return true">
  <img border=0 src="down.gif"></a>
  </td>
</tr>
```

```
</td>
</form>
</tr>
</table>
</center>
</body>
</html>
```

The `up()` and `down()` functions extract the currently selected item, and then set the `selected` property of the next or previous item, depending on the button pressed, to the logical value `true`, thus selecting the item. The list-item *currently* selected is set to `false`; otherwise multiple items will become selected as you click on an arrow.

For the `up()` function, you must ascertain when you are at the top of the list, so no action is taken to move above the first list-item, which does not exist. In this instance, all you must do is check if the `selectedIndex` value is zero (0). The `down()` function checks to see if `selectedIndex` equals the value `length-1`, where `length` is the length property of the selection list and contains the number of `<options>`s in the list. The "-1" is required because selection lists are numbered from zero (0) onwards, and the `length` property itself does not take this into account.

Dynamically Altering Selection Lists
Navigator 3.0 provides more features for dynamically updating selection lists. You can now alter which items are selected progmatically, rather than using the `selected` attribute within an `<option>` tag. Two ways currently exist to achieve this:

♦ Assigning a `true` or `false` value to an appropriate array position within the selection list using the `selected` property

♦ Assigning a numeric value to the `selectedIndex` property of an appropriate array position within the selection list concerned

For example, this script detects the current day and automatically highlights that day from within a selection-list object:

7

```
<!--
  Program 7-15
-->
<html>
<head>
<script language="JavaScript">
<!--
  function showDay() {
```

```
      today = new Date();
      day   = today.getDay(); // 0: Sunday, 1: Monday...
      if (day == 0) { document.form1.day[6].selected = true; }
      if (day == 1) { document.form1.day[0].selected = true; }
      if (day == 2) { document.form1.day[1].selected = true; }
      if (day == 3) { document.form1.day[2].selected = true; }
      if (day == 4) { document.form1.day[3].selected = true; }
      if (day == 5) { document.form1.day[4].selected = true; }
      if (day == 6) { document.form1.day[5].selected = true; }
   }
//-->
</script>
<head>
<body bgcolor="White" onLoad="showDay()">
<form name="form1">
Today is:
<select name="day">
<option>Monday
<option>Tuesday
<option>Wednesday
<option>Thursday
<option>Friday
<option>Saturday
<option>Sunday
</select>
</form>
</body>
</html>
```

When the selection list first appears the day will be set to Monday, although as soon as the document is loaded, the onLoad event-attribute will invoke the showDay() function which, in turn, updates the selected property of the selection-object. Note that this selection object was named using a name attribute, so it can be indexed as an array, rather than using the options array; updating the options array would achieve the same outcome. The getDay() method has been used to ascertain the current day; this returns a number—0 for Sunday, 1 for Monday, and so forth. You could make the code more compact. Note that this is always important because the more HTML you write, the longer it will take to load into Navigator. To make the code more compact, use the selectedIndex property to reference an array element directly, rather than assigning true or false values. This will require altering the numbering of the <select> container's <option> tags, so they are directly equivalent to the value returned by the JavaScript getDay() method. For example:

```
<!--
   Program 7-16
-->
<html>
<head>
<script language="JavaScript">
<!--
   function showDay() {
      today  = new Date();
      theDay = today.getDay();
      document.form1.day[theDay].selected = true;
   }
//-->
</script>
<head>
<body bgcolor="White" onLoad="showDay()">
<form name="form1">
Today is:
<select name="day">
<!--
   NB: These must now be in the same order as
   getDay() returns.
-->
<option>Sunday
<option>Monday
<option>Tuesday
<option>Wednesday
<option>Thursday
<option>Friday
<option>Saturday
</select>
</form>
</body>
</html>
```

As you can see, this script is more compact; not even a single `if` statement is now required, and the script runs significantly faster. Notice the reordering of the days to match the values returned by `getDay()`.

New to Navigator 3.0 is the ability to alter the `text` property of a selection-list object by assigning a new value directly to the array element of the list-item. Consider the following script, which accepts an item number and some text via a form and then uses this to update an active selection list:

```
<!--
   Program 7-17
-->
<html>
```

7

```
<head>
<script language="JavaScript">
<!--
  function updateItem() {
    var indexNum = parseInt(document.form1.myItem.value);
    var someText = document.form1.myText.value;
    document.form1.items[indexNum].text = someText;
  }
//-->
</script>
<head>
<body>
<form name="form1">
<select name="items" multiple>
<option>This is item 1
<option>This is item 2
<option>This is item 3
</select>
<p>
I want item <input name="myItem" type="text" size=3> to
be <input name="myText" type="text" size=30><p>
<input type="button" value="Update!" onClick="updateItem()">
</form>
</body>
</html>
```

The `updateItem()` function extracts the field-values from the form (note the use of the value property when you must access the actual *contents* of a field) and converts the value of the `myItem` field into an integer value using the `parseInt()` method. Array values are numbers and because you have entered the date via a text-field, the value must be converted into a numeric value—`parseInt()` is primarily used to convert strings into numeric values. This program does not validate the item number entered so, for example, entering a value higher than the actual number of list-items will result in an error (this outcome could easily be trapped in a simple validation-routine, however).

Submit Buttons

A *submit button* is used within a form to initiate the transmission of a form to a Web server. Forms can be associated with a script that complies with the CGI standard. The `action` attribute of the `<form>` tag specifies a URL, which references the script that will be accepting the form-data. JavaScript can be used to intercept a form-submission before the form is transmitted to a server for further processing, to validate the form, etc. You can refer to a submit button by using

♦ The `elements` array that represents the button element

♦ The `name` attribute of the button

For example, a form with a submit button could resemble the following:

```
<form action="http://serverat.somehost.com/cgi-bin/process.pl"
    method="POST">
Please enter your comments:<br>
<textarea cols=60 rows=5></textarea>
<input type="submit" value="Send data to server">
</form>
```

that presents a text-area field (which will be discussed next) and sends the contents of the field to the script named `process.pl`, which exists in the directory `/cgi-bin` on the server named `serverat.somehost.com`. This script is a Perl program—the ".pl" filename extension of the script is a tell-tale sign; it will accept the form-data, in this case, a single text-area field. What the script does with the data is not apparent at this stage. There is no way to see the contents of a CGI script unless it is specifically stored on the server in a plain-text file—referencing a CGI script using its URL simply invokes the script in question, rather than displaying its contents. Unlike JavaScript, whose source-code is mostly embedded within HTML files, CGI scripts are stored separately; they are always stored remotely on the server, and they are never transported to the client.

Text-Areas

A *text-area field* is similar to a text-field, except input is allowed to span over multiple lines. The `<textarea>` container is used to create the field; use the `rows` and `cols` attributes to specify the dimensions of the text-area. Text-areas can be referred to by a JavaScript application using

♦ The `elements` array that represents the text-area field

♦ The `name` attribute of the text-area field

Any text placed in between the container is reflected into the `value` property of this object; for example:

```
<!--
  Program 7-18
-->
<html>
<body>
<form>
```

7

```
<textarea name="ta" rows=5 cols=30>
This is a text-area field.
</textarea>
</body>
</html>
```

would create a text-area field with 5 rows and 30 columns. The value of the expression `ta.value` would, therefore, be `"This is a text-area field."`. You can dynamically update the contents of a text-area field by assigning a value to its `value` property; for example, using the JavaScript statement:

```
document.forms[0].ta.value = "New text";
```

would place the text `"new Text"` into the text-area field named `"ta"` which exists within the first form of the current document. See Chapter 5 for examples that illustrate a number of event-handler routines for use with text-area fields.

Text-Fields

Text-fields are primarily used to allow alphanumeric input into an application. Numeric values entered into text-fields must be coerced into their numerical equivalent using an appropriate JavaScript function, such as `parseInt()`, so you can use such input as a numeric argument to index an array, etc. A text-field is created using an `<input type="text">` tag; because `"text"` is the default type, you can optionally omit the `type` attribute when you define such fields. The `size` attribute can be used to specify the length of the field (in characters). You can refer to a text-field within a JavaScript application using

- The `elements` array that represents the text-field
- The `name` attribute of the text-field.

Values entered into a text-field can be dynamically updated by assigning an appropriate string value to the text-field object, via the `value` property. The `value` property will also be a reflection of the field's default value, which was originally assigned with the `<input>` tag's (optional) `value` attribute. Text-fields are ubiquitous in JavaScript applications that use forms; you will find them spread throughout the entire book.

User-Defined Buttons

A button is a clickable region of the screen that can be associated with a JavaScript expression, such as a function call or other statement. Buttons are form elements that are created using the `<input type="button">` tag; they can be referred to using

♦ The `elements` array that represents the button element
♦ The `name` attribute of the button

The `onClick` event-attribute (see Chapter 5) is useful to allow buttons to invoke JavaScript statements. For example, the current time and date could be displayed using the following HTML:

```
<!--
  Program 7-19
-->
<html>
<body>
<form>
<input type="button"
       value="The date and time"
       onClick="today=new Date(); alert(today)">
</form>
</body>
</html>
```

Functions can be invoked simply by naming the function in the `onClick` handler. If a function exists in the current document, simply issue its name verbatim. If it exists within another document, which is loaded into a different frame or window, be sure to add the necessary prefixes: "`parent.frames[n].`" for a frameset-document; or "`windowName`" for a particular window, where `windowName` is the variable assigned to the `window.open()` method that created the window. For example:

```
<!--
  Program 7-20
-->
<html>
<head>
<script language="JavaScript">
<!--
function callThisFunc() {
  alert("The function has been called!");
}
//-->
</script>
</head>
<body>
<form>
```

7

```
<input type="button"
       value="Invoke function"
       onClick="callThisFunc()">
</form>
</body>
</html>
```

Dynamic Button Text

Navigator 3.0 allows the text on a button-face to be dynamically altered by assigning a new string to the value attribute of the button object. For instance, you could have the following HTML:

```
<html>
<body>
<form>
<input type="button"
       value="Old value"
       onClick="this.value='New value'">
</form>
</body>
</html>
```

which awaits you to press the button labeled as "Old value," after which the value "New value" is displayed on the button. The this statement has been used here and refers to the current button object. If you did not use the this statement, you would have to refer to
document.forms[0].elements[0].value, which is longer.

If you assign a longer string than was previously assigned to the value attribute, the text will be clipped to fit within the dimensions of the button and it will not look very nice. You can expand the size of your buttons by placing spaces around the text for the button-face. Note that the button itself cannot be resized after it has been rendered, unless you completely reload the document.

Using the <input type=image> Tag

Buttons can also be images (in the GIF or JPEG format) using the type="image" attribute. For example, you could use the image named new.gif as a button with the following HTML:

```
<form>
<input type="image"
       src="new.gif"
       onClick="alert('Button Clicked!')">
</form>
```

Unless your image actually looks like a "button," you could use the alternative technique:

```
<a href="#" onClick="alert('Button Clicked!')">
<img src="new.gif">
</a>
```

which turns the image into a clickable hyperlink. The hash (#) signifies that no URL is loaded when the link is clicked. Instead, the `onClick` event-handler is used to catch the event. In this case, an `alert()` method has been used, although you would probably want to invoke a JavaScript function to perform some other task(s).

The use of image-hyperlinks instead of buttons depends on personal preferences. Both have advantages and disadvantages. Hyperlinks will introduce a status-bar message, which may not be what you require; buttons do not introduce a status-bar message. Hyperlinks that specify an `href` and `onClick` attribute can load a URL *and* activate an event; buttons can only activate one event at any one time. Note that you could write and invoke a user-defined function to simulate a hyperlink that uses both a `onClick` and `href`—the `location` property can be updated to load a new document and to simulate the `href` attribute.

 TIP: You can create your own personalized status-bar messages within Navigator using an `onMouseOver` event-attribute within a `<a href>` hyperlink. See Chapter 2 for more examples of the `window.status` property being used with hyperlinks.

Form Validation Using JavaScript

JavaScript is particularly good at form-validation, especially because it can manipulate form-elements, such as text-fields and selection lists. In its simplest form, validation involves checking input to make certain the values supplied conform to what is expected, and that the values are within acceptable bounds. Validation becomes more difficult because you are at liberty to enter just about anything you want into a form. So the programmer must check data-types and character-sequences to ensure that the input supplied is valid.

The type of validation routines you design will be the same if you are designing a "client-side" application or an application that interfaces to a CGI script (CGI is a ubiquitous standard, which facilitates the transmission of form-data between a client and a server entity over the Internet).

7

NOTE: When you design validation routines, do so on a field-by-field basis; ensure that each field, as data is entered, is validated. In some cases, the value of one field may be affected by another field, so the order of fields may be important. To overcome this problem, you can check to see if the earlier field has been populated with an appropriate value; if the field has not been populated, deny access to the current field. Navigator 3.0 has a new typeof() operator, which can be used to check the data-type of a particular object, such as a variable. This can be useful for validation routines, as you will see later.

Ensuring that a Field Is Numeric

A field is numeric if all the characters are numbers and if they are not alphabetic. Consider the following script that searches each character of an input value to test it against a range of numeric digits, from 0-9. By storing the digits that are valid within a numeric value, you can use JavaScript's indexOf() method to see if a particular digit exists in the input value (a form-field here). Each digit is then scanned against each character of the input value. The JavaScript indexOf() method returns a number that represents the starting position of a sequence of characters that we need to locate within a string, or otherwise the value -1 if the sequence cannot be located. By comparing the value of the counter variable with the length of the input value, you can test if all of the characters have been examined and are all digits:

```
<!--
  Program 7-21
-->
<html>
<head>
<script language="JavaScript">
<!--
function isNumber(data) {
  var numStr="0123456789";
  var thisChar;
  var counter = 0;
  for (var i=0; i < data.length; i++)  {
      thisChar = data.substring(i, i+1);
      if (numStr.indexOf(thisChar) != -1)
        counter ++;
  }
  if (counter == data.length) {
    // All characters are numbers
    alert("Number is OK.");
```

```
    }
    else
       alert("Number is not valid.");
}
//-->
</script>
</head>
<body>
<form>
Please enter a number:
<input name="num">
<input type="button"
       value="Submit"
       onClick="isNumber(this.form.num.value)">
</form>
</body>
</html>
```

This form of validation will also catch entries that contain numbers and letters, for example, "29a.". Appendix D contains a slightly reworked version of this program, which returns a `true` or `false` value and allows the function to be integrated into a range of other JavaScript applications more easily.

Ensuring that a Field Is Alphabetic

The `typeof()` operator runs into a few problems when it tests for purely alphabetic field values. Problems arise because text-fields are strings and testing for a string result will always be true, regardless of what characters are typed into the field. To overcome this problem, you will need to scan each character in the string to ensure it does not contain a number. Consider the following application:

```
<!--
  Program 7-22
-->
<html>
<head>
<script language="JavaScript">
<!--
function valAlpha(data) {
  var numStr="0123456789";
  var thisChar;
  for (var i=0; i < data.length; i++)  {
      thisChar = data.substring(i, i++);
      if (numStr.indexOf(thisChar, 0) != -1) {
          alert("Sorry, no numbers are allowed in this field!");
          document.forms[0].persName.value="";
```

7

```
            break;
        }
    }
}
//-->
</script>
</head>
<body>
<form>
Please enter your name:
<input name="persName" type="text">
<input type="button"
        value="Submit"
        onClick="valAlpha(this.form.persName.value)">
</form>
</body>
</html>
```

When you enter some text and press the supplied form-button, the
valAlpha() function scans through each character of the value supplied in
the text-field, using a for loop, which iterates from 0 to the value of the
string's length property. The substring() method extracts each character
and tests it against the numStr string. The numStr variable contains a list of
numbers ranging from 0 to 9—the characters you want to reject, in this
instance. JavaScript's indexOf() method returns the position of a character
within a string, or -1, if the character does not occur. By testing each digit
against the field value, you can see if a number occurs in the field.

NOTE: If a number does occur, a warning is issued and a break
statement terminates the loop at this point of the program. If no number
occurs, the loop will exit normally, and an alert-message saying "OK" will be
issued. Appendix D contains a slightly reworked version of this program,
which returns a true or false value instead, so the function can be
integrated into a range of applications more easily.

Ensuring that a Text-field Is Not Empty

A string that has the value " " is empty. You can also test the length
property of the text-field to see if it is 0, which also denotes an empty field.
Consider the following application, which tests a string's length property
and warns you if the field is empty:

```
<!--
    Program 7-23
```

```
-->
<html>
<head>
<script language="JavaScript">
<!--
function isEmpty(data) {
  if (data.length == 0) {
     // Warn the user, and refocus the field:
        alert("You must enter your full name");
        document.forms[0].persName.focus();
  }
  else {
     // Pass focus to the next field:
        document.forms[0].emailAddr.focus();
  }
}
//-->
</script>
</head>
<body>
<form>
Full name:
<input name="persName"
       type="text"
       onChange="isEmpty(this.form.persName.value)"><br>
E-mail address:
<input name="emailAddr" type="text">
</form>
</body>
</html>
```

This application differs from those previously shown because an
event-handling attribute has been specified within the first field. The
onChange event is triggered whenever the contents of the field are changed.
When a value is first entered into the field, this event is triggered and
control passes to the isEmpty() function. The value of the field is also
passed to the function as the data argument. The isEmpty() function
checks the length property of the data argument; if this equals zero, you
know the field has been left empty. In this case, the user is given a warning
and focus is placed back in the first field. If the user pressed the TAB key
while in the first field, the onChange event will also be invoked. Placing
focus back in the first field reminds the user to enter some text into the first
field now.

In fact, the onChange event can be bypassed in this application simply by
clicking on the second field as soon as the form appears within
Navigator—thus overriding the validation routine. This can be overcome by

7

altering the program to make the first field obtain focus automatically when the program loads, and then by using an `onBlur` event to check the field. An `onBlur` event is triggered when focus leaves a field, by using the TAB button or by clicking on a new form-element. Here is the entire new application:

```
<!--
  Program 7-24
-->
<html>
<head>
<script language="JavaScript">
<!--
function checkEmpty(data) {
  if (data.length == 0)
    document.forms[0].persName.focus();
}
//-->
</script>
</head>
<body onLoad="document.forms[0].persName.focus()">
<form>
Full name:
<input name="persName"
       type="text"
       onBlur="checkEmpty(this.form.persName.value)"><br>
E-mail address:
<input name="emailAddr"
       type="text">
</form>
</body>
</html>
```

When the document is loaded, focus is automatically set to the first field in the form, using the `focus()` method within an `onLoad` event in the `<body>` tag. An `onBlur` event-attribute in the first field invokes the `checkEmpty()` function with the value of the field. `checkEmpty()` passes the focus back to the first field if that field is empty, so the user cannot select the second field until data has been entered into the first field. See Chapter 5 for more examples of event attributes, such as `onBlur` and `onFocus`, and their use within JavaScript applications.

The term "empty" can be ambiguous, however. Once again, the validation in the previous program could be circumvented by placing one or more spaces into the first field. A space, even though it cannot be seen, is still a character in its own right. You may want to write a small function to check if a field is

really empty, by checking for spaces substituted as other characters. The
following example will do this; it will also check if the field is fully empty:

```
<!--
   Program 7-25
-->
<html>
<head>
<script language="JavaScript">
<!--
   function isEmpty(data) {
      for (var i=0; i < data.length; i++)  {
         if (data.substring(i, i+1) != " ") {
            alert("OK");
            return(false);
         }
      }
      alert("Please do not enter all spaces.");
      document.forms[0].persName.value="";
      return(true);
   }
//-->
</script>
</head>
<body>
<form>
Name:
<input name="persName" type="text" value="" size=30>
<input type="button"
       value="Submit"
       onClick="isEmpty(this.form.persName.value)"><br>
</form>
</body>
</html>
```

The isEmpty() function in the previous example uses a for loop to scan
through every character in the field passed to it. By using the substring()
function to step through each character, and then comparing this character
with a space, you can check if the entire field is made up of spaces. If a
non-space character is encountered, the loop is terminated and an
appropriate message is displayed. If the loop completes its cycle, it must
have scanned a space in every character and a warning is issued (the field is
also reset to an empty value). Appendix D has a smaller version of this
function, which only returns a boolean value.

7

Ensuring that a Numeric Value Is Within Certain Limits

Checking that a numeric value falls within a certain range requires the use of JavaScript's numeric operators: > (greater than), >= (greater than or equal to), < (less than), and <= (less than or equal to). The logical "and" (&&) and "or" (||) operators are also useful. For example, this simple function ensures an age field is within certain limits:

```
function checkAge(age) {
  if ((age >= 18) && (age <=30))
    alert("Age must be between 18 and 30.");
}
```

If the age is greater than or equal to 18, *and* it is less than or equal to 30, the function exits normally; otherwise, a warning-message is issued. At this stage, you could assign a empty value back to the field or take other appropriate action.

Ensuring that Only Upper- or Lowercase Values Are Supplied

You can ensure that a field is entered in upper- or lowercase by using the toUpperCase() and toLowerCase() methods. For example, when this field loses focus , its contents change to uppercase automatically:

```
<!--
  Program 7-26
-->
<form>
Name: <input type="text"
             size=30
             onBlur="this.value=this.value.toUpperCase()"><p>Ad-
             dress:<br>
<textarea cols=50 rows=5>
</textarea>
```

The value of this.value is the information entered into the text-field by the user. By reassigning the uppercase value of this field by using an onBlur event-attribute, the contents of the field will always be converted to uppercase when the user presses TAB, that is, when focus is given to another field object, such as the text-area field shown in the example. This type of validation is known as *post validation* because it is performed after the user has entered some information.

If you want to see if a field was entered in a particular case, you could use a prevalidation routine, such as:

```
<!--
  Program 7-27
-->
<html>
<head>
<script language="JavaScript">
<!--
function checkCase(txtField) {
  if (txtField != txtField.toUpperCase()) {
    alert("Please enter this field in upper-case only.");
    document.forms[0].personName.focus();   // Refocus field
    document.forms[0].personName.select();  // Select data
  }
}
//-->
</script>
</head>
<body>
<form>
Name: <input type="text"
             name="personName"
             size=30
             onBlur="checkCase(this.value)"><p>
Address:<br>
<textarea cols=50 rows=5>
</textarea>
</form>
</body>
</html>
```

This application checks to see if the `personName` is uppercase; if it is not, a warning is issued and the field is refocussed. Then its data is selected, awaiting reinput from the user.

Validation warnings can become tiresome. Consider updating the `window.status` property to display status-bar messages, rather than using `alert()` boxes; this will save you time because you will not have to press buttons to acknowledge such messages. Reselecting the field, using the `select()` method in this example, is also a useful, time-saving feature because it allows you to overwrite existing field-data immediately without having to rehighlight the field manually. Lowercase validation can be performed in the same way.

7

Summary

♦ Each <form> container tag is reflected into the JavaScript forms array. For example, document.forms[2] refers to the third form in the current document. Note that Form indexes start at zero (0) in JavaScript.

♦ If you name your <form> using a name attribute, you can refer to the form by using its name directly. For example, if you have <form name="myForm">, you could refer to this form as document.myForm, or as document.forms["myForm"]; both are equivalent.

Each form-element within a <form> container (checkbox, radio button, etc.) is reflected into an object, which is named after that element's name attribute. If a form element is unnamed, you can refer to it using the elements array. For example, the expression: document.forms[0].elements[0] is the first element within the first form of the current document. To refer to forms in other frames or windows, prefix the document property with a suitable object-name, for example, parent.frames[0] for the first frame within a frameset-document or, in the case of a window opened using the open() method, the name of the window—as assigned to the open() call.

♦ All form elements can be enhanced by including an "event-handler." An event-handling attribute specifies the type of event this form-element will detect. For example, a button created with <input type="button"> could use an onClick event handler to detect when you click on the button, and then invoke a JavaScript statement or function, etc.

♦ Most form elements have attributes that are also reflected into JavaScript object properties. For example, a checkbox can be selected by assigning a true value to the selected property of a checkbox object. This is known as "dynamic" selection because the selection is progmatic—that is, it is performed by the program, as opposed to the user.

♦ One of JavaScript's main strengths is in the handling of forms for validation. A number of routines can be used for validating form-fields to ensure they conform to the specific rules and conditions you set. If your form is being submitted to a Web server, you can ensure all data is valid before it is transmitted. This saves the server from carrying out further validation tasks, which, themselves, may require further network transmissions before the form is completely validated. Without JavaScript, form-data cannot be processed locally. JavaScript-aware applications can complement CGI scripts and, in some cases, can even replace them.

CHAPTER 8

Manipulating Windows with JavaScript

A window is an autonomous area—effectively, another browser window—into which HTML-formatted text can be written. JavaScript provides an important window-object method called `open()` that allows such a window to be opened. Multiple-windowed applications are advantageous because they allow information to be presented to the user externally, from the main browser window.

Creating Windows

Using the `open()` method, the author can open a new window, specify the appearance of the window in terms of size and interface features (toolbar, location, field, etc.), and then write text and other objects into the window as required. The use of `open()` is similar to choosing Navigator's File/New Web Browser option, except through JavaScript, you have more control over the window's appearance. You can also control what is shown within the window by dynamically updating its contents using JavaScript's `document` object methods, such as `open()`, `write()`, and `close()`.

TIP: Don't confuse `window.open()` with `document.open()`. The latter is used to open a *text-stream* and write dynamic HTML into a document. If you use `open()` by itself, a new window will still be opened because `window` is the top-level object in JavaScript and Navigator will assume you want to open a new window.

The `open()` method is a property of the `window` object and has the following syntax:

```
window.open("URL", "windowName", ["windowFeatures,..."]);
```

where URL is an optional Uniform Resource Locator to load into the new window; if left blank, as an empty string, the window is opened with no document initially loaded. `windowName` is the name of the window—although it is not the title of the window—and `windowFeatures` is an optional, comma-separated list of *features* you can add to the window. Features, in this case, include the Navigator toolbar, directory buttons, location field, menu-bar, scroll-bars, and other features, such as allowing window-resizing.

TIP: The most recently created window is given "focus," that is, is selected, although it is possible to change the focus behavior using the `window` object's new `focus()` and `blur()` methods, both of which are discussed later in this chapter.

Each window-feature is represented as an attribute with a unique name—for example, `toolbar`—and can be enabled or disabled using yes/no or 1/0 settings; no spaces are allowed in the `windowFeatures` string. The following table illustrates each attribute.

Attribute	Values	Description
`copyhistory`	`[=yes|no]  |  [=1|0]`	Copy the history? (yes/no)
`directories`	`[=yes|no]  |  [=1|0]`	Directory buttons (on/off)
`height`	`= pixelheight`	Window height (pixels)
`location`	`[=yes|no]  |  [=1|0]`	Location bar (on/off)
`menubar`	`[=yes|no]  |  [=1|0]`	Menu-bar (on/off)
`resizable`	`[=yes|no]  |  [=1|0]`	Resizable window? (yes/no)
`scrollbars`	`[=yes|no]  |  [=1|0]`	Scroll-bars? (yes/no)
`status`	`[=yes|no]  |  [=1|0]`	Status-bar (on/off)
`toolbar`	`[=yes|no]  |  [=1|0]`	Toolbar mode (on/off)
`width`	`= pixelwidth`	Window width (pixels)

All of the attribute's values default to `yes` (1) and the new window size emulates the previous, if left unspecified. The order of attributes is unimportant, and can be specified arbitrarily. The `copyhistory` attribute copies the previous window's history (the main window if you are creating your first window) into the current window. For example, you could create a new window, measuring 300 pixels wide × 200 pixels high, using the following script:

```
<!--
 Program 8-1
-->
<html>
<script language="JavaScript">
<!--
  var myUrl = "http://www.gold.net/users/ag17/index.htm";
  window.open(myUrl, "window1", "width=300,height=200");
//-->
</script>
</html>
```

where `myUrl` is the URL you want to load into the new window—in this case, the file `index.htm` that exists in the directory `/users/ag17` of the Web server `www.gold.net`. This new *child* window will inherit all of the features of the main Navigator parent window, albeit for the new dimensions.

8

TIP: The `<title>`..`</title>` container can be used to allocate a title to a window. Writing this container tag dynamically into your window will achieve this (to be described in the next section). Unless you specifically allocate a title when writing HTML-text into a window, Navigator will provide the text *"Generated by file:..."*. This text will quickly disappear when the `<title>` container takes effect, however.

By placing all of the window attributes in a single string and then passing this to the `open()` method you can make your code more readable and save precious line-space at the same time, for example:

```
winOpts = "width=500,height=250,scrollbars=0";
window.open("", "myWindow", winOpts);
```

You can refer back to `winOpts` at a later stage for any other windows you want to have the same appearance.

Frames and Windows: The Differences

JavaScript has a `window` object and a number of other synonyms that can be used, depending on the structure of your application. A separate—that is, autonomous—window is just another browser environment with its own `window`, `top`, and `self` definitions and, of course, can have other objects, such as frames, embedded within it. Do not confuse autonomous windows with window objects; they are not one and the same.

Autonomous windows are not represented as an object in JavaScript; no `windows` array exists, as such. Newly created windows can be assigned to a variable, although there is no reflection into any window-properties as yet. Frame and window objects are identical in JavaScript, although distinguishing between a document within an *autonomous* window and a frameset-document, which is part of an existing window, is very important. Autonomous windows are, in effect, clones of Navigator's main window, and can also have frames and multiple documents embedded within them. Frameset documents (see Chapter 9) are separate regions of a window that can have unique URLs, such as HTML documents, loaded into them.

Assigning an `open()` Call to a Variable

To manipulate windows and their contents, you must assign the `open()` method to a JavaScript variable. This variable can then be prefixed onto other JavaScript statements, which need to reference that window, for example, `document.write()`, etc. For example, you could create a window called `helpWin` using the single JavaScript statement:

```
helpWin = open("", "helpWindow", "width=300,height=150");
```

By building the previous line into an application, you can now write HTML-formatted text into the window dynamically, either automatically, or based upon an event associated with an object, such as a button or a hyperlink. For example, the following script presents a button, which, when clicked, opens a new window. Some HTML-formatted text is written into the window by prefixing the `document.writeln()` function with the name of the window, in this case, `helpWin`:

```
<!--
 Program 8-2
-->
<html>
<script language="JavaScript">
<!--
function CreateNewWindow() {
  helpWin = window.open("", "helpWindow",
          "width=300,height=150");
  helpWin.document.writeln("<h1>Help Window<hr></h1>");
}
//-->
</script>
<body>
<form>
<input type="button"
       value="Open a window"
       onClick="CreateNewWindow()"
</form>
</body>
</html>
```

 TIP: The `open()` method actually returns a window-id value to the variable you use to assign to any newly-created window. You can see the value in your code by placing an `alert()` method at the appropriate place, for example, `alert(helpWin)` after the `window.open()` line in the previous example, to see the value assigned. Each new window you create with `window.open()` will be assigned a unique value in this way.

Dynamically Updating Objects in a Window

Objects within a child window can be updated by the parent by dynamically writing HTML-formatted text into the `document` object of the window you require.

Updating Text Fields in Other Windows

Consider the script below, for example, which starts by creating a window and a text-field object. A form-button is then placed in the main parent window, whose `onClick` event changes the value of the field in the child window:

```
<!--
 Program 8-3
-->
<html>
<head>
<script language="JavaScript">
<!--
  // Create a window:
  var win1 = window.open("", "myWindow",
               "toolbar=0,width=300,height=100");
  win1.document.open();
  win1.document.writeln("<title>Child Window 1</title>" +
    "<form><input type='text' size=20 value='Old value' " +
    "name='aname'></form>");
  win1.document.close();
//-->
</script>
</head>
<body>
<form name="myForm">
<input
 type="button"
 onClick="win1.document.forms[0].aname.value='New value'"
 value="Change value">
</form>
</body>
</html>
```

Notice how the name of the window (`win1`) has been prefixed onto the `document` object so the `open()`, `close()`, and `writeln()` methods are applied to that specific window.

Writing Text and Graphics to Another Window

Once a window has been opened, you can write HTML-formatted text into it simply by prefixing all `document.write()` methods with the variable you assigned to the `window.open()` method. For example:

```
var myWin = window.open(...);
myWin.document.write(...);
```

Consider the following application that displays a series of thumbnail pictures of a number of products (in this case, books), and then allows the user to click on a book-cover so a new window containing details for that item can be shown. You could use a frameset document to code a similar application, although people sometimes like to minimise a window, and then examine its contents later. This is less easy to implement using a frame because the frame must always be visible somewhere on the screen. Figure 8-1 illustrates the example as seen through Navigator.

```
<!--
 Program 8-4
-->
<html>
<head>
<script language="JavaScript">
<!--
  var bookTexts = new Object();
  bookTexts[1] =
    "<img align='left' src='essjav1.gif'>" +
    "Title  : <b>ESSENTIAL JAVA*</b><br>" +
    "Author : Jason Manger<br>" +
    "ISBN   : 0-07-709292-9<hr>" +
    "A book on two of the newest technologies to hit the Web, " +
    "the <b>Java</b> and <b>JavaScript</b> languages. A guide " +
    "for novices and experts alike, and includes sections on " +
    "developing dynamic HTML, programming GUI interfaces with " +
    "Java, using threads for multitasking, and streams for " +
    "distributed Java applications. Many dozens of Java and " +
    "JavaScript programs are documented and examined within " +
    "the book, and an extensive series of appendices is also " +
    "provided.<p> <img width=30 src='cd.gif'> Contains " +
    "<b>Java Development Kit 1.0<b>";
  bookTexts[2] =
    "<img align='left' src='netnav.gif'>" +
    "Title  : <b>NETSCAPE NAVIGATOR</b><br>" +
    "Author : Jason Manger<br>" +
    "ISBN   : 0-07-709190-6<hr>" +
    "An in-depth guide to the de facto Web-browser, " +
```

8

```
        "<b>Netscape Navigator</b>. This book also covers HTML to " +
        "level 3.0, and includes details of Navigator's news and " +
        "mail facilities, as well as much more besides.";
bookTexts[3] =
        "<img align='left' src='hhcs.gif'>" +
        "Title   : <b>HITCH HIKING CYBERSPACE</b><br>" +
        "Author : Jason Manger<br>" +
        "ISBN    : 0-07-709786-6<hr>" +
        "A CD-ROM that comes in <b>two</b> parts. Part I arrives " +
        "with a copy of <b>Netscape Navigator</b> and includes a " +
        "hypertexted version of Jason's books, <i>The WWW Mosaic " +
        "and More</i>, <i>Netscape Navigator</i> and <i>The " +
        "Essential Internet Information Guide</i>. Part II " +
        "contains everything except the Navigator software.<p> " +
        "<img width=30 src='cd.gif'> No less " +
        "than 10 top tools are included, such as <b>Netmanage " +
        "Chameleon</b> TCP/IP software for Internet access.";
bookTexts[4] =
        "<img align='left' src='swwwm&m.gif'>" +
        "Title   : <b>THE WORLD WIDE WEB, MOSAIC AND MORE</b><br>" +
        "Author : Jason Manger<br>" +
        "ISBN    : 0-07-705170-6<hr>" +
        "A guide to the popular <b>Mosaic</b> browser and detailed " +
        "information on <b>CGI</b> (the Common Gateway Interface), " +
        "all in one book. CGI allows HTML to interface to back-end " +
        "databases, providing greater interactivity within " +
        "hypertext documents.";
function showBook(number) {
    if (number == null) {
        alert("This product cannot be located!");
        return;
    }
    winOpts = "toolbar=0,location=0,width=650,height=400";
    win1    = window.open("", "myWin", winOpts);
    win1.document.open();
    win1.document.write(
            "<html>" +
            "<head><title>Product Information</title>" +
            "<base href='" + location + "'></head>" +
            "<body background='back1.gif' text=White>" +
            bookTexts[number] +
            "<hr>" +
            "<img align='right' src='logo.gif'>" +
            "<form><input type=button value='Finished' " +
            "onClick='self.close()'></form>" +
            "</body></html>");
    win1.document.close();
}
```

```
//-->
</script>
</head><title>INTERNET BOOKS AND CDs FOR 1996</title>
<body text="White" background="back1.gif" link="Yellow">
<img align="left" src="mgh5.gif" hspace=12 border=0>
<font size=+3>
<img src="logo.gif"> INTERNET BOOKS FOR 1996...
</font>
<basefont size=4>
<center>
<table cellspacing=20 border=0>
<tr valign="bottom" align="middle">
 <td>
  <a href="#" onClick="showBook(1)">
  <img border=1 src="essjav1.gif">
  </a>
 </td>
 <td>
  <a href="#" onClick="showBook(2)">
  <img border=1 src="netnav.gif">
  </a>
 </td>
 <td>
  <a href="#" onClick="showBook(3)">
  <img border=1 src="hhcs.gif">
  </a>
 </td>
 <td>
  <a href="#" onClick="showBook(4)">
  <img border=1 src="swwwm&m.gif">
  </a>
 </td>
</tr>
</table>
</center>
<dl>
<dd><img src="hand.gif"> Welcome to the Internet books'
section at McGraw-Hill.<p>
<dd><img src="hand.gif"> Please click on a book cover for
more information on that book. A new window will be opened
to show the details, which you can then close or minimise
at will.
</dl>
</form>
</body>
</html>
```

8

Text is an array, containing four values. The array has been created using JavaScript's `Object()` constructor, and the values have been assigned to elements 1 to 4. Within these four elements are stored a series of HTML-formatted strings that describe four book products. Later in the script, the covers for these books will be shown, as illustrated in Figure 8-1, and you can click on a book to see its details. For example:

```
<td>
  <a href="#" onClick="showBook(4)">
  <img border=1 src="swwwm&m.gif">
  </a>
</td>
```

defines a hyperlink without a URL destination—hence the use of the hash (#)—but which, instead, invokes a user-defined function called `showBook()` when this link is clicked upon. The numeric argument passed to `showBook()`—in this case, the value 4—represents a book whose details you want to see and relates to an element in `bookText`'s array, that is, `bookTexts[4]` in this instance. The `showBook()` function then creates a new window and, in context to this example, writes the contents of the fourth `bookText`'s array element into the window, along with the book cover image and some extra HTML-formatting. Notice how all of the `document.write()` calls are prefixed with the new window name. Among the HTML written into the new window is a button with an `onClick` event-handler that shuts down the window using the expression

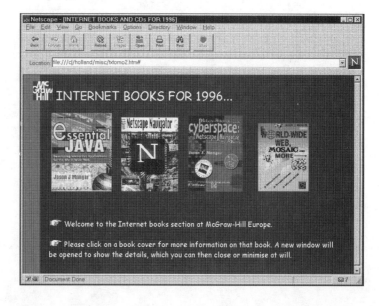

The main products screen as viewed through Navigator

Figure 8-1.

`self.close()`, where `self` refers to the current window. Figure 8-2 illustrates a newly created window that displays the details of a single book.

File-Referencing Problems

When referencing files from *within* tags, which are written dynamically into a window, such as when using the `<img src>` tag to refer to an image, you must either:

♦ Specify the *full* URL of the file to which you are referring. For example, use the `http://` or `file:` URL types—remember to use `file:///%7cdrive|/path` in the case of **local** files, where `%7c` represents the pipe character (|), to avoid a potential error message because Navigator (especially the beta versions) doesn't like the literal use of this character; *or*

♦ Place a `<base href=URL>` tag within the new window you are creating, where URL is the value of the current window location, as returned by the `location` property. Do this by concatenating the `location` property value into the string, for example, `"<base href="` + `location` + `">"`. This technique was used in the previous program example. The `<base href>` tag makes the current document the base document for all URLs that are referenced from within it.

These methods will ensure the files you reference can be found by Navigator. All new windows are associated with a new `location` object, so you must be

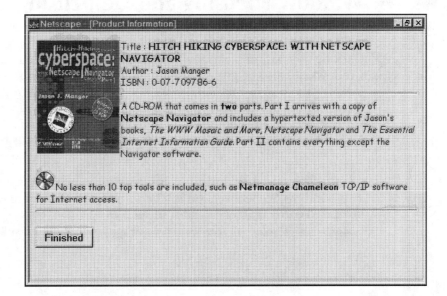

A product screen as viewed through Navigator

Figure 8-2.

8

accurate when you refer to external files, such as images and HTML documents.

Loading a New URL Into a Window

The first argument passed to the `open()` method allows a new URL to be loaded into a window. If you assign a value to the `location` object for a particular window, however, you can achieve the same effect. For instance:

```
var w1 = open("",
              "win1",
              "toolbar=0,width=700,height=400");
w1.location = "http://www.osbone.com";
```

would load the home page for Osborne's Web site into the window "w1", although in this case, it would have been easier to write:

```
var w1 = open("http://www.osbone.com",
              "win1",
              "toolbar=0,width=700,height=400");
```

Changing the contents of a window progmatically allows you to do away with "hard-coding" the URL into the `open()` call. You could also pass a string-variable as the first argument to `open()`, which holds the URL you want to load into the window.

Window Focusing and Defocusing Methods

A window that has *focus* is the currently selected window in JavaScript, and can be identified as such because the window's selection-bar is highlighted. Clicking any part of a window will give that window focus, although windows can also be given focus progmatically, through the use of the JavaScript `focus()` method. Focus can also be removed from a window by using the `blur()` method. The contents of a window can be updated without specifically allocating focus to the window; in fact, the selection of any HTML object within a window must in turn give focus to that window.

T IP: If a minimized window is focused, Navigator restores the window. The Windows 95 beta version is a bit *buggy* in this area; the window may not be resized correctly by Navigator in such cases.

It is important that you assign all newly created variables to a variable, as previously explained, so the `focus()` and `blur()` methods can be applied to a specific window; for example:

```
var w1 = window.open("","myWin",
                     "height=99,width=99,scrollbars=no");
var w2 = window.open("","myWin",
                     "height=99,width=99,scrollbars=no");
```

would create two new windows, w1 and w2. The most recently created window will be given focus; in this case, window w2 will be selected by default. However, by using the statement:

```
w1.focus();
```

focus will be passed to the first window (w1). Only one window can have focus at any given time, so blurring of all other windows will be carried out automatically by Navigator. Consider the following program that creates two child-windows: By pressing the appropriate button in the parent document, focus can be given to the appropriate window.

```
<!--
 Program 8-5
-->
<html>
<head>
<script language="JavaScript">
<!--
  function createTwoWindows() {
  var win1 = window.open("","win1","height=60," +
                             "width=175,scrollbars=no");
  var win2 = window.open("","win2","height=60," +
                             "width=175,scrollbars=no");
}
//-->
</script>
</head>
<body onLoad="createTwoWindows()">
<form>
Please click on the appropriate button:<br>
<input type=button
       value='Focus Window 1'
       onClick="win1.focus()">
<input type=button
       value='Focus Window 2'
       onClick="win2.focus()">
```

8

```
</form>
</body>
</html>
```

Another technique widely used is opening and giving focus to a window by using the same control object. For example, the following application presents a single button that opens a window. If you click on the button again, the window is immediately given focus. The option to close the window is provided *within* the window itself, using a `self.close()` function-call attached to a form-button.

Using the `opener` Property to Control Multiple Windows

The problem with manipulating the focus behavior of a window is made worse because using the `top` window-synonym to refer to variables and functions defined within the top-level Navigator window is impossible. In the case of windows opened with a `open()` method, `top` is only relative to the *current* window because these are autonomous browser-sessions. To overcome this problem, Navigator 3.0 has introduced a new `opener` property that belongs to the `window` object. The `opener` property contains the name of the window called the `open()` method and is invaluable when referring to functions and variables defined with the first Navigator window. Consider the following example, which allows you to open, and then focus, a window, and that uses the `opener` property to refer to the first Navigator window:

```
<!--
 Program 8-6
-->
<html>
<head>
<script language="JavaScript">
<!--
 var winToggle = false;
 var wt;
 function changeBut(n) {
   if (n==0) {
       winToggle = false;
       document.forms[0].elements[0].value = "Open window";
   }
   else {
       winToggle = true;
       wt = window.open("win1.htm", "wt",
                        "toolbar=0,width=300,height=100");
```

```
          document.forms[0].elements[0].value = "Focus window";
    }
  }
  function togWin() {
    if (!winToggle)
      changeBut(1);
    else
      wt.focus();
  }
//-->
</script>
</head>
<body>
<form>
<input type="button"
       value="Open window"
       onClick="togWin()">
</form>
</html>
```

The file named `win1.htm` that is loaded into the newly created window (wt) resembles the following:

```
<html>
<body>
<form>
<input type="button"
       value="Close window"
       onClick="window.opener.changeBut(0); self.close()">
</form>
</body>
</html>
```

When the main document is loaded, a form-button is created that opens a new window. The variable wt is assigned to the open() method, used later in the program, and the winToggle variable is used to track the state of the window, specifically if it is open or closed. When you click on the "Open window" button, the togWin() function is invoked. This checks the value of the winToggle variable to see if the window is already open; if so, it gives the window focus. If the window is closed, a new window must be opened. winToggle is set to false by default, so a new window is opened when the application is first started; the changeBut() function is invoked with the numeric argument "1". When the value "1" is passed to changeBut(), a new window is opened and the value of the button is changed to "Focus window", allowing the same button to focus the window, rather than to

8

open it. The value of `winToggle` is now set to `true` indicating that the window has been opened.

The button within the newly created window (as specified in the file `win1.htm`) is used to close the window. This invokes the `changeBut()` function with the argument "0", which, in this case, sets `winToggle` back to `false`, and changes the button-text back to "Open window". The current window (`self`) is then closed.

The important thing to note at this point is how the value of `window.opener`, or `self.opener` (they are the same), has been prefixed onto the `changeBut()` function. If you had used the expression `top.changeBut()`, an error would have occurred because top refers to the *current* window—autonomous windows, unlike frameset-documents, do *not* have "parents." The `opener` property, therefore, references the window that opened the current window, and in which the `changeBut()` function was originally defined. You can think of `opener` as the equivalent of the `parent` property in a frameset-document.

Closing Windows

To close a window, use a statement of the form:

```
winName.close()
```

where `winName` is the name of the window you want to close, and was the variable originally assigned to the `window.open()` method, which created the window. Alternatively, you can use a window object synonym; for example, if you need to close the current window, use `self.close()`, where `self` is a synonym for the *current* window. You could just use `close()` by itself because the current window is always assumed to exist. If you created a window without assigning it to a variable, you can only close that window from within a program when that window has focus, specifically, when a `close()` method is activated from within that window. For example, this script creates a window and provides a button to close it again:

```
<!--
 Program 8-7
-->
<html>
<head>
<script language="JavaScript">
<!--
// Create a window:
win1 = window.open("", "myWindow",
                   "toolbar=0,width=300,height=100");
```

```
//-->
</script>
</head>
<body>
<form>
<input type="button"
       onClick="win1.close()"
       value="Close window">
</form>
</body>
</html>
```

If the window in the previous example had not been assigned to a variable as in the slightly modified code example shown here:

```
<!--
 Program 8-8
-->
<html>
<head>
<script language="JavaScript">
<!--
 // Create a window:
 window.open("dummy.htm", "myWindow",
             "toolbar=0,width=300,height=100");
//-->
</script>
</head>
</html>
```

then the only way of referencing the window is to provide some code actually within the document that is eventually read into the window in order to shut it down, for example, using `self.close()`. The file `dummy.htm` has been read into the window in the previous example, so if `dummy.htm` was an HTML document resembling:

```
<html>
<body>
<form>
<input type="button"
       onClick="self.close()"
       value="Close window">
</form>
</body>
</html>
```

then the window could then be closed—here by using a form-button with an onClick event that simply closes the window using self.close().

In fact, by providing a *toggle* function, you could allow a single button to open and close a single window. Consider the following script, for example. This program defines a global variable, winToggle, which is used to create a window and also to monitor when that window is opened and closed by the user. When the program is initially loaded, the value of winToggle (a boolean variable) is set to false. When you click on the button provided, a window is opened and assigned to the wt variable. When the button is next clicked, the value of winToggle is not false (the value is set to true when the window is opened, and signifies it is open); instead, the window is closed. Notice how the value of winToggle is set back to false before the window is closed:

```
<!--
 Program 8-9
-->
<html>
<head>
<script language="JavaScript">
<!--
 var wt;
 winToggle = false;
 function togWin() {
   if (!winToggle) {
     winToggle = true;
     wt = window.open("", "wt",
                       "toolbar=0,width=300,height=100");
     document.forms[0].togBut.value = "Close window";
   }
   else {
     winToggle = false;
     document.forms[0].togBut.value = "Open window";
     wt.close();
   }
 }
//-->
</script>
</head>
<body>
<form>
<input type="button"
       name="togBut"
       value="Open window"
       onClick="togWin()">
```

```
</form>
</html>
```

Notice how the text of the button is changed, as well. This is useful when the action for the button has changed, as in the case of the toggle function in the example. The ability to change the text of a button face (via the `value` attribute) is new to Navigator 3.0.

T**IP:** Watch out! If you issue a `close()` method within the top-level Navigator document, you will shut down Netscape Navigator, just like choosing the File/Close option. The Exit and Close options within Navigator's File menu act the same when only one (top-level) window is open. This seems to be an ever-popular "gimmick" used on some Web pages at the moment.

Validating a Window

When you reference a window, check to make certain the window actually exists. You can close windows at any time, so a program should not always assume a window exists. Referencing a nonexistent window will result in an error. Validate a window *before* you attempt to write data into it or to change the value of one of its properties.

By checking to see if a specific *property* of a window exists, you can also determine if the window is currently open. In the following application, a boolean variable, `winOpen`, is created dynamically by being defined in a `<script>` container, which is dynamically written into a window. This variable is now a property of this window; it can be accessed as `win1.winOpen`. This property will remain until you close the window. If you try to access this property after the window has been closed, a `null` value will be returned.

```
<!--
 Program 8-10
-->
<html>
<head>
<script language="JavaScript">
<!--
var win1;
var scriptTags = "<html>" +
                 "<title>Sample Window</title>" +
                 "<script>var winOpen=true;</script>" +
                 "</html>";
```

8

```
function createWindow() {
  win1 = window.open("",
                     "win1",
                     "height=60,width=175,scrollbars=no");
  win1.document.open();
  win1.document.writeln(scriptTags);
  win1.document.close();
}

function validateWindow() {
  if (win1.winOpen == null)
    alert("Window does NOT exist.");
  else {
    win1.focus(); // give window focus
    alert("Window exists!");
  }
}


//-->
</script>
</head>
<body onLoad="createWindow()">
<form>
<input type=button
       value='Check Window'
       onClick="validateWindow()">
</form>
</html>
```

Notice how the `win1` variable has been defined at the top of the document, so it is available to the entire application. When the program starts, the `createWindow()` function is invoked from the `<body>` tag, and a new window is created using the `window.open()` method. A form-button within the main window can then be used to see whether or not the window still exists; this simply checks for the property `winOpen` within the newly created window, `win1`. A `null` value indicates that the property does not exist; therefore, the window cannot be open at this time. If the window does exist, it is also given focus (in case it is buried under a window, etc.).

Summary

Autonomous windows are duplicates of Navigator's main browser window, and share all of the same features. Such windows are useful in applications to allow multiple document viewing, as well as presenting user interface and other controls to the user, which can then be moved around and then maximized or minimized for the users convenience.

♦ The `window.open()` method opens a new browser window in JavaScript. Using `open()` by itself is the same as `window.open()`, since the window object is the top-level object in JavaScript. Newly created windows are known as *child windows* in JavaScript terminology, since the main browser window is the parent of all newly created windows.

♦ The `window()` method returns a window-id value, so by assigning this method to a JavaScript available it is then possible to reference that window from within a JavaScript application. For example, you can open a window and then place HTML-formatted text into it using a method such as `document.write()`, and prefixing the document object with the name of the window that you have previously created.

♦ Windows are closed using the `window.close()` method. If a `window.open()` method is not assigned to a JavaScript variable, the window must be shut down by placing an appropriate `close()` method *within* the window that has been opened—mainly because there is no way of referencing the window as its id-value has not been saved to a variable.

♦ There is no `windows[]` array in Navigator yet, which means that window validation is clumsy and difficult. You can detect whether a window is open by placing a small script in the document that is to be loaded into the window. This sets a variable. By testing if the variable is null (undefined), you can ascertain whether the window exists. This is possible because all JavaScript variables are bound to the window in which they are defined.

♦ The `opener` property was introduced with Navigator 3.0, and allows a child window to refer back to its creator, i.e. to its parent window.

Remember that when referencing variables and functions defined within a child window, you must specifiy the window name. For example, `myWindow.document.forms[0].myField.value` extracts the value of the field named `myField` from the first form of the document loaded into the window named as `myWindow`. The variable `myWindow` would need to be assigned to the `window.open()` method that created the window, e.g. `var myWindow = window.open(...)`, etc. The same access method is required for all of the elements that are defined within a child window, like frames, forms, variables, JavaScript functions, etc.

language=

CHAPTER 9

Using JavaScript with HTML Frames

Frames were introduced with Netscape Navigator version 2.0 and allow multiple regions of the browser screen (known as *frames*) to be created and manipulated. HTML-formatted documents can be read into frames using JavaScript statements, or alternatively, dynamically generated HTML can be written into a frame to simulate the loading of a document. HTML elements such as buttons and hyperlink can be used to dynamically update the contents of a frame in real-time, i.e. there and then.

Frames can also be resized by using the mouse and dragging the frame-border; scroll-bars can be also attached to individual frames to allow large documents to be scrolled vertically and horizontally. In JavaScript, each frame is referred to using JavaScript's `parent` property. JavaScript also has a `frames` array, which stores the identity of each frame within the current document and allows the programmer to reference the frame they require. Once a frame has been created an HTML-formatted document can be loaded into it, either from a local file or from a networked document using an appropriate URL. Alternatively you can write some JavaScript code to generate HTML for you—a process known as dynamic-HTML generation. Many interesting JavaScript projects located on the Web now involve the use of frame-based documents to achieve advanced navigational effects, as well as allowing multiple document viewing within a single browser environment. In this chapter, you will learn how to:

♦ Create frameset-documents and alter their characteristics

♦ Create JavaScript programs that manipulate frames

♦ Use the new `javascript:` URL to evaluate JavaScript expressions

♦ Write dynamic-HTML applications to manipulate frames

TIP: See `http://proto.netscape.com` for some interesting frameset-document prototypes created by Netscape Corporation, developers of Netscape Navigator.

Frame navigation has been altered in Netscape Navigator 3.0 (codenamed *Atlas).* In particular, the Navigator *Back* button now loads the previous *frame* rather than the previous *document.* The navigation methods in JavaScript such as `back()` etc., also reflect this important new change.

Creating a Frame Using `<frameset>`

The term *frameset-document* refers to an HTML document that uses the Navigator 2.0 `<frameset>..</frameset>` container tag. The HTML `<frameset>` container has the following syntax:

```
<frameset [rows="rowspec" | cols="colspec" ]>
<frame [ name="frameName" ]
       src="fileName|URL"
       [ marginwidth=w ]
       [ marginheight=h ]
       [ onLoad="JsCommand" ]
```

```
          [ scrolling=yes|no ]
          [ noresize ]
</frameset>
```

The `<frameset>` tag identifies the current document as a frameset-document and renders the frame onto the screen. Each of the nested `<frame>` tags specifies a specific document to load into each frame area. The `rows` and `cols` attributes specify the dimensions of the frames within the current document, and can accept both percentage and pixel measurements. All numbers that do not end with a "`%`" (percent) sign are considered pixel measurements, note. Both of these attributes are string values and, in the case where multiple frames are required, a list of frame-dimensions for each of the frames must be specified as a comma-separated list. The size of a frame can be specified in any of three different ways—the order is unimportant and combinations are also possible:

♦ Pixel measurements

♦ Percentage measurements

♦ Wildcard measurements

Using Pixel Measurements

A number specified by itself is assumed to be a pixel value, for example:

```
<frameset rows="300,200">
```

creates two horizontal frames: One frame is 300 pixels in height, and the other frame is 200 pixels. This method is considered the least attractive of the three frame-measurement methods. The size of the main Navigator window cannot yet be controlled by JavaScript (although subsequently created windows can); therefore, if pixel values are used, it would make sense to allow the user to resize the frame, that is, by not specifying the `noresize` attribute. Fixed pixel-width frames that have a `noresize` attribute may obscure HTML elements loaded into that frame because the pixel measurement is not relative to the window's size. Navigator can override a pixel measurement to ensure that the total dimensions of the frame are 100% of the width and height of the main Navigator window.

Using Percentage Measurements

A percentage measurement value ranges from 1 to 100% (the "`%`" sign at the end of the value signifies this form of measurement) and creates a frame whose size is relative to the main Navigator window. For example:

```
<frameset rows="50%,50%">
```

creates two horizontal frames of equal size. When specifying percentages for multiple frames, it is always wise to ensure that the summed value of percentages for each frame equals 100. If the total is greater than 100, all of the other frame's percentages will be scaled down. Likewise, if the total is less than 100, and one or more relative-sized frames exist, extra space will be given to these, accordingly. If there are no relative-sized frames, all percentages will be scaled up to match a total of 100%.

Using Wildcarded Measurements

To specify a wildcard the * character (asterisk) is used. Wildcards can be used by themselves or in conjunction with another value. A frame whose size is specified *only* as a single * character requests Navigator to allocate all *remaining* space to the frame. If any other wildcarded frames exist, all remaining space is divided evenly between them accordingly. For instance:

```
<frameset rows="70%,*">
```

creates one frame, which is 70% of the width of the main Navigator window and allocates as much space as remains to the other frame—30% in this case. If a value is placed in front of the *, then this frame receives that much more relative space. For example,

```
<frameset rows="2*,*">
```

would give two thirds of the space to the first frame (2*) and one third to the second frame (*).

Frames can also be nested inside one another—a feature you can use if you want to break up single frames into smaller regions.

Both filenames and full URLs are allowed in the src attribute of the <frame> tag, a compulsory attribute that must be specified, which allows individual frames to be populated with both local and remote hypertext documents. The marginwidth and marginheight specify the size of the margins within each frame—in relation to the first object placed in the frame: text, form, image, etc. The name attribute of each frame is optional and specifies the name of the current frame. When this is omitted, you must refer to a frame with JavaScript by passing a numeric argument (starting from zero) to the frames property, an array structure that contains the name of each frame: frames[0] is the first frame in a frameset-document; frames[1] is the second, etc. The onLoad attribute is a JavaScript event-handler, which is invoked when the current frame is loaded with a document and can be used to execute a JavaScript statement, such as a function-call, etc. The `scrolling` attribute specifies whether or not a scroll-bar is placed within the frame; `noresize`, if specified, stops the user from resizing the frame (frames can otherwise be resized by positioning the mouse over the frame border until the up and down arrow cursor appears, and then holding down the left mouse-button and dragging the frame accordingly).

Also important to remember is that frameset-documents are unlike conventional HTML documents, in that the document body actually *is* the `<frameset>` container. You cannot nest a `<frameset>` within the `<body>` container of an HTML file; doing so will simply make Netscape render an empty document in place of the frameset-document. Be sure to replace `<body>` with `<frameset>` in all such instances. Furthermore, mixing *raw* HTML-text within a frameset-document is not a good idea because the main portions of text will be located in separate files, which are then loaded within individual frames (in fact this statement is not completely true because it *is* actually possible to write text dynamically into a frame using JavaScript without populating frames with separate HTML files).

TIP: To allow a hyperlink to target a given frame, the `<a href>` tag has been extended with the addition of the new `target` attribute. See examples of a frame using a hyperlink in the section entitled *"Targeting a Frame Using a Hyperlink."*

Navigator (especially version 2.*x*) is sometimes reluctant when reloading a frameset document after the *Reload* button has been pressed. When you are making changes to your code you must use *Reload* to see the new results. By clicking on Navigator's main *Location:* field at the top of the screen and then pressing the ENTER key the document should then load properly. Pressing the SHIFT key down while pressing *Reload* is another popular method, and one that I'd recommend. You may also consider looking at Navigator's options (via the Options menu) and then looking at the caching options to ensure that documents are verified each time they are loaded, rather than once per session.

Here are some examples of some simple frameset-documents in general use:

```
<!--
  Program 9-1
-->
<html>
<frameset rows="100%" cols="50%,50%">
```

```
<frame src="file1.htm" name="frame1">
</frameset>
</html>
```

The previous example illustrates how a single frame is rendered onto the screen. The frame occupies half of the browser's screen. The second column is simply blanked out and left unselectable by the user. The file named `file1.htm`, which is loaded into the frame, resembles the following:

```
<html>
<body>
<font size=+1>
This is a HTML-formatted file called <tt>file1.htm</tt>
which is loaded into the frame in this example.<p>
Here are some fancy bullets:
<dl>
<dd><img hspace=3 src="internal-gopher-menu">Bullet 1
<dd><img hspace=3 src="internal-gopher-text">Bullet 2
<dd><img hspace=3 src="internal-gopher-unknown">Bullet 3
</dl>
</font>
</body>
</html>
```

In the following example, the concept of a *nested* frame is illustrated:

```
<!--
  Program 9-2
-->
<html>
<frameset rows="50%,50%">
<frame src="1.htm" name="frame1">
<frameset cols="70%,30%">
  <frame src="2.htm" name="frame2">
  <frame src="3.htm" name="frame3">
</frameset>
</frameset>
</html>
```

A "nested" frame is simply one set of `<frameset>` tags placed inside another set of `<frameset>` tags. In the previous example, two horizontal rows of equal size are created, and the file `1.htm` is loaded into the first. The second frame does not contain a file, but contains another `<frameset>` container with two column definitions, one `70%` in width, and the other `30%`. The files `2.htm` and `3.htm` are then loaded into these two frames, respectively. You will learn how to create nested-frames dynamically later in this chapter.

Targeting a Frame Using a Hyperlink

To make a frame the destination for a hyperlink, the <a href> tag that implements the hyperlink must include a target attribute. The target attribute specifies the name of the frame you want as the "destination" when you load a new document, or URL. For example, the tag:

```
<a href target="frame2" src="http://www.infoseek.com">
```

loads the URL http://www.infoseek.com—the home page for the popular Infoseek browser—into the frame with the name "frame2". Individual frames are named using the name attribute of the <frame> tag, for example, using the <frame name="frame2" ...> tag. Here is a hypothetical frameset-document, named index.htm, using two vertically aligned frames:

```
<!--
  Program 9-3
-->
<html>
<frameset cols="50%,50%">
<frame src="c1.htm" name="column1">
<frame src="c2.htm" name="column2">
</frameset>
</html>
```

The file c1.htm could include a hyperlink to load a document into the second frame (column2) and may resemble the following:

```
<html>
<body>
<a href="http://www.osborne.com" target="column2">Osborne's Site</a>
</body>
</html>
```

Finally, the file c2.htm is left empty awaiting some data to be loaded, and is, therefore, structured as an empty <body> container:

```
<html>
<body>
</body>
</html>
```

When the hyperlink *"Osborne's Site"* is clicked upon, the URL http://www.osborne.com is loaded into the second frame. The new URL could be loaded over the current frame by specifying the target as "column1." In pure-HTML, specifying anything but the name of the frame is unnecessary; JavaScript is stricter in respect to this, and you will have to use the parent property and frame's array to specify the frame you want to reference.

TIP: When you load a null document—that is, an empty document—ensure the document is not physically empty and has the bare minimum of tags, for example, `<body></body>`, `<html></html>`, or `<html><body></body></html>` , etc. If you try to load an empty—that is, zero bytes length file—Netscape will return the dreaded *"Document has no data"* error message.

If you don't like the idea of using external documents to populate frames, read the later section on using the `javascript:` URL, which shows how this can be avoided (useful for keeping your HTML documents compact, perhaps even with a single file).

Loading a Nonframed Document

If you need to load a nonframed document into a whole window, simply use the special name "_top" in the `target` attribute of your `<a href>`tag. For example, if a frame had the tag:

```
<a  target="_top" href="nonframe.htm">
Click here for no frames
</a>
```

then clicking on the link *Click here for no frames* would load a new document, `nonframe.htm`, into a complete window, erasing any frames currently on the screen.

Using Other Reserved Frame Names

When using the `target` attribute with a tag such as `<a href>` Navigator also understands the following reserved frame names (synonyms):

Reserved Name	Description
_blank	Always load this link into a new, unnamed window. A new window is actually treated as a single frame.
_self	Always load this link over the current frame.

Reserved Name	Description
_parent	Always load this link over the parent frame. This becomes _self if no parent exists.
_top	Always load this link at the top level. If you are already at the top level, this becomes _self.

For example, a hyperlink defined as:

```
<a href="file.htm" target="_self">
```

would load the file named file.htm into the current frame.

Anchors and Frames

Anchors warrant a separate discussion. The src attribute of the <frame> tag cannot contain an anchor. Anchors are created using the <a name=anchorName> tag; they are used with a <a href> hyperlink of the form <a href="#anchorName"> where anchorName is the anchor created by <a name=...>. Anchors are a navigational aid, which allows sections of a document to be targeted and moved using a hyperlink. Remote anchors are <a name> tags, which refer to anchors in different documents. In Netscape, the following HTML tag is impossible:

```
<frame src="http://www.wombat.com/file.htm#myanchor">
```

although you can create a *hyperlink* of the form:

```
<a href="file.htm#sec1>Section 1</a>
```

where file.htm is the file you want to load, and sec1 is the anchor you want to move to within this document when it is fully loaded into Navigator. The hyperlink can be placed in the file you load into the frame, but frames can only specify a URL that relates to a single HTML page , and not a document and an anchor together; for example:

```
<frame src="http://www.wombat.com/marsupial.htm#wombat">
```

is not valid since an anchor name has been specified (#wombat) within the src attribute of the <frame> tag—this part needs to be omitted since anchors are not supported in such URLs. In fact, the anchor will be ignored. To load a frame and than move to an anchor you could use the JavaScript location.hash property.

Selecting and Reloading a Frame

Netscape allows you to select a frame by clicking on it by using the mouse (click on an empty area within the frame). This makes the frame active, or *modal*. To reload a single frame, you can click on the frame, and then use Netscape's View menu. Then select the Reload Frame option, as illustrated in Figure 9-1.

Use this as a useful shortcut instead of reloading the entire document. If code has changed in different frames, though, you will need to completely refresh the document. In order to reload a frame you must regenerate the frame from scratch (see later sections). You can make Netscape reload a frame using JavaScript by simply assigning the current page back to the location.href property. This will have the effect of reloading the current page. For example, here is a form-button using an <input type="button"> tag, which invokes a JavaScript function to reload the current page:

```
<form>
<input type="button"
       value="Reload page"
       onClick="window.location.href=document.location">
</form>
```

In the previous example, the JavaScript event-handler, onClick, has been used to assign a value to the window.location.href property. The location.href property stores the URL (page address) of the document currently loaded. If this HTML is placed within a frame, clicking the *Reload page* button will act the same as pressing Netscape's *Reload* button in the main toolbar or by pressing CTRL-R. You could remove the button and make the code dependent on some other event, such as a time-out event (see Chapter 10 for more details) so the page is refreshed at a regular

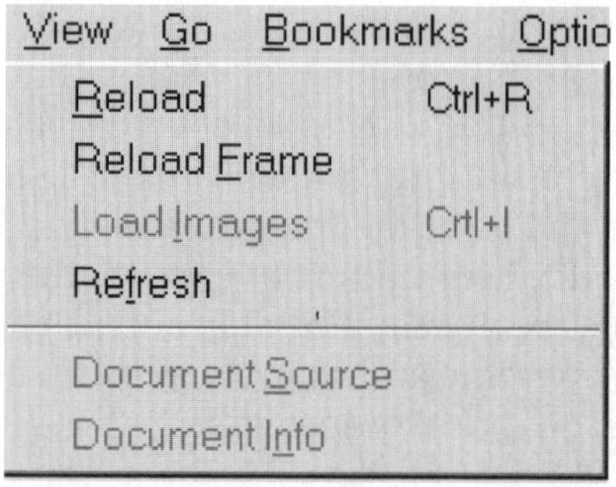

The
View/Reload
Frame menu
option in
Navigator
Figure 9-1.

time-interval. If a server-side CGI script was updating a file on a regular basis, you could refresh this file periodically into a frame.

Clearing a Frame's Contents

Clearing a frame—that is, removing the document held within the frame—can be achieved by opening and closing the frame using `document.open()`, and then `document.close()` together. The `document.clear()` method did not function in Navigator 2.*x* and the beta versions of Atlas. You can also clear a frame by "dynamically" creating a new frame, thus overwriting the other one. This technique is discussed in a later section of this chapter.

Keeping Your Code After Clearing a Frame

The only disadvantage to clearing a frame using the previous method is any JavaScript code in that document will be lost when the document is cleared; this means any functions defined within that frame will be lost. Obviously, you may only want to clear the visible content within the frame, and *not* the actual JavaScript code embedded within the document. Rather than regenerating the JavaScript code from scratch, which is one solution, you can alter your documents so the main portion of JavaScript code is placed in the frameset-document—that is, the HTML document that has the `<frameset>` container, also known as the *parent* document—and then use the `parent` property to refer to the function(s) you defined in the parent. For example, you could have the following HTML, which defines the JavaScript function `DontGoAway()`:

```
<!--
   Program 9-4
-->
<html>
<head>
<script>
<!--
function DontGoAway() {
   alert("See, it still works after the frame " +
         "has been cleared since the function " +
         "is in the parent document.");
}
//-->
</script>
</head>
<frameset rows="50%,50%">
<frame src="1.htm" name="frame1">
</frameset>
</html>
```

9

The `DontGoAway()` function is placed into memory when this document is initially loaded by Netscape. The frames are then created and the HTML document `1.htm` is loaded into the frame. Within the file `1.htm` is a form that contains a simple form-button to clear the frame, coded as follows:

```
<html>
<body>
Here is some text in frame 1.<p>
<form>
<input type="button"
       value="Clear frame 1"
       onClick="parent.frames['frame1'].document.open();
                parent.frames['frame1'].document.close();
                parent.DontGoAway();">
</form>
</body>
</html>
```

Notice how the `onClick` event-handler within the form-button opens and closes the frame (thus, clearing it) and then calls the `parent.DontGoAway()` function. Calling `DontGoAway()` by itself will not work because this particular function is not defined within the *current* document; instead, it is defined in the parent frameset-document. To refer to the top-level document, the `parent` property must precede the name of the function you are calling.

The end result of the previous example is you can now define functions that can be called from *any* frame, and you can safely regenerate a document without losing precious code in the process. By trying this example in your browser, you can see the `DontGoAway()` function is called successfully.

TIP: A JavaScript function is bound to the document in which it is created, that is, the *scope* of the function is the current document (or frameset-document in context to the previous example). You must use `parent.funtionName()` to refer to a function defined in the parent frameset-document. This effectively makes the function "globally" defined rather than "locally" defined, allowing you to call it from any document or program. Note that the `parent` property is only used with frame-based HTML documents. If you have nested frameset-documents that are created dynamically, the `top` property can be used to access top-level variables, etc.; this is discussed in a later section of this chapter. If you need to refer to a function or variable within another document loaded into a separate frame, you must explicity define the name of the frame in which the variable or function exists, for example, `parent.frameName.variable`, etc.

Using the `Javascript:` URL to Populate a Frame's Contents

Navigator 3.0 introduces a number of new Uniform Resource Locators, one being `javascript:` URL. The `javascript:` URL allows a JavaScript expression to be evaluated and its results displayed within a document (or frameset-document). The use of this URL is becoming important within the design of frame-based Web sites. You can use the `javascript:` URL by itself within Netscape's *Location:* field, along with any JavaScript function or expression. For example:

```
javascript:alert("Hello World!")
```

which would display the message *Hello World!* on the screen, although the use of this URL really comes into its own when used within JavaScript programs, especially in scripts that manipulate frameset-documents. Until recently, all of our frames have been populated by data arriving from a file or from the network using a `http://` URL, etc. The use of external files and URLs can be done away with by using the new `javascript:` URL. Consider the following example, which creates two horizontal frames of equal size, and then uses the javascript: URL to display two text-variables that contain some HTML-formatted text:

```
<!--
  Program 9-5
-->
<html>
<head>
<script language="JavaScript">
<!--
var f1="<body bgcolor=Blue>This is frame 1</body>";
var f2="<body bgcolor=Black>This is frame 2</body>";
//-->
</script>
</head>
<frameset rows="50%,50%">
<frame src="javascript:parent.f1">
<frame src="javascript:parent.f2">
</frameset>
</html>
```

The scope of the variables f1 and f2 is "global," i.e. they can be examined anywhere in the script, because they are defined outside of any `function` declaration. By using the `parent` property, you can refer to the variables. In this context, the *parent* document is, in fact, the current document because this is where the `<frameset>` container is located. Remember the scope of the variables must be global for this to work properly. The variables f1 and f2 are the equivalent of two separate HTML files, with the added bonus that they can be updated at any time (the ability to manipulate external files is something not provided in JavaScript, and may never be provided because of security concerns).

In addition to using variables within the `javascript:` URL, you can also use function-calls. For example:

```
<frame name="f1" src="javascript:parent.showResults()">
```

where `showResults()` is a JavaScript function defined within the `<script>` container of the frameset-document, perhaps resembling the following:

```
function showResults() {
  var results="<body>Here are some <b>HTML</b> " +
              "results</body>";
  return(results);
}
```

in which case the frame named as f1 will contain the text: "Here are some **HTML** results." The `return()` statement allows a JavaScript function to return a value, such as the HTML-formatted string in this example.

T IP: When you are using a variable to populate a frame with the `javascript:` URL it is safe to leave the variable empty because a file is not being physically loaded locally from a disk, or from the network. This would be impossible with an empty file loaded with the `<frame src=..>` tag, without an error message first being displayed by Netscape. In context to the previous example, the statement `var f1=""` would, therefore, load an empty frame.

By using a target-frame expression in an `<a href>` tag of the form:

```
<a href="mydoc.htm" target="javascript:parent.frames[1]">
Click here
</a>
```

you can load the document `mydoc.htm` into a *new* browser window, rather like using JavaScript's `open()` method. This happens because the `javascript:` URL loads a new document after evaluating the expression, by default. In this case, the expression is `parent.frames[1]`, which refers to the second frame in a frameset-document. You can use the `close()` method to close the window.

Dynamically Creating Frameset-Documents Using JavaScript

You can also create a frameset-document *dynamically* by using `document.write()` statements to generate the required HTML `<frameset>` tags. Such a facility is useful if you want to generate a frame-based document "on the fly" without hard-coding it into an HTML document. Dynamically creating frames also saves you from maintaining external HTML files that contain the necessary frameset tags. Consider the following example, which creates a frameset-document dynamically:

```
<!--
  Program 9-6
-->
<html>
<script language="JavaScript">
<!--
function genFrames() {
  var frameSpec = "<frameset cols='50%,50%'>" +
                  "<frame src='1.htm' name='f1'>" +
                  "<frame src='2.htm' name='f2'>" +
                  "</frameset>";
  document.open();
  document.write(frameSpec);
  document.close();
}
genFrames();
//-->
</script>
</html>
```

In this script, the variable `frameSpec` has some HTML-formatted text containing some frame tags. A stream is opened to the browser and the text is written out using a `document.write()` statement, thus creating the new frameset-document in the process. The `open()` and `close()` methods are required if you intend to regenerate a document, that is, if you want to write a completely new document into the browser's current window, or frame. When you generate dynamic frameset-documents, referring to external

9

HTML files when you populate various frames can be clumsy because the files may be difficult to locate, or they may not exist at all. To overcome this, simply use the `javascript:` URL within the `src` attribute of the `<frame>` tag, as illustrated earlier in this chapter. This will allow you to populate a frame from the value of a variable or from the value returned by a user-defined JavaScript function, etc.

Dealing with Browsers that Do Not Support Frames

Navigator 2.0 was the first Web client to support frameset-documents. Microsoft's Internet Explorer also recently built support for frames; other Web clients are expected to follow in the near future. To deal with a person reading a frameset-document who is not using Navigator 2.0, or other "frames-capable" browser, `<noframes>..</noframes>` can be provided. However, because `<noframes>` is only supported by Netscape Navigator, other browsers may be unable to interpret this tag and, as a result, may render a completely blank screen. The HTML-text placed with the `<noframes>` container should inform you that your Web browser does not support frames and you should consider upgrading to one that does. For instance, by extending the previous example to the following:

```
<!--
  Program 9-7
-->
<html>
<frameset rows="50%,50%">
<frame src="1.htm" name="frame1">
<frameset cols="70%,30%">
  <frame src="2.htm" name="frame2">
  <frame src="3.htm" name="frame3">
</frameset>
</frameset>
<noframes>
<hr>Sorry, you need a frames-compatible browser such as Netscape
2.0 to view these pages. Click <a href="index2.htm">here</a> for
a non-frames version.<hr>
</noframes>
</html>
```

you can check to see if you can use frames and, if not, you are given the option of loading a nonframes version of the site. Building a nonframes version of a Web site can be a time-consuming process although, usually, this only involves changing the main frameset-document itself because all the actual hyperlinks will still be intact. Any `<a href target=...>` tags will also still work, that is, they will still load the document(s) mentioned.

TIP: The `<noframes>..</noframes>` container is *only* currently recognized by Netscape (Navigator 1.1+ and 2.0), and this can be used to some advantage. All non-Netscape browsers will not render a `<frameset>` or `<frame>` tag; indeed, they will not render any tag that is unrecognized. However, because Netscape 1.2 (a nonframeset browser) will recognize `<noframes>`, you can include the HTML-text for a normal, nonframeset body within this container, thus providing compatibility for two browser-audiences at once (albeit, Netscape and perhaps Microsoft Internet Explorer audiences). For example, the following:

```
<!-- This will be seen by Netscape 2.x users -->
<frameset rows="50%,50%">
<frame name="f1" src="http://www.osborne.com">
<frame name="f1" src="http://www.mcgraw-hill.com">
</frameset>
<!-- This can be seen by Netscape 1.x users -->
<noframes>
<body>
This is the body of the document.<p>
</body>
</noframes>
```

The previous example illustrates the exception to the rule, where a `<body>` container *can* be included in a `<frameset>` document. When a Netscape 1.*x* user loads this page, he or she will see the text in between the `<noframes>..</noframes>` container, whereas a Netscape 2.*x* user will see a series of frames rendered onto the screen (the `<noframes>` container will be ignored by Navigator 2.0 because it is designed to handle frameset-documents).

Generating a frameset-document dynamically can also be useful when people may have different browser capabilities, some of which may not support frames. JavaScript, as an open standard, will eventually be integrated into a number of other Web clients. Currently, Netscape's Navigator and Microsoft's Internet Explorer are the only JavaScript-aware clients. By using JavaScript's `navigator` object with the `appName` and `appVersion` properties, you can create HTML, depending on the actual browser-version (which would otherwise require a server-side solution, such as a CGI Perl script, etc.). For example, In JavaScript, you could have the following code:

```
<!--
  Program 9-8
-->
<html>
<head>
<script language="JavaScript">
<!--
function checkBrowser() {
  var TheBrowser = navigator.appName + " " +
                   navigator.appVersion.substring(0,3);
  if (TheBrowser == "Netscape 2.0") {
    var frameSpec="<frameset cols='50%,50%'>" +
                  "<frame src='1.htm' name='f1'>" +
                  "<frame src='2.htm' name='f2'>" +
                  "</frameset>";
    document.open();
    document.write(frameSpec);
    document.close();
  }
  else {
        document.open();
        document.write("<body><hr>Sorry, you need" +
                       "<a href=http://home.netscape.com>" +
                       "Netscape 2.0</a> to use this " +
                       "site.<hr>");
        document.close();
  }
}
// Check what browser the person is using:
checkBrowser();
//-->
</script>
</head>
</html>
```

In the previous code excerpt, the variable `TheBrowser` contains values
returned by the `navigator` object's properties, `appName` and `appVersion`.
These are concatenated (joined) together and are then used in an `if`
statement to test whether or not Navigator 2.0 is being used by the user. If it
is, the frameset-document is created; otherwise, a message is displayed
telling the user a frames-compatible browser is required. The message
provides a hyperlink to the Netscape home page, so if the user is interested
they can download Netscape at a later stage. You could also redirect the user
to a nonframes set of pages instead, of course.

Watch for later tips and techniques on using Netscape's
`<noframes>..</noframes>` container for dealing with Netscape 1.*x* users.

Loading Different URLs into a Frame

Another common requirement is to load a different URL into a given frame. To achieve this, the `location` property of the frame should be altered by assigning it a valid URL value. This will cause Netscape to load the URL accordingly. Both networked and local documents can be loaded in this way. Consider the following example, which creates two frames and allows you to select a search engine of your choice (Infoseek or AltaVista), in this case by clicking an appropriate button. Depending on which button is clicked, the search engine is then loaded into the lower frame for you to see, and you can switch back and forth simply by reclicking :

```
<!--
  Program 9-9
-->
<html>
<head>
<script language="JavaScript">
<!--
var result = "<html><body>Your search engine will " +
             "be loaded here<p></body></html>";
function changeUrl1() {
  parent.frames['bot'].location="http://www2.infoseek.com";
}

function changeUrl2() {
  parent.frames['bot'].location =
         "http://altavista.digital.com";
}

function buttons() {
  var but = "<html><body><form>" +
            "<input type='button' value='Infoseek'" +
            "onClick='parent.changeUrl1()'>" +
            "<input type='button' value='Alta Vista'" +
            "onClick='parent.changeUrl2()'>" +
            "</form></body></html>";
  return(but);
}
//-->
</script>
</head>
<frameset rows="10%,90%">
<frame name="top"
       src="javascript:parent.buttons()"
       scrolling="no">
<frame name="bot"
```

9

```
        src="javascript:parent.result">
</frameset>
</html>
```

In the previous example, the document contains two frames, named `top` and `bot`, respectively. Both frames are loaded using variables via the `javascript:` URL. The top frame is populated with some buttons, while the bottom frame is initially set to a simple message. Each button in the first frame has an `onClick` event-handler associated with it, and each button calls a separate JavaScript function. For example, the first button invokes the `changeUrl1()` function, which simply contains the statement:

```
parent.frames['bot'].location="http://www2.infoseek.com";
```

that changes the URL in the second frame (named `bot` in this instance) to Infoseek's home page.

Loading Local Files into a Frame

Local file access requires a workaround in Navigator 2.01 and Atlas. First, a local file *cannot* be mentioned literally, that is, by itself as a valid URL (something you *can* do within a `<a href>` hyperlink), so a JavaScript assignment statement, such as:

```
parent.frames['bot'].location="myfile.htm";
```

will not work, at least not until a fix arrives—perhaps in a later Navigator release. Instead, you can use a local-file URL of the form `file:/drive|/dir/file` URL (or `file:///drive|/dir/file`). This technique, however, presents a further problem because the pipe character (|) seems to have been causing Netscape some grief on the Windows platform version, and an error may occur. To work around this problem the pipe character can be replaced with the code `%7c`, where `7c` is the hexadecimal representation of the decimal number 124, and where the ASCII value of 124 is the "|" character, which we require. Hexadecimal numbers span 0-9 and A-F; they must be preceded by a percent sign (%) when used within a URL-formatted string.

 TIP: The use of hexadecimal characters is highly beneficial because some filenames require special treatment. For example, a Macintosh file system can contain filenames that have spaces in them, something not allowed in DOS or Windows 95. Spaces are not allowed in URLs either, so an equivalent must be used. The space character has the ASCII value 32 (in hexadecimal this would be `%20`); so, a file named exactly as `"Java Script"` could be referenced within a URL as `"Java%20Script"`, which would allow the file to be loaded into Navigator. To use the `file:` URL to load the *local* hypertext file located at the URL,

```
c:\dir\myfile.htm
```

use a javascript statement of the form:

```
parent.frames['bot'].location="file:/c%7c/dir/myfile.htm";
```

where `frames['bot']` is the name of the lower frame, in context to the previous example. You can alter the directory names to work with your own application accordingly.

Working with "Nested" Frameset-Documents

JavaScript can also deal with nested frameset-documents, that is, frames that are nested within existing frames. Such a capability is important because the window-structure of an application can be changed dynamically, without recreating the entire HTML document; you can allow the user to open and shut down various frames dynamically. Nested-frames are slightly more complicated to understand because you are dealing with two frame *layers*, rather than one. You will also find frame object properties, such as `parent`, are no longer valid in some cases. Because the `parent` document refers to the *current* frameset-document, dynamically writing a completely new `<frameset>` container into an existing frameset-document will have the effect of altering Navigator's internal frame references to the extent that you cannot refer to the new nested frame using `parent`. Instead, window properties, such as `top`, must be used.

Consider the following HTML document and embedded JavaScript program, which, when loaded, has two frames, `frames[0]` and `frames[1]`, as illustrated in Figure 9-2.

```
<!--
  Program 9-10
-->
<html>
<head>
<script language="JavaScript">
<!--
function pop2() { return("This is frame 2"); }
function pop3() { return("This is frame 3"); }
var frame1 = "<body>This is frame 1<p><form>" +
```

```
                    "<input type=button value='Change Frames' "+
                    "onClick='parent.changeFrames()'>" +
                    "</form></body>";
var frame2 = "";
var frame3 = "<frameset cols='50%,50%'>" +
                    "<frame name=newf2 src='javascript:top.pop2()'>" +
                    "<frame name=newf3 src='javascript:top.pop3()'>" +
                    "</frameset>";

function changeFrames() {
   parent.frames['f2'].document.open();
   parent.frames['f2'].document.write(parent.frame3);
   parent.frames['f2'].document.close();
}
//-->
</script>
</head>
<frameset rows="50%,50%">
<frame name=f1 src="javascript:parent.frame1">
<frame name=f2 src="javascript:parent.frame2">
</frameset>
</html>
```

When the document is first loaded, the `<frameset>` container at the end of the file is read into Navigator:

```
<frameset rows="50%,50%">
<frame name=f1 src="javascript:parent.frame1">
<frame name=f2 src="javascript:parent.frame2">
</frameset>
```

The frameset-document as seen when the example is first loaded

Figure 9-2.

which, in turn, creates two horizontal frames of equal size named `f1` and `f2`, and which are reflected into the `forms` array in JavaScript as `forms[0]` and `forms[1]` (or `forms['f1']` and `forms['f2']`), respectively. The contents of both frames are taken from JavaScript variables `frame1` and `frame2`, rather than from separate files. The `parent` property has been used to refer to the variables because they are defined within the *current* frameset-document.

The top frame (`f1`) also contains a form-button that has an `onClick` event-attribute, which invokes a function called `changeFrames()`. The `changeFrames()` function is also defined within the current frameset document; it has been referred to using the `parent` property. When this button is clicked upon by the user, the following statements are executed:

```
...
parent.frames['f2'].document.open();
parent.frames['f2'].document.write(parent.frame3);
parent.frames['f2'].document.close();
```

which opens a new data-stream to the lower frame (`f2`), and then writes the contents of the variable `frame3` into the frame. The stream is then closed and the contents of the new frame appear shortly thereafter. In this instance, the new frame content is a new `<frameset>` document, which is defined within the variable `frame3`:

```
var frame3 = "<frameset cols='50%,50%'>" +
             "<frame name=newf2 src='javascript:top.pop2()'>" +
             "<frame name=newf3 src='javascript:top.pop3()'>" +
             "</frameset>";
```

As you can see, this new `<frameset>` container defines two vertical frames. At this stage, Navigator already has two frames defined. This new frameset-document is nested within the existing, lower frame, and appears as shown in Figure 9-3.

Now the document has three frames, but notice how the `top` property was used within the `src` attribute of the `<frame>` tags in the variable `frame3`. The `top` property refers to the topmost window: the main Navigator window. In Navigator, all variables are actually properties of this window. The `parent` property can no longer be used to refer to the variables created within the document because `parent` refers to the current frameset-document, and the current frameset-document is the `<frameset>` container, which is defined in the variable `frame3`, and which is now nested inside the lower frame of Figure 9-3, shown previously. Instead, the `top` property can be used to go up another *level* within the frameset-document hierarchy because this

9

This is frame 1

<button>Change Frames</button>

This is frame 2

This is frame 3

The new
frameset-
document as
seen when the
button is
clicked

Figure 9-3.

is where the functions `pop2()` and `pop3()` exist. These latter two functions simply return some text to place in the two new frames.

Referring to all these new frames now becomes slightly more complicated because instead of dealing with two frames, there are now four frames. Note that two new frames (`newf2` and `newf3`) are now embedded, or *nested*, within the original lower frame (`f2`). To refer to the frame `newf3`, you must use *a fully-qualified* expression, which starts from the topmost object (the main `window` object, in this case), then moves to the lower frame, `f2`, and then refers to the second frame within this, namely, `newf3`. In JavaScript, this would be either of the following (starting from the topmost JavaScript object) object-expressions:

♦   `top.frames[1].frames[1]`
♦   `top.frames['f2'].frames['newf3']`

TIP: If you lose track of your frames, or the syntax you should be using to refer to them, you can type a `javascript:alert()` expression into Navigator's *Location:* field (at the top of the window) with an appropriate expression to see the results. For example:

`javascript:alert(window.frames[1].frames[1])`

will show you the name attribute of the nested second frame, in this example, `newf3`. The output will be `<object newf3>`, which is the internal representation of a JavaScript object named `newf3`, a window object, in this case.

NOTE: Remember window objects and frame objects are the same, although you must use the correct property to refer to them, that is, `top` or `parent`. A *null* or *undefined* value will be displayed if the expression you type does not evaluate to any known object.

To load a new URL into the window (frame) `newf3`, you could have used the `src` attribute of the `<frame>` tag to load an appropriate page; otherwise, you could have written a user-defined function, such as the following modified version of `pop3()`:

```
function pop3() {
   return("<form><input type=button value='load file' " +
          "onClick='self.location=\"http://www.osborne.com\"'>" +
          "</form>");
}
```

which returns some HTML-formatted text that creates a form-button using an `onClick` event. The button, when clicked, updates the current frame's `location` property, thus loading the new URL specified into the current frame. The `self` property is a synonym for `top.frames[1].frames[1]` in this case; that is, it is a shorthand synonym for the current frame.

TIP: Sometimes you will run out of quotation marks during an expression. Not all attribute-values require quotation marks around them, although if you assign a value to a property, the value must be placed within quotes (as in the previous example where a URL was assigned to the `location` property of the current frame). In such a case, you should *escape* the quote, so it does not interfere with the rest of the statement. For instance, `\"` specifies a double quote. Because double quotes are already used in the `return` statement to return a string value, the use of a double quote without the preceding `\` character will make JavaScript think the string has ended when, in fact, it has not ended.

Pressing on the button in the example will, therefore, make Navigator load the home-page for the Web site named as `www.osborne.com`. Loading files locally from a disk requires a local-file URL of the form: `file:///drive%7c/dir/filename`, for example, `file:///d%7c/file/myfile.htm` to load the file named `d:\file\myfile.htm` from disk (`D:` is most probably a CD-ROM drive in this case). See the previous section that discusses the loading of local file URLs into frames for more information.

If you want to load a URL into the frame automatically, the simplest way is to use the `src` attribute of the `<frame>` tag. Or you could use the `onLoad` event-hander attribute to load different URLs. Consider the modified example of the previous program. This program uses the `body1` and `body2` variables to store HTML `<body>` tags that use the `onLoad` attribute to load new URLs into each frame:

```html
<!--
  Program 9-11
-->
<html>
<head>
<script language="JavaScript">
<!--
  var body1 = "<body onLoad=" +
              "'self.location=\"http://www.osborne.com\"'>" +
              "</body>";
  var body2 = "<body onLoad=" +
              "'self.location=\"http://www.mcgrawhill.com\"'>" +
              "</body>";
  var frame1 =
      "<body>This is frame 1<p><form><input type=button " +
      "value='Change Frames' onClick='parent.changeFrames()'>" +
      "</form></body>";

  var frame2 = "";
  var frame3 =
      "<frameset cols='50%,50%'>" +
      "<frame name=newf2 src='javascript:top.body1'>" +
      "<frame name=newf3 src='javascript:top.body2'>" +
      "</frameset>";

  function changeFrames() {
    parent.frames['f2'].document.open();
    parent.frames['f2'].document.write(parent.frame3);
    parent.frames['f2'].document.close();
  }
//-->
</script>
</head>
<frameset rows="50%,50%">
 <frame name=f1 src="javascript:parent.frame1">
 <frame name=f2 src="javascript:parent.frame2">
</frameset>
</html>
```

HTML-formatted text can be written into a nested frame by using the JavaScript `open()`, `write()`, and `close()` routines, as before, but with the name of the nested frame prefixed onto each statement, for example:

```
top.frames[1].frames[1].document.open();
top.frames[1].frames[1].document.write("Some <b>HTML</a>" +
    "-formatted text<p>");
top.frames[1].frames[1].document.close();
```

The previous statements could be invoked by a user-activated event, such as a button click, using an `onClick` event that calls a function, such as those shown earlier. In fact, all of the frame-based manipulation routines remain the same for nested frames, as they do for normal frameset-documents, albeit for the new referencing techniques mentioned in this section.

Further Frameset-Document Examples

This section contains a number of additional frameset-document examples that use facilities discussed earlier in the chapter.

♦ **Example 1:** Creating a simple frame with two columns

The following example uses both the `cols` and `rows` attributes at the same time. These attributes are not mutually exclusive, so they can be used together in this way. In this case, the final document will have two frames of equal size set side by side in two columns. The second row attribute will be empty and unselectable; the inclusion of the second row ensures only half the screen is used for the two frames. If the second `50%` in the `rows` attribute is omitted, the entire screen would be used (Navigator allocates the largest size possible, even though the percent stated is `50%` in this case):

```
<html>
<frameset rows="50%,50%" cols="50%,50%">
<frame src="1.htm" name="frame1">
<frame src="2.htm" name="frame2">
</frameset>
</html>
```

TIP: When using column-based frames, remember each frame will be numbered in an ascending clockwise order. In the previous Example 1, the top left-hand frame is `frames[0]`, and the top right-hand frame is `frames[1]`. If you name your frames at the beginning, you will avoid confusing the numbers (you can still use numbers to index frames after allocating names).

♦ **Example 2:** Loading frames with local and networked-data

In the following Example 2, two frames of equal size and horizontal alignment are defined. The `src` attribute of the first `<frame>` specifies the home page for the Web site at the URL `http://www.mcgraw-hill.co.uk` is to be loaded, while the second frame loads the local file named `test.htm`. Local files can be loaded using their name relative to the current directory:

```
<html>
<frameset rows="50%,50%">
<frame name="frame1" src="http://www.mcgraw-hill.co.uk">
<frame name="frame2" src="test.htm">
</frameset>
</html>
```

In this example, the first frame can be referenced using the JavaScript expression `parent.frames[0]`, or as `parent.frames['frame1']`—the latter is possible because the frame has been named as `"frame1"` using the `name` attribute of the `<frame>` tag.

TIP: Avoid using numeric index values to refer to frames; naming the frame using `<frame name=...>` is much easier, and then refer to the frame using `frames['name']` rather than `frames[0]`, etc. This is especially true for long and complex documents where counting each frame is difficult.

♦ **Example 3:** Appending data into a frame

The following Example 3 illustrates how data can be *appended* dynamically into a frame, and uses three HTML files: the first file, `ex_3.htm`, is a frameset-document that loads the HTML documents, named `ex_3a.htm` and `ex_3b.htm` respectively. This example also has some JavaScript code to carry out the frame-updating. Here is the code for file `ex_3.htm`:

```
<!--
  Program 9-12
-->
<html>
<frameset rows="50%,50%">
<frame src="ex_3a.htm" name="f1">
<frame src="ex_3b.htm" name="f2">
</frameset>
</html>
```

The code for file `ex_3a.htm` resembles the following:

```
<html>
<!--
  * ex_3a.htm
  * A document with some form button to generate
  * some HTML and place it in the second frame.
-->
<form>
<input type="button"
       value="Click me!"
       onClick="parent.frames[1].document.writeln('Hello<p>');">
</form>
</html>
```

Finally, the code for file ex_3b.htm resembles the following:

```
<html>
<!--
  * ex_3b.htm
  * Null document
-->
<body>
</body>
</html>
```

The file ex_3b.htm is an empty file, containing nothing but a comment and an empty <body> container. This will be used to load an empty frame in the example because without a src attribute in the <frame> tag, Navigator will not render the frame; i.e. it will not display the frame. When ex_3a.htm is loaded into the top frame, a button is rendered using the <input type="button"...> tag, with the words "Click Me!" shown on it. This button is associated with an onClick event so, when the button is clicked upon, a JavaScript command is executed; the command in question is

```
parent.frames['f2'].document.writeln('Hello<p>');
```

which writes the HTML-formatted text "Hello<p>" into the lower frame (frame2). Notice how the expression frames['f2'] has been used. You could also use frames[1] instead. To write text into a frame, and then *commit* it—that is, render it—a paragraph break (<p>) or equivalent—for example, <hr>—must be used; otherwise the text will not be shown. This can be a useful feature in itself because you can build up tags and then commit them at some later stage.

TIP: When writing data without using `open()` and `close()`, you must *commit* the data you are writing into a frame using a tag, such as `<p>` or `<hr>`.

The end result of this example is the text `"Hello!"` will be appended to the lower frame every time the button in the top frame is clicked upon. To overcome this and to regenerate the entire frame, a *data-stream* to the frame must be opened, a concept illustrated in the example below.

TIP: Without a `src` attribute mentioned within the `<frame>` tag, Netscape will not create the frame.

♦ **Example 4:** Refreshing a document with new data

Example 4 shows how to refresh a frame so a completely new document is generated: The `document.open()` and `document.close()` methods must be used. These function-calls must encapsulate the `write()` or `writeln()` statements you use to write information into the frame, as demonstrated in the following example.

The first file in this example, `ex_4.htm`, is a frameset-document, the parent document, which loads two documents named `ex_4a.htm` and `ex_4b.htm` into two frames. The frame structure has been changed slightly to display a column-based output. The file `ex_4a.htm`, the main frameset parent document, resembles the following:

```
<!--
  Program 9-13
-->
<html>
<frameset rows="50%" cols="50%,50%">
<frame src="ex_4a.htm" name="frame1">
<frame src="ex_4b.htm" name="frame2">
</frameset>
</html>
```

The code for file `ex_4a.htm`, the first frameset-document, resembles the following:

```
<html>
<!--
  * ex_4a.htm
```

```
    * Write a data-stream to another frame.
-->
<form>
<input type="button"
       value="Click me!"
       onClick="parent.frames['frame2'].document.open();
       parent.frames['frame2'].document.writeln('Hello<p>');
       parent.frames['frame2'].document.close();">
</form>
</html>
```

Finally, the file ex_4b.htm (the final frameset-document) resembles the following—this is a null document that is used to display an empty frame:

```
<html>
<!--
   * ex_4b.htm
   * Null document
-->
<body>
</body>
</html>
```

When the button in the top frame is pressed, the text in the lower frame is now shown only once on each press of the button. When writing more complex JavaScript applications, you will need to refresh a complete frame, rather than appending data to it; remember to use open() and close() accordingly. You should use open() and close() to encapsulate a group of write() or writeln() statements; everything in between these statements is *buffered* by Navigator, and then written out quickly as one large chunk of text into the browser's display area, such as a frame area, in this instance.

TIP: Remember a document refresh, which empties all frames, will also remove any JavaScript code previously loaded into a document. See the earlier section on how to use the parent property to refer to global JavaScript functions.

Rather than using multiple write() or writeln() statements, you can concatenate your text together using the string concatenation operator, "+", using a single JavaScript statement, for example:

```
document.write("This is how two strings can be " +
               "joined together");
```

♦ **Project 1:** USENET newsgroup selection script

This is the first of two projects in this chapter. This project implements a simple newsgroup launching script. Netscape's ability to read USENET (USErs NETwork) news is achieved though use of the `news:` URL. The `news:` URL has been modified and enhanced in Netscape Navigator, allowing article selection, newsgroup selection, and unsubscribing (see my book, *Netscape Navigator* (McGraw-Hill Europe), for more information on Netscape's news URLs). At a simple level, a `news:` URL resembles `news://news-server/group-name`, for example, `news://news.funet.fi/comp.lang.java`, where `news.funet.fi` is a USENET news server, and `comp.lang.java` is a popular group discussing the Java programming language. Netscape now has a fully integrated news-reader that allows server and group selection, and does this much better than a JavaScript application. The purpose here is to demonstrate JavaScript techniques, so you understand how such scripts are structured. Figure 9-4 illustrates the script running within Navigator:

The application itself is basically a frameset-document (split into two frames). You will need to understand how JavaScript treats HTML forms using the `forms` array property, although this is all quite straightforward (see Chapter 7).

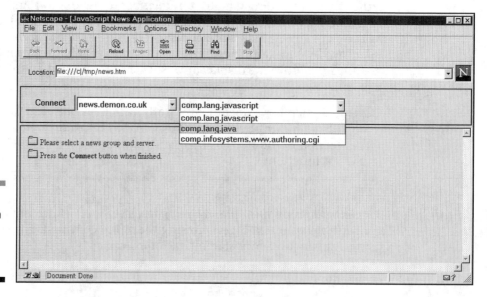

Project 1 running within Netscape Navigator

Figure 9-4.

```
<!--
  Program 9-14
-->
<html>
<head>
<title>JavaScript News Application</title>
<script language="JavaScript">
<!--
var results =
      "<html><body><font size=+1>" +
      "<img src='internal-gopher-menu' " +
      "hspace=5>Please select " +
      "a news group and server.<br>" +
      "<img src='internal-gopher-menu' hspace=5>Press the " +
      "<b>Connect</b> button when finished." +
      "</font></body></html>";

function chooseServer() {
  var botFrame=parent.frames['bot'];
  var idxs=parent.frames[0].document.forms[0].ns.selectedIndex;
  var idxg=parent.frames[0].document.forms[0].ng.selectedIndex;
  var nServ =
      parent.frames[0].document.forms[0].ns.options[idxs].text;
  var nGroup =
      parent.frames[0].document.forms[0].ng.options[idxg].text;
  var newsUrl = "news://" + nServ + "/" + nGroup;

  if (confirm("Shall I connect to: " + newsUrl)) {
      // Load --> news://servername/groupname
      parent.frames[1].location = newsUrl;
  }
}

function buttons() {
  var but = "<html><body>" +
            "<form name='f1'>" +
            "<input type='button' value='Connect'" +
            "onClick='parent.chooseServer()'> " +
            "<select name='ns'>" +
            "<option selected>news.demon.co.uk" +
            "<option>news.funet.fi" +
            "<option>news.cityscape.co.uk" +
            "</select> " +
            "<select name='ng'>" +
            "<option selected>comp.lang.javascript" +
            "<option>comp.lang.java" +
            "<option>comp.infosystems.www.authoring.cgi" +
            "</select>" +
```

```
                    "</form>" +
                    "</body></html>";
      return(but);
     }
//-->
</script>
</head>
<frameset rows="12%,88%">
<frame name="top"
        src="javascript:parent.buttons()"
        scrolling="no">
<frame name="bot"
        src="javascript:parent.results"
        scrolling="yes">
</frameset>
</html>
```

The previous HTML document and script use a number of form-properties to access values from two `<select>` tags. The `<select>` container tag was introduced in Chapter 7 and allows a pull-down list of options to be shown, one or more of which can then be selected by the user. In this project, the two selection-lists contain a list of news-servers and news-groups, each of which is placed with an `<option>` tag within the `<select>` container. The two selection-lists are named `ns` and `ng`, respectively, and are used within the `chooseServer()` function to extract the options chosen by the user. The `selectedIndex` property contains the item selected in a selection-list tag and is used with the name of the required selection-list to retrieve the item the user has chosen. Once the two selection-list items have been ascertained, a relatively long-winded process, the variable `newsUrl` is created that contains the `news:` URL required, and which is based upon the user's selections. The URL is then launched by altering the lower frame's `location` property. Because a news-based URL doesn't actually constitute an HTML document in Navigator 2.0 the statement instead launches Navigator's news-reading system and this appears shortly in a new browser window (assigning a URL to the frame is necessary just to actually *launch* the URL, note).

♦   **Project 2:** A document navigation system

The second project shows how a series of pages can be created, which can be navigated back and forth at will. This project uses a number of HTML files—not all of which are shown—that represent a number of pages, which can be viewed in succession. The page-updating is done by frame-manipulation using a series of buttons placed in an upper frame, whereas the main document is shown in the middle frame. A lower frame, or *footer*, is also included, and contains a field that shows the current page number.

The use of frameset-documents for page-movement is becoming more widespread on Navigator 2.0-compliant Web sites all across the Web. The navigation buttons in the frame named `frame1` are created using simple `<input type="button">` tags and have an associated `onClick` attribute to launch a navigation function that checks to see which page the user is on, and updates the frames accordingly. This is contained in the file `buttons.htm`. Each HTML "page" is called `page1.htm`, `page2.htm`, and so forth. Here is the main frameset-document, `index.htm`:

```
<!--
  Program 9-15
-->
<html>
<frameset rows="13%,74%,13%">
<frame name="frame1" src="buttons.htm" scrolling="no">
<frame name="frame2" src="page1.htm">
<frame name="frame3" src="footer.htm"  scrolling="no">
</frameset>
</html>
```

The file `buttons.htm` contains the JavaScript functions `left()`, `right()`, and `jump()`. The `left()` and `right()` functions allow left and right page movement, respectively; the `jump()` function allows a specific page number to be loaded; that is, `"3"` would load `page3.htm`, etc.

The variable `page` contains the current page number value, starting at 1, when the document initially loads. Whenever you click on a button, this variable is checked and updated accordingly. This system works for a maximum of three pages (`page1.htm`, `page2.htm`, and `page3.htm`), although this can be changed quite easily to any number of pages that you require. If you try to move past page 3, a warning message is displayed. Likewise, if you try to move before page 1, another warning message results—these are displayed using JavaScript's `alert()` method. When the script is loaded, the page number is set to 1; the value of the footer field is also set to 1. Notice how the `value` property is used to assign a value to a `<input>` field:

```
<html>
<!--
  buttons.htm
-->
<head>
<script language="JavaScript">
<!--
  page = 1;
  parent.frames[2].document.forms[0].pageNum.value = "1";
```

```javascript
// Jump to a specific page, and validate the user input:
function jump() {
  var pageNum = prompt("Enter a page number:", "");
  if (pageNum != page) {
  if (pageNum > 3) {
     alert("Page number " + pageNum + " does not exist!");
  }
  else {
     // abs() returns an unsigned number i.e. -1
     // becomes 1:
     pageNum = Math.abs(pageNum);
     page = Math.abs(pageNum);
     // Page names 'page1.htm', 'page2.htm' ...
     parent.frames[2].document.forms[0].pageNum.value =
            pageNum;
     parent.frames[1].location = "page" + pageNum +
            ".htm";
  }
  }
}


// Move left a page (-1):
function left() {
  if (page==1) {
     alert("You are at the first page!");
  }
  if (page==2) {
     page --;
     parent.frames[2].document.forms[0].pageNum.value="1";
     parent.frames[1].location="1.htm";
  }
  if (page==3) {
     page --;
     parent.frames[2].document.forms[0].pageNum.value="2";
     parent.frames[1].location="2.htm";
  }
}


// Move right a page (+1):
function right() {
  if (page==3) {
     alert("You are at the last page!");
  }
  if (page==2) {
     page ++;
     parent.frames[2].document.forms[0].pageNum.value="3";
     parent.frames[1].location="3.htm";
  }
```

```
      if (page==1) {
         page ++;
         parent.frames[2].document.forms[0].pageNum.value="2";
         parent.frames[1].location="2.htm";
      }
   }
//-->
</script>
</head>
<body>
<table border=0 cellpadding=0 cellspacing=1>
<tr>
<td align="left">
    <form><input type="button" value="<<"
                 onClick="left()"></form>
</td>
<td align="left">
    <form><input type="button" value=">>"
                 onClick="right()"></form>
</td>
<td align="left">
    <form><input type="button" value="Goto"
                 onClick="jump()"></form>
</td>
</tr>
</table>
</body>
</html>
```

The files `page1.htm`, `page2.htm`, and `page3.htm` contain the HTML-text you want to display within the main (middle) frame of the browser. To allow the script to function properly, `page1.htm` simply contains the following *bare-bones* HTML:

```
<html>
<!--
  page1.htm
-->
<body>
<img src="internal-gopher-menu"> This is page 1 of 3<p>
</body>
</html>
```

In these pages, you can place your own application's main body part, including text, graphics, and even other JavaScripts, applets, etc.

The file `footer.htm` contains a page-number field and whatever other HTML-formatted text (logos, etc.) you require in your application, for example:

```
<html>
<!--
   footer.htm
-->
<body>
<form>
PAGE NUMBER <input name="pageNum"
                     type="text"
                     size=7>
</form>
</body>
</html>
```

Figure 9-5 illustrates the application running within Navigator (with page-jump option selected).

Summary

Frameset-documents are an important concept for the JavaScript developer, since they allow more advanced document display and navigation techniques that would otherwise not be possible.

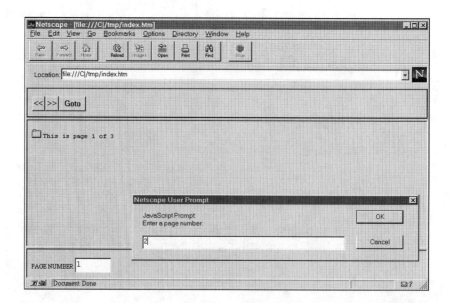

Project 2
running under
Navigator
Figure 9-5.

♦ Frameset-documents can be identified by use of the `<frameset>` container *instead* of a `<body>` container. Do not mix the `<frameset>` and `<body>` tags together within a single HTML document.

♦ The `frames` array is used to reference a frame within JavaScript. You must use the `parent` property to access this; for example, `parent.frames[0]` refers to the first frame, that is, the first `<frame>` tag.

♦ If you use the `name` attribute of the `<frame>` tag, you can refer to a frame using the expression `parent.frames['textname']` rather than `parent.frames[n]`, etc., where `textname` is the name of a frame allocated within the `name` attribute of the HTML `<frame>` tag.

♦ The `javascript:` URL is new to Navigator 2.0 and allows a JavaScript expression, such as a command, function call, etc., to be evaluated and to have its result displayed. This is a useful URL for creating dynamic frame contents (see previous examples).

♦ The `parent` property refers to the document that contains the `<frameset>` container. This may even be the *current* document if the `javascript:` URL has been used to populate a frame from a JavaScript variable.

♦ The `src` attribute of the `<frame>` tag specifies either a filename—for example, `file.htm`—or a Uniform Resource Locator (URL) of a file—for example, of the form `http://hostname/filenameOrPath`.

♦ To clear a frame, use the `document.open()` and `document.close()` methods immediately after one another. Note that any JavaScript code in the document being cleared will be lost in the process, so define functions in the *parent* document, and then call these using the `parent` property, as illustrated previously. When dynamically writing data into a frame to *replace* that frame with new information, remember to encapsulate any `document.write()` or `document.writeln()` statements inside a `document.open()` and `document.close()`. If you are not using `open()` and `close()`, issue an HTML paragraph break (`<p>`) to *commit* the data to the frame. The only problem with this latter approach is that data will be *appended* to the frame, which may not be the effect you require. The `open()` and `close()` methods open a *stream* to the frame, refreshing the entire document on each occasion. Remember to use `document.open()`, not `open()` by itself; using `open()` by itself will open a new browser window because the `window` object is the top-level object in JavaScript.

♦ When you need a hyperlink to target a frame, use the `target=frameName` attribute of the `<a href>` tag, where `frameName` is the name of the frame, as defined in the `name` attribute of the `<frame>` tag. Use the special frame synonym called `"_top"` to load a document into a completely new, top-level window, that is—a single browser window rather than a window with separate frames—and `"_self"` to load a document into the currently active frame.

CHAPTER 10

Using JavaScript's Time-Out Mechanisms

A *time-out* is a JavaScript-initiated event, which is created using the `setTimeout()` method. Time-outs are useful in applications that need to generate events that occur independently and, perhaps, with a certain regularity. A time-out is a *countdown* to a user-specified action, in this case, a function-call or a series of other JavaScript statements.

In this chapter you will learn how to

♦ Create and remove time-out events

♦ Build time-out events into your HTML applications

♦ Build recursive time-out applications

♦ Embed real-time clocks, animation scripts, and more into your applications

An Introduction to Time-Out Events

Time-outs can be used for many purposes, including real-time clocks, simple animation techniques, and updating pages within a Web site on a regular basis.

Creating a Time-Out Using `setTimeout()`

To initiate a time-out event, simply use the setTimeout() method with the following syntax:

```
var timeoutID = setTimeout(expression, msecs);
```

The setTimeout() method returns a time-out identification value that identifies this particular time-out event. Note that you should always assign setTimeout() to a variable in this way, so you can disable the event at a later stage with the clearTimeout() method. The expression can be any valid JavaScript statement or statements; multiple statements must be separated by semicolons (;). You can also specify a JavaScript function; this is useful for making your code more readable, rather than bunching groups of statements together. All time-out events happen in the future, as specified by the msecs argument, which represents the number of milliseconds after which the expression is invoked: One second is equivalent to 1,000 milliseconds. Note that the msecs argument must be specified in milliseconds.

TIP: When a time-out event is active, moving to a new page will cancel the time-out. When you return to the page, the time-out will be reactivated *only* if the code in your script specifically restarts the event, that is, in a <body onLoad> or by executing the necessary code from within a <script> statement.

Removing a Time-Out Using `clearTimeout()`

To disable a time-out event created with `setTimeout()`, use the `clearTimeout()` method, which has the syntax:

```
clearTimeout(timeoutID)
```

where `timeoutID` is the identification number of the time-out event you want to disable. Such values are returned by `setTimeout()` when a time-out event is first created.

TIP: A time-out variable will contain the value `null` if it has not yet been set (as will all variables). You can test if a particular time-out exists before canceling it, although cancellation of a nonexistent time-out will not result in an error message from Navigator.

Consider the following example, which creates a time-out event that issues an *alarm-call* within a specified number of minutes into the future. Notice how the user's input is modified to represent the number of milliseconds passed to the `setTimeout()` function.

```
<!--
  Program 10-1
-->
<html>
<head>
<title>Alarm Call Script</title>
<script language="JavaScript">
<!--
  var alarmId;
  function alarmFunc() {
    // Sound the alarm call. You could play a sound here
    // as well, by using location=soundfile, etc.
    alert("ALARM CALL!");
  }
  function startTimeout(id) {
    var minutes = prompt("How many minutes?",0);
    // Time-outs are measured in milliseconds, so if the
    // user enters 1 minute, we need to multiply by 6000.
    alarmId = setTimeout("alarmFunc()", minutes*6000);
  }
//-->
</script>
</head>
```

```
<body>
<form>
<input type=button
       value="Start"
       onClick="startTimeout()">
<input type=button value="Cancel"
onClick="clearTimeout(alarmId)">
</form>
</body>
</html>
```

When this script is loaded into Navigator, two form-buttons are created: The first creates a new time-out event; the second cancels the event. The prompt() method is used to obtain the number of minutes for the alarm-call; it is stored in the variable minutes. The setTimeout() method is then invoked. Notice how the value for minutes is converted into milliseconds. alarmFunc() is the name of the function called when the time-out event occurs. It displays a simple message using the alert() method. By clicking on the Cancel button, the current time-out event will be stopped using clearTimeout(). The event identification number is held in the variable alarmId and is passed to the clearTimeout() method to clear the time-out event.

Real-Time Clocks

Time-outs are especially useful for creating real-time clocks, which update either by the second or by the minute. This section explores how JavaScript can be used to create both text-based and graphical clocks, which can be embedded within your HTML application.

Creating a Text-Based Clock

By updating a text-field within a form that is constantly set to the current time, you can display a real-time clock within a text-field in your HTML document. Consider the following application:

```
<!--
  Program 10-2
-->
<html>
<head>
<script language="JavaScript">
<!--
function showTime() {
  // Get the current time and then extract the
  // hours, minutes and seconds:
```

```
    var timeNow = new Date();
    var hours   = timeNow.getHours();
    var minutes = timeNow.getMinutes();
    var seconds = timeNow.getSeconds();
    // Alter the time format so it is a 12-hour clock:
    var timeString = "" + ((hours > 12) ? hours - 12 : hours);
    // Break up the time as HH:MM:SS, making sure that
    // each field has at least two digits:
    timeString  += ((minutes < 10) ? ":0" : ":") + minutes;
    timeString  += ((seconds < 10) ? ":0" : ":") + seconds;
    // Add an A.M./P.M. indicator based on the current hour
    timeString  += (hours >= 12) ? " P.M." : " A.M.";
    // Update the time-field in the document:
    document.htmlClock.timeField.value = timeString;
    // Update the clock every 1 second:
    timerID = setTimeout("showTime()", 1000);
}
//-->
</script>
</head>
<body onLoad="showTime()">
<form name="htmlClock">
<input type="text"
       name="timeField"
       size=14>
</form>
</body>
</html>
```

When this script is loaded into Navigator, the function showTime() is invoked from an onLoad attribute, which is referenced in the <body> tag. showTime() creates a Date object and from this, extracts the hours, minutes, and seconds, and then stores these in three variables of the same name. JavaScript stores the time in a 24-hour format; to change this to a 12-hour clock, you must test to see if the hours are greater than 12. If they are, 12 hours are simply taken away to leave the 12-hour equivalent. The variable timeString is used to store the combined hours, minutes, and seconds as a text-string of the form HH:MM:SS. The only form within the document is named htmlClock, which has a single text-field named timeField. This text-field is set to the value of the timeString variable and the current time appears within the field.

To keep updating the time second-by-second, a time-out event is used to call the current function repetitively. This is known as a recursive time-out because a time-out is being used to call the current function. The time-out delay is specified as 1,000 milliseconds, thus updating the clock every second. Text-fields are ideal for the continuous updating of text because they can be rendered onto the screen quickly by Navigator.

Instead of using a text-field, you can create a graphical clock based on small GIF images used to represent each digit of the time. While this has no speed advantages, the display is more attractive within a Web page.

Creating a Graphical Clock

Consider the next application, based around a frameset-document. A single frame is used to display the clock, and a time-out event refreshes the frame every minute. This application consists of four files: `10-3.htm`, the main frameset-document; `clocka.htm`, the upper-left frame; `clockb.htm`, the upper-right frame; and `clockc.htm`, the lower frame, making a total of three frames. The clock will appear in the upper-left frame—named `topLeftFrame` in the example.

The digits for the clock are small image files stored in the GIF format. They were found on the Internet (see Appendix C), and they are also included in the disk that accompanies this book, so you can create your own version of the program. The digits are named `dg0.gif` to `dg9.gif`, respectively. In addition to the digits 0-9, there is also a field separator (`dgc.gif`), and an A.M. and P.M. indicator (`dgam.gif` and `dgpm.gif`, respectively). The main frameset-document, `clock.htm`, is structured as follows, and contains the code for the clock:

```
<!--
  Program 10-3
-->
<html>
<head>
<script language="JavaScript">
<!--
  var timerId, bodyString, timeString, result;
  var urlPrefix = "file:///c%7c/clock/";
  var imgStart = "<img height=20 width=15 src=" +
      urlPrefix+"dg";
  var colon = "<img height=20 width=15 src=" +
      urlPrefix+"dgc.gif>";
  var amind = "<img height=20 width=15 src=" +
      urlPrefix+"dgam.gif>";
  var pmind = "<img height=20 width=15 src=" +
      urlPrefix+"dgpm.gif>";
  var imgEnd = ".gif>";
  function showTime() {
    var today        = new Date();
    var hours        = today.getHours();
```

```
        var minutes     = today.getMinutes();
        var indicator   = amind;|
        if (hours >= 12) {
            hours = (hours-12);
            indicator = pmind;
        }
        if (hours == 0)
            hours = 12;
        hours = "" + hours;
        if (minutes < 10)
            minutes = ("0" + minutes);
        else
            minutes = ("" + minutes);
        minutes = "" + minutes;
        var hourLen = hours.length;
        var minLen  = minutes.length;
        bodyString  = "";
        timeString  = "";
        // Hours:
        for (var n=0; n < hourLen; n++) {
            timeString += imgStart + hours.substring(n, n+1) +
                        imgEnd;
        }
        timeString += colon;
        // Minutes:
        for (var n=0; n < minLen; n++) {
            timeString += imgStart + minutes.substring(n, n+1) +
                        imgEnd;
        }
        timeString += indicator;
        bodyString = "<html><body bgcolor=Black><center>" +
                    timeString +
                    "</center></body></html>";
        return(bodyString);
    }
    function setTimer() {
      result = showTime();
      parent.frames[0].document.open();
      parent.frames[0].document.write(result);
      parent.frames[0].document.close();
      // Update the clock every minute:
      timerId = setTimeout("setTimer()", 60000);
    }
  function removeTimer() {
      clearTimeout(timerId);
    }
//-->
</script>
```

```
</head>
<frameset rows="11%,*">
  <frameset cols="14%,*">
    <frame name="topLeftFrame"
         src="clocka.htm"
         noresize
         scrolling="no">
    <frame name="topRightFrame"
         src="clockb.htm"
         noresize
         scrolling="no">
  </frameset>
  <frame name="botFrame" src="clockc.htm">
</frameset>
</html>
```

Document `clocka.htm` is loaded into the upper-left frame and uses an `onLoad` event to call the `setTimer()` function defined with the parent window; hence, the use of the `parent` synonym.

```
<html>
<head>
</head>
<body onLoad="parent.setTimer()">
</body>
</html>
```

The other frames—`clockb.htm` and `clockc.htm`—are just *stubs*, into which you can place your own HTML-formatted text later. These frames occupy the upper-right and lower frames, and resemble the following:

```
<html>
<body bgcolor="Black">
</body>
</html>
```

Or you can just place a hash (#) or a `javascript:` call in the `<frame>` tag's `src` attributes to load an empty frame. The tags that relate to the digit separator and A.M./P.M. indicators are hard-coded HTML tags, which are stored within JavaScript variables.

The variable `urlPrefix` contains a URL that specifies where the images for the clock are physically stored—in this case, the local directory `C:\CLOCK` on my own hard-disk, although they could be referenced from another Web server using a `http://`-prefixed URL. If you upload this application, and all the GIF images that belong with it, to a Web server at the URL:

```
http://www.somehost.com/main/
```

be sure to store the value `"http://www.somehost.com/main/"` into the variable `urlPrefix`—note the final slash. If you use the application locally, use a local `file:`-based URL of the form `file://drive%7c/directory`, where `drive` is the disk drive, and `directory` is the path to the directory in which the application and digits reside. The `%7c` is a hexadecimal value, which places the pipe (|) character into the URL (the literal placement of this character causes an error under Navigator 2.0 and Atlas—try it on your system, and change it accordingly).

In this application, the images start with the letters `"dg"` (for *digit*), although you can change this prefix. The idea is to examine each digit, and then integrate this, via some simple string-manipulation, into a string that references the required image-digit, that is, `"0"` maps to `"dg0.gif"`, and so forth. All times are shown using a 12-hour notation in this application, so you must examine the hour and minute values to see if they need alteration. For example, if the current hour is greater than or equal to 12, you would simply subtract 12 hours (for a 12-hour clock). At this stage, it has been determined that it is P.M. (`hours >= 12`), so you can change the indicator type as well:

```
if (hours >= 12) {
    hours = (hours-12);
    indicator = pmind;
}
if (hours == 0)
    hours = 12;
```

You should also check for the situation where the hour value is zero—that is, twelve o'clock—and reassign the literal value of `"12"`. So all variables are treated as strings, a null string is prefixed onto all values, for example:

```
hours = "" + hours;
```

which turns the numeric variable `hours` into a string-typed variable. The same is done for the `minutes` variable. String-values are needed because you will use the `substring()` method to scan through each digit to allocate a corresponding image-file; for example, for an hour value of `"12"`, you will need `dg1.gif` (1) and `dg2.gif` (2), respectively. Scanning through the `hours` and `minutes` variables is done with a `for` statement. The `hours` string resembles the following:

```
for (var n=0; n < hourLen; n++) {
    timeString += imgStart + hours.substring(n, n+1) +
```

```
                imgEnd;
}
```

where `hourLen` is the length of the `hours` string variable (assigned from `hours.length`). The variable `timeString` is then used to build up a series of HTML-formatted tags, which contain each of the required digits. The value of `timeString` after processing one digit, say `"1"`, as in 1 P.M., is the string:

```
"<img height=20 width=15 src=" +
"file:///c%7c/clock/" +
"dg" +
"1" +
".gif>"
```

or when concatenated together, the HTML-text:

```
<img height=20 width=15 src=file:///c%7c/clock/dg1.gif>
```

that references the image-file named `dg1.gif`, in this instance. Remember to change this URL to your own requirements. After processing the `hours`, a separator image is appended (this is just an image of a colon character) so the hours and minutes are not set directly next to one another:

```
timeString += colon;
```

where `colon` is a variable that stores the HTML tag to load the separator image. In context to our example, the `timeString` variable would now store the value:

```
<img height=20 width=15 src=file:///c%7c/clock/dg1.gif>
<img height=20 width=15 src=file:///c%7c/clock/dgc.gif>
```

The same operation is carried out for the `minutes` variable, after which an A.M./P.M. indicator image is added. The end-result is a long string of text, which contains each of the image-files that make up the current time. All this text is then placed within a `<body>` container and returned from the function as a string-value. The function `setTimer()` invokes the `showTime()` function when the document is loaded via an `onLoad` event-attribute. `setTimer()` simply invokes the `showTime()` function and assigns the return-value to the variable `result`, which is then written out to the browser using the `document.write()` method. It is important to use the `open()` and `close()` methods to ensure the document in the upper-left frame is completely replaced when the time changes.

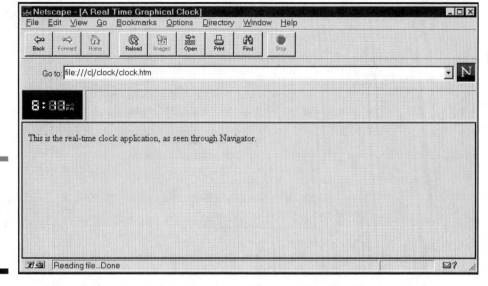

The graphical
clock
application as
seen through
Navigator
Figure 10-1.

To make the clock actually *tick*—that is, update itself—a `setTimeout()` method reinvokes the `setTimer()` function with an interval of `60000` milliseconds, or 60 seconds—all clock-based applications need such a *recursive* time-out event. To display each second using this method would be impractical because the overhead of updating the frame and reloading the appropriate digit(s) would take longer than a second, even on a very fast computer. You could use a text-field, as in the case of the previous real-time clock, which used a form field. Figure 10-1 illustrates the clock in action, as seen through Navigator.

Updating Frames Using Time-Out Events

Time-out events are also useful for updating the contents of individual frames within a frameset-document, allowing pages to be rotated or updated on a regular basis; this allows the pages of a Web site to be shown to you without any further interaction—this is known as a *walk-through*. In the following example, a frame is updated at a regular time interval. The main parent frameset, `10-4.htm`, is structured as follows and contains the code to perform the walk-through:

```
<!--
  Program 10-4
-->
<html>
<head>
```

```
<script language=JavaScript">
<!--
 var thisPage = 1;
 var timerId;
 var textMessage = new Object();
 textMessage[1] = "<body>This is message 1 of 3<p></body>";
 textMessage[2] = "<body>This is message 2 of 3<p></body>";
 textMessage[3] = "<body>This is message 3 of 3<p></body>";
 function scrollPage() {
   // Load the current message:
   var thisMsg = textMessage[thisPage];
   // Write a stream of text into the top frame (f1):
   parent.f1.document.open();
   parent.f1.document.write(thisMsg);
   parent.f1.document.close();
   // Update page counter:
   thisPage ++;
   if (thisPage > 3)
     thisPage = 1;
   // Call this function again in 30 seconds time:
   timerId = setTimeout("scrollPage()", 30000)
 }
//-->
</script>
</head>
<frameset rows="15%,*">
<frame name="f1" src="rotate.htm" scrolling="no">
<frame name="f2" src="bottom.htm" scrolling="yes">
</frameset>
</html>
```

The file, `bottom.htm`, is a blank HTML file in this instance; it would normally contain some text to be placed in the lower-frame. The upper-frame is loaded with the file, `rotate.htm`, and contains the code that invokes the `scrollPage()` function defined in the parent document:

```
<html>
<body onLoad="parent.scrollPage()">
</body>
</html>
```

Notice how the `parent` property prefixes the `scrollPage()` function. Because this function is defined within the parent frameset-document, and not the current document, this ensures the function is located, and then invoked. The current page number is also defined as the variable `thisPage`.

When `index.htm` is loaded, a number of global variables are created. The `thisPage` variable tracks the current page; this application will load a frame in three stages, that is, 1, 2, 3, 1, 2 . . ., etc. The HTML-formatted text that is actually loaded into the upper-frame is held within the `textMessage` array, as elements `textMessage[1]`, `[2]`, and `[3]`, respectively. The `scrollPage()` function carries out the frame-update and updates the page-counter variable to ensure all three values within the `textMessage` array are displayed. Finally, a recursive time-out event is set to update the frame in 30 seconds, that is, 30000 milliseconds. The effect seen within Navigator is an updated frame that is updated indefinitely until a new page is loaded.

TIP: You may find a recursive time-out event doesn't run when the code to update a frame is not placed within the parent (or top-level) document. This seems due to a bug in Navigator. Place all your time-out code in the top-level frameset document, and then call this from a child document using a tag such as: `<body onLoad="top.functionName()">`, where `functionName()` is the function in the top-level document you want to call, as shown in the previous digital-clock example. Use this technique when you need to update a frame continually using a recursive time-out function.

Using the `<meta>` Tag to Perform Updates

Navigator also implemented a similar feature for loading URLs after a prespecified time, using a modified form of the `<meta>` tag. A `<meta http-equiv="Refresh">` tag of the form: `<meta http-equiv="Refresh"; content="30; url=file2.htm">` will cause Navigator to load the file named `file2.htm` in 30 seconds time. This method can be used to reload a frame with new data in the same way as the previous JavaScript program, although a complete HTML document must be loaded (JavaScript can load HTML-formatted text-variables, which can be changed at any time). The `<meta http-equiv>` tag also suffers badly because once it is parsed by Navigator, the countdown starts at *this* precise moment. If a complicated page takes a longer time to download, the `<meta>` tag has no way to know this. As a result, the next page will be loaded before the previous page has been fully loaded. JavaScript time-outs do not suffer from this problem because you can more accurately control the placing of the time-out within the program; that is, you can ensure the time-out occurs after a document has been loaded, as previous examples demonstrate.

Scrolling Text-Fields and Status Bars

A scrolling message is another effect that can be implemented with a time-out. Scrolling messages can be implemented in text-fields or by using the Navigator status bar. They are useful to show long messages, which occupy more space (vertically) than the screen. Scrolling indicators such as these are known as *ticker-tape* applications.

Scrolling Status Bars

The Navigator status bar is used to present system messages to you. The status bar is reflected into the `window.status` property within JavaScript, so it can be used as a scrolling area to present messages. Consider the following script:

```
<!--
  Program 10-5
-->
<html>
<head>
<script language="JavaScript">
<!--
 var timerId;
 var msg = "This is an example of a scrolling message";
 var counter = 0;

 // Is the timer already running?
 if (timerId != null)
    clearTimeout(timerId);

 function pad() {
  var padding = "";
   for (var n=0; n <= (100+msg.length); n++)
      padding += " ";
   return(padding);
 }

 function scroll() {
  newMsg = pad() + msg + " ";
  window.status = newMsg.substring(counter, newMsg.length);
  if (counter == newMsg.length) {
     window.defaultStatus="Netscape";
     clearTimeout(timerId);
  }
  counter ++;
  timerId = setTimeout("scroll()", 500); // 0.5 seconds
  return true;
 }
```

10

```
 // Start the scroller function:
 scroll();
//-->
</script>
</head>
</html>
```

When this script is loaded, the `scroll()` function is automatically invoked. This takes the message you want to display, as stored in the `msg` variable, and prepends (prefixes) a string of 100 spaces using the `pad()` function. These characters must be added so the message scrolls from the right-hand side of the status bar to the left—the initial spaces ensure this happens; otherwise, the message will appear flush left to the status bar, and will then scroll to the left. If this is the effect you are after, you can omit the calling of the `pad()` function entirely. The *scrolling* effect itself is nothing more than a continuous update of the status bar using the `substring()` method. By continually extracting a smaller substring of the message (from left to right) you can portray the scrolling effect on the screen. The time-out event is set to one half second in this example (500 milliseconds), ensuring a rapid scroll-rate, which you can alter accordingly.

The time-out is cleared when the message has fully scrolled off the screen, at which time the status bar is set back to the value `"Netscape"`. Note that you can change this to any value you require. Notice how the `defaultStatus` property has been used here.

TIP: The `window.defaultStatus` property in the status bar message is a transient property whose value is shown only when the status bar is empty. The `window.status` property represents the current active message shown. You *must* return a `true` value after altering the value of these properties to ensure the value is placed into the status bar. You can see an example of a transient message by placing the mouse briefly over one of the navigation toolbar buttons within Navigator—the status bar message changes to show you what action the button performs, and then changes back when you move away from the toolbar.

HTML-formatted text cannot be used in the scrolled-message because the status bar is not part of the browser's HTML viewing area. You can concatenate other variables and object properties into the message if required.

TIP: Remember to update the status bar dynamically instead of creating a new string object on each pass of the loop. The latter method causes Navigator to create a new string object, and you may run out of memory or, at least, notice a decrease in performance.

Scrolling status bars work best with long messages. Another good idea is to place a large gap in-between successive messages so you can see something new is coming along. For example, in context to the previous script, you could consider a message-string set as:

```
var msg = "This is the first scrolling message" + pad() +
          "This is the second scrolling message";
```

If you need the scrolling effect to continue, simply change the following portion of code within the program that resembles:

```
if (counter == newMsg.length) {
   window.defaultStatus="Netscape";
   clearTimeout(timerId);
}
```

to the following:

```
if (counter == newMsg.length)
   counter = 0;
```

Unfortunately, the message itself must be held statically, that is, it must be hard-coded. The presentation of nonstatic information is difficult because the message variable (msg) cannot extract dynamic information from another source within the current script. It is possible to use a frameset-document to update a single frame continually by using a CGI script, which is referenced in a time-out event. The HTML document returned by the CGI script could contain embedded JavaScript code that sets a cookie (see Chapter 13), which is then placed into the message variable, and then is scrolled along the status bar. The CGI script would need to be quite *intelligent* because it would need to pick out real-time information from a server, such as information from a continually updated file, database, etc. Real-time information of this kind could include updates to a log-file that tracks accesses to a Web server, etc. The CGI script could also employ other features on the server, such as extracting information from system files.

TIP: Consider placing Pause buttons in your scroll-functions to allow people to stop the scrolling effect, so they can read messages. Stopping and restarting a time-out event will achieve this.

Scrolling Text-Fields

The method employed in the previous section can also be used for text-fields. Consider the following script:

```
<!--
  Program 10-6
-->
<html>
<head>
<script language="JavaScript">
<!--
 var timerId;
 var msg = "This is an example of a scrolling message";
 var counter = 0;

 // Is the timer already running?
 if (timerId != null)
    clearTimeout(timerId);

 function pad() {
   var padding  = "";
   // Prepend 50 spaces to the message:
   for (var n=0; n <= (50 + msg.length); n++)
       padding += " ";
   return(padding);
 }

 function scroll() {
  newMsg = pad() + msg + " ";
  document.forms[0].elements[0].value =
          newMsg.substring(counter, newMsg.length);
  if (counter == newMsg.length) {
     counter = 0;
  }
  counter ++;
```

```
  timerId = setTimeout("scroll()", 1);
  return true;
 }
//-->
</script>
</head>
<body onLoad="scroll()">
<form>
<center>
<input type="text" size=70></center>
</form>
</body>
</html>
```

With this script, you simply update a text-field, rather than the status bar property. The text-field is defined within the body of the document and the `scroll()` function is called from within the body. The value of `forms[0].elements[0]` is the first HTML object within the first form, namely the text-field. Because the text-field has not been named with a name attribute, the `elements[]` array is the only way to refer to it. Remember to use the `value` property of the field when you update its contents.

TIP: Notice how the `scroll()` function in this example is called from within the <body> tag. This is essential because the `onLoad` event is not triggered until the *complete* document has been loaded. To refer to a field within the body, the document must have been completely loaded from disk; otherwise, you will receive an error message stating the field you are trying to update does not exist. If you start the `scroll()` function from within the <script> container, as with the status bar scroller-application previously presented, the body of the document will not yet have been loaded, hence the error. This is a common and frustrating error you can now safely avoid.

Image Animation

Time-outs are also useful for creating simple animation, particularly when using Navigator's internal GIF images (that have no loading-time overhead). Consider the following script that displays two GIF images, one after the other, to give the impression of animation. The script starts by defining an array using the `Array()` constructor and allocates the names of the two images that will be animated—in this case, `rb.gif` and `yb.gif`—two balls, red and yellow in color, respectively. Both images are the same size in this instance, although you could make the images differ in size to give the impression of size reduction or enlargement. The `alternate` variable tracks whichever image is currently displayed and alternates between the values 0 and 1.

Navigator allows images on the page to be dynamically altered by assigning the name of an image to the `src` property of the image. The first image in the document is the contents of `images[0]` or, rather, the first `<img>` tag; it is a new array property of the `document` object, which has been introduced with Navigator 3.0.

```
<!--
  Program 10-7
-->
<html>
<head>
<script language="JavaScript">
<!--
  var images = new Array("rb.gif", "yb.gif");
  var alternate = 0;
  var timerId;
  function showIcon() {
     alternate = (alternate == 0) ? 1 : 0;
     document.images[0].src = images[alternate];
     timerId = setTimeout("showIcon()", 1000);
  }
//-->
</script>
</head>
<body bgColor="White" onLoad="showIcon()">
<img src="rb.gif"><p>
The above image will change color every second
</body>
</html>
```

A time-out is then created that recalls the `showIcon()` recursively, ensuring the images are continually updated. A time-out period of `1000` milliseconds, one second, has been allocated to ensure a swift animation in this case. The animation routine is started by using an `onLoad` event-attribute in the `<body>` tag, which invokes the `showIcon()` function. An image must already exist within the document to allow the animation to begin, so an `<img>` tag to load the first image has been placed in the body of the document. This could be placed anywhere within the document, even in another frame or in a separate window (in which case you would need to ensure you prefix "`document.images`" with the window or frame name). See Chapter 11 for greater details on frameset-documents: See Chapter 8 for more information on JavaScript's window manipulation routines.

You could also make an animation active only while the document is loading. This would simply involve starting the animation automatically when the script is loaded, and then canceling the time-out event when the document has been fully loaded, that is, within a <body onLoad=...> tag. Note that without a significantly long document, the animation will not last long. For this reason, the time-out period has been made shorter to make the animation more vigorous and eye-catching. Here is a slightly modified script, which animates an icon during a program-load. From a local disk, the animation will be shorter, although over a network connection (via a http://-based URL), a greater delay will be likely as the file is transferred over to your machine via the Internet. In this example, a delay has been introduced by placing an <img> tag that looks up a nonexistent Internet host for an image, thus causing a (purposeful) lengthy delay. Placing a few hundred lines of text into the example will be sufficient to see the animation while the document loads locally from disk. Using the example off-line will also increase the delay, of course:

```
<!--
  Program 10-8
-->
<html>
<head>
<script language="JavaScript">
<!--
  var images = new Array("rb.gif", "yb.gif");
  var alternate = 0;
  var timerId;
  function showIcon() {
     alternate = (alternate == 0) ? 1 : 0;
     document.images[0].src = images[alternate];
     timerId = setTimeout("showIcon()", 100);
  }

  function clearEvent() {
    clearTimeout(timerId);
    document.images[0].src = images[0];
  }

  // Create an image...
  document.write("<img src="rb.gif"><p>");

  // Start the animation...
  showIcon();
//-->
</script>
```

```
</head>
<body onLoad="clearEvent()">
The above ball-image will animate while the current
document is being loaded, whereupon the time-out event
will be canceled and the animation will halt.
<b>Ensure</b> that this document has a few hundred lines
of text to delay the loading, or keep the line below to
make a network lookup to a nonexistent host.<p>
<img src="http://www.no-where.com/nothing.gif">
</table>
</body>
</html>
```

Another important point to note is that an image needs to exist within the document before the animation function is started. In this example, a `document.write()` method creates an image by dynamically writing an `<img>` tag into the browser beforehand. An `OnLoad` event will only be triggered *after* the current document has been loaded; because the animation should take place *while* the document-load is taking place, the existence of an image is paramount—otherwise, Navigator will issue an error message saying the `images[0]` array reference does not exist. This would be true because the whole document has not been loaded, and Navigator hasn't yet set up the required JavaScript objects in memory. The placement of the image may be a problem, but you could use a frameset-document and place the image in another frame, animating it while a lower frame is being loaded with a document. The `clearEvent()` function cancels the time-out event and draws the first icon back into the image area (the text-icon) to indicate the load has completed—you can alter this accordingly.

Summary

Time-outs are essentially user-initiated events that occur in the future, and have many uses in JavaScript applications.

♦ A time-out event specifies a JavaScript statement or function you want to invoke at a later time. When you create a time-out event, use `setTimeout()` and assign the function-call to a variable so you can refer to the time-out. Referring to a time-out is required when you clear a time-out, in which case you use `clearTimeout()` and pass it the variable to which you originally assigned the time-out event.

♦ Time-out events require a time at which to invoke the event, and this time is specified in milliseconds, where one thousand milliseconds is equal to one second.

♦ Time-out events are useful for real-time activities, such as clocks and animations. They are also useful for updating frame contents at a period interval, bringing an application alive without the need for user input.

CHAPTER 11

LiveConnect:
Interfacing JavaScript
with Java

Up until the release of Navigator 3.0, applet-JavaScript
communication was difficult and clumsy. Navigator 3.0
has made the task more concrete by allowing JavaScript
programs to access the public classes and variables of a
Java applet running within the Navigator browser.
Netscape announced their new LiveConnect system that
facilitates communication between applets, JavaScript
programs, and plug-ins. LiveConnect opens up a whole

new world of possibilities because JavaScript programs can invoke, interact with, and even change the behavior of an applet while it is active within the current hypertext page (and vice-versa).

This chapter presents a number of applications that demonstrate how Java and JavaScript interface with one another, specifically, to allow variables to pass between different environments, and to allow JavaScript programs to invoke classes stored within applets running within the current application. In this chapter, you will learn how to:

♦ Use Java's `showDocument()` method with the `javascript:` URL to pass information from a Java applet to a JavaScript application running within the same hypertext document

♦ Implement applet and JavaScript communication using the new Navigator 3.0 `document.applets` property and the LiveConnect system built into Netscape Navigator

T IP: When you test HTML applications that use Java applets, make sure that you reload your document using the SHIFT–*Reload,* where you press the SHIFT key while you click on the *Reload* button. This will ensure that all applets are reloaded without using the internal cache. Navigator caches the JavaScript program and applet classes, that is, writes them to disk, to improve performance. Sometimes, though, this has the negative effect of not reloading an applet when it has been changed and recompiled during testing. If you still have problems, try disabling and re-enabling Java using the Options/Network Preferences/Languages menu; then reload your document normally.

To code in Java, you will need access to the Java Developer's Kit (JDK). The JDK comprises all of the Java classes, plus an applet compiler for converting your source-code applets into class files (compiled "byte code"). It is beyond the scope of this chapter to cover the Java language in any great detail. My earlier book, *Essential Java**, serves as a good introduction. Look out for the program names in this chapter, so that you can identify the examples on the accompanying book disk. These are located at the top of each program.

Using the `Javascript:` URL for Applet-JavaScript Communication

Java has a number of objects similar to those found in HTML, including radio-buttons, check-boxes, selection-lists, text-areas, etc. By extracting a value from an object, such as a string or a number, this can be passed to the browser using Java's `showDocument(URL)` method.

The Java `showDocument()` method writes HTML-formatted text into the Navigator browser, much in the same way as the `document.writeln()` method does within a JavaScript application. To access the applet's "environment," the `getAppletContext()` method is used with the `showDocument()` method to call a JavaScript function, using the `javascript:` URL. This method is not the easiest to use and much better alternatives are now available in the form of Netscape's LiveConnect system, which allows applets and JavaScript programs to communicate with one another. The use of `showDocument()` is considered the "old way" of implementing applet-JavaScript communication; it is only included here for completeness.

Consider the following HTML/JavaScript application, `selectcolor.htm`, which allows you to enter a color-code via a text-field provided by a Java applet, and then sends this value to a JavaScript function, which uses the value to change the background color of a frameset-document. This method allows an applet to send information to a JavaScript application, although sending data back to the applet is not possible.

```
<!--
   selectcolor.htm
-->
<html>
<head>
<title>How to Call JavaScript from Java</title>
<script language="JavaScript">
<!--
var top =
    '<body><base href=' + location + '><basefont size=4>' +
    'How to Call JavaScript from Java<hr>' +
    'Enter a color code in to the text field below and then ' +
    'press the button to see the value reflected into ' +
    'JavaScript as a background color.<p>' +
    '<applet code="selectcolor.class" width=100% height=40>' +
    '<param name="paramArg" value="parent.show">' +
    '</applet>' +
    '</body>';

var bot = '';

function show(value) {
  bot = '<body bgcolor="' + value + '"></body>';
  frames['botFrame'].location = "javascript:parent.bot";
}
```

```
//-->
</script>
</head>
<frameset rows="150,*">
<frame src="javascript:parent.top" name="topFrame">
<frame src="javascript:parent.bot" name="botFrame">
</frameset>
</html>
```

Taking the first statement, we have:

```
var top =
    '<body><base href=' + location + '><basefont size=4>' +
    'How to Call JavaScript from Java<hr>' +
    'Enter a color code in to the text field below and then ' +
    'press the button to see the value reflected into ' +
    'JavaScript as a background color.<p>' +
    '<applet code="selectcolor.class" width=100% height=40>' +
    '<param name="paramArg" value="parent.show">' +
    '</applet>' +
    '</body>';
```

which we can see is a JavaScript `var` statement defining a variable named top—a string object—assigned some HTML-formatted text. This text will eventually end up within the top frame of the application. The text, in this case, contains two important parts that *all* Java/JavaScript communication programs require, namely:

◆ The `<base href=' + location + '>'`... part
◆ The `<applet>..</applet>` container

The `<base href=URL>` tag specifies the *base URL* of a document, meaning all links from this page are *relative* to this URL, rather than the URL that actually loaded the current HTML document. In this example, no actual HTML documents exist; instead, they exist as variables in a JavaScript program and are loaded into frames within a `<frameset>` tag. Frames are windowed areas of the Navigator browser, which can contain documents with unique URLs. The `javascript:` URL is central to the applet/JavaScript communication because it allows a frame to be populated with HTML (the `javascript:` URL allows an HTML document to access a scripts variables and functions etc.). In this case, the HTML includes an `<applet>` tag that invokes the applet named `selectcolor.class`, the source code for which is contained in `selectcolor.java`, illustrated later in this section. Next is the statement:

```
var bot = '';
```

which will eventually contain more HTML-formatted text to populate the lower frame in the application. At this stage, it is empty, but it will store a `<body bgcolor=colorSpec></body>` tag, where `colorSpec` is a color-code string, such as `"#0000ff"` (a red-green-blue color-code triplet) or `"Blue"` (a color verb). The value of `colorSpec` will be chosen by the user within the Java applet.

The only user-defined function within `selectcolor.htm` is the `show()` function, which resembles:

11

```
function show(value) {
  bot = '<body bgcolor="' + value + '"></body>';
  frames['botFrame'].location = "javascript:parent.bot";
}
```

As you can see, the `bot` variable is assigned some HTML-formatted text—in this case, a `<body>` container with the `bgcolor` attribute specified. The argument passed to this function (`value`) is concatenated into the string, and the lower frame is assigned a new URL using `javascript:`. The `javascript:` URL does not represent the location of a Web resource but, instead, it evaluates the expression passed to it and places this within a new document. Hence the statement:

```
frames['botFrame'].location = "javascript:parent.bot";
```

is saying: "set the location of the lower frame (`botFrame`) to the value of the variable `bot`". The `parent` property must be used when you refer to variables defined within a `<frameset>` document, as explained in the discussion of frameset-documents in Chapter 9. For example, if the function `show(value)` was called with the argument `"#0000ff"`—that is, as `show("#0000ff")`—the value of the lower frame will be set to `<body bgcolor="#0000ff"></body>` and the frame's background color will then turn blue, proving both programs have communicated.

How does Java invokes the `show()` function with an actual color-code? This is the task of the `selectcolor.java` applet, as the following shows:

```
/*
** selectcolor.java
*/
import java.awt.*;
import java.net.*;
public class selectcolor extends java.applet.Applet {
  TextField tf1;
```

```
String butName = "See value in Navigator";
String js = "javascript:", paramArg;

// Send javascript: URL to the browser:
private void send(String str) {
  if (str != null) {
    try {
      getAppletContext().showDocument(new URL(js + str));
    } catch(MalformedURLException e) {}
  }
}

// Applet initilisation:
public void init() {
  if ((paramArg = getParameter("paramArg")) == null)
      paramArg = "textarea";
  Panel Panel1 = new Panel();
  add("North", Panel1);
  Panel1.add(tf1 = new TextField("", 30));
  Panel1.add(new Button(butName));
  Panel1.show();
}

public boolean action(Event evt, Object arg) {
  if ((String)arg == butName) {
    // The button has been pressed.
    send(paramArg + "('" + tf1.getText() +"')");
  }
  return true;
}
}
```

All the Java language cannot be covered in this chapter, although a section-by-section breakdown of this particular program is given here to make r the explanation complete and to explain some key Java program concepts. For more information on the Java language, refer to my book, *Essential Java**, published by McGraw-Hill Europe (http://www.mcgraw-hill.co.uk).

All Java programs start with a series of import statements, such as:

```
import java.awt.*;
import java.net.*;
```

which load various Java classes to perform tasks, such as creating graphical objects and performing network operations. The java.awt.* class refers to the Abstract Window Toolkit (AWT) classes, which are used by Java to provide the programmer with the facilities to create graphical user-interface (GUI) components, such as buttons, input-fields, etc. The asterisks (*) are wildcards that load all the libraries for AWT, of which there are many. The `java.net.*` classes control, among other things, the loading of URLs into Java. The application developed does not need to be "online" in order to function because some URLs can be used *without* an Internet connection. Nevertheless, the classes must still be imported for the compilation of the program. Think of classes as libraries of pre-written Java code—an Applications Programmers Interface (API) class library, in effect.

Next, an applet class called `selectcolor` is defined, which is derived from the Applet class named `java.applet.Applet`. This particular class has not been `imported`, although, if it had, it could have been referred to as just `Applet`, rather than by its full name. The top-level class in Java is "`Applet`," just like `window` is within JavaScript:

11

```
public class selectcolor extends java.applet.Applet {
   TextField tf1;
   String butName = "See value in Navigator";
   String js = "javascript:", paramArg;
```

The `TextField tf1` entry defines an object known as a text-field. This is the equivalent of an `<input type="text" name="tf1">` container in JavaScript, and will allow you to enter a color-code in this example. Next, three string variables are defined, using the `String` constructor. These are named `js`, and `paramArg`, respectively. The `butName` variable has been assigned the value `"See value in Navigator"` and will be used for the face of a button later in the applet. The `js` variable contains the `"javascript:"` URL. `paramArg` is another string that will be used later in the program.

Some methods are now defined: The first is called `send()`; it is defined as `void`. A *void method* is one that does not return a value. All methods must state their return-type, even void methods (hence, the provision of the `void` keyword). The method itself accepts a string as an argument named `str`. If the `str` value exists—that is, if it isn't `null`—the Java `showDocument()` method is invoked. This method is called with the argument `new URL(js + str)`, where the `URL()` method is a valid URL. In this case, the `js` string's value `"javascript:"` is prefixed (prepended) onto the `str` argument and then sent to the Navigator browser to be displayed. The `try` and `catch` parts of the statement allow a malformed URL error to be caught:

```
// Send javascript: URL to the browser:
private void send(String str) {
   if (str != null) {
```

```
    try {
        getAppletContext().showDocument(new URL(js + str));
    } catch(MalformedURLException e) {}
  }
}
```

As you can see, Java is strict about its data-typing, and catching exceptions (errors) is made compulsory. JavaScript is much more loosely implemented in this respect; essentially, this is because it is a much simpler language.

All applets undergo a series of "milestones" during their lifetime within the browser. The `init()` function, or *initialization* function, is called first and allows the programmer to set-up the applets environment. The Navigator message `"Loading applet"` is displayed when this code is being loaded into Navigator. The `init()` method in this applet resembles the following:

```
public void init() {
  if ((paramArg = getParameter("paramArg")) == null)
     paramArg = "textarea";
  Panel Panel1 = new Panel();
  add("North", Panel1);
  Panel1.add(tf1 = new TextField("", 30));
  Panel1.add(new Button(butName));
  Panel1.show();
}
```

The first statement assigns the value of the `getParameter()` method to the string variable `paramArg`. `getParameter()` and allows Java to access a value from a `<param value=...>`. The `<param>` tag must be specified within the `<applet>` container, as within the `selectcolor.htm` file. In the case that the `paramArg` value is not set within the `<param>` tag, a value (`"textarea"`) is provided accordingly. The value of the `<param>` tag is `"parent.show"`, which is a reference (as opposed to a function-call) to the name of the function you want to call to update the color of the lower frame. Instead of specifying the `parent.show` within the Java program in this instance, a `<param>` tag *must* be used because the expression `parent.show` can only be interpreted by a JavaScript program, and *not* by a Java applet.

TIP: You can use the JavaScript `alert()` method to print out the value of expressions, such as `parent.show`. The value of `parent` by itself is, in fact, a window object of the `for <object windowNumber>`, where `Number` is the unique numeric identifier for that window. If you typed: `javascript:parent.show` into the *Location:* field of Navigator while `selectcolor.htm` was loaded, you would see a literal representation of the method `show()`.

To lay out user-interface objects, a *panel* must be created in Java. This is done with the Java statement:

```
Panel Panel1 = new Panel();
```

Panels cannot actually be seen within an applet; they are merely boundaries for various Graphical User Interface (GUI) objects such as text-fields, buttons, etc. The statement:

```
add("North", Panel1);
```

specifies the objects within the panel are to be displayed towards the top of the applet's display area, in the Northern region. The display-area of the applet is dictated by the `<applet>` tag, coincidentally (see `setcolor.htm`). Next, you have a text-field and a button object, defined with the two statements:

```
Panel1.add(tf1 = new TextField("", 30));
Panel1.add(new Button(butName));
```

The `add()` method adds a new object to a panel; the text field is created using Java's `TextField()` constructor. The text field has no initial value (`""`) and it has a default size of 30 characters. This would be equivalent to `<input type="text" size=30 value="">` within HTML. The button is created using the `Button()` constructor and takes the argument `butName` for the text displayed on the face of the button.

Finally, an `action()` method exists, a standard method in Java that implements an event-handling routine, which intercepts events you generate. The only event generated in this applet is pressing the button object. This, in turn, will trigger the `action()` statement, and then you can examine which object has been triggered. This has been done with a single `if` statement in this applet, which checks the button value:

```
public boolean action(Event evt, Object arg) {
   if ((String)arg == butName) {
      // The button has been pressed.
      send(paramArg + "('" + tf1.getText() +"')");
   }
   return true;
}
```

The end-result of pressing the button within the applet is invoking the `send()` function. This function is called with the argument:

```
paramArg + "('" + tf1.getText() + "')"
```

which is, basically, building a function-call of the form:

```
parent.show('color-code')
```

to call the function `show()` within the JavaScript program. The `paramArg` value is the value `parent.show`, a reference to the `show()` function within the JavaScript program embedded within `setcolor.htm`; then come the function arguments. A `"('"` string is then joined onto the front of the value returned in the applet's text-field (`tf1`)—the Java `getText()` method returns this particular value—and finally another `"')"` is added, completing the function-call. All of this text is then sent to the `send()` function, which uses the Java `showDocument()` method to write the text into the browser. The end result is a `<body>` tag with the color-code entered into the applet which is written into the Navigator browser. Navigator then renders this text accordingly, which results in the lower frame having a new background color allocated to it.

The features you actually build into an applet are up to you, although as long as they return meaningful values, such as strings, numbers, etc., you can pass these back to the browser by forming a JavaScript function call with the `javascript:` URL, and then using `showDocument()` to write this into the Navigator browser.

TIP: You can see when an applet is running within Navigator by looking at the status bar. The message "Applet *appletname* is running" will periodically be shown, where *appletname* is the name of your applet, as set with the `name` attribute of the `<applet>` tag. The Java Console option in Navigator's Options menu will also show you details of the applet(s) that is currently active.

Using Navigator 3.0's New LiveConnect System

LiveConnect allows for two-way communication between Java applets and JavaScript programs (as well as Netscape plug-ins). The new `document.applets` property of Navigator 3.0 allows a JavaScript program to reference the public variables and methods of an applet and vice-versa. The following sections demonstrate a number of applications that illustrate how values can be passed from JavaScript programs to Java applets, and how applets can communicate values to a JavaScript function.

The `document.applets` property is a reflection of each `<applet>` tag in the current HTML document. In order to allow an applet to use the facilities of LiveConnect, a new `<applet>` tag attribute called `mayscript` has been introduced. Be sure to include this attribute in your `<applet>` tags when the applet in question needs to use LiveConnect, i.e. when it interfaces to a JavaScript program.

Passing Values from Java to JavaScript

The `document.applets` property within Navigator 3.0 allows a public class of a Java applet to be invoked simply by appending the name of the applet, along with any arguments, onto the object. For example, if you had the following HTML that defined an applet called `myApplet`:

11

```
<applet mayscript
        name="myApplet" code="example.class"
        width=200 height=100>
</applet>
```

then the JavaScript expression:

```
document.applets.myApplet
```

would refer to this applet within the browser. Furthermore, if a public method was stored within this Java applet, which resembled the following (and, in this case, which returns a string value):

```
public String myFunc() {
  return "Hello world!";
}
```

you could assign the value returned by this method to a JavaScript variable by issuing the JavaScript statement:

```
var JavaVar = document.applets.myApplet.myFunc();
```

You could also invoke Java methods that do not return values, which perhaps perform other tasks, such as starting an animation, playing a sound, etc.

Consider the following example, which is a rework of the previous application. This program displays two text-area fields: the first arrives from a Java applet and the second is defined within HTML using a `<textarea>` container tag. By pressing a form button, the text entered into the applet's text-area field is copied into the HTML-defined text-area. This action is performed by assigning the value of a Java method to the `value` attribute of

the HTML text-field. The HTML file resembles the following and is named
JavaToJs2.htm:

```html
<html>
<!--
  JavaToJs2.htm
-->
<head>
<title>Sending Java variables to JavaScript</title>
<script language="JavaScript">
<!--
  // This function runs a public method that exists within
  // a Java applet. The applet returns a text-area value
  // which then updates an HTML text-area field.
  function fromJava() {
      document.forms[0].javadata.value =
              document.applets.JavaToJs2.retString();
  }
//-->
</script>
</head>
<body>
This application demonstrates how a public Java method can be
invoked from within JavaScript using the <b>document.applets</b>
property. The value returned by the applet is used to update
an HTML text-area field dynamically.<p>
<hr>
<applet code="JavaToJs2.class"
        name="JavaToJs2"
        mayscript
        width="100%"
        height=175>
</applet>
<hr><center>
<form>
<textarea name="javadata" cols=50 rows=5>
</textarea>
<p>
<input type="button"
        value="Press to update field from applet"
        onClick="fromJava()">
</form>
</center>
</body>
</html>
```

The application is very small and the main JavaScript code consists of only a few lines of code, namely a function definition that resembles:

```
function fromJava() {
      document.forms[0].javadata.value =
              document.applets.JavaToJs2.retString();
}
```

which updates the text-area file called `javadata` with the value returned by the Java method named `retString()`. The `retString()` method is defined within the following applet, `JavaToJs2.java`:

```
/*
** JavaToJs2.java
*/
import java.applet.*;
import java.awt.*;
public class JavaToJs2 extends Applet {
  TextArea data=new TextArea("Enter some text to send",5,60);
  public void init() {
    setLayout(new BorderLayout());
    Panel pan1 = new Panel();
    pan1.add("Center", data);
    add("South", pan1);
  }
  public String retString() {
    return (String) data.getText();
  }
}
```

This applet displays a text-area field, and then allows you to input some text. No other functionality is provided; there isn't even a button. The Java `getText()` method has been used to extract the value of the text-area field and to return it as a string value in this instance—nothing more complex than this is required.

Passing Values from JavaScript to Java

Passing data from a JavaScript program to a Java applet is simply a matter of reversing the behavior of the previous application. By using the `document.applets` property, you can invoke a Java method and pass it an argument, which represents a value defined within the current JavaScript program.

Consider the following application that allows you to enter some text into a text-field via an `<input>` tag, and then reflect this value into a text-field defined with a Java applet running within the same document. The HTML and JavaScript code resembles the following:

```html
<html>
<!--
  jstojava.htm
-->
<head>
<title>Sending JavaScript variables to Java</title>
<script language="JavaScript">
<!--
  // This function calls the updateField() method
  // in the Java applet and passes the text-string
  // argument through the 'val' argument.
  function sendToApplet(val) {
    document.applets.JsToJava.updateField(val);
  }
//-->
</script>
</head>
<body>
<center>
<form>
Please enter the data that you want to send to the
Java applet, and click on the <b>Send</b> button.<p>
Data to send to applet:
<input name="jsdata"
       type="text"
       size=40><p>
<input type="button"
       value="Send"
       onClick="sendToApplet(this.form.jsdata.value)">
</form>
<hr>
This is the data <b>sent</b> from the JavaScript program
above.<br>
<applet code="JsToJava.class"
        name="JsToJava"
        mayscript
        width="100%"
        height=50>
</applet>
</center>
</body>
</html>
```

The text-field and button are created using `<input>` tags. The function `sendToApplet()` is invoked by an `onClick` event-attribute and is passed the value of the text-field (`this.form.jsdata.value`). The `sendToApplet()` function invokes the Java applet method named `updateField()`; once again, the value of the text-field is passed as an argument. The `JsToJava.java` applet resembles the following:

```
/*
** JsToJava.java
*/
import java.applet.*;
import java.awt.*;
public class JsToJava extends Applet {
  TextField txtField  = new TextField(40);
  public void init() {
    setLayout(new BorderLayout());
    Panel p1 = new Panel();
    p1.add("Center", txtField);
    add("Center", p1);
  }
  public void updateField(String arg) {
    txtField.setText(arg);
  }
}
```

This applet creates a text-field, `txtField`, and provides a single public method, `updateField()`, which sets the value of the text-field to the value of the string argument, which is passed to the method. The value of the argument is passed from the JavaScript program that references this applet. The end-result of this application is, by calling the Java method from within a JavaScript program (using an appropriate string argument, in this case), the value of a Java variable can be changed, and even updated, dynamically.

11

Accessing Java Features from Within JavaScript

The beauty of interfacing JavaScript programs with Java is that all of Java's features can be made available to JavaScript developers, with a few exceptions. Security concerns will still stop you from using Java to access local files from within an applet, although you can use Java to display windows, create animations, and play sounds, and control all of these functions from within a JavaScript program. Java sports an extensive API and has a range of classes that handle networking and GUI facilities.

Consider the following application that uses a Java applet to retrieve information about the current screen resolution. This information can then be used by a JavaScript application that needs to open a window, to the maximum possible size. JavaScript has no methods or properties that return such information, so Java can be put to great use in this scenario. Screen resolutions are an important area for the Web developer because they ultimately dictate the appearance of an application and control the placing of objects within the page. The HTML/JavaScript application consists of the following:

```
<html>
<!--
  checkScr.htm
-->
<head>
<script language="JavaScript">
<!--
  var w, h, w1;
  function getSize() {
    // Retrieve the width/height values from the applet:
    w = document.applets.checkScr.getScr(1);
    h = document.applets.checkScr.getScr(0);
    // Open the largest window possible:
    w1 = open("", "w1", "height=" + h + ",width=" + w);
  }
//-->
</script>
</head>
<body>
<h2>Accessing screen dimensions from JavaScript</h2>
<applet align="right"
        name="checkScr"
        code="checkScr.class"
        mayscript
        width=1
        height=1>
</applet>
This application returns the current screen resolution
using a Java applet via the Java <b>ToolKit</b> class and
<b>getScreenSize()</b> method.<p>
<form>
<input type="button" value="Click me" onClick="getSize()">
</form>
</body>
</html>
```

The script references an applet, checkScr.class, and calls it with two arguments, 0 and 1: The first returns the height; the second returns the width of your screen. The applet itself does not have a "display area" because it creates no output—it simply returns some values. For this reason, the width and height attributes have been set to just 1 pixel (you could also set them to zero). A form button invokes the user-defined function getSize(), which invokes the Java getScr() method to retrieve the width and height of the screen. A JavaScript open() method then uses the "w" and "h" variables returned by getScr() and concatenates them into a string, which is passed to the window-options argument in the open() call, thus setting the size of the window.

11

The checkScr.java applet resembles the following:

```
/*
** checkScr.java
*/
import java.applet.*;
import java.awt.*;
public class checkScr extends Applet {
  Dimension scrsize =
      java.awt.Toolkit.getDefaultToolkit().getScreenSize();
  public int getScr(int val) {
    // 0 returns the height, 1 the width:
    if (val==0)
      return(scrsize.height);
    else
      return(scrsize.width);
  }
}
```

Java's Toolkit class contains a getScreenSize() method that returns width and height values, which represent the current screen size. You can examine the source code for the Toolkit.class file (Toolkit.java) by looking at the SRC.ZIP file that accompanies the Java Developer's Kit.

A multitude of other Java methods exist that you can incorporate into your JavaScript applications. McGraw-Hill's book, *Esssential Java**, covers the Java language in more detail and explains how applets can use "streams" to communicate with distant Internet servers, create animations, manipulate windows and other GUI components, etc..

Summary

We have only scratched the surface of LiveConnect's features in this chapter, although you can see how easy it now is to make applets and JavaScript programs communicate with each other within Netscape Navigator.

♦ You can place an applet into an HTML document "dynamically" by writing an `<applet>` tag into the Navigator browser. Use the `<param>` tag within an `<applet>` container to pass arguments; Java's `getParameter()` method will pick up these values.

♦ Remember to use the new `mayscript` attribute of the `<applet>` tag when referencing applets that need to use LiveConnect, i.e. for applets that interface to JavaScript programs (the `mayscript` attribute was introduced with Navigator version 3.0).

♦ The `applets` property of the `document` object can be used to refer to an applet's public classes, allowing JavaScript applications to call Java methods. Not all Java methods can be used, however. For example, if you try to open a local file, a security exception will be raised from within Navigator, thus halting the process. Access to local files via an applet raises security concerns, although nearly any other public Java method can be called.

♦ Security problems are to be addressed in Navigator 4.0, code-named "Galileo," whereby the concept of "trusted applets" is introduced. These applets should be able to access local file systems.

CHAPTER 12

Using JavaScript with Netscape Plug-ins

Plug-ins were introduced with Navigator 2.0. In concept, plug-ins are similar to "helper applications"—autonomous software applications installed alongside Navigator, which allow multiple file formats to be viewed and incorporated into a Web page. Plug-ins differ from helper applications.

They are not actually stand-alone applications that can be run outside Navigator; instead plug-ins are stored as Windows' Dynamic Link Library (DLL) files, and they are referenced when required. Plug-ins, like Java applets, run *within* the browser environment. Well over 40 plug-in applications now exist for Navigator. These support a wide range of file-formats, including spreadsheets and word-processing documents (see Appendix F for a recent list).

Plug-ins allow you to incorporate effectively a rich mixture of file-formats that Navigator cannot deal with otherwise. Because plug-ins are controlled by a plug-in application, they can also interact with the user, through the use of a mouse, etc. Netscape's new LiveConnect system, discussed in Chapter 11, also allows plug-ins to communicate with both Java applets and JavaScript programs, and vice-versa. In this chapter you will learn how to

♦ Detect the presence of a plug-in application within a JavaScript application

♦ Invoke plug-ins dynamically using JavaScript

♦ Use the <embed> tag to invoke a plug-in application

♦ Use special <embed> tag parameters to control Netscape's plug-in applications

Plug-ins currently come in three flavors, namely:

♦ Hidden plug-in—also known as a "background" plug-in

♦ Partial-screen plug-in—also known as an "embedded" plug-in

♦ Full-screen plug-in—this occupies the full screen

A *hidden* plug-in is one that occupies no space within a Web page. Such plug-ins include applications that play sounds and perform background tasks that do not require a visible portion of the screen. Partial-screen plug-ins occupy a rectangular area of the browser page, as specified in the width and height attributes of the <embed> tag. The majority of plug-ins fall into this category. Full-screen plug-ins occupy the entire browser screen automatically, although some can be confined to a specific frame (see Chapter 9 for more information on frameset-documents).

JavaScript's Plug-ins and MIME Types Properties

Plug-ins are an important concept to the JavaScript developer because Navigator 3.0 has new facilities for detecting and manipulating plug-ins, using the new `navigator.plugins` property. The `plugins` property belongs to the `navigator` object; it is an array of plug-in applications that are installed when you install Navigator. The `navigator.mimeTypes` property is also provided and contains a list of MIME types supported by Navigator. Because the vast majority of plug-ins are not part of the Navigator browser, not everyone will have access to a particular plug-in application. Navigator arrives with a number of "default" plug-in applications, however, including: "LiveAudio," a streamed audio-player, which allows you to hear sounds in real-time, that is, as a file is being downloaded; "LiveVideo," an Audio Visual Interleave (AVI) animation viewer; and a QuickTime animation file viewer. The AVI and QuickTime formats are popular on the Internet for animated content; sound is also included in such formats and is synchronized to the imagery in the file. These default plug-ins are special because they have support in JavaScript, which allows the content of the plug-in to be controlled; for example, an animation can be stopped or replayed progmatically. Each plug-in application is stored as a DLL (library) file in the `PROGRAM\PLUGINS` subdirectory, below the directory in which Netscape Navigator 3.0 is installed.

12

How does a plug-in application actually get invoked? Each plug-in is associated with a range of MIME file-type extensions. MIME is a standard way of categorizing different file-formats. For example, a GIF image is represented by the MIME name `image/gif`, whereas an HTML file would be represented by the name `text/html`, and so forth. The first part of the MIME type is called the "file-type;" the part mentioned after the "/" is referred to as the "subtype." Within Navigator, a range of filename extensions are also associated with each MIME type. Multiple MIME sub-types can also exist for the *same* filename extension. Because a variety of different developers are actively writing plug-in applications, some perhaps for the same data-formats, a range of filename extensions and MIME sub-types are in use. Each plug-in application you install will update Navigator so it recognizes the new MIME type. Navigator's Options/General settings menu has a "helper" section, which specifies the MIME types and is launched when a specific filename extension is encountered. Plug-in applications are also specified here.

Figure 12-1 illustrates this screen. The highlighted entry `x-world/x-vrml` is a MIME type for a Virtual Reality Modeling Language (VRML) application. Notice how this MIME type supports the filename extensions ".`wrl`", ".`wrz`", and ".`flr`" in this instance. Some of the files that plug-in applications reference can be very large, especially those of an audio/visual nature. For this reason, some files are compressed at the source; the plug-in can then decompress the file when it has been fully downloaded from the network. A ".`wrz`" file is an example of this—the *z* indicates the file is compressed.

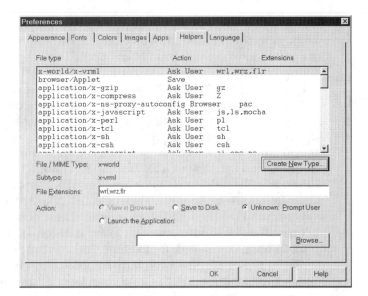

The Navigator
Options/General/
Helper menu
Figure 12-1.

The HTML <embed> tag is used to reference the file you want to place within your page; in fact, "embed" accurately describes the effect you require. This invokes the plug-in associated with the filename extension of the file referenced within the <embed> tag. The <embed> tag is covered later in this chapter, along with syntax descriptions and examples.

JavaScript's `navigator.plugins` property is a reflection of all the plug-in applications you have installed. This is a complex property and contains a multidimensional array. This array-structure is required because multiple plug-ins, and multiple MIME types and sub-types can be associated with each particular plug-in. Remember, different operating systems can use longer filename extensions—a classic example is ".htm" and ".html". The `navigator.plugins` property has the following subproperties:

Property Description	Property Format
Number of plug-ins installed.	`navigator.plugins.length`
The name of the i'th plug-in.	`navigator.plugins[i].name`
The name of the i'th plug-in application, as stored in the Navigator PROGRAM\PLUGINS directory.	`navigator.plugins[i].filename`
A description of the i'th plug-in application.	`navigator.plugins[i].description`

Property Description	Property Format
The number of MIME subtypes this plug-in recognizes.	`navigator.plugins[i].length`
The array element `j` contains a description of the primary filename extension that plug-in `i` contains. Multiple filename extensions can be supported by plug-in `i`.	`navigator.plugins[i][j].description`
The MIME type associated with the current filename extension. This links into the `navigator.mimeTypes` (array) property.	`navigator.plugins[i][j].type`
Similar to `description` but is a comma-separated list of filename extension pairs for plug-in number `i`.	`navigator.plugins[i][j].suffixes`

12

All of these properties can seem confusing, although you will learn the structure of each property after you see some examples and a slightly larger application that uses them. As mentioned, Navigator can support multiple plug-in applications. For example, the JavaScript expression:

```
navigator.plugins[0]
```

refers to the first plug-in. To access some further subproperties of this plug-in, you can add on the specific properties, or subproperties, as they are known, that are required. For example:

```
navigator.plugins[0].name
```

yields the name of the first plug-in. By default, this will be the value `"Navigator QuickTime Plug-In"` because this is automatically installed with Navigator 3.0 at the time of installation (it is known as a default plug-in). You could also find a description of the plug-in and the actual location of the plug-in application on your hard-disk using the JavaScript expressions:

```
navigator.plugins[0].description
navigator.plugins[0].filename
```

To ascertain the MIME types and filename extensions is slightly more tricky because you must deal with two arrays: The first indexes the plug-in, as you saw with the first plug-in (`plugins[0]`); the second indexes the MIME types and filename suffixes. Individual plug-ins can recognize a range of filename extensions and MIME subtypes, so the use of two arrays is a necessity. You can determine how many MIME types are supported by the first plug-in by using the JavaScript expression:

```
navigator.plugins[0].length
```

When you develop JavaScript programs that query plug-ins, this expression will crop up often. The first plug-in, the QuickTime player, recognizes only one filename extension—namely ".mov"—so the value of `navigator.plugins[0].length` will be 1. To see the MIME type and filename suffix, you would use the expressions:

```
navigator.plugins[0][0].type
navigator.plugins[0][0].suffixes
```

which would yield the values "`video/quicktime`" and "`mov`" respectively, where `video` is the file type, `quicktime` is the MIME type (both parts comprise the MIME type for this plug-in), and `mov` is the filename extension this plug-in recognizes. For example, `jaws3.mov` might be a clip from the well-known film with the nasty fish that goes around eating people. The `suffixes` property contains a comma-separated list of filename extensions this plug-in recognizes, although with the first plug-in, only a single filename extension is used across all platform implementations. You may also want to consider using:

```
navigator.plugins[0][0].description
```

to access filename extensions because comma-separated lists are difficult to process—you must work with string-manipulation routines to extract the information required. The `description` property contains each filename extension by itself, in uppercase. In this example, the value of the JavaScript expression `navigator.plugins[0][0].description` would be "`MOV`".

If a plug-in application supports multiple filenames and multiple MIME types, you must specify the correct array indexes to access the appropriate plug-in details. For example, `navigator.plugsin[1]`, the second Navigator plug-in, is the Netscape LiveAudio sound-player. The value of the JavaScript expression `navigator.plugins[1].length` will be 7, meaning eight (arrays start at position 0) MIME subtypes are associated with the LiveAudio plug-in. These could be displayed using a simple script, such as:

```
<!--
  Program 12-1
-->
<html>
<head>
<script language="JavaScript">
<!--
  var plugStr = "";
  for (var n=0; n < navigator.plugins[1].length; n++) {
      plugStr += navigator.plugins[1][n].type + " = " +
                 navigator.plugins[1][n].suffixes + "\n" + );
  }
  alert(navigator.plugins[1].name + ":\n" + plugStr);
//-->
</script>
</head>
</html>
```

12

The preceding script loops through each element of the second-array, extracts the `type` and `description` properties, and adds them to a string (`plugStr`), which is then displayed on the screen using the `alert()` method. The MIME types supported in this instance are: "audio/basic", "audio/x-aiff", "audio/aiff", "audio/x-wav", "audio/wav", "audio/mid", "audio/x-midi", and "audio/midi". The filename extensions associated with these MIME types were "au", "aiff", "aif, aiff", "wav", "mid" and "midi, mid", respectively.

Consider the following, more extensive application that displays a list of all the installed plug-ins, including a description of the plug-in, the filename extensions it recognizes, and the MIME types associated with each filename extension.

```
<!--
  Program 12-2
-->
<html>
<head>
<script language="JavaScript">
<!--
document.write("There are <b>" + navigator.plugins.length +
               "</b> plug-ins installed.<p>");
document.write("<table border=1 width='100%' cellpadding=5>" +
               "<tr valign='top'>" +
               "<td bgcolor='Aqua' width='25%'>Name</td>" +
               "<td bgcolor='Aqua' width='25%'>Description</td>" +
               "<td bgcolor='Aqua' width='25%'>Filename</td>" +
               "<td bgcolor='Aqua' width='15%'>Suffixes / MIME " +
```

```
                    "type</td>" +
                    "</tr>");
// Scan through each plug-in:
for (n=0; n < navigator.plugins.length; n++) {
    document.write("<tr valign='top'>" +
                    "<td><b>" + navigator.plugins[n].name +
                    "</b></td>" +
                    "<td>" + navigator.plugins[n].description +
                    "</td>" +
                    "<td>" + navigator.plugins[n].filename +
                    "</td><td>");
    // Scan through this plug-in's suffixes array:
    for (m=0; m < navigator.plugins[n].length; m++) {
        document.write(navigator.plugins[n][m].suffixes +
                    " = " +
                    navigator.plugins[n][m].type +
                    "<br>");
    }
    document.write("</td></tr>");
}
document.write("</table>");
//-->
</script>
</head>
</html>
```

The `navigator.mimeTypes` property is an array of MIME types known to Navigator, although this list does not imply a plug-in application exists for each such MIME type—only `navigator.plugins` contains such information. To access a given MIME type, use the syntax:

```
navigator.mimeTypes[n].type
```

where *n* is the index value of the `mimeTypes` array required, for example:

```
navigator.mimeTypes[0].type
```

would yield the value:

```
audio/aiff
```

which denotes an audio subtype for AIFF-formatted files (other audio formats are also supported). Navigator supports around 100 different MIME types, spanning a range of media content types. The `mimeTypes` array has limited uses, mainly because it is simply a list of MIME types that are recognized rather than actually supported by Navigator. Note that the `navigator.plugins` property links into the `navigator.mimeTypes` property to retrieve the MIME types supported by each plug-in. The following script will show each MIME type within a selection list for convenient viewing:

```html
<!--
  Program 12-3
-->
<html>
<head>
<script language="JavaScript">
<!--
   var htmlString= "MIME types <form><select size=25>";
   function showTypes() {
      for (var i=0; i < navigator.mimeTypes.length; i++)
         htmlString += "<option>" +
                           navigator.mimeTypes[i].type;
      htmlString += "</select></form>";
      document.write(htmlString);
      document.close();
   }
//-->
</script>
</head>
<body onLoad="showTypes()">
</body>
</html>
```

12

Using the `<embed>` Tag

To embed a file within a document, use the `<embed>` tag. This tag will cause a plug-in to invoke the referenced file, assuming it exists on your machine. The general syntax of the `<embed>` tag is:

```html
<embed src="fileOrUrl"
       name="embedFileName"
       [ border=n ]
       [ align=[left|middle|right] ]
       width=w
       height=h
       vspace=v
       hspace=h>
```

where `fileOrUrl` is the name of a file with which a plug-in is associated, and it is the file you want to "embed" within the current page. A URL to the file can be specified or you can issue the name of the file. If you issue the name of the file, it is assumed to exist within the same directory as the current HTML file, which contains the <embed> tag.

Plug-ins are installed separately although they are not "stand-alone" applications; instead, plug-ins use a dedicated API, which seamlessly links into the Navigator browser. The name attribute allows you to name the embedded file, then refer to it at a later stage.

NOTE: Naming your plug-in is important because JavaScript provides a suite of standard functions—to be discussed later—that can control each plug-in progmatically, rather than through the <embed> tag.

The document.plugins property contains a list of embedded files; document.plugins.length will tell you how many. The <embed> tag has undergone many extensions, mainly because of the new default plug-ins Navigator supports, for example, LiveAudio, LiveVideo, and the QuickTime animation player. The appearance of the embedded file is controlled by the border, align, and width attributes. The vspace and hspace attributes accept pixel values that control the vertical and horizontal spacing of the plug-in's display area and the other HTML objects that exist around it, such as text or images.

You can dynamically create an <embed> tag using the document.write() method, perhaps after you detect which plug-ins have actually been installed—as described in the next section. For example, you could embed a Adobe Portable Document Format (PDF) file into an HTML page using Adobe's Amber plug-in with the following line:

```
<embed src="jsess.pdf" border=0 align="left" width=500>
```

In the <embed> tag, the file jsess.pdf has the filename extension ".pdf". Navigator will check this against its list of supported filename extensions to see if the plug-in exists. Adobe's Amber plug-in allows PDF files to be embedded with Navigator; if it is installed on your machine, the file will be loaded and displayed accordingly. The <embed> tag will ignore a file for which a plug-in application cannot be found. If a plug-in's application exists, but the file it references cannot be located, a warning message will be issued. Navigator also warns you when an embedded file is about to be downloaded—although you will be given the chance to disable this message after the first warning is displayed.

TIP: Appendix F contains a list of Navigator plug-in applications, descriptions, and location details. Plug-ins, like Navigator, are available free for downloading and evaluation during testing. Some plug-ins will eventually become commercial products once they leave the testing stage, although many are expected to remain available at no cost to the end user.

The New `<embed>` Syntax and JavaScript Plug-in Functions

12

The syntax for `<embed>` has been extended significantly to deal with Navigator's default plug-ins, specifically the LiveAudio and LiveVideo applications. For example, you can now control QuickTime animations directly via the `<embed>` tag. A JavaScript application can also control a plug-in using a number of standard JavaScript methods. Many plug-ins also have specific *call-back methods*. A call-back method is a JavaScript function, which is called by the plug-in automatically if the user defines it. For example, an animation would invoke this function automatically every time a new frame of that animation is displayed.

TIP: The attributes used within the `<embed>` tag depend on the plug-in application. Not all attributes work for every plug-in; in fact, some are irrelevant, for example, a magnification factor for an audio-file, etc. In general, the standard attributes are `name`, `src`, `width`, `height`, `vspace`, and `hspace`. Some attributes, such as `pluginspace`, `autostart` and `loop`, are plug-in specific. The documentation that accompanies the plug-in should have an example of the `<embed>` tag syntax that can be used.

LiveAudio

The LiveAudio plug-in will play audio files in the AIFF, AU, MIDI, and WAV formats—the most ubiquitous sound formats available. LiveAudio will also provide a series of button-controls, but only if a plug-in's display-area is large enough—for example, you can omit the controls if you specify a zero width. The syntax of the `<embed>` tag has been modified to allow LiveAudio to control the actual playing of the embedded audio file. It resembles the following:

```
<embed src=fileOrUrl
       name=pluginName
       width=w
       height=h
       [ autostart = [true|false] ]
       [ loop = [true|false] ]
       [ vspace=v ]
       [ hspace=h ]>
```

The `autostart` attribute controls whether or not the file is played automatically when first loaded, and the `loop` attribute allows the audio file to be played in repetition. A number of JavaScript methods are also supported for LiveAudio files, namely: `play()`, which starts the video file at the current position; `stop()`, which halts the currently playing video; `rewind()`, which rewinds the video to the starting frame; and `seek(secs)`, which moves forward `secs` seconds into the file, and then starts playing it. The LiveAudio plug-in will provide controls for starting, stopping, and movement within the file, although these only appear if the `width` attribute is large enough—that is, zero `width` and `height` attribute values will omit the controls—then you must use the JavaScript functions to control the playing of the file. For example, an `<embed>` tag structured as:

```
<embed name="greet"
       width=0
       height=0
       autostart=false
       src="hello.wav">
```

would load the file `hello.wav`. No controls are displayed because the `width` attribute and `height` attribute are set to `0`, and the file is not played when it is first referenced. To start playing the file, you must use the JavaScript statement:

```
document.greet.play();
```

where "`greet`" is the name of the embedded file in this instance. You could now play the file whenever you invoke a specific action or event, for example, when you click on a button or when a field loses focus, etc.

LiveVideo
The LiveVideo plug-in will play video files that are stored in the Audio Visual Interleave (AVI) format. Note that this plug-in is not the same as the QuickTime plug-in—QuickTime is covered later in this chapter. The `<embed>` tag's extended syntax for LiveVideo content is similar to LiveAudio:

```
<embed src=fileOrUrl
       name=pluginName
       width=w
       height=h
       [ autostart=[true|false] ]
       [ loop=[true|false] ]
       [ align=[left|middle|right] ]
       [ border=n ]
       [ controls=[true|false] ]
       [ vspace=v ]
       [ hspace=h ]>
```

12

The `controls` attribute accepts a `true` or `false` value, which determines whether or not controls are displayed for the plug-in. You can disable the controls and use this plug-in's JavaScript methods instead. `play()` starts the video file at the current position; `stop()` halts the currently playing video; `rewind()` rewinds the video to the starting frame; and `seek(frameNum)` moves to the frame number `frameNum` within the video file. `autostart` controls the automatic playing of the file when the plug-in is loaded (this accepts a boolean value: that is, `true` to start playing the sound automatically, and `false` not to play the sound), and where `loop` controls the looping, that is, repetition of the file—if set to `true`, the audio file is played continuously from start to end. A number of JavaScript functions are also available: `play()` starts playing the audio file from the current position; `stop()` stops playing the file; `rewind()` sets the current position to the beginning of the audio file; and `seek(secs)` sets the current position to the given number of seconds (`secs`) into the audio file. For example, `seek(10)` would move 10 seconds forward into the file. Once a plug-in has been named using the `name` attribute, it can be referenced via the `document` object. For instance, a plug-in defined with an `<embed>` tag as:

```
<embed name="movie1"
       src="alien.avi"
       width=400
       height=300>
```

you could start the movie named "`movie1`" using the JavaScript statement:

```
document.movie1.play();
```

You could have made the movie start by itself, using the `<embed>` tag with the `autostart` attribute set to `true`. For example:

```
<embed name="movie1"
       src="alien.avi"
```

```
width=400
height=300
autostart=true>
```

although with the dedicated JavaScript plug-in methods, you can start and stop the animation when and where you require. You can even do so on the basis of other JavaScript-based events.

TIP:　The LiveVideo (AVI player) has a `AviFrameCallback()` call-back function, which is invoked whenever the video advances. This is called with a single numeric argument that represents the current frame number. For example, if you had a plug-in defined with the tag `<embed width=400 height=300 src="alien.avi">` a function defined as:

```
function AViFrameCallback(f) {
    ...
}
```

would be called automatically by the LiveVideo plug-in and would pass the current frame number as the parameter named `f`. You could update a text-field or invoke some other condition based upon this value; that is, when the video reaches a specific frame, you can update a text-field or other HTML object.

QuickTime

QuickTime is a popular video format that incorporates both audio and/or image content. The `<embed>` tag for this particular file format is extensive, and takes account of all the features in the QuickTime format, such as tilt and panning angles:

```
<embed src=[fileOrUrl]
       name=pluginName
       width=w
       height=h
       [ autoplay=[true|false] ]
       [ controller=[true|false] ]
       [ loop=[true|false|palindrome] ]
       [ playeveryframe=[true|false] ]
       [ href=[fileOrUrl] ]
       [ target=[frameName|_self|_top] ]
       [ hidden=[true|false] ]
       [ pluginspace=[fileOrUrl] ]
       [ pan=[integer] ]
```

```
    [ tilt=integer] ]
    [ fov=[integer] ]
    [ node=[integer] ]
    [ vspace=v ]
    [ hspace=h ]>
```

The `width` and `height` attributes control the size of the display-area for the movie; `autoplay`, if set to `true`, plays the movie as soon as the plug-in is loaded. The `controller` attribute controls whether or not movie-controls are displayed within the plug-in display area. `loop` controls the repetition of the movie, while `playeveryframe` is used to control the quality of the video—over slow connections, you may want to set this attribute to `false`, so less frames are played. The `href` attribute allows a URL to be associated with the plug-in; then, when it is clicked, the URL specified is loaded. Use the `target` attribute to specify a frame into which to load the URL after clicking on the movie—you can use frame synonyms, such as `_self` and `_top`, or a specific frame-name , named with the `<frame>` tag (see Chapter 9 for more details on frameset-documents). The boolean `hidden` attribute, when set to `true`, tells Navigator not to display the movie when only an audio track is contained within the video—this will override the `width` and `height` settings, if specified (some QuickTime files may not contain both audio and video content). The `pluginspace` attribute is the name of a URL that links to the plug-in software if you have not installed a QuickTime plug-in—this can be a normal HTML document with links to the necessary software.

You can remove Navigator's default plug-ins by deleting the appropriate plug-in from the PLUGINS subdirectory. If a plug-in cannot be found, this attribute allows you to visit the site where the QuickTime plug-in is stored to download and run it. This is currently the URL `http://quicktime.apple.com`. Finally, the `pan`, `tilt`, `fov`, and `node` attributes specify a pan angle, tilt angle, file-of-view value, and node number, respectively (QuickTime movies can have *node* values, which denote specific parts of a movie). The QuickTime specification is currently being updated; it now supports more features and enhanced audio/video support. Visit Apple's Web site at `http://www.apple.com` for further information.

Detecting a User's Plug-in Capability

Using embedded files in an ad-hoc manner is the sign of a poor JavaScript application. A better solution is to detect which plug-ins are required *before* referencing the file with an `<embed>` tag. Knowing which plug-ins are supported beforehand allows you to prepare for the client environment being used to view your JavaScript/HTML application. Indeed, the whole

12

purpose of having a `navigator.plugins` property is to allow JavaScript to query which plug-ins are actually installed on your machine. A JavaScript application may warn you that you do not have the required plug-in. Or, more wisely, you may alter the page according to your capabilities; that is, if you haven't installed a particular plug-in, you look for an alternative, and then reference a different file. You interrogate your system to see which plug-ins you have by examining the filename suffixes supported by the plug-ins currently installed.

Consider the following application that uses a function, `findPlugin()`, to search through the filename extensions of the `navigator.plugins` property to see if a plug-in application can be found for a particular file. The required filename extension can then be passed to `findPlugin()` as a string. For example, the statement:

```
findPlugin("midi")
```

attempts to seek a plug-in that supports ".`midi`" files (Netscape's LiveAudio plug-in supports this file-format). The `findPlugin()` function could return a boolean value—that is, `true` or `false`—depending on whether or not the plug-in exists for this file. Consider the following application that does this:

```
<!--
  Program 12-4
-->
<html>
<head>
<script language="JavaScript">
<!--
var extNeed, namePlug;
function findPlugin(ext) {
  var thisExt, findExt;
  extNeed = ext;
  for (var n=0; n < navigator.plugins.length; n++) {
      for (var m=0; m < navigator.plugins[n].length; m++) {
          thisExt =
            navigator.plugins[n][m].description.toLowerCase();
          findExt = thisExt.substring(0, thisExt.indexOf(" "));
          if (findExt == ext) {
             namePlug = navigator.plugins[n].name;
             return(true);
          }
      }
  }
  return(false);
}
```

```
// Search for a plug-in that can handle .midi files:
if (findPlugin("midi")) {
   alert("A plug-in for " + namePlug +
         " is installed.");
   // etc...
}
else {
      alert("A plug-in application to play ." +
            extNeed +
            " files is not installed!");
}
//-->
</script>
</head>
</html>
```

12

The `findPlugin()` uses one loop to search through each plug-in and another to search through each of the supported filename extensions—a *nested* loop. By extracting the `description` subproperty, you can retrieve the filename extension supported by that plug-in. Then you can compare it against the `ext` argument, which is passed to the `findPlugin()` function (this argument contains a string value representing the filename extension required here. Note that no leading periods are used for the extension here). This example is longer because warnings have been output to the user. A more brief version, which only returns a `true false` value depending on whether or not the plug-in is available, is presented in Appendix D. Using the example from Appendix D creates a JavaScript application that places an embedded file within the current document based upon the availability of a plug-in:

```
<!--
  Program 12-5
-->
<html>
<head>
<script language="JavaScript">
<!--
function findPlugin(ext) {
  var thisExt, findExt;
  for (var n=0; n < navigator.plugins.length; n++) {
      for (var m=0; m < navigator.plugins[n].length; m++) {
          thisExt =
            navigator.plugins[n][m].description.toLowerCase();
          findExt = thisExt.substring(0, thisExt.indexOf(" "));
          if (findExt == ext)
```

```
                return(true);
        }
    }
    return(false);
}

// See if the user has a PDF compatible plug-in, i.e., Amber,
// if this exists, dynamically create the HTML to invoke the
// plug-in application:
if (findPlugin("pdf")) {
    // The user can view the PDF file, so embed one within the
    // current page
    document.open();
    document.write("<embed src='jsess.pdf' width='100%'>");
    document.close();
}
else {
    // The user cannot view the PDF file, so show the user a
    // HTML-only version of the file instead:
    location = "essjava.htm";
}
//-->
</script>
</head>
</html>
```

In this application, the findPlugin() function looks for a plug-in that can view PDF files. If such a plug-in is found, an <embed> tag is dynamically created to invoke the plug-in on the file jsess.pdf. Otherwise, an HTML version of the file is displayed—this is read into the current browser window by assigning the URL of the file to the location property of the document object.

Summary

Plug-ins are applications that allow different file formats to be viewed by Navigator. Plug-ins are not stand-alone applications like the older "helper applications." Instead, they allow content to be embedded *within a* Web page, that is, executable content. A wide variety of plug-in applications are now available, as documented in Appendix F.

♦ Use the HTML <embed> tag to place an embedded file within the current Web page. This will invoke a plug-in application for the file based upon that file's filename extension. For example, an <embed width=400 src="ding.aiff"> tag would invoke an audio-player such as LiveAudio (by default) because the ".aiff" extension denotes an audio file. Navigator is equipped with a default plug-in for this filename extension, which has the MIME type `audio/aiff`.

♦ The `<embed>` tag has been enhanced considerably to allow for new file-formats. The QuickTime plug-in installed by default with Navigator 3.0 can be configured to a detailed level, using a number of enhanced tag attributes. Navigator has also defined a series of call-back functions, which are essentially JavaScript functions called by a plug-in. If a function is defined with the same name in your application, it will be called automatically. This will allow for closer interaction between the plug-in application and the JavaScript program.

♦ JavaScript supplies two useful properties to the programmer designing "plug-in aware" applications, namely: `navigator.plugins` and `navigator.mimeTypes`. Both of these properties belong to the `navigator` object; they are structured as arrays. Of these two properties, the `plugins` property is the most useful because it will tell you which plug-ins are installed and, therefore, which file-formats you can view. The `mimeTypes` property is a reflection of the MIME types Navigator supports and *not* a list of plug-in applications actually supported, that is, installed.

♦ By scanning through the `navigator.plugins` array *before* invoking a plug-in, you can test to see whether or not the user viewing your page can actually view any plug-in file(s) you may have embedded in your hypertext document. Note that placing `<embed>` tags in a document on an *ad hoc* basis is not a good idea. Instead, create the `<embed>` tags dynamically after you detect which plug-ins have been installed. Plug-ins, unlike Java applets, do not travel over the Internet, so the client must have the plug-in application installed in advance, before a particular file-format can be played or viewed.

♦ Navigator 3.0 has introduced a series of "default" plug-in applications for this purpose. These default plug-ins allow audio and video file-formats—the most common content types—to be embedded without the need for further software installation.

12

CHAPTER 13

Using JavaScript's Cookie Mechanism

A *cookie* is a small item of information stored on a client machine, which can be retrieved by a JavaScript program using the `document.cookie` property. Cookies are a useful feature because they allow state-information to be stored and accessed; for example, the number of visits to a particular HTML document could be recorded, as could user-preferences for a particular interface. Persistent objects are difficult to implement in JavaScript, although cookies provide a good solution to a tricky problem.

By using cookies you can do away with server-side solutions, such as the need for CGI scripts that interface to back-end databases. Cookies are also useful as temporary repositories for variable values that exist during the lifetime of a JavaScript program. At the end of the day a cookie is not going to replace a structured server-side database, although it will go some of the way toward storing client-side information for use within JavaScript applications. In this chapter you will learn

♦ What cookies are and how they can help the JavaScript developer

♦ How to create, read, and delete cookies from the Netscape `cookies.txt` file

♦ What "temporary" and "persistent" cookies are

♦ How to use cookies to create hit-counters and to store user-input

Navigator first introduced the concept of a *client-state cookie*. Until this time, cookies could only be set by the server through the use of a CGI script. JavaScript now allows read-write actions on cookies, allowing developers to store state information from previous sessions with JavaScript applications. An example of a cookie-based application is presented later in this chapter, along with other code samples. Navigator can deal with a maximum of 300 cookies, each of which can be up to 4 Kilobytes in size. Navigator will *intelligently* purge—that is, delete—cookies that fall outside these limits. For example, it will purge a least-used cookie when resources run low. The full cookie specification can be found at Netscape's Web server located at the URL: `http://home.netscape.com/newsref/std/cookie_spec.html`.

Cookie Syntax

To create a cookie, you must first decide on the name of the cookie. Cookies must adhere to the following general syntax:

```
name=value; [expires=date;]
```

where `name` names the cookie, and `expires` sets a date when the cookie should *expire*; the latter is optional. By allocating a value beyond the current day, the cookie is said to *persist* into the future. *Persistent cookies,* or cookies that are kept after the current Navigator session, are stored in the `cookies.txt` file installed with Navigator. When you leave Navigator, your cookies remain intact; when you next visit a JavaScript page, which originally created the cookie, it can reread it and take the necessary action, that is, use the value with a JavaScript function, etc. As you will see, cookies are very useful at personalizing Web pages because they can store information from past Navigator sessions, in effect, providing Navigator with a *memory*.

Naming a Cookie

The `name` argument is a string that cannot contain semicolons (`;`), commas (`,`), or spaces. If you need to place such characters within the cookie, use the hexadecimal code for that character of the form `%nn`, where `nn` is the hexadecimal representation of the ASCII value for the character; for example, a semicolon has the ASCII (decimal) value `59`, which is `%3b` in the hexadecimal JavaScript representation. You can use the decimal to hexadecimal converter in Appendix D if you do not have access to a calculator with this conversion capability. Valid cookie names include: `_counter`, `hitCount`, and `user_Name`, although `user;Name` would not be valid—use `user%3bName` in this case where you need to use a semicolon. Semicolons are used to separate cookie arguments, note.

Providing a Cookie Expiry Date

Expiry dates are slightly more complex to allocate because they are based upon a JavaScript `Date` object. If the `expires` attribute is not present, the cookie expires at the end of the current Navigator session. Such cookies are useful as temporary variables within JavaScript programs. Using cookies in this way is helpful when dealing with frameset-documents (see Chapter 9), whose values may be lost when a document is emptied or reloaded by the user or by a script. An expiry date must adhere to a particular syntax, namely:

```
Weekday, Month hh:mm:ss Year GMT
```

for example, a valid date could be:

```
Fri, Apr 19:13:06 1996 GMT
```

The JavaScript `toGMTString()` method will create a date in this format, as you will see later. To set an expiry date for a persistent cookie, take the following steps:

♦ Establish how many days you want to keep the cookie—for example, seven (7) for one week, etc.—and then store it in a variable, for example, `days`

♦ Create a new JavaScript `Date` object and store it in a variable, for example, `todayDate`

♦ Use the `setDate()` method to alter the date variable previously created—use the `addDate()` method to add the number of days required for the expiry date

13

♦ Convert the date to Greenwich Mean Time (GMT) format or Universal Time Coordinated (UTC) format

Some JavaScript code to do this could resemble:

```
var todayDate = new Date();
todayDate.setDate(todayDate.getDate() + days).toGMTString();
```

where `todayDate` stores the current date, and `setDate()` updates a `Date` object. The `getDate()` method returns the current day of the month; it can be used when adding days to dates. Date objects can be updated in this way, which vastly simplifies many of the date-manipulation functions. Better still, you could place this in a JavaScript function to make the code accessible whenever you need to create an expiry date. Consider the following `returnExpiry()` function:

```
function returnExpiry(days) {
  var todayDate = new Date();
  todayDate.setDate(todayDate.getDate() + days);
  return(todayDate.toGMTString());
}
```

We can now call the `returnExpiry()` function using a statement, such as:

```
daysToExpire = returnExpiry(7);
```

which returns a `Date` object representing next week's date, that is, seven days into the future.

Generating the Cookie

This is the time to create the cookie, using the `document.cookie` property. Once you decide upon a name and you work out an expiry date for the cookie, you must decide *what* you want to store in the cookie. Assume you have a variable called `browsVers`, which stores the name and version of Navigator with which you are viewing the current page. The value of `browsVer` could be a JavaScript expression such as:

```
appVers = navigator.appName + " " +
          navigator.appVersion.substring(0,3);
```

which would return `"Netscape 3.0"` if you are viewing the current page with Navigator version 3.0. A value can now be assigned to the cookie as follows, taking into account the cookie syntax previously shown:

```
document.cookie = "browsVer=" +
                  appVers +
                  "; expires=" +
returnExpiry(7) + ";";
```

which, assuming the date was July 10, 1996 at 8:00 P.M., would create a cookie of the form:

```
browsVer=Netscape 3.0; expires=Fri Jul 10 20:00:00 GMT 1996;
```

This cookie will now be stored in the `cookies.txt` file. The next time you reload the JavaScript page that created this cookie, you can test to see if the cookie exists; if it does, you can take appropriate action. In this case, you would know Navigator 3.0 was previously used. You could have stored any other value in the cookie. The `extractCookie()` function, which will be discussed later in this chapter, can be used to recover the value in this or any other cookie. You could now write some small JavaScript functions to automate the cookie-creation procedure, for example:

```
function createCookie(name, value, expiredays) {
  var todayDate = new Date();
  todayDate.setDate(todayDate.getDate() +
                    expiredays);
  document.cookie = name +
                    "=" +
                    value +
                    "; expires=" +
                    todayDate.toGMTString() +
                    ";"
}
```

13

The `createCookie()` function is passed a cookie-name, a value, and a value specifying the number of days in which to expire the cookie; it could be called using a statement of the form:

```
createCookie("Jason",
             "wombat@spuddy.mew.co.uk",
             30);
```

which creates a cookie called `Jason`, which expires in 30 days and has one of my e-mail addresses contained within it. See Appendix D for a `createTempCookie()` function that creates a cookie without an expiry date.

Cookies are not written to disk—that is, to the `cookies.txt` file—*until* the current Navigator session ends, although once a cookie has been created, it can be accessed immediately. When the cookie is written to disk, the name, value, and URL (or document) associated with the cookie are all written to disk. The URL information written to the cookie-file is known as *state information* because it specifies the range of states under which this cookie is valid, that is, the URL of the document(s) for which this cookie is valid.

TIP: Cookies may contain valuable data, so you may want to consider backing-up the `cookies.txt` file periodically. Navigator has one cookie-protection mechanism that can be used to alert you when a cookie is about to be accepted. This can be found in the Options/Network Preferences/Protocols menu. A "malicious" JavaScript program could easily examine the cookies on your system via the `document.cookie` property, and then expire or corrupt these: a "*cookie monster*," in the literal sense. ;-)

Creating a Temporary Cookie

By assigning a value to the `document.cookie` property, you can create a temporary cookie that can be used throughout the current Navigator session, for example:

```
document.cookie.myCookie = fullName;
```

where `fullName` is a variable you want to store in the cookie called `myCookie`. You can now access the value of the cookie `myCookie` simply by using the expression:

```
document.cookie.myCookie
```

This undocumented feature, where a new property is allocated to `document.cookie`, can be useful because you do not need any additional JavaScript code to create the cookie.

Reading an Existing Cookie

All the cookies are contained within the `document.cookie` property as one continuous text string. Reading the value of a single cookie involves searching through the `cookie` property to extract each cookie-entry, and then comparing this with the cookie name you require. If the name matches, you can extract the `value` part, which occurs after the = character. Unfortunately, the `cookie` property is not an array, so individual cookie-entries cannot be accessed as separate values. Instead, you must write some string-processing functions to extract the cookie's value part.

The following illustrations of ReadCookie() and extractCookieValue() functions will extract a cookie value. The main function, ReadCookie(), takes a cookie name as an argument, and then scans through the cookie property using the Java substring() method. If a cookie name matches the one passed to the function, the cookie value is extracted using the extractCookieValue() function. If no cookie name matches the one you specify, a null value is returned:

```
function ReadCookie(cookiename) {
  var numOfCookies = document.cookie.length;
  var nameOfCookie = cookiename + "=";
  var cookieLen = nameOfCookie.length;
  var x = 0;
  while (x <= numOfCookies) {
      var y = (x + cookieLen);
      if (document.cookie.substring(x, y) == nameOfCookie)
          return(extractCookieValue(y));
      x = document.cookie.indexOf(" ", x) + 1;
      if (x == 0)
          break;
  }
  return null;
}

function extractCookieValue(val) {
  if ((endOfCookie =
      document.cookie.indexOf(";", val)) == -1) {
    endOfCookie = document.cookie.length;
  }
  return unescape(document.cookie.substring(val,endOfCookie));
}
```

Expiring (Removing) a Cookie

Cookie deletion is synonymous with the expiration of that cookie. A cookie can be expired simply by rewriting it with an expiry date that occurred in the past. Cookie deletion is an important task because cookie-resources are finite, as are all disk-based resources. Consider the following JavaScript function, deleteCookie():

```
function deleteCookie(name) {
  var todayDate = new Date();
  todayDate.setDate(todayDate.getDate() - 1);
  document.cookie = name +
                "=" +
```

```
value +
"; expires=" +
todayDate.toGMTString() +
";"
}
```

In this function, the value of `todayDate` is put *back* one day; the cookie is then rewritten, thus expiring it. This cookie can no longer return a value through the `document.cookie` property.

A Sample Cookie-Based Application

Many of the best cookie-based applications are used to store state information, which is likely to change when you revisit a particular JavaScript-enabled page or pages. Consider the following application that implements a page-hit application. *Page-hit applications*, or *hit-counters*, are extremely popular across the Web, and are used to count the number of visits to a particular Web site. The vast majority, if not all, of these applications require server-side solutions, such as Perl scripts running a CGI-based interface. The JavaScript equivalent can be used to track a *specific* user's (client's) visits to a page by using a cookie to store the number of visits made. Remember, because JavaScript is embedded within the client, that is, the browser, the hit-count can be confined only to the user visiting the current page, and not to any other users—not without using additional facilities, such as CGI or Java applets, etc. The following script uses the cookie-manipulation functions introduced earlier in this chapter.

```
<!--
   Program 13-1

-->
<html>
<script language="JavaScript">
<!--
// Number of visits variable:
var visits = 0;
// Standard cookie functions:
function extractCookieValue(val) {
  if ((endOfCookie =
      document.cookie.indexOf(";", val)) == -1) {
          endOfCookie = document.cookie.length;
  }
  return unescape(document.cookie.substring(val,endOfCookie));
}

function ReadCookie(cookiename) {
```

```javascript
        var numOfCookies = document.cookie.length;
        var nameOfCookie = cookiename + "=";
        var cookieLen = nameOfCookie.length;
        var x = 0;
        while (x <= numOfCookies) {
            var y = (x + cookieLen);
            if (document.cookie.substring(x, y) == nameOfCookie)
                return (extractCookieValue(y));
                x = document.cookie.indexOf(" ", x) + 1;
                if (x == 0)
                    break;
        }
        return (null);
}

function createCookie(name, value, expiredays) {
    var todayDate = new Date();
    todayDate.setDate(todayDate.getDate() + expiredays);
    document.cookie = name +
                        "=" +
                        value +
                        "; expires=" +
                        todayDate.toGMTString() +
                        ";"
}

function showHits() {
    // First we'll check if the user has visited this
    // page before by examining the _visitSite cookie:
    userCookie = ReadCookie("_visitSite");
    if (userCookie == null)
        visits = 1;  // This is the first visit
    else
        visits = parseInt(userCookie) + 1;
        // Create or update existing cookie:
        createCookie("_visitSite", visits, 30);
        document.write("You have visited this site on <b>" +
                        visits +
                        "</b> occasions<hr>");
}
//-->
</script>
</head>
<body>
<script>
<!--
  Call the hit counter...
```

13

```
-->
showHits();
</script>
This is where the body of the actual document
appears.<p>
</body>
</html>
```

This page-hit program is straightforward. When loaded, a <script> tag invokes the showHits() function, which checks to see if a persistent cookie exists by the name of "_visitSite". If the cookie exists, you know the user has visited this page before, so you extract the value of the cookie and add one to it—the extra value is today's visit. The cookie is then updated by rewriting it back to disk with a expiry date of 30 days into the future. A document.write statement is then used to print out the cookie to tell the user how many times he or she has visited—that is, loaded—this particular page into Navigator.

T IP: Pressing the Navigator *Reload* button will also update the cookie because the script will be reinvoked—another reason why hit-counts should always be taken with a pinch of salt. You could update the cookie by assigning a literal value to it at any time. In order to make a cookie take only a single value, simply check to see if the cookie is empty (or null). Persistent cookies can be overwritten if you reload the script that sets the cookie, so it is always wise to specifically check to see if the cookie exists before you overwrite it (assuming you do not want the cookie to be overwritten). In this way you can gain access to a real "persistent object" in that its value is static throughout the lifetime of a JavaScript application.

By creating a temporary cookie—that is, one without an expiry date—you could also count the number of hits to the current page within the current Navigator session.

Summary

Cookies are repositories for simple alphanumeric data, and are stored either persistently or temporarily. Temporary cookies have no expiry date and will be purged at the end of the current Navigator session. Persistent cookies have a future expiry date associated with them, after which they are no longer valid; i.e. they are no longer given out by Navigator when requested by a JavaScript application.

♦ Persistent cookies can be used to store information locally on the client's hard-disk. The `document.cookie` property yields a string containing each cookie. You can access each cookie using the cookie manipulation routines previously shown in the chapter, as well as in Appendix D.

♦ Use cookies to store state information, such as the details of a user's visits to a particular page or the options selected in a form, etc. You could also store user-preferences, such as window sizes and screen colors, so these settings can be restored, ready for that user's next visit to your site. The code required is small, but the possibilities for applications are endless.

13

APPENDIX A

Questions & Answers

This appendix contains a series of questions and answers that are related to all aspects of the JavaScript language.

General JavaScript Questions

This section contains questions and answers that relate to the JavaScript and HTML languages generally.

Q: What is JavaScript?

A: JavaScript (previously known as *LiveScript*) is a Java-like programming language that allows closer interaction with the browser. With JavaScript, the tags that make up an HTML document are "reflected" into a series of objects whose properties can then be changed or manipulated. JavaScript is especially good at generating dynamic HTML based upon external events and values, like dates and times. It can also be used to automate many repetitive tasks. With JavaScript, you can make a Web site change its appearance automatically at set intervals, or even program a database or a game that is viewed within the browser. JavaScript can also interface to Java applets and plug-in applications via the new LiveConnect system in Netscape Navigator 3.0 (see Chapter 11 for information on LiveConnect).

Q: How do HTML and JavaScript integrate?

A: Netscape-enhanced HTML has been altered significantly to include new attributes for integration with JavaScript. Most tags are now treated as *objects* within Netscape, so, for example, an anchor created using <a name>...</a> is now called an *anchor object,* etc. Such tags have also been given a `name` attribute so that they can be named as JavaScript objects. HTML forms are now "JavaScript-aware," in that objects such as text-fields, text-areas, checkboxes, radio buttons, and selection lists all *trigger* JavaScript events. For example, a text field that uses the `onChange` attribute will trigger an event when that field is changed by the user.

Q: What is a JavaScript alert box?

A: An "alert box" is a window that appears when an error in the current JavaScript program is detected. Click on the OK button to continue and make a note of the line-number for the error so you can locate and correct it. Multiple windows can appear in succession if more than one error is detected. Appendix I contains a list of JavaScript error messages and descriptions of some common error causes.

Audio and Sound

This section covers the integration of audio content into JavaScript/HTML applications.

Q: How can I embed sounds within my applications?

A: There are two ways of embedding sound within a hypertext page using JavaScript. The first method involves embedding the sound file within a page using the HTML <embed> tag, and requires the user to have a sound player configured as a plug-in applications. This method is suited to Navigator 3.0. For example:

```
<embed src="screech.au" width=25 height=25>
```

The second method involves using the location property to load a sound file. This will launch the default sound player NAPLAYER.EXE that comes with Navigator 3.0, for example:

```
<script language="JavaScript">
location = "screech.au";
</script>
```

By placing this script at an appropriate point within your application, Navigator will play the sound file. The appropriate helper application must be installed for this to work. You must also have hardware capable of playing such sounds, namely a sound card and speakers. The Microsoft Internet Explorer (MSIE) Web browser also supports "background sound playing" via a number of dedicated HTML tags, although it is not covered here since our discussion is primarily Netscape-based (see http://www.microsoft.com for more details on MSIE).

A

JavaScript Variables

This section contains questions and answers that relate to JavaScript variables.

Q: What "scope" does a newly created variable have?

A: In JavaScript, a variable is associated with a document loaded into the current window; therefore, if a new document is loaded any previously created variables will be lost. To overcome this problem you can use a frameset-document and define your variables within the top-level (*parent*) document. In this way, your top-level window will always remain in memory, while other windows (frames) can be used to load documents, etc.

Use the `top` and `parent` properties of the window object to enable this function. Alternatively, you can use JavaScript's "cookie" mechanism, which allows information to be stored to disk on both a temporary and permanent basis. Cookies are discussed in Chapter 13; frameset-documents are covered in Chapter 9. Variables defined in different documents are not "global;" in order to access a variable (or indeed a function) defined in another window or frame, you must use the appropriate expression to access that variable, e.g. `parent.frames[i].document.variableName` for a frameset-document, or `windowName.document.variableName` for an autonomous window opened using the JavaScript `open()` method.

Q: Do I have to use the `var` statement to create a variable?

A: No. The `var` statement is optional, although if you want to create a new variable and do not want to assign a value to it, the `var` statement must be used. Otherwise you can just assign value as required; for example,

```
var myVar = 68;
```

and

```
myVar = 68;
```

are equivalent.

Frameset-documents

This section contains questions and answers that are related to frameset-documents.

Q: None of the files (such as images) I refer to from *within* a frame can be found. What is wrong?

A: If you are writing HTML into a newly created window using the `window.open()` method, you must refer to the file either by using its "fully qualified" URL—i.e. `http://host/path` for networked documents—or by using the URL `file:///drive|c/path` for local files. Alternatively, you can use a `<base href=URL>` tag. When you dynamically write this tag into your window using a statement such as

```
myWin.document.write("<base href=" + location + ">");
```

your files will then be located by Navigator.

Q: How can a frame be loaded without using a separate file?

A: You can use the `javascript:` URL to load the frame by defining a variable that contains HTML-formatted text and then referring to this in the `<frame>`'s `src` attribute. For example:

```
var topFrame = "<body>Some <b>HTML</b> text</body>";
...
<frame src="javascript:parent.topFrame">
```

Please see Chapter 9 for more information on using the `javascript:` URL with frameset-documents.

Q: How can I load an empty frame?

A: Use the `javascript:` URL to load an empty HTML body, for example:

```
var emptyFrame = "</body></body>";
...
<frame src="javascript:parent.emptyFrame">
```

You can also use a hash mark (#) as a value for the `src` attribute, as in the following example.

```
<frame src="#">
```

This syntax should also provide an empty frame. This method has been known to cause some problems, such as frame-replication, however. To avoid that problem, you may want to consider the following syntax,

```
<frame src="javascript:">
```

which uses the `javascript:` URL to return a blank page, although this has been known to cause a few system crashes. The `javascript:` URL evaluates a JavaScript expression and returns a document. Using `parent:variable` is the recommended solution.

A

Q: What is the "anonymous" error I keep getting when referring to a field within a window?

A: If you are referring to a form field within a window or frame, and you receive an error with the "anonymous" message, it may be that you are trying to refer to a form field *before* the entire document has loaded. If you call a function that tries to access such a field within the `<script>` container, this may be the problem. To avoid this error, simply use an `onLoad` event-attribute in the `<body>` tag and call the function from here instead. This will ensure that all of the fields (and tags) within the current document are safely reflected into the necessary JavaScript objects before the function tries to refer to them prematurely.

Q: How do I access functions defined in different frames?

A: Use the standard syntax:

```
parent.framename.functionName()
```

It may be better to define functions within a *single* document, the parent frameset-document (the file with the `<frameset>` container) in this case, and then use `parent.functionName()`, where `parent` refers to the parent window, a synonym for the window object, but which refers to the Navigator window that contains the `<frameset>` tag. The synonym "`top`" can also be used, and will be the same as `parent` in this case, although `top` will need to be used when dealing with dynamically-created frameset-documents that are nested inside each other. See Chapter 9 for more details.

Q: Can I detect which frame is "active", i.e. which has focus?

A: Not yet. There is no boolean property of a frame object that allows the user to detect which frame has focus, although there has been talk of providing this in later versions of Navigator. The `focus()` method allows an autonomous window to be focused, although a frame (which is a window object) cannot use this method to gain focus. The progmatic selection of HTML elements in other frames—i.e. by assigning values to fields in other frames, etc.—does not give that frame focus either.

Q: When I return to a frameset-document using a hyperlink, the frames are duplicated. Why?

A: You must use a `target` attribute in the `<a href>` tag that you are using to return to the top-level (frameset) document. This will ensure that the original frameset-document is loaded into a "whole" window, rather than just one frame, which is what is happening in this particular case. See Chapter 9 for more details on using the `target` attribute of the `<a href>` tag. There has been a long-running bug in this area, so the problem may lie here.

The <script> and <noscript> Container Tags

This section contains information on the new `<script>` and `<noscript>` tags.

Q: Why does the <script>..</script> container need to be enclosed inside comments?

A: In a phrase: for *backward compatibility* with other Web browsers. Your JavaScript code will be written to the screen verbatim if comments are not used. JavaScript-aware browsers can scan the program code contained within a comment, although non-JavaScript browsers will ignore both the `<script>` tag *and* the contents of the script. For example, we could have

A

```
<!--
  Program A-1
-->
<script language="JavaScript">
<!--
alert("Hello, World!");
//-->
</script>
```

If the "`<!--`" and "`//-->`" were omitted, the statement "`alert("Hello, World!")`" would appear within the browser. Notice how the final comment is "`//-->`" rather than just "`-->`". Why is this? Well, since the final comment exists within the body of the script, the "`-->`" has no significance, since normal HTML is not recognized at this point. Instead, we have to use a JavaScript comment ("`//`") and then append an HTML comment onto this.

Q: Is the `language` attribute compulsory?

A: The `language` attribute is compulsory unless the `src` attribute has been specified. The use of the `src` attribute allows JavaScript code to be referenced from a remote Internet Web server.

Q: Where can `<script>` containers be placed within an HTML document?

A: A script can occur anywhere within an HTML document. Many scripts are placed in the `<head>` container because this occurs near to the top of the HTML document and will be read into memory as soon as the document is loaded. This is useful if you need to load function definitions or variables, etc. You can also use the `<script>` container within the `<body>` part of a document. In this way you can *dynamically* incorporate HTML text into your application "on the fly" as required; for example,

```
<!--
  Program A-2
-->
<html>
<body text="White">
<table bgcolor="Blue" width="100%">
<tr>
<td>
<script language="JavaScript">
<!--
 document.write(Date().substring(0, 10));
//-->
</script>
</td>
</tr>
</table>
</body>
</html>
```

would display the current date within a table row. The table background color has been set with the new `bgcolor` attribute, which is new to Atlas (Navigator 3.0) and is a good technique to use when displaying a header bar within a document.

Q: What is the `<noscript>` container used for?

The `<noscript>..</noscript>` container will be displayed when JavaScript support has been disabled from within Navigator. Non-JavaScript browsers may not recognize `<noscript>`, so this remains a Netscape-only tag until other browser manufacturers build this support into their browsers. By placing some HTML-formatted text into the `<noscript>..</noscript>` container you can provide some alternative text and/or graphics. The `<noscript>` container works in a similar manner to `<noframes>` (see Chapter 9).

Q: What is the `src` attribute for?

A: The `src` attribute of the `<script>` tag specifies the source location for a JavaScript program that is stored separately from the current HTML document. Navigator 3.0 allows JavaScript programs to be stored in separate files, in much the same way as the `<applet>` tag works with Java. Be sure to name your files with a `.js` filename extension, such as `cookie.js`, so that the files are properly imported by Navigator.

JavaScript Statements

JavaScript statements are the topic of this question and answer session.

Q: Are semicolons (`;`) required at the end of all JavaScript statements?

A

A: This is a yes and no answer. Semicolons are optional in JavaScript statements that exist on separate lines. However, if you use statements within event-handling attributes (as part of a string) you will need to terminate each statement with a semicolon (excluding the final statement). For example, the code

```
<a href="http://www.host.com/dir/page1.html"
   onClick="window.status='Click here for page 1';
            return true">
Click me!
</a>
```

requires a semicolon to separate the two JavaScript statements within an `onClick` event attribute; however, the two statements

```
tortoiseAge = 102
PetName = "Tortoise"
```

do not require semicolons. They are optional in this case because both statements occupy single lines. However, when a semicolon is introduced, you could also say

```
tortoiseAge = 102; PetName = "Joey"
```

because the JavaScript interpreter now knows where one statement ends and another begins, even though both statements occupy the same line in this case.

Q: How can I use the same quotation mark within a single statement?

A: Preface the quotation mark with a backslash ("\"), for example:

```
<a href="http://www.host.com/dir/page1.html"
   onClick="window.status=\"Click here for page 1\";
            return true">
Click me!
</a>
```

At some point you actually find yourself running out of quotation marks! If you do run out of quotes you should look for an alternative solution, such as invoking a separate function to perform the operation you require.

Obtaining User Input with JavaScript

This section considers the topic of obtaining user input via JavaScript.

Q: How can I obtain input from the user into my JavaScript application?

A: The first method involves using the JavaScript prompt() method, for example:

```
var name = prompt("Enter your e-mail address", "user@host");
```

where "user@host" is the default value placed into the prompt box in this instance.

The only other method requires the use of an HTML form and defining the necessary fields for user input. JavaScript can access, and even modify, form fields dynamically by direct assignment to the field. See Chapter 7 for more information on HTML forms.

JavaScript Events

This section considers the topic of JavaScript events.

Q: Can I invoke a JavaScript function *after* a page is loaded?

A: Yes, you can do this by using the new onLoad attribute within an HTML <body> tag. For example:

```
<html>
<body onLoad="updateFrame()">
. . .
</body>
</html>
```

will call the function updateFrame() when the current document has loaded. In this case "loaded" means when all HTML elements have been parsed, i.e. read into Navigator (the very definition of a *loaded document* has been causing much discussion since the onLoad event was sometimes triggered when images within the document were still loading). The meaning of onLoad can be confusing because the event is not triggered when the document is *initially* loaded, but when the document has finished loading (see the next Q&A). OnLoad is useful for calling functions from within a script after the document has been fully loaded.

Q: The onLoad event-handling attribute doesn't do what I want it to, which is to create HTML documents *dynamically* when a document is loaded. How do I do this in JavaScript?

A: If you need to write a function that writes data into an HTML document when it is first loaded, start by creating a simple function that writes out a <body> tag (and whatever other HTML-formatted text and HTML attributes you need), then call the function immediately after you have defined it (a compulsory call). Now you can put a literal </body> tag into your text at the end of your document, and you are done. For example:

```
<!--
  Program A-3
-->
<html>
<head>
<script language="JavaScript">
<!--
 function startBody() {
   document.writeln("<html><body " +
                    "background=back1.gif text=#0000ff>");
 }
 // Call the function to start the body:
 startBody();
//-->
</script>
</head>
This is where your actual HTML body text goes...
</body>
</html>
```

defines a function, `startBody()`, that dynamically creates the first part of a
`<body>.</body>` container.

Q: How can I invoke a JavaScript function using an event?

A: Defining a button within an HTML form is one solution, whereby you use
the event-handler attribute `onClick` to reference the JavaScript function.
For example,

```
<form name="myForm">
<input type="button"
       value="Click me"
       onClick="myFunc()">
</form>
```

would create a button on the page; when clicked, the button activates the
JavaScript function named `myFunc()`. You can also invoke a JavaScript
function automatically, without user involvement. This is done by defining
a function and then calling it immediately; for example, the code

```
<script language="JavaScript">
<!--
 function myFunc() {
   ...
 }
```

```
myFunc();
//-->
</script>
```

calls the user-defined function called `myFunc()`. Watch out when using this method, because if you try to refer to a JavaScript object—for example, a text-field defined with a `<input type>` tag—you may get an error message saying that the object is "anonymous." This happens because object reflection happens *after* a document is fully loaded. If a `<body>` tag houses all of the fields you are referring to, calling a function to access these fields *before* Navigator has even scanned them will cause a "*property not found*" error. Another solution to this problem involves calling the function from a `<body>` tag using the `onLoad` attribute; for example,

```
<body onLoad="myFunc()">
...
</body>
```

ensures that the function `myFunc()` is invoked when the document containing this function has been fully loaded.

JavaScript and Forms

This question and answer section concentrates on JavaScript's interactions with HTML forms.

Q: How can I refer to a form within a document?

A: Forms are accessed using the `forms` array, which belongs to the `document` object, so

```
document.forms[0]
```

is the first form within the *current* document. To refer to a form within a frame, prefix the name of the frame onto the `document` object. For example,

```
parent.frames[0].document.forms[0]
```

is the first form within the first frame of a frameset-document. The `parent` object must be specified when referring to individual frames (see Chapter 9). Referring to a form by itself is not enough in this case, however, because in order to access the literal information *within* a form—data within the fields of a form, for example—you must add the name of the field required, followed by the `value` property. For example,

```
document.forms[0].myField.value
```

would extract the value of the field `"myField"` from the first form within the current document.

If a `<form>` tag is named using the `name` attribute, as in `<form name="myForm">`, then you do not have to use the `forms` array to specify a form. Simply replace this with the value of the `name` attribute, for example:

```
document.myForm.myField.value
```

Q: I am receiving an error message that says a form field does not exist. What is wrong?

A: First, check all spellings and the ordering of objects. If you are calling a function within the `<script>` container that refers to a field defined within the `<body>` of your document, this may be causing the problem, because the whole document has not yet been loaded into Navigator. Place the function-call within a `<body onLoad=...>` tag in this case. A tell-tale sign is the Navigator error message *"anonymous field has no properties"* (or words to this effect). You may also wish to check the `name` attribute of the field to see if it is not misspelled, etc. Remember that JavaScript is case-sensitive, so check the case of the field as well to see if it matches. If the field does not have a `name` attribute you can use the `elements` array to refer to it (see Chapter 7).

Also, when using the `open()` and `close()` methods, to dynamically create documents, you should check to see that you are not overwriting the document that contains the variable you are having problems trying to reference. Refreshing a document removes all previously defined variables and functions, unless you use a frameset document and keep all variables and functions in the top-level parent document. See Chapter 9 for more information on frameset-documents and "persistent" objects.

Q: When performing numeric calculations using form fields, I receive very large numbers. How can I round these numbers sensibly?

A: Use the `roundValue()` function shown in Appendix D. This will allow you to convert a number like `14.9999995` to `15.0`, etc.

Dynamic HTML Generation

The topic of dynamic HTML generation is covered in this Q&A section.

Q: How can I send HTML-formatted text from JavaScript into the Netscape browser?

A: By using the `document.write()` and `document.writeln()` functions. The latter sends a carriage-return code at the end of the string that is written. For example,

```
document.writeln("<table><tr><td>This is some HTML-formatted " +
                 "text within a table</td></tr></table>");
```

sends an HTML-formatted string—that creates a simple table structure—into the Navigator browser. Because you can control the exact HTML that is sent to the browser, it is possible to alter the appearance of documents according to prespecified rules. That is, you could return differently formatted HTML-documents depending on the output of a JavaScript function. It is also a good idea to use `document.open()` and `document.close()` around the `write()` methods, especially if you want to regenerate a complete document or update a complete frame's contents. When generating documents dynamically be sure not to write data *indiscriminately* into a document, otherwise you may crash Navigator. Always try and use a document-stream; that is, use the `document.open()` and `document.close()` methods to write a stream of HTML-formatted text to the browser, i.e. to a specific frame—for example, using an expression such as `parent.frames[0].document.open()` to open a stream to the first frame within a frameset-document. Be sure to close the stream afterwards.

A

Q: What is inline JavaScript evaluation?

A: Navigator 3.0 introduced a very important concept known as inline JavaScript evaluation. Basically, this is a way of allowing HTML to evaluate JavaScript expressions when assigning values to HTML attributes. The syntax `&{ expression };` is used for this, where `expression` is a JavaScript expression, such as a reference to a JavaScript variable, or object, or a mathematical expression. For example, rather than saying

```
<body bgcolor="Blue">
```

which hard-codes the value "Blue" into the tag, you can now "soft-code" such tags; for example, you could have

```
<!--
  Program A-4
-->
```

```
<html>
<script language="JavaScript">
<!--
  function getTheDay() {
    var dateToday = new Date();
    var dayToday  = dateToday.getDay(); // Day number 0-6
    if (dayToday >= 3)
       backcolor = "Blue";
    else
       backcolor = "Black";
  }
  getTheDay();
//-->
</script>
<body bgcolor="&{ backcolor };">
This is the body of the document.<p>
</body>
</html>
```

which in this case assigns a background color to the current page based upon the current day. The day is ascertained by using the JavaScript `getDay()` method, so if it is Wednesday or later, the background color will be Blue; otherwise it will be Black. Notice how the inline evaluation uses the `backcolor` variable to substitute a color-verb string into the `<body>` tags `bgcolor` attribute. There are unlimited uses for inline evaluation. For example, I like to allocate different fonts to different documents based upon a `<font face="&{ parent.globalFont }">` expression, where `parent.globalFont` is a variable containing the name of a font—e.g. `"Helvetica"`—that is defined within a parent frameset-document in this instance.

Evaluation of expressions can only take place when assigning values to HTML attributes, remember. Note also that you cannot place JavaScript program statements within a `&{};` since this is not "evaluation" as such, but rather "execution."

Q: Is it possible to create scripts and applets dynamically?

A: Yes. Simply output a `<script>` or `<applet>` container using the `document.write()` method. and Navigator should interpret them accordingly, just as if they had been typed literally into a document and then read into the browser.

Q: Can documents be appended to when they have been fully displayed?

A: It is not advisable to use the `document.write()` and `document.writeln()` methods to add text to a document that has been fully displayed. The entire document should ideally be refreshed or regenerated from scratch and they redisplayed. The `document.open()` and `document.close()` methods can be used to write *streams* of HTML-formatted text to the browser in one continuous chunk. You should be able to append data to a document by using successive `document.writeln()` methods, just as long as an `open()` has not been issued, i.e. so that the document is not expecting a "stream" of data to arrive.

Anchors and Hyperlinks

This Q&A section examines JavaScript's ability to work with anchors and hyperlinks.

Q: Is there an equivalent to the `<a href="#anchor">` tag?

A: Yes. Use the `hash` property of the `location` object; for example, the JavaScript statement,

```
location.hash = "section1";
```

would position the current document at the `<a name="section1">` tag (assuming it exists). This technique requires the document to be reloaded, so I wouldn't recommend it for very large documents.

A

Q: Is it possible to create anchors and links dynamically?

A: Yes. The `anchor()` and `link()` methods are provided for this very purpose. Please refer to Chapter 2 for more information and examples.

Properties

This section examines JavaScript object properties.

Q: How can I change document-based properties within JavaScript, rather than using HTML?

A: Some of the *read-write* properties of JavaScript allow direct modification; for example, if you placed the JavaScript statement,

```
document.bgColor="Black";
```

into your application, the background-color would be set to black. This saves having to use the <body bgColor=...> tag, and thus saves you from loading a new document just to change the document colors. *Read-write* properties are properties that can be assigned values. Not all of JavaScript's properties have this particular capability, however. Appendix B contains a list and description of each JavaScript property.

Window Manipulation

Window manipulation is the topic of this Q&A session.

Q: How can I open a new window?

A: Use the window.open() method, as described in Chapter 8.

Q: I want to access variables and functions in the "parent" window. How do I do this?

A: A new browser window is opened using the JavaScript window.open() method. In this case, however, the concept of a "parent" window is not the same as when dealing with frameset-documents created with the <frameset> container. You must use the opener property to refer to the parent window that *created* the current window, that is, to the window that invoked the open() call. Using parent or top will *not* work with autonomous windows. If your parent window is a frameset-document, be sure to mention the name of the variable or function within the frame that you require. For example, opener.frames[0].document.myFunc(), when used *within* a window created by an window.open() call, refers to the function myFunc() defined within the first frame of the parent frameset-document. If you have defined functions and variables in other frames, use the example in Chapter 8 that *loops* through each window to find the function and/or variable that you require. It makes sense to define functions and variables within a single frame, such as a parent frameset-document, and then refer to this frame only (multiple functions in different frames can make JavaScript applications overly complicated).

Q: How can I load a URL into a window?

A: Pass the URL to the first argument in `open()`. Alternatively, you can dynamically update the URL of the window by assigning a value to its `location` property, for example,

```
w1 = open("", "myWin", "height=300,width=500"););
w1.location = "newfile.htm";
```

which is the same as:

```
w1 = open("newfile.htm", "myWin","height=300,width=500");
```

You can use the `location` property of a window to read a new file (or URL) into that window at any time, perhaps via a form element like a button that the user can select.

File Access

The topic of file-access is discussed in this Q&A session.

Q: How can you access files locally from within JavaScript?

A: JavaScript under Navigator 2.0 and 3.0 has no standard methods for allowing access to a local file-system, for security reasons. Java programs have been written that allow local file access, although this approach is not recommended since it may not work in future releases of Navigator. Netscape's new Galileo project, which represents a major new release of the Netscape Navigator client, will have a "trusted applet" scheme, whereby Java applets can write to a server machine, or to a local disk. For more information you are directed to the URL:

```
http://home.netscape.com/comprod/at_work/white_paper/
intranet/vision.html
```

A

APPENDIX B

A-Z of JavaScript's Methods and Properties

You can use this appendix to refer to methods and properties that are used throughout the examples in this book.

♦ **Part 1** of this appendix is an A-Z guide to JavaScript's standard object methods and properties.

♦ **Part 2** is a guide to each of JavaScript's object properties (objects themselves are discussed in Chapters 4 and 6).

Part 1: A-Z of JavaScript Methods

This appendix details each JavaScript method in an A-Z manner. Each entry has a syntax description, a return value (if applicable), and the object family that the method belongs to.

abs()

Syntax:

```
Math.abs(val)
```

Returns: The absolute value of the numeric argument `val`.

Object family: `Math`.

The absolute value of a number is that number with any preceding sign removed; for example, the value `-36` has an absolute value of `36`, which can be seen using the simple script:

```
<!--
  Program B-1
-->
<html>
<script language="JavaScript">
<!--
var val = -36;              // Negative value
var newVal = Math.abs(val);  // Positive value
//-->
</script>
</html>
```

acos()

Syntax:

```
Math.acos(val)
```

Returns: The arc cosine value of the argument `val`.

Object family: `Math`.

The `acos()` method returns the arc cosine (in radians) of the numeric argument `val`.

alert()
Syntax:

```
alert(string | expression);
```

Returns: Nothing.

Object family: `window`.

The `alert()` method allows a string of text to be displayed within a window on the users screen. The window is autonomous from the main Navigator window, although while the alert window is active, Navigator cannot be selected. An exclamation mark icon will be shown at the side of the message and an OK button is provided to close the window. The user must therefore acknowledge the window. HTML-formatted text will be shown literally within `string` and should not be used. Since `window` is a top-level object you do not need to prefix the `alert()` method with "window." In order to break up lines in the alert box, use the `\n` (*new line*) code; for example,

```
alert("Welcome to my Home Page!\n\nThis page requires " +
      "Navigator 3.0.");
```

Navigator places the text `"JavaScript Alert:"` at the top of the window to distinguish the message from a standard Windows 95 dialog box (this text cannot be removed and is provided automatically by Navigator). `alert()` is useful mainly as a warning mechanism; for example, by defining a function that validates a particular field of an input-form:

```
function validateName(name) {
  if (name.length > 30) {
     alert("Names must be less than 30 characters.");
  }
}
```

you can warn the user of any problems with the input they have entered:

```
<form>
<input type="text"
       name="aname"
       onBlur="validateName(this.form.aname)">
...
</form>
```

B

anchor()

Syntax:

```
String.anchor(anchName);
```

Returns: Nothing.

Object family: String.

Anchors are the targets for `<a href="#anchorName">..</a>` hyperlink tags. They are points within a hypertext document that can be moved by using a hyperlink that addresses that particular anchor, and are useful for creating indexes and for providing the user with a way of moving around to specific portions of a document. Anchors can exist locally, within the same file, or externally within other files. The target for an anchor can also be a URL such as another Web server on the Internet.

The `anchor()` method is used to make a string-object (`String`) into a named anchor, where `anchName` is the name for the anchor. Consider the following example:

```
<!--
  Program B-2
-->
<html>
<head>
<script>
<!--
anchorName = "Section1";
anc        = anchorName.anchor(anchorName);
document.writeln("Click <a href=#Section1>here</a> " +
              "for section 1.");
/*
** More of the current document appears
** inbetween here ...
*/

// Section 1:
document.writeln("<a name=" + anchorName + ">" +
              "<h1>Section 1<hr></h1></a>");
document.writeln("This is the text for section 1.");
//-->
</script>
</head>
<body>
</body>
</html>
```

which implements a named-anchor using the `anchor()` method to create the anchor "`Section1`" (noting that spaces are not allowed in anchor names). The variable `anchorName` is a string-object that contains the name of the anchor, and `anc` is an anchor-object that creates the anchor. By clicking on the hyperlink named *here* the user is then positioned at the anchor named "`Section1`," effectively moving the user to that part of the document just as if he or she had navigated his or her way manually to this region of the document using the cursor keys, etc. If you need to specify an anchor in another HTML file, use the syntax:

```
<a href="filename.html#anchorName">Click here</a>
```

The `<a href>` code can also be replaced by a JavaScript equivalent, namely the `link()` method, which is used to create a hyperlink. See the later section on `link()` for more information.

asin()
Syntax:

```
asin(val)
```

Returns: The arc sine of the argument passed as `val`.

Object family: `Math`.

The `asin()` function is passed a numeric value (specified in radians) and produces the arc sine of that value.

atan()
Syntax:

```
atan(val)
```

Returns: The arc tangent of the argument `val`.

Object family: `Math`.

back()
Syntax:

```
history.back()
```

Returns: Nothing.

Object family: `history`.

B

The `history.back()` method simulates the pressing of the *Back* button in
Netscape Navigator, allowing the previous hypertext document to be loaded.
In the case of a frameset-document the previous frame will be loaded
instead. This method performs the same action as a `go(-1)` method. If you
use the *Reload* button in Netscape with a document containing a `back()`
statement, Netscape will continue to load the previous URL from the history
buffer; i.e. you will retrieve a unique document upon each reload. You could
implement a simple *Back* and *Forward* button of your own in JavaScript,
implemented as:

```
<!--
  Program B-3
-->
<html>
<body>
<form>
<input type="button"
       value="Back"
       onClick="history.back()">
<input type="button"
       value="Forward"
       onClick="history.forward()">
</form>
</body>
</html>
```

where the `forward()` method invokes the opposite action to `back()`.
Emulating Netscape's *Back* and *Forward* buttons can be useful in allowing the
user to still have basic page navigation controls in the event of a disabled
toolbar. Disabling Navigator's main toolbar allows a larger display area to be
used, especially if Navigator's directory buttons and location field are
disabled. Netscape's toolbars can be disabled by opening a new window
using an `open()` method with the `toolbar=no` attribute. See `open()` for
more details.

big()
Syntax:

```
String.big()
```

Returns: Nothing.

Object family: String.

Use `big()` with a string to make that string appear in a large font. This makes use of Netscape's `<big>..</big>` container tag; for example,

```
document.writeln("This is " + "big".big() + " text");
```

would place the word `"big"` in a `<big>..</big>` container, thus making this word appear in a larger font than the rest of the sentence. Notice how the string-object `"big"` has been placed literally in the text; this could be replaced with a string-variable if required, of course.

The actual font size rendered by a `<big>` tag will depend on the settings in Navigator's Options/Preferences/Fonts setup screen, and will be relative to the base font set within Navigator's Preferences.

blink()
Syntax:

```
String.blink()
```

Returns: Nothing.

Object family: String.

Use `blink()` with a string object to make that string blink. This makes use of Navigator's HTML `<blink>..</blink>` container.

```
document.writeln("This is " + "blinking".blink() +
           " good!");
```

blur()
Syntax:

```
objName.blur()
```

Returns: Nothing.

Object family: `password, text, textArea`.

`blur()` removes focus from a given object (`objName`). *Focus* is the term applied to the object that is currently selected, e.g. a text field within an HTML form. `objName` can be a password, a select object, text object, or text area object.

B

bold()

Syntax:

```
string.bold()
```

Returns: Nothing.

Object family: String.

This method makes the specified string object **bold** by encapsulating the string in HTML .. (bold) tags. Ensure that the case of the function is kept as shown. For example, we could have the following code:

```
myVar = "bold";
document.writeln("This is "+ myVar.bold() + " text");
```

which writes the string 'This is **bold** text' into the Navigator browser.

ceil()

Syntax:

```
Math.ceil(val)
```

Returns: The next largest integer (whole number) that is greater than `val`. If `val` is already an integer, the same value is returned.

Object family: `Math`. For example:

```
alert(Math.ceil(45.67));    // Displays 46
alert(Math.ceil(45.0));     // Displays 45
```

charAt()

Syntax:

```
string.charAt(index);
```

Returns: A character at the string-index indicated by the numeric value of `index`.

Object family: `string`. `charAt()` is used to return a character at a given position within a string; for example,

```
myString = "Wombat";
m_Pos = myString.charAt(2);
```

would set the variable `m_Pos` to the value "m".

NOTE: Strings start at position 0 in JavaScript.

clear()
Syntax:

```
document.clear()
```

Returns: Nothing.

Object family: document.

The clear() method clears a document loaded into a frame or window. Navigator can be reluctant to clear the document on most platforms, so it is recommended that you use document.open() and document.close() in succession, which should have the same effect. clear() did not function in Navigator 3.0.

clearTimeout()
Syntax:

```
clearTimeout(timeout-ID)
```

Returns: Nothing.

Object family: window.

The clearTimeout() method clears a time-out event created with setTimeout(), where timeout-ID is the value returned from an earlier call to setTimout(). For example,

```
var id = setTimeout("alert('Hello!')", 60000);
clearTimeout(id);
```

would clear the time-out event named as id before it was invoked in 60 seconds time.

B

click()
Syntax:

```
formObject.click()
```

Returns: Nothing.

Object family: checkbox, radio button, submit, reset, and button.

Mouse-clicks on a specific object within an HTML-form can be simulated using the `click()` method in JavaScript, thus allowing clickable objects to be activated from within a JavaScript program. The effect of a `click()` action will alter according to the `formobject` specified. The objects currently supported include those shown in the object family description above. For radio buttons and checkboxes the elements are selected/checked. Buttons include `submit` and `reset` objects.

Navigator's `click()` method was not functioning at the time of writing (Navigator 3.0). It is expected to be fixed in later versions. You can check radio buttons and checkboxes by assigning a `true` or `false` value to the `checked` property of the object. Under Navigator 3.0 the `clear()` method can be used to highlight a button, although it will not invoke the button—this may actually be a security consideration, so that programs can not invoke certain actions without the user's involvement.

close()
Syntax:

```
document.close()
window.close()
```

Returns: For a window object, the window-id value.

Object family: `window` and `document`.

When used with a window object the window is closed, and the parent window is given focus. For document objects, the `document.close()` method closes a text stream opened with the `document.open()` method. If `close()` is used by itself, `window.close()` is assumed. For example,

```
var w1 = window.open("", "w1", "width=300,height=100")
w1.document.open();
w1.document.write("<form>" +
                "<input type='button' value='Close' " +
                "onClick='self.close()'>" +
                "</form>";
w1.document.close();
```

creates a window using `window.open()` and then writes some HTML into the window to create a form button that allows the current window (using the `self` window object synonym) to be closed.

confirm()

Syntax:

```
confirm(String);
```

Returns: `true` (for OK button) and `false` (for CANCEL button)

Object family: `window`.

The `confirm()` function displays a user-defined message within a window and presents an OK and CANCEL button that the user can click on. The function returns a boolean (logical) value depending on the button pressed by the user, which can be used as a test condition for a task or action. For example, we could have the following code:

```
var result = confirm("Are you sure?");
if (result) {
    alert("You clicked on the 'OK' button");
}
else {
    alert("You clicked on the 'CANCEL' button");
}
```

In this small JavaScript example, the variable `result` is assigned the value returned from the `confirm()` function. Upon clicking an appropriate button, an `if` statement shows a simple message indicating the button pressed (although any valid JavaScript statements can be placed in these code-blocks, of course). Below is the `confirm()` window from the above example. Notice how the text "JavaScript Confirm:" is placed in the window so that you know this dialog box originates from the Netscape JavaScript interpreter.

B

It is possible to shorten your code somewhat when using `if` statements with the `confirm()` function. Consider the following code, for example, where the `confirm()` function has been integrated into an `if` statement in the same line:

```
var result;
if ((result=confirm("Are you sure?")) == true) {
    // User pressed on 'OK' button
    alert("You pressed OK");
}
```

If you wish to be even more compact, however, you can omit the equality testing criterion completely,

```
if (confirm("Are you sure?")) {
    // User pressed on 'OK' button
    alert("You pressed OK");
}
```

since `confirm()` is a boolean method and specific variables do not need to be set in order to test the value that it actually returns.

cos()
Syntax:

```
Math.cos(val);
```

Returns: The cosine of the argument `val`.

Object family: `Math`.

escape()
Syntax:

```
escape("String")
```

Returns: The ASCII code for the argument `String` of the form `"%nn"`.

Object family: Internal method.

The `escape()` method returns the ASCII code of the character passed to the method; for example,

```
var ascChar = escape("%");
```

places the value `"%25"` into the variable `ascChar`. Alphanumeric characters that are passed to `escape()` are returned unchanged.

eval()
Syntax:

```
eval(String)
```

Returns: The value of the evaluated expression.

Object family: Internal.

`eval()` evaluates expressions that can include variables and object-properties. It is not used to evaluate arithmetical expressions, since these are handled by JavaScript automatically (this feature has changed from Navigator 2.0). The `eval()` method is highly useful in JavaScript applications that need to invoke function-calls that are constructed dynamically; for example,

```
var val = "0-07-709292-9";
var funcCall = "lookUpIsbn('" + val + "')";
eval(funcCall);
```

would call the function `lookUpIsbn()` with the variable argument 'val'.

exp()
Syntax:

```
exp(val)
```

Returns: The exponent of the numeric argument `val`.

Object family: `Math`.

This mathematical method returns Euler's constant (*e*) to the power of the argument `val`.

B

```
e = exp(1);   // Returns 2.71828...
```

The `Math.E` property also returns the same value as `exp(1)`.

fixed()
Syntax:

```
String.fixed()
```

Returns: Nothing.

Object family: String.

The `fixed()` method causes a text string, `String`, to be displayed in a fixed-pitch (monospace) font by encapsulating the string argument in a `<tt>..<./tt>` (teletype monospaced text) container. `<tt>`, unlike `<pre>`, does not issue a paragraph break after the closing tag.

floor()
Syntax:

```
Math.floor(val)
```

Returns: The greatest whole number (integer) that is less than or equal to `val`.

Object family: `Math`. For example:

```
alert(Math.floor(43.4));    // Displays 43
```

focus()
Syntax:

```
obj.focus();
```

Returns: Nothing.

Object family: window, password, text, text area, and select.

This method moves focus to the object `obj`, that is to say that object `obj` becomes the currently selected object within the browser. For example, a text-area field created and named using the HTML `<textarea>..</textarea>` tag could be given focus so that the cursor appears within that field ready for the user to enter or change a value within it. Windows can now be given focus (a feature new to Navigator 3.0).

fontcolor()
Syntax:

```
String.fontcolor(RGB-color | color-verb)
```

Returns: Nothing.

Object family: String.

This method sets the color of a string using the `<font color="#rrggbb">..</fontcolor>` container. The argument `RGB-color` can be a red-green-blue triplet specified in hexadecimal notation, `#FFFF00` being yellow and `"#0000ff"` being Blue, for example, or alternatively can be a color verb such as "`Yellow`." See Appendix G for a list of color codes supported by Navigator 3.0.

fontsize()

Syntax:

```
fontsize(size)
```

Returns: Nothing.

Object family: String.

The `fontsize()` method allows text to be changed in size. This is done by encapsulating a string in Netscape `<font size=size>..</font>` tags; for example, to print a string of text with a font size of 14 the following statement could be used.

```
var MyString = "Example text";
document.writeln(MyString.fontsize(14));
```

You can also increase and decrease the font size using `+size` and `-size` values. For example, `+1` would increase the size of the font by one level. The `<basefont size=n>` tag specifies a default font size in HTML, to which all other +/- settings are relative.

forward()

Syntax:

```
forward()
```

Returns: Nothing.

Object family: `history`.

Use the `forward()` method to simulate the pressing of the Netscape Navigator *Forward* button. The Forward button is a navigation button in Netscape's toolbar that allows the user to move between previously loaded documents. This method is the same as issuing a `go(1)` statement. See the `back()` method as well.

getDate()

Syntax:

```
dateObject.getDate()
```

B

Returns: The day of the month (a number between 1 and 31) for the object named `dateObject`.

Object family: `Date`.

This method can be used to extract the current day number from the current month. Be sure to apply the function to a `Date` object, such as the one provided by the JavaScript `Date()` method; for example,

```
theDate = new Date("August 8, 1996 08:08:08");
theDay = theDate.getDate();
```

would store the value 8 in to the variable `theDay`.

getDay()
Syntax:

```
dateObject.getDay()
```

Returns: The day of the week for the date object named `dateObject`. The following integer values are returned from `getDay()`: **0** for Sunday, **1** for Monday, **2** for Tuesday, **3** for Wednesday, **4** for Thursday, **5** for Friday, and **6** for Saturday.

Object family: `Date`. For example,

```
theDate = new Date("December 28, 1995 11:00:00");
DayNum = theDate.getDay();
```

would store the value 4 in the variable `DayNum`, since December 28, 1995 was a Thursday.

getMinutes()
Syntax:

```
dateObject.getMinutes()
```

Returns: The minutes in the date object named as `dateObject`.

Object family: `Date`.

For example, if we had

```
theDate = new Date("December 28, 1995 11:33:00");
Mins = theDate.getMinutes();
```

the value 33 would be stored in the variable `Mins`.

getMonth()
Syntax:

```
dateObject.getMonth()
```

Returns: The month in the date object named as `dateObject`. Months are represented by the numbers **0** to **11** (January to December).

Object family: `Date`.

getSeconds()
Syntax:

```
dateObject.getSeconds()
```

Returns: The seconds (**0-59**) in the date object named `dateObject`.

Object family: `Date`.

getTime()
Syntax:

```
dateObject.getTime()
```

Returns: The number of milliseconds since the JavaScript *epoch date* (1 January, 1970 00:00:00).

Object family: `Date`.

getTimezoneOffset()
Syntax:

```
dateObject.getTimezoneOffset()
```

Returns: The time zone difference (in minutes)—e.g. the difference between local time (on the client machine) and Greenwich Mean Time (GMT).

Object family: `Date`.

For example, we could have

```
theDate = Date();
Localtime = theDate.getTimezoneOffset();
```

B

The value returned `getTimezoneOffset()` cannot be constant due to daylight saving time in various countries.

getYear()
Syntax:

```
dateObject.getYear()
```

Returns: The year value from the date object `dateObject`.

Object family: `Date`.

go()
Syntax:

```
object.go(val | "String")
```

Returns: Nothing.

Object family: `history`.

`go()` is a method that belongs to the `history` object that moves the user to a different hypertext document based upon the current Netscape history. The `go()` method can be passed one of two arguments: (1) an integer value `val` that represents the number of history entries to move backward or forward (use negatively signed integers like -3 for backward movement); or (2) a `String` representing a URL to move to, based upon that string matching a substring of the `String` argument. For example, you can search for a URL in the history list using a substring search, upon which Netscape will then load the URL for that particular history entry (strings are not case-sensitive). For example,

```
history.go(-3);
```

would move backward three history entries, according to the current Netscape document history, whereas,

```
history.go("users/ag17");
```

would search the current Netscape history for a string containing `"users/ag17"` and then load that URL accordingly, i.e. `http://www.gold.net/users/ag17/index.htm`. If multiple URLs are matched, only the first is returned.

If you use a zero value for the `val` argument—e.g. `history.go(0)`—the current document is re-loaded, rather like pressing the *Reload* button in

Navigator. This can be useful to refresh a document, for example, after changing a font face or font size, etc.

indexOf()
Syntax:

```
String.indexOf(char, [index])
```

Returns: The index (an integer) representing the position of the first character, char, optionally starting from position index.

Object family: String.

indexOf() is a string-based method that is used to search for instances of a particular character in a string object; for example,

```
aString = "wombat@marsupial.somehost.au";
PosAt = aString.indexOf("@");
```

would place the value 6 into the variable named PosAt, because the character @ lies at position six within the string stored in variable aString. Remember that in JavaScript, index-positions start at zero (0). So, for example, we could extract the hostname from the above string with,

```
HostName = aString.substring(PosAt, aString.length);
```

which uses JavaScript's substring() method to extract the part of the string we need. The index argument is used when you want to start the search from a specific character within a string. You could use indexOf() to ascertain this value.

isNaN()
Syntax:

```
isNaN(testValue)
```

Returns: true or false.

Object family: Internal.

The isNaN() function is a platform-specific function (Unix, at the time of writing) that is used to determine whether a given value is "not a number." The parseInt() and parseFloat() methods that are implemented on all other platforms, apart from Windows 95, return the value "NaN" when they encounter a value that isn't a number. Under the Unix version of Netscape Navigator isNaN() returns true if the outcome is non-number, and false

B

otherwise. `isNan()` can be useful in validation routines that need to test for numeric results.

italics()
Syntax:

```
String.italics()
```

Returns: Nothing.

Object family: String.

`italics()` changes the appearance of the string-object named `String` so that it is *italicized*. The effect is made using an HTML `<i>..</i>` (italics) container that encapsulates the `String` object. For example, we could have,

```
document.write("This is displayed in italics".italics());
```

which would display *"This is displayed in italics"* within the Navigator browser's document area.

lastIndexOf()
Syntax:

```
String.lastIndexOf(char | [,index])
```

Returns: The index within the calling string of the *last* occurrence of the specified character, or `-1` if the character does not exist.

Object family: String.

The calling string (`String`) is searched in a backward manner, optionally starting at position `index` (which can range from `0` to `String.length-1`). For example,

```
var myUrl="ftp://www.wombat.com/wombats/";
var lastCharPos=myUrl.lastIndexOf("/");
```

would store the value `28` in the variable `lastCharPos` because this is the position at which the last `"/"` sign appears.

link()
Syntax:

```
String.link(UrlString)
```

Returns: Nothing.

Object family: String.

The `link()` method makes the string-object `String` into an HTML hyperlink by encapsulating the entire string within an HTML `<a href>..</a>` container. The method is used to dynamically create hyperlinks from within JavaScript programs, rather than using raw HTML. The `UrlString` object must therefore be a valid URL, and `String` is the text for the hyperlink, which the user sees within Navigator. For example, we could use the following code to create a hyperlink to the URL `http://www.gold.net/users/ag17/index.htm`.

```
<!--
  Program B-4
-->
<html>
<head>
<script language="JavaScript">
<!--
  myUrl = "http://www.gold.net/users/ag17/index.htm";
  ref    = "here";
  document.open();
  document.writeln("Click " + ref.link(myUrl) +
                   " to visit my home page.");
  document.close();
//-->
</script>
</head>
<body><hr></body>
</html>
```

In this case the variable `ref` is a string-object that contains the single word `here`, and which represents the text of the hyperlink that the user will click on. The actual URL is stored in the string-object named `myUrl`; therefore, the expression `ref.link(myUrl)` creates the link required. In order to display the link within the current HTML document, the `document.writeln()` method is used.

In order to provide an anchor for a *local* hyperlink—a link to another part of a document, for example—use a URL of the form `filename#anchorname` (or just `#anchorName` for the current document) with the JavaScript `anchor()` method.

`log()`
Syntax:

B

```
log(val)
```

Returns: The natural logarithm (base *e*) of the numeric argument `val`.

Object family: `Math`.

max()
Syntax:

```
max(val1, val2)
```

Returns: The larger numeric argument, `val1` or `val2`.

Object family: `Math`.

The `max()` method should be used to return the greater of two arguments; for example,

```
number1 = 100;
number2 = 101;
largest = max(number1, number2);
```

places the value `101` into the numeric variable `largest`.

min()
Syntax:

```
min(val1, val2)
```

Returns: The lesser numeric argument, `val1` or `val2`.

Object family: `Math`. The `min()` method works in the opposite manner to the `max()` method, as described above.

open()
Syntax:

```
document.open(documentURL);
window.open("URL", "windowName", ["WindowFeatures,..."]);
```

Returns: Window ID value.

Object family: `window` and `document`.

The `open()` method in JavaScript works in two modes, the first for document-based objects and the second for window-based objects (URLs loaded into a new browser window).

Window-Based Objects

For a *window*-based object, open() opens a new window, rather like selecting the *File / New Web Browser* option in Navigator. The "URL" argument is the Uniform Resource Locator that you want to load, such as the address of another Web site or alternative service. If left blank, open() opens a blank window with no URL initially loaded. The "windowName" argument names the new window, although you can refer to the window by assigning the window.open() call to a JavaScript variable.

The optional windowFeatures argument is a comma-separated list of *optional* values that control the appearance of the new window and are documented fully in Chapter 8. For example,

```
var w1 = window.open("http://www.osborne.com",
                     "w1",
                     "height=500,width=800,toolbar=no");
```

creates a window measuring 500x800 pixels and disables the Navigator toolbar. The URL "http://www.osborne.com" is loaded into the window when it is opened.

The window object prefix is optional because the window object is always assumed, as it is the top-level object in JavaScript; all open() calls default to window.open() and *not* document.open(), note.

If you need to ascertain the size of the users screen (in pixels) in order to determine the size of your newly created windows, please refer to Chapter 11 on LiveConnect, where a Java applet is provided for this purpose.

Document-Based Objects

In a *document*-based object, the document.open() method is used to open a text stream. The document().close() method is used to close the stream. Streams are mainly used to send HTML-formatted text into the browser in one large chunk, refreshing the *entire* document in the process. For example,

```
document.open();
document.write("<hr><center>This is some HTML text" +
               "</center></hr>");
document.close();
```

refreshes the current document with the HTML enclosed in the write() method, effectively placing this HTML text in a new document by itself.

If you need to write text into a specific window or frame, use the appropriate object prefix; for example,

B

```
w1.document.write("...");
```

would write some HTML text into the separate browser window (see Chapter 8) named as 'w1', where `w1` is assigned to a `window.open()` call, whereas,

```
parent.frames[1].document.write("...");
```

would write text into the second frame of a frameset-document (see Chapter 9).

parse()
Syntax:

```
Date.parse(dateString)
```

Returns: The number of milliseconds in a date string since the epoch date (January 1st, 1970 00:00:00 local time).

Object-family: `Date`.

parseFloat()
Syntax:

```
parseFloat(String)
```

Returns: A floating point number.

Object family: Internal.

The `parseFloat` method parses a string argument and returns a floating point number based upon that string value. This method therefore coerces one data-type, a string, into a number. For example,

```
var myNum = "8.68";
car numericNum = parseFloat(myNum);
```

stores the numeric value `8.68` in the variable named `numericNum`.

parseInt()
Syntax:

```
parseInt(String [,radix])
```

Returns: An integer of the specified radix (or *base*).

Object family: Internal.

The `parseInt()` method parses a string and attempts to return a whole number (an integer) of the specified base (`radix`). Example bases include 10 for decimal and 16 for hexadecimal, the latter of which uses the numbers 0-9 and letters A-F to represent a numeric value, e.g. FF (hexadecimal, base 16) is the value 255 (decimal, base 10). For example,

```
parseInt("A", 16)
```

returns 10 since A is the value 10 in hexadecimal. Appendix D contains a number of hexadecimal conversion programs written in JavaScript.

pow(val1, val2)
Syntax:

```
pow(val1, val2)
```

Returns: `val1` to the power of `val2`.

Object family: `Math`.

The power function is represented in JavaScript by the `pow()` method. For example:

```
tenTimesten = pow(10, 10);   // Same as 10 * 10
```

prompt()
Syntax:

```
prompt("message", input-default)
```

Returns*:* A string entered by the user.

Object family: `window`.

The `prompt()` method is JavaScript's primary data-input method, allowing keyboard input from the user to be stored into a variable. The `prompt()` method provides a window and input field automatically when it is invoked. The `"message"` argument represents a string to display when showing the initial input prompt, and `"input-default"` is a default value that is placed within the input field. For example, we could define and invoke a simple JavaScript function as follows:

```
function goSomewhere() {
  // Ask the user to input a URL, and suggest a default:
  goHere = prompt("Where do you want to go?",
              "http://wombat.doc.ic.ac.uk"); // default
```

B

```
  // Load the URL into a new Navigator window:
  myWin = window.open(goHere, "", "width=600");
}
```

You can make your code more compact by omitting the assignment of a variable to the `prompt()` method completely, for example by using a statement of the form:

```
window.open(prompt("Where do you want to go?",
                   "http://wombat.doc.ic.ac.uk"), "",
                   "width=600");
```

which integrates the `prompt()` method directly into the `window.open()` function call. Windows are discussed in more detail within Chapter 8. More information on the `open()` method can be found earlier in this Appendix.

random()
Syntax:

```
Math.random()
```

Returns: A pseudo-random number between zero and one.

Object family: `Math`.

The `random()` function works across all Navigator platforms. Numbers are seeded from the current time. For example, the statement,

```
var randNum = random();
```

could return a value ranging from between 0 and 1, such as 0.759796175311911153.

round()
Syntax:

```
Math.round(val)
```

Returns: The argument, `val`, rounded to the nearest integer (whole number).

Object family: `Math`.

The `round()` method is used to round a number to the nearest whole number. The rules for rounding are as follows: If the argument `val` has a fractional part greater than or equal to `0.5` the number is rounded to `val+1`, otherwise `val` is returned without the fractional part—but also as an integer. For example:

```
MyValue1 = 68.5;
MyValue2 = 68.3;
rounded1 = Math.round(MyValue1);   // Result: 69
rounded2 = Math.round(MyValue2);   // Result: 68
```

select()
Syntax:

```
object.select();
```

Returns: Nothing.

Object family: `text`, `textArea`, `Password`.

Highlights an input area of an HTML form (a text-field, password-field or text-area).

TIP: Selection and focus are not the same thing in JavaScript. Use both `select()` and `focus()` to select and then allow user-input within a form-field. The `select()` method highlights the text within a field.

setDate()
Syntax:

```
dateObject.setDate(day)
```

Returns: Nothing.

Object family: `Date`.

The `setDate()` method is used to set the day of the month for the date object `setDate()`; for example,

```
myDate = new Date("7th August, 1996 12:00:00");
myDate.setDate(8);
```

changes the day from the 7th to the 8th of August (updating variable `myDate` in the process), where `day` is a value ranging from `1` to `31`.

B

setHours()
Syntax:

```
dateObject.setHours(hours)
```

Returns: Nothing.

Object family: Date.

Sets the hours in the date object dateObject, in much the same way as with the previous example, which sets the day number in a month (hours = 0-23)

setMinutes()
Syntax:

```
dateObject.setMinutes(mins)
```

Returns: Nothing.

Object family: Date.

Sets the minutes in the date object dateObject (where mins is a value ranging from 0 to 59).

setMonth()
Syntax:

```
dateObject.setMonth(month)
```

Returns: Nothing.

Object family: Date.

Sets the months in the date object dateObject, where month is a value ranging from 1 to 12.

setSeconds()
Syntax:

```
dateObject.setSeconds(secs)
```

Returns: Nothing.

Object family: Date.

Sets the seconds in the date object `dateObject`, where `secs` is a number ranging from 0 to 59.

setTime()
Syntax:

```
dateObject.setTime(timeString)
```

Returns: Nothing.

Object family: `Date`.

Sets the time value within the date object named `dateObject`.

setTimeout()
Syntax:

```
setTimeout(expression, millisecs)
```

Returns: A time-out identifier code.

Object family: `window`.

The `setTimeout()` method sets a time-based event (`expression`) that will be triggered in a given number of milliseconds, specified as `millisecs`. The `clearTimeout()` method can be used to cancel a time-out event. For example,

```
var t = setTimeout("alert('Hello World!')", 30000)
```

displays the text "Hello World!" in 30 seconds' time. The time-out events internal identification number is stored in the variable 't' allowing the time-out event to be cleared using `clearTimeout(t)`. See Chapter 10 for more information on time-out events.

B

setYear()
Syntax:

```
dateObject.setYear(year)
```

Returns: Nothing.

Object family: `Date`.

Sets the year value in the date object `dateObject`. The `year` value must be greater than `1900`.

sin()
Syntax:

```
sin(val)
```

Returns: The sine of argument `val`.

Object family: `Math`.

small()
Syntax:

```
String.small()
```

Returns: Nothing.

Object family: String.

Sets the string identified by `String` in a small font using an HTML `<small>..</small>` container to encapsulate the string object. Use this with a method such as `document.write()` when generating dynamic HTML.

sqrt()
Syntax:

```
sqrt(val)
```

Returns: The square root of argument `val`.

Object family: `Math`.

strike()
Syntax:

```
String.strike()
```

Returns: Nothing.

Object family: String.

Causes a string to be displayed in Navigator as being struck out. The `<strike>` container is used to render the effect. Use this with a method such as `document.write()` when generating dynamic HTML.

sub()

Syntax:

```
String.sub()
```

Returns: Nothing.

Object family: String.

Causes the string-object named `String` to be set in a subscript font using a Netscape HTML `<sub>..</sub>` container to encapsulate the string. Use this with a method such as `document.write()` when generating dynamic HTML.

submit()

Syntax:

```
submit()
```

Returns: Nothing.

Object family: `form`.

Simulates the pressing of a submit button in an HTML `<form>..</form>` container. The HTML tag `<input type="submit">` is always provided in a form that sends its user-input to a Web server for processing. JavaScript can simulate the pressing of this button using `submit()`.

substring()

Syntax:

```
String.substring(start,length)
```

Returns: The substring of string object `String`.

Object family: String.

The `substring()` method is used to extract substrings from a string-object. The `start` argument specifies the index-position of the string (starting at 0 for the beginning of the string, remember), whereas `length` specifies the

B

number of characters to actually extract after position `start`. For example if we had the statement,

```
aString = "http://www.gold.net/users/ag17/index.htm";
```

the JavaScript statement,

```
theHost = aString.substring(7, aString.length);
```

would retrieve the characters from position seven onward (the string of text `"www.gold.net/users/ag17/index.htm"`). If the `start` argument is greater than the `length` argument JavaScript still returns the same substring; for example, the expressions `aString.substring(0,4)` and `aString.substring(4,0)` return the string `"http"`.

sup()
Syntax:

```
String.sup()
```

Returns: Nothing.

Object family: String.

Causes the string-object named `String` to be set in a superscript font using a Netscape HTML `<sup>..</sup>` container to encapsulate the string. Use this with a method such as `document.write()` when generating dynamic HTML.

tan()
Syntax:

```
tan(val)
```

Returns: The tangent of argument `val` (where `val` is specified in radians).

Object family: `Math`.

toGMTString()
Syntax:

```
DateObject.toGMTString()
```

Returns: Nothing.

Object family: `Date.`

Converts a date to a string using GMT data-formatting conventions.

toLowerCase()
Syntax:

```
String.toLowerCase()
```

Returns: Nothing.

Object family: String.

Converts the string-object named `String` to lowercase.

toLocaleString()
Syntax:

```
DateObjectString.toLocaleString()
```

Returns: Nothing.

Object family: `Date.`

Converts a `Date` object to a string using local time conventions.

toString()
Syntax:

```
DateObject.toString()
```

Returns: Nothing.

Object family: `Date.`

Converts the date object `DateObj` to a string-object.

toUpperCase()
Syntax:

```
String.toUpperCase()
```

Returns: Nothing.

Object family: String.

Converts the string-object named `String` to uppercase.

B

typeof()
Syntax:

```
typeof(val)
```

Returns: A string object indicating the type of the object referenced in argument `val`. The operand `val` is not evaluated, as in the `eval()` method.

Object family: Internal.

The `typeof()` operator is new to Navigator 3.0 and allows the "type" of an object to be retrieved. Values returned from `typeof()` include `undefined` (object does not exist), `function` (object is a JavaScript function), `object` (object is a JavaScript object), `number` (object is numeric), `boolean` (object has a `true` or `false` value), and `string` (string object). Chapter 6 has more information on the new `typeof()` operator.

unescape()
Syntax:

```
unescape("String")
```

Returns: The ASCII string of the argument provided.

Object family: Internal.

The `unescape()` method accepts a string of the form `"%c"`, where `c` is an integer between 0 and 255 (hexadecimal 0 - FF). For example,

```
unescape("%25")
```

returns the value `"%"`. Values without a preceding `%` are assumed to be in hexadecimal notation `0x00` to `0xff` (0 - 255 decimal).

UTC()
Syntax:

```
Date.UTC(year, month, day [, hours] [,mins] [,secs])
```

Returns: The number of milliseconds in a date object since the epoch date (January 1st, 1970 00:00:00 GMT).

Object family: String.

write()

Syntax:

```
document.write(string);
```

Returns: Nothing.

Object family: String.

The `document.write()` function writes a `string` of text to the browser without sending a line-feed code. The text string should ideally be HTML-formatted, containing the appropriate HTML tags.

Variables can also be joined together to form a single string, for example:

```
document.write("The code for product " + productName +
               " is " + productCode);
```

Numeric values can also be concatenated by treating them as strings to begin with; JavaScript can perform numeric calculations on strings, remember, so specific casting (the changing of a variable data-type) is not actually required. If you need to join a string with a numeric value, the "+" signs can be changed to commas (,), as shown in the following example.

```
var HoursInYear = 365 * 24;
document.write("Hours in a year = ", HoursInYear, ".");
```

TIP: You can shorten your code by using the `with` statement so that the "`document.`" prefix can be omitted, as in the example

```
with (document) {
    open();
    writeln("This is some <b>HTML-text</b>.");
    writeln("Here is another sentence.");
    close();
}
```

B

writeln()

Syntax:

```
document.writeln(string);
```

Returns: Nothing.

Object family: String.

This operates in the same way as `document.write()` except a line-feed code is generated automatically after the string. Again, the `string` argument should be HTML-formatted.

TIP: If you need to write text into a window created using JavaScript's `open()` method, prefix the `document.write()` function with the name of the window. For example,

```
myWin.document.write("HTML-text...") ;
```

where myWin is the name of your window variable assigned to the `open()` method, as in `myWin = open(...)`.

Part 2: A-Z of JavaScript Properties

JavaScript has approximately 60 standard properties—values that belong to various objects and which are used to determine their behavior. All objects have properties, and this section documents each property and the objects upon which they act. A good tip to remember is that you can dynamically change some of Netscape's standard properties by simply assigning the property a new value. For example,

```
document.bgColor="Blue";
```

would change the current document's background color to blue (see the `bgColor` property for more details). This saves having to use specific HTML tags to achieve the same effects. Look out for the properties that can be set in this way—these are known as *read-write properties*. Read-only properties cannot be altered in this way. Property names are case-insensitive because they are part of the HTML language. For example, `bgColor` is the same as `bgcolor`; the former has been used in this appendix to improve readability.

Action Property

Description: A reflection of the `action` attribute in a `<form>` object.

Applies to object(s): `form`.

Type: Read-only.

alinkColor Property

Description: Active hyperlink color.

Applies to object(s): `document`.

Type: Read-write.

This property represents the color of an active hyperlink within the current hypertext document as set by the `<body alink="#RRGGBB">..</body>` tag, where `"#RRGGBB"` is a hexadecimal-encoded red-green-blue triplet representing the active-link color combination. `"#0000BB"` (blue) is the default. For example:

```
document.alinkColor="#ff0000";  // Active-links are red
```

Anchors Array Property

Description: An array of hyperlinks that exist within the current hypertext document.

Applies to object(s): `document`.

Type: Read-only.

Applets Property

Description: A reference to a Java applet, as defined with an `<applet>` container tag.

Applies to object(s): `document`.

Type: Read-only.

Use the `name` attribute of the `<applet>` tag to name an applet and then refer to the applet from JavaScript as `document.applets.appletName`, or even to access (run) a public method within the applet as:

```
document.applets.appletName.functionName()
```

See Chapter 11 for more information on this property for use in applications that require Java/JavaScript interaction.

appName Property

Description: The code name of the current browser.

Applies to object(s): `navigator`.

B

Type: Read-only.

appVersion Property

Description: The version number of the current browser in the format:

```
release-number (platform, country)
```

Applies to object(s): `navigator`.

Type: Read-only.

bgColor Property

Description: The background color of the currently loaded hypertext document.

Applies to object(s): `document`.

Type: Read-write.

This property represents the background color of the current hypertext document as set by the `<body bgcolor="#RRGGBB">..</body>` tag, where `"#RRGGBB"` is a hexadecimal-encoded red-green-blue triplet representing the foreground color, for example:

```
document.bgColor="#0000ff"; // Blue background color
```

You could phase in a series of colors using a simple `for` loop, as in the example:

```
<!--
  Program B-5
-->
<html>
<script language="Javascript">
<!--
var hex = new makeArray(17);
for (var i = 0; i < 10; i++) {
    hex[i] = i;
    hex[10]="a"; hex[11]="b"; hex[12]="c";
    hex[13]="d"; hex[14]="e"; hex[15]="f";
}

function makeArray(n) {
  this.length = n;
  for (var i = 1; i <= n; i++)
```

```
        this[i] = 0;
    return(this);
}

function toHex(i) {
  if (i < 0)
     return("00");
  else
  if (i > 255)
     return("ff");
  else
     return "" + hex[Math.floor(i / 16)] +
               hex[i % 16];
}

function setbgColor(r, g, b) {
  var hr = toHex(r); var hg = toHex(g); var hb = toHex(b);
  document.bgColor = hr+hg+hb;
}

function fade(r1, g1, b1, r2, g2, b2, n) {
  for (var i = 0; i <= n; i++) {
     setbgColor(Math.floor(r1 * ((n-i)/n) + r2 * (i/n)),
             Math.floor(g1 * ((n-i)/n) + g2 * (i/n)),
             Math.floor(b1 * ((n-i)/n) + b2 * (i/n)));
  }
}

// Fade in from Black to White (00,00,00 to FF,FF,FF);
fade(0, 0, 0, 255, 255, 255, 50);
//-->
</script>
<body>
Watch closely...<p>
</body>
</html>
```

B

Checked Property

Description: A boolean value indicating whether a checkbox or radio button object is checked.

Applies to object(s): checkbox and radio button.

Type: Read-write.

The checked property returns a boolean value indicating whether a radio button or checkbox object is selected by the user.

Cookie Property

Description: A cookie is a small item of information that can be stored locally on the user's machine for later reference. The `cookies.txt` file stores each cookie.

Applies to object(s): `document`.

Type: Read-write.

See Chapter 13 for more information on cookies in Netscape Navigator.

default Checked Property

Description: A boolean value indicating whether the default checkbox/radio button object is checked.

Applies to object(s): checkbox and radio button.

Type: Read-write.

The `defaultChecked` property returns `true` if the checkbox or radio button being examined is the default button, as set by the `checked` attribute (see `<input type="radio|checkbox">` syntax).

defaultSelected Property

Description: A boolean value indicating whether the default option in a `<select>` tag is selected.

Applies to object(s): `select`.

Type: Read-write.

`defaultSelected` is a boolean property that returns true if an `<option selected>` tag within an HTML `<select>..</select>` container is currently selected by the user, meaning that the default selection has been made. When assigning a value to this attribute, the select object does not visibly update itself.

defaultStatus Property

Description: The default status-bar message.

Applies to object(s): `window`.

Type: Read-write.

The `defaultStatus` property contains the default status-bar message that appears in Netscape (not to be confused with the `status` property—see later). The `defaultStatus` value appears when no other messages are displayed in the status bar.

defaultValue Property

Description: Default text-field value.

Applies to object(s): text, text-area, and string.

Type: Read-write.

Contains the default contents of a text field according to the value supplied by the `value` attribute. The contents of the field do not change until you actually assign a string to the `value` attribute.

Encoding Property

Description: The encoding type of a form—a reflection of the `<form enctype>` attribute.

Applies to object(s): `form`.

Type: Read-write.

E Property

Description: Euler's constant.

Applies to object(s): `Math`.

Contains the value of Euler's mathematical constant *e*, the base of the natural logarithm (2.718...), for example:

```
exp = Math.E;  // Store e in variable exp
```

B

Elements Array Property

Description: Form elements array.

Applies to object(s): `form`.

Type: Read-only.

The `elements` property is an array of objects that contain each element of an HTML form (in the order that they are defined within the HTML file), such as the text-fields, text-areas, radio buttons, and/or checkboxes that comprise the form. For example,

```
document.forms[0].elements[0]
```

refers to the first element in the first form of the current document.

fgColor Property

Description: The foreground color of the currently loaded hypertext document.

Applies to object(s):   `document`.

Type: Read-write.

This property represents the foreground color of the current hypertext document as set by the `<body fgcolor="#RRGGBB">..</body>` tag, where `"#RRGGBB"` is a hexadecimal-encoded red-green-blue triplet representing the current foreground color. For example,

```
document.fgColor="#FFFF00";
```

sets the current documents foreground color to yellow.

Frames Array Property

Description: Frame elements array.

Applies to object(s):   `window`.

Type: Read-write.

The `frames` property is an array for each frame in the current window. Frames are regions of a window that can contain separate HTML documents (and therefore separate URLs). To refer to the first frame of a frameset-document, you would therefore use the expression:

```
parent.frames[0]
```

The number of frames in the current HTML document can be returned using the expression `parent.frames.length`.

Please refer to Chapter 9 for more information on frameset-documents, and frame addressing techniques.

Hash Property

Description: The anchor name following the # sign.

Applies to object(s):   `location`.

Type: Read-write.

The `hash` property is used to extract a local hyperlink from an HTML <a href> tag.

Host Property

Description: The hostname and port property.

Applies to object(s): `location`.

Type: Read-write.

Contains the hostname and port of the current URL in the format `host:port`.

Hostname Property

Description: The current URL hostname.

Applies to object(s): `location`.

Type: Read-write.

Contains just the hostname from the currently loaded URL. For example, if `http://www.wombat.com` is loaded into Navigator, the JavaScript statement,

```
hname = location.hostname;
```

would store the string value `"www.wombat.com"` into the variable `"hname"`.

href Property

Description: The current URL property.

Applies to object(s): `location`.

Type: Read-write.

The value of `location.href` contains the current URL, as loaded into Navigator.

Images Array

Description: An array of images that exist within the current document (Navigator 3.0).

Applies to object(s): `document`.

Type: Read-write.

B

Each `<img src>` tag within a document is reflected into the `images` array. The total number of images is reflected into `document.images.length`. You can use the `src` attribute of an image object to load a new image; for example,

```
document.images[0].src = "newimage.gif";
```

would place a new image, `myimage.gif`, over the first image in the current document.

Index Property

Description: A value representing a position in a `<select>` object such as an `<option>` that has been selected by the user.

Applies to object(s): `select`.

Type: Read-only.

lastModified Property

Description: Document modification date.

Applies to object(s): `document`.

Type: Read-only.

This property contains the date on which the current hypertext document was last modified.

Length Property

Description: Object lengths.

Applies to object(s): `history`, radio button, string, anchors, `forms`, `frames`, `links`, and `options`.

Type: Read-only.

For a `history` object, the length of the history list is returned; for a `string` object, the length of the string (in characters) is returned (`null` strings return a zero length); for a radio button object, the number of radio buttons is returned. For `anchors`, `frames`, `forms`, `option` and `link` objects, the number of elements in each structure is returned.

linkColor Property

Description: Hyperlink color.

Applies to object(s): `document`.

Type: Read-write.

The `linkColor` property contains the current hypertext document's hyperlink color, expressed as a hexadecimal-encoded red-green-blue triplet of the form `"#RRGGBB"`, as set by the HTML `<body link="#RRGGBB">..</body>` container. You can assign a value directly to this property to change its color. Color-verbs can also be used, e.g. `"Yellow"` instead of `"#ffff00"`, etc.

LN2 Property

Description: The natural logarithm value.

Applies to object(s): `Math`.

Type: Read-only.

A mathematical constant, here the natural logarithm (~`0.693`).

LN10 Property

Description: The natural logarithm of 10.

Applies to object(s): `Math`.

Type: Read-only.

Another mathematical constant, here the natural logarithm of 10 (~`2.302`).

Location Property

Description: The full URL of the current document.

Applies to object(s): `document`.

Type: Read-only.

The `document.location` property contains the full URL of the current hypertext document. Do not confuse this property with `window.location` (or `location` by itself), or even `frames[n].location`, the latter of which *can* have its `location` properties changed (and thus reload a new document).

Log2_E Property

Description: The base 2 logarithm of *e*.

Applies to object(s): `Math`.

B

Type: Read-only.

A mathematical constant with the value ~1.442.

Log10_E Property

Description: The base 10 logarithm of *e*.

Applies to object(s):   Math.

Type: Read-only.

A mathematical constant with the value ~0.434.

Method Property

Description: Form posting method property.

Applies to object(s):   form.

Type: Read-write.

Contains the form transmittal method of a form "post" or "get", as set via the method attribute of the <form> tag.

Name Property

Description: Object name property.

Applies to object(s):   All objects.

Type: Read-only.

The name property is a reflection of an HTML tag's name attribute. Window and frame objects are treated slightly differently. An open() method that is assigned to a variable gains its name from that variable, and this is reflected into the name property for the window. A frame that is part of a frameset-document is named via the name attribute in the <frame> tag; for example, parent.frames[0].name returns the name of the first frame.

Options Array Property

Description: A list of options in a <select> tag.

Applies to object(s):   select.

Type: Read-only.

The options property contains details of the elements within an <option> tag of an HTML <select>..</select> container. It is an array of such objects, so for a selection-object named as `browser`, like `<select name="browser">`, the expression,

```
browser.options[0]
```

would store the first `<option>` selection value. The number of selection-objects can be returned using the `length` property (`browser.options.length`). See also the `selected` and `text` properties for more information.

Parent Property

Description: The parent frame window property.

Applies to object(s): `window`.

Type: Read-only.

In a *frameset*-document (i.e. one that defines a framed window using the `<frameset>..</frameset>` container), the `parent` property returns the name of the parent window. The `top` property (a synonym) can also be used.

Pathname Property

Description: Pathname/URL information property.

Applies to object(s): `location`.

Type: Read-write.

The `pathname` property returns the file or path after the third slash ('/' or '\') in the current URL; for example if the current URL was `http://www.gold.net/users/ag17/index.htm`, the expression

```
location.pathname
```

returns "`users/ag17/index.htm`".

B

PI Property

Description: Mathematical constant *pi*.

Applies to object(s): `Math`.

Type: Read-only.

The mathematical constant *pi* (3.1415).

Port Property

Description: The current URL's port number.

Applies to object(s):   `location`.

Type: Read-write.

The `port` property returns the current port number from the URL (if specified). For example, if the current URL was `http://www.somehost.com:8080/index.html`, then the value of `location.port` would be `8080`.

Protocol Property

Description: Protocol access method.

Applies to object(s):   `location`.

Type: Read-write.

Returns the protocol access method, based upon the current URL (including colon), as in `http:`, `gopher:`, `news:`, etc. Appendix E contains a list of protocol service-types that can be used with Navigator 3.0.

Referrer Property

Description: The referring URL.

Applies to object(s):   `document`.

Type: Read-only.

The `referrer` property contains the URL of the calling document after the user has clicked on a hyperlink—for example, the document that contained the hyperlink, and which referred to the new document mentioned in the link.

Selected Property

Description: Boolean value of an option within a `<select>` container.

Applies to object(s):   `select`.

Type: Read-only.

The `selected` property returns a `true` value if the current `<option>` within a `<select>` container has been selected by the user, and `false` otherwise.

selectedIndex Property

Description: The index value of the current option in a `<select>` container.

Applies to object(s): `select`.

Type: Read-write.

The `selectedIndex` property returns an integer that represents the current `<option>` that has been selected by the user in a `<select>` container. When assigning a value to this property, the select object is updated immediately. Values start from zero (0), not 1, note. See Chapter 7 for more information on selection lists.

self Property

Description: The current window (or frame) property.

Applies to object(s): `window`.

Type: Read-only.

The `self` property is a synonym that refers to the current `window` or `frame` object.

Status Property

Description: Transient status-bar message.

Applies to object(s): `window`.

Type: Read-write.

The `status` property represents a transient message in the Netscape status bar at the bottom of the current window (not to be confused with the `defaultStatus` property, which stores the default status-bar message).

For example we could have the following JavaScript/HTML document:

```
<!--
  Program B-6
-->
<html>
<body>
<a href="http://www.gold.net/users/ag17/index.htm"
   onMouseOver="self.status='Please click me!'; return true">
<img src="image1.gif" border=0>
</a>
</body>
</html>
```

B

The above script defines an image (`image1.gif`) as a hyperlink and then launches the URL specified within the `<a href>` tag when the user clicks on the hyperlink. As the user moves over the hyperlink, the message *"Please Click Me!"* is displayed (this message stays in the status bar until a new message replaces it).

Target Property

Description: The window targeted for form response.

Applies to object(s): `form` and `link`.

Type: Read-write.

The `target` property returns the value placed in the `target` keyword of the HTML `<form>` tag. This specifies a window that is to be used for any feedback after the form has been submitted, and works in conjunction with a `<frameset>` tag.

Text Property

Description: The text after an `<option>` tag.

Applies to object(s): `select`.

Type: Read-write.

The `text` property contains the text placed after an `<option>` tag within a `<select>..</select>` container, and could be used to extract the option that has been selected by the user. For example we could have,

```
<!--
   Program B-7
-->
<html>
<script language="JavaScript">
<!--
function CheckSelect(f) {
   alert("You selected: " + f.text);
}
//-->
</script>
</head>
<body>
<form name="myForm" method="POST"
action="http://some.host.com/scripts/myscript.cgi"
onSubmit="CheckSelect(myForm.sel)">
Have you ever used JavaScript before
```

```
<select name="sel">
<option>Yes
<option>No
</select>
<hr>
<input type="submit" value="Submit form">
</form>
</body>
</html>
```

which uses the `text` property to ascertain which option has been selected by the user, in this case the value `"yes"` or `"no"`. This form has a `submit` button and will be sent to a server script for further processing. Since the `text` property is read-write, you can overwrite an existing option with a new description. For example, in context to the above example, the statement,

```
document.forms[0].sel[0].text = "Maybe";
```

would change the first items option-text from "No" to "Maybe".

Title Property

Description: Document title.

Applies to object(s): `document`.

Type: Read-only.

The `title` property contains the document title as set by the `<title>..</title>` container within the current HTML file loaded into Navigator.

Top Property

B

Description: A synonym referring to the top-most Navigator window.

Applies to object(s): `window`.

Type: Read-only.

The `top` property is often confused with `parent`. The `top` property can be used instead of `parent` since both synonyms refer to the top-level window. Autonomous windows created using `window.open()` cannot use `top` to refer to the parent window. The `opener` property should be used in such cases. The `top` property, when used with an autonomous window, simply refers to the top-most window within the *current* window. Chapters 8 and 9 have many more examples of both autonomous windows and frames.

Type Property

Description: The type of a form-element.

Applies to object(s): `form`.

Type: Read-only.

The `type` property is new to Navigator 3.0 and is a reflection of the type of a particular form-element. Each form-element has its own `type` property. For example, a `<select multiple>` container has the type 'select-multiple.' Chapter 7 examines the `type` property in more detail.

userAgent Property

Description: The user-agent (browser) name, as sent in an HTTP header.

Applies to object(s): `navigator`.

Type: Read-only.

value Property

Description: The value of a form-field.

Applies to object(s): button, checkbox, reset, submit, radio button, password, selection, text, and text-area.

Type: Read-write.

The `value` property returns a string value based upon the `value` attribute when used with `button`, `reset`, and `submit` objects. With a checkbox the string-value `"on"` is returned if an item is checked, and `"off"` if it is not checked. Radio buttons and selection lists will return the literal value of the `value` attribute with which they are created; `text` and `textArea` objects will yield a verbatim copy of the string (or strings) that has been entered within them.

vlinkColor Property

Description: The color of a 'visited' hyperlink.

Applies to object(s): `document`.

Type: Read-write.

The `vlinkColor` property returns a red-green-blue hexadecimal-encoded triplet that represents the color of all visited hyperlinks. A *visited* hyperlink is one that has been clicked upon in the past, and which is stored in the Netscape URL history file, `NETSCAPE.HST`. Visited link colors are initially set using the HTML <body vlink="#RRGGB"> tag, or if not specified here, internally in Netscape's *Options/Preferences* menu.

window Property

Description: A synonym for the current window (or frame).

Applies to object(s):   window.

Type: Read-write.

Refers to the current window or frame within a <frameset> document.

B

APPENDIX C

JavaScript Resources

Part 1 of this appendix contains details of JavaScript resources located on the Internet, World Wide Web, and USENET. All entries in this appendix are rated out of five stars (☆ = poor, ☆☆☆☆☆= excellent).

Part 2 of the appendix documents miscellaneous resources that readers may find useful for inclusion in their JavaScript applications, such as graphics and other files.

Part 1—JavaScript Resources

Resources in this section are broken down into different categories, namely Web sites, USENET groups, and mailing lists.

Web Sites

The following Web sites are among the best resources for JavaScript developers. Many new sites appear daily, so you are advised to use a search-engine to locate the most recent additions.

GameLan ☆☆☆☆☆

A new JavaScript section is now on GameLan, with access to many hundreds of Java/JavaScript programs.

◆   `http://www.gamelan.com`

JavaScript Debugger ☆☆☆

A debugging system for JavaScript programs.

◆   `http://www.media.com/users/public/jsdb.html`

JavaScript Resources Page ☆☆☆☆

In my opinion, one of the best JavaScript Web resources. Contains hundreds of links for new scripts, books, resources, and general Mocha-lite *gossip*.

◆   `http://www.c2.org/~andreww/javascript`

Java Documentation via Windows ☆☆

A series of Windows-based help files with JavaScript documentation (downloadable files are available).

◆   `http://www.jchelp.com/javahelp/javahelp.htm`

Netscape's JavaScript Pages ☆☆☆☆

These pages contain all of the JavaScript documentation, as well as examples of JavaScript running under Netscape Navigator 3.0.

◆ http://home.netscape.com/comprod/products/navigator/
   version_3.0/script/index.html

◆ http://home.netscape.com/comprod/products/navigator/
   version_3.0/script/script_info/index.html

Miscellaneous Web Resources

A multitude of sites now contain JavaScript-related information, including sample programs and information. These sites are best viewed usng Navigator 3.0 because many use frames and JavaScript-embedded commands.

◆ http://flamenco.icl.dk:8000/~sjm/java/index.en.html

◆ http://www.cs.rit.edu/~atk/JavaScript/javascriptinfo.html

◆ http://porthos.phoenixat.com/~warreng/WWWBoard/
   wwwboard.html

◆ http://rummelplatz.uni-mannheim.de/~skoch/js/script.htm

◆ http://websys.com/javascript/

◆ http://ws2.scripting.com/playingwithjavascript.html

◆ http://www.c2.org/~andreww/javascript/docs.html

◆ http://www.center.nitech.ac.jp/ml/java-house/hypermail/
   0000

◆ http://www.cris.com/~raydaly/javatell.html

◆ http://www.dannyg.com/

◆ http://www.freqgrafx.com/411/

◆ http://www.gatech.edu/amnesty/writingtest.html

◆ http://www.hotwired.com/davenet/95/47/index3a.html

◆ http://www.metrowerks.com/products/announce/java.html

◆ http://www.webacademy.com/jscourse

◆ http://www.wineasy.se/robban/jsindex.htm

◆ http://www.winternet.com/~sjwalter/javascript/

◆ http://www.zdnet.com/~pcmag/dvorak/jd1211.htm

◆ http://www.zeta.org.au/~rodos/JavaScript.html

Mailing lists (LISTSERVs)

This list collects USENET postings from the USENET group `comp.lang.javascript` (see below). It mainly consists of questions from developers, although solutions to many JavaScript problems are also provided, making this probably the best e-mail based resource currently available for JavaScripters.

♦   `http://www.obscure.org` ☆☆☆☆

Mail to: `javascript-list@inquiry.com`

Message body: `subscribe javascript`

USENET Groups

The main USENET groups at the time of writing are

♦   `news://comp.lang.javascript` ☆☆☆☆☆

♦   `news://secnews.netscape.com/netscape.devs-javascript` ☆☆☆

♦   `news://news.livesoftware.com/livesoftware.javascript.examples` ☆☆☆

♦   `news://news.livesoftware.com/livesoftware.javascript.developer` ☆☆☆

Part 2—Miscellaneous Program Resources

Some of the JavaScript applications in this book require external tools and/or files to properly function. This section lists these resources and how they can be of use.

Digits for Clock-based JavaScript Applications

Some of the JavaScript applications in this book make use of graphical digits for time and date displays. The URLs below contain a selection of freeware graphical digits (GIF files) that can be used in your JavaScript applications.

♦   `http://cervantes.learningco.com/kevin/digits`

♦   `http://www-hppool.cs.uni-magdeburg.de/HTMLDevelopment/Counter.html`

♦   `http://www.datasync.com/waidsoft/wsnumbers.html`

♦   `http://www.digits.com/charsets.html`

♦   `http://www.ganesa.com/Ganesa/Museum/index.html`

♦ http://www.issi.com/people/russ

♦ http://www.ugrad.cs.ubc.ca/spider/q6e192/cgi/COUNTER.HTM

The mapedit Program

The mapedit program, by Thomas Boutell, allows imagemap coordinates to be created, and is useful in the design of client-side imagemaps for use within HTML/JavaScript applications. mapedit is a shareware package (for Windows 3.x at the moment) and can be evaluated prior to usage. See

♦ http://boutell.com

Alternatively, visit the FAQ (Frequently Asked Questions) document at:

♦ http://sunsite.unc.edu/boutell/faq/www_faq.html

You can also find mapedit using a Web search-engine or via an Archie server.

Animated GIF Images

The GIF89a image standard, developed by Compuserve, allows multiple GIF images to be displayed in succession, allowing simple image animation to take place. The "GIF Convertor" (GIFCON) tool will facilitate the creation of such images and can be found on the Internet on a variety of anonymous FTP servers. The primary site for this software is

♦ http://www.mindworkshop.com/alchemy/gifcon.html

Searching for "GIFCON" or "animated GIF" using a search-engine, such as Alta Vista, will locate other servers that also have access to the GIFCON software. GIFCON is available for Windows 95 (GIFCON32, a 32-bit application) and Windows 3.x (a 16-bit application).

C

APPENDIX D

Ready-to-Use JavaScript Programs

This appendix contains a selection of prewritten JavaScript programs that perform a number of general routines useful to the developer.

Ready-to-Run Functions

The entries in this appendix have been provided mainly as JavaScript functions to allow direct integration into a JavaScript application, and are categorized according to the task they perform.

Array Creation

```
<!--
  Function D-1
-->
function makeArray(n) {
    this.length = n;
    for (var x=0; x <= n; x++) {
        this[x] = 0;
    }
    return(this);
}
```

The `makeArray()` function creates a one-dimensional array structure of the size specified as argument n. For example, you could create an array, called `marsupials`, with two elements, referred to as `marsupials[0]` and `marsupials[1]`, respectively, using the JavaScript statement:

```
marsupials = makeArray(2);
```

and then populate the array using assignment statements of the form:

```
marsupials[0] = "Wombat";
marsupials[1] = "Kangaroo";
```

Accessing the array is then a matter of specifying the index; for example, `alert(marsupials[0])` would display the value `"Wombat"`. You can also construct an array using the `Object()` method, which is used to create a *generic* object, for example:

```
var myArray = new Object();
myArray[0] = "Value 1";
myArray[1] = "Value 2";
...
```

Netscape Atlas (Navigator 3.0) now supports additional facilities for array creation, including the `Array()` and `Object()` constructors, both of which allow you to create arrays using more compact and faster code. See Chapter 6 for more information.

Decimal to Hexadecimal Number Conversion

The functions in this section convert decimal (base 10) numbers in the range 0–255 to their equivalent value in hexadecimal (base 16); for example, 255 in decimal is FF in hexadecimal. Both of the DecToHex() functions presented in this section are useful for color-code manipulation programs that have decimal RGB (red-green-blue) arguments. Although the first version of the function is longer, it is a useful insight into how JavaScript works with arrays and strings. The second version is much shorter and runs slightly faster.

Conversion Based Upon a Hex-Table

This function requires the makeArray() function previously detailed. The conversion process is based upon a hexadecimal conversion table, many of which exist on the Internet at math-related Web sites. The array hexTable[] represents the columns and rows of such a table spanning decimal values 0 to 255. The program, upon being passed a decimal value, works out the row and column location of the number within the table (table rows are made up of 16 decimal values, 0–15, 16–31, 32, 48, . . . 240–255), and then retrieves the row and column headers. These headers contain hexadecimal values for the low- and high-order parts of a number; for example, the rows range from 00, 01, 02 . . . 0F, and the columns range from 00, 10, 20, . . . F0. The decimal value of 100, therefore, consists of the values 60 and 04 in the table, column and row, respectively. By stripping away the superfluous zeroes, the number 64 emerges, which is the resulting hexadecimal value required.

```
<!--
  Function D-2
-->
function DecToHex(decval) {
  var r=0, g=0, b=0, inc=0, cnt=0, cnt2=0;
  var part1 = "", part2 = "";
  var hexTable = makeArray(16);
  hexTable[1]  = "00:00";
  hexTable[2]  = "10:01";
  hexTable[3]  = "20:02";
  hexTable[4]  = "30:03";
  hexTable[5]  = "40:04";
  hexTable[6]  = "50:05";
  hexTable[7]  = "60:06";
  hexTable[8]  = "70:07";
  hexTable[9]  = "80:08";
  hexTable[10] = "90:09";
  hexTable[11] = "A0:0A";
```

D

```
hexTable[12] = "B0:0B";
hexTable[13] = "C0:0C";
hexTable[14] = "D0:0D";
hexTable[15] = "E0:0E";
hexTable[16] = "F0:0F";
inc = 0;
cnt = 1;
while ((inc += 16) <= decval) {
      cnt ++;
}
inc   = inc - 16;
cnt2  = Math.abs(decval - inc) + 1;
part1 = hexTable[cnt].substring(0,2);
part2 = hexTable[cnt2].substring(3,5);
// Trim off any trailing and leading 0's
if (part1.substring(2,1) == "0") {
   part1 = part1.substring(0,1);
}
if (part2.substring(0,1) == "0") {
   part2 = part2.substring(2,1);
}
return(part1+part2);
}
```

Navigator 3.0 Hex Conversion Program

This version of `DecToHex()` is a more compact, faster version, which requires Navigator 3.0. The program works by storing the digits of the hexadecimal numbering system (`0 ... 9, A-F`) in an array created by an `Array()` constructor. The program uses the `Math.floor()` method to find the greatest number, less than or equal to the decimal value you entered, when divided by `16` (the base value of the hexadecimal numbering system). By using the JavaScript modulus operator with the value supplied, you can find the high- and low-order parts of the resulting hexadecimal number. These are used to index the `hexDigits` array to present the converted value. For example, the decimal number `38` divided by `16` is `2.375`, which when passed through `floor()` returns `2`. This value is then used to index the `hexDigits` array, which also yields the value `2`. The value of `38` modulo `16` is `6`, which when used to index the `hexDigits` array yields the value `6`, so `38` (decimal) is `26` in hexadecimal.

```
<!--
  Function D-3
-->
function DecToHex(decValue) {
```

```
var hexDigits = new Array("0","1","2","3","4",
                          "5","6","7","8","9",
                          "A","B","C","D","E","F");
if (decValue >= 255) { return "FF"; }
if (decValue <= 0)   { return "00"; }
return("" + hexDigits[Math.floor(decValue / 16)] +
          hexDigits[decValue % 16]);
}
```

Cookie Functions

The functions in this section perform simple cookie-manipulation routines.
Cookies are pieces of information stored locally to disk, which are accessed
via the JavaScript `document.cookie` property.

`ReadCookie()` reads a cookie-name based on a cookie that is assumed to
exist in the `cookies.txt` file, which requires the `extractCookie()`
function. The `createCookie` function, as the name implies, creates a
persistent cookie and allows an expiry date based on a specific number of
days into the future, which you will supply. `createTempCookie()` is
similar, although it omits the `expires=` attribute, creating a *temporary*
cookie, which lasts only for the duration of the current Navigator session.
Cookie deletion, performed by the `deleteCookie()` routine, can be used to
expire a cookie. If you need to manipulate dates, the
`returnExpiry()` function can be used to return a future expiry date for a
cookie based on a prespecified number of days.

```
<!--
  Function D-4
-->
function ReadCookie(cookiename) {
  var numOfCookies = document.cookie.length;
  var nameOfCookie = cookiename + "=";
  var cookieLen = nameOfCookie.length;
  var x = 0;
  while (x <= numOfCookies) {
        var y = (x + cookieLen);
        if (document.cookie.substring(x, y) == nameOfCookie)
           return(extractCookieValue(y));
        x = document.cookie.indexOf(" ", x) + 1;
        if (x == 0)
           break;
  }
  return null;
}

function extractCookieValue(val) {
```

D

```
if ((endOfCookie=document.cookie.indexOf(";",val))==-1)
    endOfCookie = document.cookie.length;
    return unescape(document.cookie.substring(val,
        endOfCookie));
}

function createCookie(name, value, expiredays) {
  var todayDate = new Date();
  todayDate.setDate(todayDate.getDate() + expiredays);
  document.cookie=name + "=" + value + "; expires=" +
        todayDate.toGMTString() + ";"
}

function createTempCookie(name, value) {
  var todayDate = new Date();
  todayDate.setDate(todayDate.getDate() + expiredays);
  document.cookie=name + "=" + value + ";";
}

function returnExpiry(days) {
  var todayDate = new Date();
  todayDate.setDate(todayDate.getDate() + days);
  return(todayDate.toGMTString());
}

function deleteCookie(name) {
  var todayDate = new Date();
  todayDate.setDate(todayDate.getDate() - 1);
  document.cookie=name + "=" + value + "; expires=" +
        todayDate.toGMTString() + ";"
}
```

Clocks

This section has a number of applications that manipulate date objects and time values.

Document Load Time Application—Graphical Display

This application displays the time at which the current document was loaded. Graphical digits are used to display all time-values and are assumed to reside in the files dg0.gif to dg9.gif. Other images include dgc.gif (a colon separator graphic) and the A.M./P.M. indicators dgam.gif and dgpm.gif. These images can be found on the Web at various locations as documented in Appendix C.

```
<!--
  Function D-5
-->
<html>
<head>
<script language="JavaScript">
<!--
  var imgStart    = "<img height=20 width=15 src=dg";
  var colon       = "<img height=20 width=15 src=dgc.gif>";
  var amind       = "<img height=20 width=15 src=dgam.gif>";
  var pmind       = "<img height=20 width=15 src=dgpm.gif>";
  var imgEnd      = ".gif>";
  var timeString = "";
  function showTime() {
    document.bgColor = "Black";
    document.fgColor = "White";
    var today       = new Date();
    var hours       = today.getHours();
    var minutes     = today.getMinutes();
    var indicator   = parent.amind;
    if (hours >= 12) {
       hours = "" + (hours-12);
       indicator = parent.pmind;
    }
    else
       hours == (""+hours);
    if (hours == 0)
       hours = "12";
    if (minutes < 10)
       minutes = ("0"+minutes);
    else
       minutes = (""+minutes);
    // Hours:
    for (var n=0; n < hours.length; n++) {
        timeString += parent.imgStart +
                      hours.substring(n, n+1) +
                      parent.imgEnd;
    }
    timeString += parent.colon;
    // Minutes:
    for (var n=0; n < minutes.length; n++) {
        timeString += parent.imgStart +
                      minutes.substring(n, n+1) +
                      parent.imgEnd;
    }
    timeString += (indicator + "<p>");
    document.write("<body bgcolor=Black>" +
                   "<basefont size=4>" +
```

D

```
          "You loaded this document at " +
          timeString +
          "<hr></body>");
   }
   showTime();
//-->
</script>
</head>
<body>
<basefont size=4>
Here is the main body text for this document.<p>
</body>
</html>
```

Real-Time Digital Clock (Frameset-Based)

The following script implements a real-time digital clock that is updated
every minute. To use this function, incorporate the code into your top-level
frameset document, that is, the document with the first `<frameset>`
container within it. Then place a call to the `setTimer()` function from
within the frame in which you want the clock to appear, using a `<body`
`onLoad="top.showTimer()">` tag. The digits for the image are assumed to
exist with the `c:\clock` directory in this example. Change the `urlPrefix`
variable to a valid URL that contains the digit-images; remember to include
the directory and the final "/" character. For example, if you upload your
digit images to the host `www.somehost.com/clock`, change the
`urlPrefix` variable to `"http://www.somehost.com/clock/"`
accordingly. If the images simply appear in the same directory as the script,
you can omit the `urlPrefix` completely. You will need to place a `<base`
`href=URL>` tag in your HTML file (in the header) that points to the URL
containing the images, including the directory, etc. This program also needs
to be told within which frame the clock should be displayed. You can
modify the `frames[]` array value to change this—a comment marks the
frame-name you will need to alter.

```
<!--
   Function D-6
-->
<html>
<head>
<script language="JavaScript">
<!--
   var timerId, bodyString, timeString, result;
   var urlPrefix = "file:///c%7c/clock/";
   var imgStart = "<img height=20 width=15 src=" +
                   urlPrefix +
                   "dg";
```

```javascript
var colon = "<img height=20 width=15 src=" +
            urlPrefix +
            "dgc.gif>";
var amind = "<img height=20 width=15 src=" +
            urlPrefix +
            "dgam.gif>";
var pmind = "<img height=20 width=15 src=" +
            urlPrefix +
            "dgpm.gif>";
var imgEnd = ".gif>";

function showTime() {
  var today       = new Date();
  var hours       = today.getHours();
  var minutes     = today.getMinutes();
  var indicator   = amind;
  if (hours >= 12) {
     hours = (hours-12);
     indicator = pmind;
  }
  if (hours == 0)
     hours = 12;
  hours = "" + hours;
  if (minutes < 10)
     minutes = ("0"+minutes);
  else
     minutes = (""+minutes);
  minutes = "" + minutes;
  var hourLen = hours.length;
  var minLen  = minutes.length;
  bodyString  = "";
  timeString  = "";
  // Hours:
  for (var n=0; n < hourLen; n++) {
     timeString += imgStart +
                   hours.substring(n, n+1) +
                   imgEnd;
  }
  timeString += colon;
  // Minutes:
  for (var n=0; n < minLen; n++) {
     timeString += imgStart +
                   minutes.substring(n, n+1) +
                   imgEnd;
  }
  timeString += indicator;
  bodyString = "<html><body bgcolor=Black><center>" +
               timeString +
```

D

```
                   "</center></body></html>";
     return(bodyString);
   }

   function setTimer() {
     result = showTime();
     //
     // I am assuming frames[0] is where the clock
     // should be displayed. Change accordingly:
     //
     parent.frames[0].document.open();
     parent.frames[0].document.write(result);
     parent.frames[0].document.close();
     // Update the clock every minute:
     timerId = setTimeout("setTimer()", 60000);
   }
   function removeTimer() {
     clearTimeout(timerId);
   }
//-->
</script>
</head>
</html>
```

Games and Pastimes

Since JavaScript is a general-purpose scripting language, you can write just
about anything, including games. The game of Tic-Tac-Toe is shown here.

Tic-Tac-Toe ("Noughts & Crosses")

The following JavaScript program implements the game of noughts and
crosses. Most of the work is done updating and modifying the grid, and
detecting which moves the player makes. Ensure that the `imageUrl` variable
points to a directory where the `cross.gif` and `tick.gif` images can be
located. In this case, they are loaded from disk, although they could arrive
from the network via a `http://`-prefixed URL. Player 1 uses a check mark;
player 2 uses a cross. You can change the images accordingly, or you can
even use internal GIFs (see Appendix H to speed things up further). The
`random()` method could also be used to build some randomness into the
program, perhaps to allow the player to play against Navigator.

```
<!--
  Function D-7
-->
<html>
<script language="JavaScript">
```

```
<!--
  // GIF images for both players. You could change these
  // to internal GIFs to speed things up:
  var imageUrl  = "file:///c%7c/"; // URL to images
  var player1Gif = "<img border=0 src='" +
                    imageUrl +
                    "tick.gif'>";
  var player2Gif = "<img border=0 src='" +
                    imageUrl +
                    "cross.gif'>";
  // Game status variables:
  var gameOver = false;
  var noMoves  = 0;
  // Set player (0 = player1):
  var thisPlay = 0;
  // Fill the frames upon loading:
  var top = "<body><basefont size=4>" +
            "<font size=+1>N</font>OUGHTS & " +
            "<font size=+1>C</font>ROSSES<p>" +
            "</body>";
  // Assign some blank images to the grid at the start:
  var a1_val = a2_val = a3_val = b1_val = b2_val = b3_val =
      c1_val = c2_val = c3_val = ("<img border=0 src='" +
                                    imageUrl + "blank.gif'>");
  // Bottom frame:
  var bot = parent.Grid(a1_val, a2_val, a3_val,
                        b1_val, b2_val, b3_val,
                        c1_val, c2_val, c3_val,
                        "<b>Player 1</b>: Please select a " +
                        "square");
  // Coordinates:
  var _a1, _a2, _a3, _b1, _b2, _b3, _c1, _c2, _c3;
  var _a12, _a22, _a32, _b12, _b22, _b32, _c12, _c22, _c32;
  function setUpGrid() {
    var Win1 = false;
    var Win2 = false;
    var _a1  = false;
    var _a2  = false;
    var _a3  = false;
    var _b1  = false;
    var _b2  = false;
    var _b3  = false;
    var _c1  = false;
    var _c2  = false;
    var _c3  = false;
    var _a12 = false;
    var _a22 = false;
    var _a32 = false;
```

D

```
    var _b12 = false;
    var _b22 = false;
    var _b32 = false;
    var _c12 = false;
    var _c22 = false;
    var _c32 = false;
}
// Button to start a new game (reloads file):
function reLoadBut() {
    parent.frames[1].document.write("<center><form>" +
        "<input type='button' value='New Game' " +
        "onClick='parent.frames[1].location" +
        "=document.location;" +
        "parent.setUpGrid()'>" +
        "</form></center>");
}
function a1() {
  if (gameOver) {
     alert("This game has finished " +
           "please click the\n" +
           "'New Game' button.");
     return;
  }
  if ((!_a1) && (!_a12)) {
     // This space is not taken...
     if (thisPlay == 0) {
        a1_val = parent.player1Gif;
        _a1 = true;
     }
     else {
        a1_val = parent.player2Gif;
        _a12 = true;
     }
     noMoves ++;
     parent.checkWinner();
  }
  else
     alert("Sorry, this space is taken!");
}
function a2() {
  if (gameOver) {
     alert("This game has finished, please " +
           "click the\n'New Game' button.");
     return;
  }
  if ((!_a2) && (!_a22)) {
     // This space is not taken...
     if (thisPlay == 0) {
```

```
                    a2_val = parent.player1Gif;
                    _a2 = true;
                }
                else {
                    a2_val = parent.player2Gif;
                    _a22 = true;
                }
                noMoves ++;
                parent.checkWinner();
            }
            else
                alert("Sorry, this space is taken!");
        }
        function a3() {
            if (gameOver) {
                alert("This game has finished, please " +
                    "click the\n'New Game' button.");
                return;
            }
            if ((!_a3) && (!_a32)) {
                // This space is not taken...
                if (thisPlay == 0) {
                    a3_val = parent.player1Gif;
                    _a3 = true;
                }
                else {
                    a3_val = parent.player2Gif;
                    _a32 = true;
                }
                noMoves ++;
                parent.checkWinner();
            }
            else
                alert("Sorry, this space is taken!");
        }
        function b1() {
            if (gameOver) {
                alert("This game has finished, please " +
                    "click the\n'New Game' button.");
                return;
            }
            if ((!_b1) && (!_b12)) {
                // This space is not taken...
                if (thisPlay == 0) {
                    b1_val = parent.player1Gif;
                    _b1 = true;
                }
                else {
```

D

```
            b1_val = parent.player2Gif;
            _b12 = true;
         }
         noMoves ++;
         parent.checkWinner();
      }
      else
         alert("Sorry, this space is taken!");
   }

   function b2() {
      if (gameOver) {
         alert("This game has finished, please " +
               "click the\n'New Game' button.");
         return;
      }
      if ((!_b2) && (!_b22)) {
         // This space is not taken...
         if (thisPlay == 0) {
            b2_val = parent.player1Gif;
            _b2 = true;
         }
         else {
            b2_val = parent.player2Gif;
            _b22 = true;
         }
         noMoves ++;
         parent.checkWinner();
      }
      else
         alert("Sorry, this space is taken!");
   }

   function b3() {
      if (gameOver) {
         alert("This game has finished, please " +
               "click the\n'New Game' button.");
         return;
      }
      if ((!_b3) && (!_b32)) {
         // This space is not taken...
         if (thisPlay == 0) {
            b3_val = parent.player1Gif;
            _b3 = true;
         }
         else {
            b3_val = parent.player2Gif;
```

```
            _b32 = true;
         }
         noMoves ++;
         parent.checkWinner();
      }
      else
         alert("Sorry, this space is taken!");
   }

   function c1() {
      if (gameOver) {
         alert("This game has finished, please " +
               "click the\n'New Game' button.");
         return;
      }
      if ((!_c1) && (!_c12)) {
         // This space is not taken...
         if (thisPlay == 0) {
            c1_val = parent.player1Gif;
            _c1 = true;
         }
         else {
            c1_val = parent.player2Gif;
            _c12 = true;
         }
         noMoves ++;
         parent.checkWinner();
      }
      else
         alert("Sorry, this space is taken!");
   }

   function c2() {
      if (gameOver) {
         alert("This game has finished, please " +
               "click the\n'New Game' button.");
         return;
      }
      if ((!_c2) && (!_c2)) {
         // This space is not taken...
         if (thisPlay == 0) {
            c2_val = parent.player1Gif;
            _c2 = true;
         }
         else {
            c2_val = parent.player2Gif;
            _c22 = true;
         }
```

D

```
      noMoves ++;
      parent.checkWinner();
   }
   else
      alert("Sorry, this space is taken!");
}

function c3() {
   if (gameOver) {
      alert("This game has finished, please " +
            "click the\n'New Game' button.");
      return;
   }
   if ((!_c3) && (!_c32)) {
      // This space is not taken...
      if (thisPlay == 0) {
         c3_val = parent.player1Gif;
         _c3 = true;
      }
      else {
         c3_val = parent.player2Gif;
         _c32 = true;
      }
      noMoves ++;
      parent.checkWinner();
   }
   else
      alert("Sorry, this space is taken!");
}

function Grid(arg1,arg2,arg3,arg4,arg5,arg6,arg7,
   arg8, arg9, msg) {
   return("<body><center>" +
         "<table border=1>" +
         "<tr align='middle'>" +
         "<td width=75 height=75>" +
         "<a href='javascript:parent.a1()'>" +
         arg1 + "</a></td>" +
         "<td width=75 height=75>" +
         "<a href='javascript:parent.a2()'>" +
         arg2 + "</a></td>" +
         "<td width=75 height=75>" +
         "<a href='javascript:parent.a3()'>" +
         arg3 + "</a></td></tr>" +
         "<tr align='middle'>" +
         "<td width=75 height=75>" +
         "<a href='javascript:parent.b1()'>" +
         arg4 + "</a></td>" +
```

```
                  "<td width=75 height=75>" +
                  "<a href='javascript:parent.b2()'>" +
                  arg5 + "</a></td>" +
                  "<td width=75 height=75>" +
                  "<a href='javascript:parent.b3()'>" +
                  arg6 + "</a></td></tr>" +
                  "<tr align='middle'>" +
                  "<td width=75 height=75>" +
                  "<a href='javascript:parent.c1()'>" +
                  arg7 + "</a></td>" +
                  "<td width=75 height=75>" +
                  "<a href='javascript:parent.c2()'>" +
                  arg8 + "</a></td>" +
                  "<td width=75 height=75>" +
                  "<a href='javascript:parent.c3()'>" +
                  arg9 + "</a></td></tr>" +
                  "</table>" +
                  msg + "<br>" +
                  "<center></body>");
      }


      function checkWinner() {
        // These are the winning permutations:
        Win1a = _a1 && _a2 && _a3;
        Win1b = _a1 && _b2 && _c3;
        Win1c = _c1 && _b2 && _a3;
        Win1d = _b1 && _b2 && _b3;
        Win1e = _c1 && _c2 && _c3;
        Win1f = _a1 && _b1 && _c1;
        Win1g = _a2 && _b2 && _c2;
        Win1h = _a3 && _b3 && _c3;
        Win2a = _a12 && _a22 && _a32;
        Win2b = _a12 && _b22 && _c32;
        Win2c = _c12 && _b22 && _a32;
        Win2d = _b12 && _b22 && _b32;
        Win2e = _c12 && _c22 && _c32;
        Win2f = _a12 && _b12 && _c12;
        Win2g = _a22 && _b22 && _c22;
        Win2h = _a32 && _b32 && _c32;

        // Update the frame; redraw the table:
        var thisMsg = (thisPlay == 0) ?
            "<b>Player 2</b>: Please select a square" :
            "<b>Player 1</b>: Please select a square";
        parent.frames[1].document.open();
        parent.frames[1].document.write(parent.Grid(a1_val,
            a2_val, a3_val, b1_val, b2_val,
            b3_val, c1_val, c2_val, c3_val,
```

D

```
                    thisMsg));
        parent.frames[1].document.close();

        // Have we now run out of squares?...
        if (noMoves >= 9) {
           gameOver = true;
           alert("Stalemate, neither player has won.")
           parent.reloadBut();
        }

        // No, so has anyone won in this game yet?...
        Win1 = (Win1a || Win1b || Win1c || Win1d ||
                Win1e || Win1f || Win1g || Win1h);
        Win2 = (Win2a || Win2b || Win2c || Win2d ||
                Win2e || Win2f || Win2g || Win2h);
        if (Win1) {
           gameOver = true;
           alert("Player 1 has won!");
           reLoadBut();
           return;
        }
        if (Win2) {
           gameOver = true;
           alert("Player 2 has won!");
           reLoadBut();
           return;
        }

        // ...not yet, so change players:
        if (thisPlay == 0)
           thisPlay = 1;
        else
           thisPlay = 0;
     }
   setUpGrid();
//-->
</script>
<frameset rows="10%,*">
<frame name="top"    src="javascript:parent.top" scrolling="no">
<frame name="bottom" src="javascript:parent.bot" scrolling="no">
</frameset>
</html>
```

Mathematical Functions

A number of miscellaneous mathematical functions can be found here.

A Number-Rounding Function

The following `roundValue()` function rounds a number to two decimal places. Numbers whose fractional part is greater than `.50` are rounded up to the next whole number. This function can be used for form-based calculations, where Navigator tends to return excessively accurate numbers. Using `roundValue()`, a number such as `14.9999995` will be returned as `15.0`. You can change the precision by altering the program accordingly.

```
<!--
  Function D-8
-->
function roundValue(val) {
  if (val == 0)
     return("0");
  var inputVal = ("" + val);
  if (inputVal.indexOf(".") == -1)
     inputVal += ".0";
  var decPart =
     inputVal.substring(0, inputVal.indexOf("."));
  var fracPart =
     parseInt(inputVal.substring(inputVal.indexOf(".")+1,
              inputVal.indexOf(".")+3));
  // Precision > 0.50 results in next largest number.
  if (parseInt(fracPart) > 50) {
     return("" + (parseInt(decPart)+1) + ".00");
  }
  else {
     fracPart = "" + Math.round(val * 100);
     newfracPart = fracPart.substring(fracPart.length-2,
                                      fracPart.length);
     return("" + decPart + "." + newfracPart);
  }
}
```

Validation Routines

These routines can be used to validate a range of values, such as form-fields or values supplied by the JavaScript `prompt()` method.

Ensuring a Value is Numeric

The `isNumber()` function returns `true` if the `data` argument is numeric, and `false` otherwise.

```
<!--
  Function D-9
-->
```

D

```
function isNumber(data) {
  var numStr="0123456789";
  var thisChar;
  var counter = 0;
  for (var i=0; i < data.length; i++)  {
      thisChar = data.substring(i, i+1);
      if (numStr.indexOf(thisChar) != -1)
          counter ++;
  }
  if (counter == data.length)
     return(true);
  else
     return(false);
}
```

Ensuring a Value is Alphabetic

The isAlpha() function returns true if a value is alphabetic, and false otherwise.

```
<!--
  Function D-10
-->
function isAlpha(data) {
  var numStr="0123456789";
  var thisChar;
  for (var i=0; i < data.length; i++)  {
      thisChar = data.substring(i, i+1);
      if (numStr.indexOf(thisChar, 0) != -1)
          return(false);
  }
  return(true);
}
```

Ensuring a String is Not Empty

The following isEmpty() function returns true when a string or form-field is empty, even when spaces have been substituted for other characters, and false in all other cases. For example, the string " " would return a true value, although " hello" would return false because not all of the characters are spaces.

```
<!--
  Function D-11
-->
function isEmpty(data) {
  for (var i=0; i < data.length; i++)  {
```

```
        if (data.substring(i, i+1) != " ")
            return(false);
        }
        return(true);
    }
}
```

Plug-in Routines

Plug-ins are applications that allow Navigator to deal with a variety of external file formats. Appendix F contains a list of plug-in applications that are available for use with Navigator 3.0.

Detecting if a Plug-in Exists for a Given File Format

The following `findPlugin()` function accepts a filename extension as an argument; it returns `true` if a plug-in application is installed that can view this file format, and `false` otherwise. See Chapter 12 for more information on plug-in applications.

```
<!--
  Function D-12
-->
function findPlugin(ext) {
  var thisExt, findExt;
  for (var n=0; n < navigator.plugins.length; n++) {
      for (var m=0; m < navigator.plugins[n].length; m++) {
          thisExt =
            navigator.plugins[n][m].description.toLowerCase();
          findExt = thisExt.substring(0, thisExt.indexOf(" "));
          if (findExt == ext)
              return(true);
      }
  }
  return(false);
}
```

D

APPENDIX E

JavaScript/Navigator URL Formats

The *URL*, or Uniform Resource Locator, is an address of a resource based on the Internet. Netscape Navigator understands a number of URL prefixes, or "service types," and these can be used accordingly within JavaScript applications.

A-Z of Uniform Resource Locators Supported by Navigator 3.0

Restrictions have been placed on some URL prefixes so that the information they produce cannot be intercepted and sent to another user, etc. Such entries are marked with the **✗** symbol:

about:✗

Syntax:

- ♦ `about:document`
- ♦ `about:cache`
- ♦ `about:global`
- ♦ `about:image-cache`
- ♦ `about:license`
- ♦ `about:authors`
- ♦ `about:security`

Description

The `about:` prefix, when used by itself, shows information about the current version of Navigator, including copyright information. A number of extensions are supported, including `license`, which shows license information, and `security`, which displays security-related information. The `about:` URL prefix cannot be used in JavaScript applications for security reasons. If, for example, you try to assign an `about:` URL to the JavaScript `location` object, an error will occur.

file:

Syntax:

- ♦ `file:///drive|/directory/filename`
- ♦ `file://hostname/directory/filename`

Description

You have two choices of syntax for the `file:` URL prefix, the first of which is used to load a local file from the user's hard-disk, and the second of which is used to connect to an FTP site (see below). The `ftp:` and `file:` URLs work similarly in this respect. When loading local files, the drive-letter, directory, and/or files must be specified. Therefore, `file:///c|/` would show a list of files that exist in the root directory of drive C, whereas `file:///c|/tmp/myfile.htm` would load the file `myfile.htm` that exists in the `c:\tmp` directory directly into Navigator.

ftp:

Syntax:

◆   `ftp://hostname`

◆   `ftp://hostname/filename`

Description

The `ftp:` URL prefix allows the user to connect to a computer on the Internet using FTP, or File Transfer Protocol. Thousands of public FTP sites exist on the Internet, and they can be used to download files such as documents, images, and programs. It is possible to connect to the root directory of an FTP server using a URL of the form `ftp://hostname`, as in `ftp://ftp10.netscape.com`. In this case, you will be logged into the computer `ftp10.netscape.com`, and you can browse that computer's file-system (all directories and files will be shown as hyperlinks, etc.). Alternatively, you can immediately download a file directly to your computer by specifying the name of the file; for example: `ftp://somehost.com/dir1/myfile.zip` would download the file `myfile.zip` from the directory `dir1` that exists on the hypothetical host computer named `somehost.com`.

gopher:

Syntax:

◆   `gopher://hostname`

◆   `gopher://hostname/filename`

Description

Gopher is an information-retrieval tool that allows users to log in to a Gopher server and then browse the system for information. All information on a Gopher server is stored in a hierarchical manner, so you navigate your way around using hyperlinks, etc. A system called 'veronica' indexes Gopher servers from all around the world, allowing global Gopher searching. Searches can be carried out locally, on a particular Gopher server, or globally (the veronica option will be offered to you on a menu). If you specify just

E

the `hostname`, you will be logged in to the root directory (or main-menu) for that server. If you know the name of a specific file you want to load, use the `filename` to take a more direct route to the desired file.

javascript:

Syntax:

◆   `javascript:expression`

Description

The `javascript:` URL prefix allows a JavaScript expression to be evaluated and displayed accordingly. If the expression equates to a literal value, the value is displayed within the browser. A new document is generated as a result of the evaluation of the expression. Any JavaScript method, object, or property can be examined in this way; for example: `javascript:10*10` would show the value `100` in the browser, because 100 is the result of 10 multiplied by 10 ('`*`' being the multiplication operator in JavaScript); likewise, `javascript:alert("Hello World!")` would display an alert box with the value "Hello World!" The `javascript:` URL prefix is useful in JavaScript applications that need to create frames—see Chapter 9 for more information.

mailbox:X

Syntax:

◆   `mailbox:`
◆   `mailbox:folderName`
◆   `mailbox:folderName?compress-folder`
◆   `mailbox:folderName?empty-trash`
◆   `mailbox:folderName?deliver-queued`

Description

The `mailbox:` URL invokes Navigator's mail-reading program and allows the user to receive and read e-mail messages. This URL prefix cannot be used in JavaScript because of e-mail security considerations. The mail in a specific folder (`folderName`) can be read if required, although messages are, by default, stored in the `Inbox` folder.

`mailto:`

Syntax:

- `mailto:`
- `mailto:username@hostname`
- `mailto:username@hostname?subject=subjectLine`
- `mailto:username@hostname?cc=ccPerson`
- `mailto:username@hostname?bcc=bccPerson`

Description

The `mailto:` URL prefix allows an e-mail message to be composed and sent to a mail-server (as specified in Navigator's *Options* menu) for delivery to a recipient located on the Internet. The simplest form of syntax is `mailto:username@hostname`. For example, you could type: `mailto:wombat@spuddy.mew.co.uk`. Subject lines and carbon-copy recipients can also be specified using the `cc` and `bcc` parts of the URL—these can also be joined together just as long as ampersands (`&`) separate each part. A question mark (`?`) must follow the `username@hostname` part of the URL. The `cc` part specifies a "carbon copy" user; i.e. this user will also receive the message. The `bcc` part specifies a "blind carbon copy" user—one who will also receive the message but not see a list of other recipients.

`news:`

Syntax:

- `news:`
- `news:groupname`
- `news://hostname/groupname`

Description

The `news:` URL allows users to connect to a USENET (USErs NETwork) news-server so they can read and participate in newsgroups. More than 15,000 such newsgroups now exist and cover just about every subject. Using `news:` by itself loads a default news-server, as specified in the *Options / Mail and News* menu within Navigator. You can specify an alternative news-server if you wish, although you must have permission to use it. Public news-servers are rare—although they do exist. You may want to search for a list of them using a search-engine like Alta Vista. For example: `news:` will load a default news-server as you have specified, and will show a list of groups that you have subscribed to, whereas

E

`news:comp.lang.javascript` would load articles in the USENET group `comp.lang.javascript` (the JavaScript programmers forum on USENET).

pop3:X

Syntax:

◆   `pop3:`

Description
POP3 (Post Office Protocol 3) is used by Navigator to collect e-mail from a POP server. This URL prefix works in the same way as `mailbox:`, which we discussed earlier, and cannot be used in JavaScript applications for security reasons.

snews:

Syntax:

◆   `snews:`
◆   `snews://hostname/groupname`
◆   `snews:groupname`

Description
The `snews:` URL prefix works in much the same way as the `news:` URL except that a "secure" channel is established for all communication. You must connect to a secure news-server when using this URL.

telnet:

Syntax:

◆   `telnet://hostname`

Description
The `telnet:` URL prefix invokes a Telnet (virtual terminal protocol) utility that allows the user to log in to a remote computer and communicate with and control that system just as if they were using it locally. The *Options / General Preferences / Helpers* menu allows users to specify a telnet application, of which there are many freeware and shareware versions available from the Internet.

tn3270:

Syntax:

♦ `tn3270://hostname`

Description

The `tn3270:` URL works in the same way as `telnet:`, although a different telnet utility can be specified. This is normally a telnet utility for connecting to IBM 3270 mainframes, which use a different screen emulation. If your telnet application supports such emulations, this URL prefix can be left unused, and you can use `telnet:` instead.

E

language=

APPENDIX F

Navigator Plug-ins

Plug-in applications allow Navigator to deal with a multitude of files, such as spreadsheets, animation, video, audio, word-processing documents, 3-D graphics, VRML, AutoCad images, vector-drawings, and a host of other proprietary file-formats.

A-Z of Plug-in Applications for Netscape Navigator

Each plug-in will arrive with its own installation program. In the following entries, the first URL shown is the main home-page for the company that has developed the plug-in. Note that you should visit the site and read the documentation to ascertain which hardware platforms and software environments are supported, etc., before downloading any software. The following icons denote each category of plug-in, for easy reference.

Graphical software, for example, graphics-file viewers, VRML browsers, etc.

Document plug-ins, for example, word-processor file viewers

Communications-related plug-ins, for example, BBS connectivity, etc.

Audio-based plug-ins, for example, real-time sound.

Acrobat Amber

A plug-in for viewing, navigating, and printing Portable Document Format (PDF) files:

♦ `http://www.adobe.com/Amber`

♦ `http://w1000.mv.us.adobe.com/Amber/amexamp.html` (sample files)

Action

Plays Motion Pictures Expert Group (MPEG) animations with synchronized sound:

♦ `http://www.open2u.com/action/action.html`

♦ `http://www.open2u.com/action/tg.html` (sample files)

Animated Widgets

Image animation plug-in:

♦ `http://www.internetconsult.com`

♦ `http://www.progtools.com` (sample files)

F

Argus Map Viewer
A geographic plug-in viewer that supports vector graphics:

◆ `http://www.argusmap.com`

◆ `http://www.argusmap.com/vwintro.htm` (sample files)

ASAP WebShow
A plug-in that views documents created by SPCs ASAP WordPower report and presentation software tool:

◆ `http://www.spco.com/asap/asapwebs.htm`

◆ `http://www.spco.com/asap/asapgall.htm` (sample files)

Astound Web Player
A plug-in that plays both Astound and Studio-M Multimedia files:

◆ `http://www.golddisk.com/awp.html`

◆ `http://www.golddisk.com/awp/demos.html` (sample files)

Carbon Copy/Net
An interesting plug-in that allows you to control by remote another PC via the Web:

◆ `http://www.microcom.com/cc/ccdnload.htm`

◆ `http://www.microcom.com/cc/ccdnload.htm` (sample files)

Chemscape Chime
A plug-in primarily for scientists that presents chemical information, such as 3-D protein models, etc.:

◆ `http://www.mdli.com/chemscape/chime/chime.html`

◆ `http://www.mdli.com/chemscape/chime/sample.html` (sample files)

CMX Viewer
A plug-in that allows Corel CDX files (vector files) to be viewed in a Web page:

◆ `http://www.corel.com`

♦ `http://www.corel.com/corelcmx/realcmx.htm` (sample files)

CoolFusion

An extensive plug-in for creating multimedia presentations, incorporating video, animation, and sound:

♦ `http://webber.iterated.com/coolfusn/download/cf-loadp.htm`

Crescendo

Sound Crescendo plays MIDI formatted sound files, for listening to audio within a Web page:

♦ `http://www.liveupdate.com/crescendo.html`

CyberSpell

A plug-in that spell checks e-mail messages sent using Netscape Navigator's e-mail interface:

♦ `http://www.inso.com/consumer/cyberspell/democybr.htm`

DWG/DFX Viewer

A plug-in that allows DWG, DFX, and SVF (vector) AutoCad files to be viewed within a Web page:

♦ `http://www.softsource.com/softsource`
♦ `http://www.softsource.com/softsource/plugins/plugins.html` (sample files)

EarthTime

A plug-in that displays the local time in eight locations around the world, all updated in real-time:

♦ http://www.starfishsoftware.com/getearth.html

EchoSpeech

A plug-in for playing high-quality compressed speech (audio):

♦ `http://www.echospeech.com/plugin.htm`
♦ `http://www.echospeech.com/speech.htm` (sample files)

Emblaze 🖥

Displays real-time (streamed) animation files:

♦ `http://geo.inter.net/Geo/technology/emblaze/`
`downloads.html`

♦ `http://www.geo.Inter.net/technology/emblaze/`
`animations.html`(sample files)

Envoy 📖

A plug-in for reading Envoy-formatted documents within a Web page:

♦ `http://www.twcorp.com/plugin.htm`

FIGleaf Inline 🖥

A plug-in for viewing multiple graphics-file formats, for example, CGM. A "lite" version is also available:

♦ `http://www.ct.ebt.com/figinline`

♦ `http://www.ct.ebt.com/figinline/demofrm.html` (sample files)

Formula One/Net 🖥

An important plug-in for viewing spreadsheet documents:

♦ `http://www.visualcomp.com/f1net/download.htm`

Fractal Image 🖥

A plug-in for viewing Fractal Image Format (FIF) files:

♦ `http://www.iterated.com/cnplugin.htm`

♦ `http://www.iterated.com/gonline.htm` (sample files)

FutureSplash 🖥

A graphical plug-in that views vector graphics and animations:

♦ `http://www.futurewave.com`

Galacticomm Worldgroup ☎

An interesting plug-in that allows Navigator to communicate with a Galacticomm-based Bulletin Board System:

♦ http://www.gcomm.com

Lotus Notes Inline

A plug-in that links Lotus Notes into Navigator. This plug-in requires Notes and the Lotus Openscape software to function:

♦ http://www.braintech.com/grpdemo.htm (sample files)

HistoryTree

An innovative plug-in that tracks your journeys on the Web, recording all URLs visited, and allowing you to revisit sites. Journeys are logged in a tree-like structure for fast navigation:

♦ http://www.smartbrowser.com

IChat

An Internet Relay Chat (IRC) plug-in that allows Web pages to include an IRC-client for global chatting:

♦ http://www.ichat.com

InterCAP InLine

A graphical plug-in that allows the viewing, magnification, panning, and animation of Computer Graphics Metafile (CGM) vector files:

♦ http://www.intercap.com/about/DownloadNow.html
♦ http://www.intercap.com (sample files)

ISYS Hindsite

A Web-tracking plug-in that saves all of the URLs you have visited within a specific time-frame. Its added bonus is saving the contents of the sites as well, rather like a glorified file cache system:.

♦ http://www.isysdev.com/hindsite.html

Jet Form

Jet Form is a form-filling plug-in that adds advanced form controls to HTML documents:

♦ http://www.jetform.com/product/web/jfwebov.html

KEYview

An extensive plug-in that can view, print, and convert between nearly 200 different file-formats:

♦ `http://www.ftp.com/mkt_info/evals/kv_dl.html`

KM's Multimedia Plug

A video viewer, mainly for playing QuickTime movies, although other formats are also supported:

♦ `ftp://ftp.wco.com/users/mcmurtri/MySoftware`

Koan

A plug-in that plays embedded audio files, which are stored in the format created by the software tool "Koan Pro." Real-time sound-playing is also supported:

♦ `http://www.sseyo.com`

Lightning Strike

A graphical plug-in for playing compressed image files (which are stored in LSs own format):

♦ `http://www.infinop.com/html/infinop.html`
♦ `http://www.infinop.com/html/comptable.html` (sample files)

Liquid Reality

A Virtual Reality Modeling Language (VRML) player. Allows VRML worlds to be explored within the Navigator browser's environment:

♦ `http://www.dimensionx.com/products/lr/index.html`

ListenUp

A sound-player for Apple's "PlainTalk" format:

♦ `http://snow.cit.cornell.edu/noon/ListenUp.html`

Live3D 🖥 🔔

A VRML viewer for Netscape Navigator. Live3-D allows 3-D VRML worlds to be viewed and explored, and incorporates animation, sound, and video effects:

♦ `home.netscape.com/comprod/products/navigator/live3d/`

♦ `download_live3d.html`

♦ `http://home.netscape.com/comprod/products/navigator/live3d/cool_worlds.html` (sample files)

Look@Me 🖥 ☎

An interesting plug-in that allows you to see and share the desktop of another person's computer remotely, via the Net:

♦ `http://collaborate.farallon.com/www/look/ldownload.html`

mBED 🖥 🔔

A popular multimedia plug-in for Navigator:

♦ `http://www.mbed.com`

Splash 🖥

A multimedia plug-in that allows animated and interactive Web pages to be constructed and viewed:

♦ `http://www.powersoft.com/media.splash/product/index.html`

♦ `http://www.powersoft.com/media.splash/action/index.html` (sample files)

MIDIPlugin 🔔

A plug-in for playing MIDI-formatted files:

♦ `http://www.planete.net/~amasson/midiplugin.html` (sample files)

MovieStar 🖥 🔔

A QuickTime file viewer that allows streamed downloads; that is, data is played as it is being read from the Net:

♦ `http://www.beingthere.com`

◆ http://130.91.39.113/product/mspi/mspi.htm (sample files)

NCompass

A plug-in for allowing Object Linking and Embedding (OLE) controls to function within Netscape Navigator:

◆ http://www.excite.sfu.ca/NCompass

◆ http://www.excite.sfu.ca/NCompass/home.html (sample files)

NetSlide 95 ⌨

An AutoCad file viewer:

◆ http://www.archserver.unige.it/caadge/ao/SOFT.HTM

Play3D ⌨

Allows for the creation and viewing of 3-D graphics and scenes within a Web page:

◆ ftp://magna.com.au/pub/users/mark_carolan/HeadsOff.html

PointPlus ⌨

Allows Microsoft PowerPoint files to be embedded and viewed within Web pages:

◆ http://www.net-scene.com

PreVU ⌨ 🔔

An MPEG motion viewer (streamed) for Netscape Navigator:

◆ http://www.intervu.com/prevu.html

QuickSilver ⌨

Allows graphics created with ABC QuickSilver and ABC Graphics Suite to be viewed within Navigator:

◆ http://www.micrografx.com/quicksilver.html

RapidTransit 🔔

An audio-based plug-in that decompresses and plays music with high compression rates. Capable of CD-quality sound:

- ♦ `http://monsterbit.com/rapidtransit/download.html`
- ♦ `http://monsterbit.com/rapidtransit` (sample files)

RealAudio 🔔

This plug-in allows you to listen to quality audio while it is being downloaded:

- ♦ `http://www.realaudio.com/products/player2.0.html`
- ♦ `http://www.realaudio.com/products/ra2.0/plugin.html` (sample files)

ShockTalk 🔔

This plug-in allows for speech recognition with a Web page. It is primarily of use for people with the ShockWave/Director plug-in (see the following entry):

- ♦ `http://www.emf.net/~dreams/Hi-Res/index.html`
- ♦ `http://www.emf.net/~dreams/Hi-Res/shocktalk/index.html` (sample files)

Shockwave/Director 💻 🔔

This well-known plug-in allows multimedia content to be viewed in Navigator. Shockwave files are created using Macromedia's Director software:

- ♦ `http://www.macromedia.com/Tools/Shockwave/index.html`
- ♦ `http://www.macromedia.com/Tools/Shockwave/Gallery/index.html` (sample files).

Shockwave/Freehand 💻

The Shockwave/Freehand plug-in allows you to view Freehand Graphic files within a Web page:

- ♦ `http://www.macromedia.com/Tools/FHShockwave`
- ♦ `http://www.macromedia.com/Tools/FHShockwave/Gallery/index.html` (sample files)

Sizzler 💻 🔔

A plug-in that allows you to view sizzler (multimedia) files within a Web page:

- ♦ `http://www.totallyhip.com`

♦ `http://www.totallyhip.com/hipstuff/5_stuff.html`
(sample files)

Speech Plug-In

An innovative plug-in allows the contents of a Web page to be read out aloud to you, and requires Apple's "Text to Speech" software to function:

♦ `http://www.albany.net/~wtudor`

Summus

A multimedia plug-in that allows the viewing of compressed graphics and video data:

♦ `http://www.summus.com`
♦ `http://www.summus.com/i_demo.htm` (sample files)

Superscape

A 3-D graphics viewer that allows interaction with VRML worlds:

♦ `http://www.superscape.com`
♦ `http://www.us.superscape.com/supercity/3d.htm` (sample files)

SVF Viewer

A plug-in for viewing Simple Vector Format (SVF) files:

♦ `http://www.softsource.com/softsource/svf/svftest.html`

"Table Of Contents"

A plug-in that is a glorified bookmark system, allowing "point-and-click" access to URLs:

♦ `http://www.InternetConsult.com`

TEC Player

A QuickTime movie-player:

♦ `http://www.tecs.com/TECPlayer_docs`

TMS ViewDirector

A plug-in that allows TIFF images to be embedded within a Web page:

♦ `http://www.voxware.com/download.htm`

♦ `http://www.voxware.com/voxmstr.htm` (sample files)

ToolVox (Audio)
A speech-player plug-in, supporting multiple audio formats and data-streaming:

♦ `http://www.voxware.com/download.htm`

♦ `http://www.voxware.com/voxmstr.htm` (sample files)

TrueSpeech
Another audio-player with streaming capabilities:

♦ `http://www.dspg.com/plugin.htm`

VDOLive
A video-player plug-in:

♦ `http://www.vdolive.com`

♦ `http://www.vdolive.com/newsite/watch` (sample files)

ViewDirector
A TIFF-format image viewer with panning, zooming, and rotation facilities, etc.:

♦ `http://www.tmsinc.com/plugin/download.htm`

♦ `http://www.tmsinc.com/plugin/sample/sample.htm` (sample files)

ViewMovie
A QuickTime movie viewer plug-in:

♦ `http://www.well.com/user/ivanski/download.html`

♦ `http://www.well.com/user/ivanski/viewmovie/viewmovie_sites.html` (sample files)

VR Scout
A VRML viewer plug-in:

♦ `http://www.chaco.com/vrscout`

♦ `http://www.chaco.com/vrml` (sample files)

VRealm 🖥
Another VRML viewer:

♦ `http://www.ids-net.com`

♦ `http://www.ids-net.com/ids/explore.html` (sample files)

WebActive 🖥
A 3-D clip-art viewer for embedding clip art within Web pages:

♦ `http://www.3d-active.com/pages/WebActive.html`

♦ `http://www.usit.net/hp/omniview/omniview.htm` (sample files)

WIRL 🖥
A VRML plug-in for Navigator:

♦ `http://www.vream.com`

♦ `http://www.vream.com/2cool.html` (sample files)

Word Viewer 📖
This plug-in allows embedded Microsoft Word documents (versions 6.0 and 7.0) to be included in a Web page:

♦ `http://www.inso.com/plug.htm`

♦ `http://www.inso.com/plugsamp.htm` (sample files)

Wurlplug 🖥
A plug-in that allows Apple QD3D (3D images) to be embedded within a Web page:

♦ `ftp://ftp.info.apple.com/Apple.Support.Area/QuickDraw3D/Test_Drive/Viewers`

language=

APPENDIX G

Navigator's HTML Color Codes

This appendix documents Navigator 3.0's HTML color codes. These codes can be used in a variety of HTML tags, as well as with JavaScript's color properties. Color codes are represented in one of two ways:

- By using a red-green-blue (#RGB) triplet that is encoded in the hexadecimal numbering system ranging from 00 to FF (0 to 255), 00 being the minimum color intensity, and FF the maximum

- By using a color code verb, e.g. "Yellow"

For example, the color blue could be represented using the hexadecimal code 0000FF (that is, no red, no green, and the maximum blue intensity), or just as the word "Blue". When using hexadecimal triplets, the hash (#) is *optional* in Netscape Navigator 2 and above (both within JavaScript and HTML).

A-Z of Color Codes

A variety of standard HTML and JavaScript-enhanced tags in Navigator 3.0 can specify color codes. The font container <font color="#rrggbb">..</font> is one such example, where rrggbb specifes the color code (use the Table G-1 to identify each RGB value). The HTML <body>..</body> container also uses a number of color-related attributes including bgcolor (background color), fgcolor (foreground color), link (hyperlink color), alink (active hyperlink color), vlink (visited hyperlink color), and text (text color).

JavaScript color properties such as document.alinkColor, document.bgColor, document.fgColor, document.linkColor, and document.vlinkColor can also make use of the color codes documented in Table G-1.

As well as RGB codes, specific color *names* can also be used within tags. For example, rather than specifying <font color="#008000">..</font> for the color green, you could use <font color="green">..</font> instead. Color names are shown in the first column of Table G-1. This table has four columns, the first of which shows the textual color name. Columns two through four show the decimal and hexadecimal representation of that color (in the format: dec/hex). The decimal values are useful to know because they can be used with JavaScript functions such as parseInt() to convert between decimal (base 10) and hexadecimal (base 16). If you are using color codes of the form #rrggbb, be sure to use the right-hand (hexadeximal) entry. So for example, if you wanted to use the color aquamarine, you could use the RGB code #7FFFD4.

Color Name	Red (dec/hex)	Green (dec/hex)	Blue (dec/hex)
aliceblue	240 / F0	248 / F8	255 / FF
antiquewhite	250 / FA	235 / EB	215 / D7
aqua	0 / 00	255 / FF	255 / FF
aquamarine	127 / 7F	255 / FF	212 / D4
azure	240 / F0	255 / FF	255 / FF
beige	245 / F5	245 / F5	220 / DC
bisque	255 / FF	228 / E4	196 / C4
black	0 / 00	0 / 00	0 / 00
blanchedalmond	255 / FF	235 / EB	205 / CD
blue	0 / 00	0 / 00	255 / FF
blueviolet	138 / 8A	43 / 2B	226 / E2
brown	165 / A5	42 / 2A	42 / 2A
burlywood	222 / DE	184 / B8	135 / 87
cadetblue	95 / 5F	158 / 9E	160 / A0
chartreuse	127 / 7F	255 / FF	0 / 00
chocolate	210 / D2	105 / 69	30 / 1E
coral	255 / FF	127 / 7F	80 / 50
cornflowerblue	100 / 64	149 / 95	237 / ED
cornsilk	255 / FF	248 / F8	220 / DC
crimson	220 / DC	20 / 14	60 / 3C
cyan	0 / 00	255 / FF	255 / FF
darkblue	0 / 00	0 / 00	139 / 8B
darkcyan	0 / 00	139 / 8B	139 / 8B
darkgoldenrod	184 / B8	134 / 86	11 / B
darkgray	169 / A9	169 / A9	169 / A9
darkgreen	0 / 00	100 / 64	0 / 00
darkkhaki	189 / BD	183 / B7	107 / 6B

Color Names and Their Code Representations **Table G-1.**

G

Color Name	Red (dec/hex)	Green (dec/hex)	Blue (dec/hex)
darkmagenta	139 / 8B	0 / 00	139 / 8B
darkolivegreen	85 / 55	107 / 6B	47 / 2F
darkorange	255 / FF	140 / 8C	0 / 00
darkorchid	153 / 99	50 / 32	20 / 14
darkred	139 / 8B	0 / 00	0 / 00
darksalmon	233 / E9	150 / 96	122 / 7A
darkseagreen	143 / 2B	188 / BC	143 / 2B
darkslateblue	72 / 48	61 / 3D	139 / 8B
darkslategray	47 / 2F	79 / 4F	79 / 4F
darkturquoise	0 / 00	20 / 14	20 / 14
darkviolet	148 / 94	0 / 00	211 / D3
deeppink	255 / FF	20 / 14	147 / 93
deepskyblue	0 / 00	191 / BF	255 / FF
dimgray	105 / 69	105 / 69	105 / 69
dodgerblue	30 / 1E	144 / 90	255 / FF
firebrick	178 / B2	34 / 22	34 / 22
floralwhite	255 / FF	250 / FA	240 / F0
forestgreen	34 / 22	139 / 8B	34 / 22
fuchsia	255 / FF	0 / 00	255 / FF
gainsboro	220 / DC	220 / DC	220 / DC
ghostwhite	248 / F8	248 / F8	255 / FF
gold	255 / FF	215 / D7	0 / 00
goldenrod	218 / DA	165 / A5	32 / 20
gray	128 / 80	128 / 80	128 / 80
green	0 / 00	128 / 80	0 / 00
greenyellow	173 / AD	255 / FF	47 / 00
honeydew	240 / F0	255 / FF	240 / F0

Color Names and Their Code Representations *(continued)*
Table G-1.

Color Name	Red (dec/hex)	Green (dec/hex)	Blue (dec/hex)
hotpink	255 / FF	105 / 69	180 / 50
indianred	20 / 14	92 / 5C	92 / 5C
indigo	75 / 4B	0 / 00	130 / 1E
ivory	255 / FF	255 / FF	240 / F0
khaki	240 / F0	230 / 1E	140 / 8C
lavender	230 / 1E	230 / 1E	250 / FA
lavenderblush	255 / FF	240 / F0	245 / F5
lawngreen	124 / 7C	252 / FC	0 / 00
lemonchiffon	255 / FF	250 / FA	20 / 14
lightblue	173 / AD	216 / D8	230 / 1E
lightcoral	240 / F0	128 / 80	128 / 80
lightcyan	224 / E0	255 / FF	255 / FF
lightgoldenrodyellow	250 / FA	250 / FA	210 / D2
lightgreen	144 / 90	238 / EE	144 / 90
lightgrey	211 / D3	211 / D3	211 / D3
lightpink	255 / FF	182 / B6	193 / C1
lightsalmon	255 / FF	160 / A0	122 / 7A
lightseagreen	32 / 20	178 / B2	170 / AA
lightskyblue	135 / 87	20 / 14	250 / FA
lightslategray	119 / 77	136 / 88	153 / 99
lightsteelblue	176 / B0	196 / C4	222 / DE
lightyellow	255 / FF	255 / FF	224 / E0
lime	0 / 00	255 / FF	0 / 00
limegreen	50 / 32	20 / 14	50 / 32
linen	250 / FA	240 / F0	230 / 1E
magenta	255 / FF	0 / 00	255 / FF
maroon	128 / 80	0 / 00	0 / 00

Color Names and Their Code Representations *(continued)*
Table G-1.

G

Color Name	Red (dec/hex)	Green (dec/hex)	Blue (dec/hex)
mediumaquamarine	102 / 66	20 / 14	170 / AA
mediumblue	0 / 00	0 / 00	20 / 14
mediumorchid	186 / BA	85 / 55	211 / D3
mediumpurple	147 / 93	112 / 70	219 / DB
mediumseagreen	60 / 3C	179 / B3	113 / 71
mediumslateblue	123 / 7B	104 / 68	238 / EE
mediumspringgreen	0 / 00	250 / FA	154 / 9A
mediumturquoise	72 / 48	20 / 14	20 / 14
mediumvioletred	199 / C7	21 / 15	133 / 85
midnightblue	25 / 19	25 / 19	112 / 70
mintcream	245 / F5	255 / FF	250 / FA
mistyrose	255 / FF	228 / E4	225 / E1
moccasin	255 / FF	228 / E4	181 / B5
navajowhite	255 / FF	222 / DE	173 / AD
navy	0 / 00	0 / 00	128 / 80
oldlace	253 / FD	245 / F5	230 / 1E
olive	128 / 80	128 / 80	0 / 00
olivedrab	107 / 6B	142 / 2A	35 / 23
orange	255 / FF	165 / A5	0 / 00
orangered	255 / FF	69 / 45	0 / 00
orchid	218 / DA	112 / 70	214 / D6
palegoldenrod	238 / EE	232 / E8	170 / AA
palegreen	152 / 98	251 / FB	152 / 98
paleturquoise	175 / AF	238 / EE	238 / EE
palevioletred	219 / DB	112 / 70	147 / 93
papayawhip	255 / FF	239 / EF	213 / D5
peachpuff	255 / FF	218 / DA	185 / B9

Color Names and Their Code Representations *(continued)*
Table G-1.

Color Name	Red (dec/hex)	Green (dec/hex)	Blue (dec/hex)
peru	20 / 14	133 / 85	63 / 3F
pink	255 / FF	192 / C0	20 / 14
plum	221 / DD	160 / A0	221 / DD
powderblue	176 / B0	224 / E0	230 / 1E
purple	128 / 80	0 / 00	128 / 80
red	255 / FF	0 / 00	0 / 00
rosybrown	188 / BC	143 / 2B	143 / 2B
royalblue	65 / 41	105 / 69	225 / E1
saddlebrown	139 / 8B	69 / 45	19 / 13
salmon	250 / FA	128 / 80	114 / 72
sandybrown	244 / F4	164 / A4	96 / 60
seagreen	46 / 2E	139 / 8B	87 / 57
seashell	255 / FF	245 / F5	238 / EE
sienna	160 / A0	82 / 52	45 / 2D
silver (default)	192 / C0	192 / C0	192 / C0
skyblue	135 / 87	20 / 14	235 / EB
slateblue	106 / 6A	90 / 5A	20 / 14
slategray	112 / 70	128 / 80	144 / 90
snow	255 / FF	250 / FA	250 / FA
springgreen	0 / 00	255 / FF	127 / 7F
steelblue	70 / 46	130 / 1E	180 / 50
tan	210 / D2	180 / 50	140 / 8C
teal	0 / 00	128 / 80	128 / 80
thistle	216 / D8	191 / BF	216 / D8
tomato	255 / FF	99 / 63	71 / 47
turquoise	64 / 40	224 / E0	20 / 14
violet	238 / EE	130 / 1E	238 / EE
wheat	245 / F5	222 / DE	179 / B3

Color Names and Their Code Representations *(continued)*
Table G-1.

G

Color Name	Red (dec/hex)	Green (dec/hex)	Blue (dec/hex)
white	255 / FF	255 / FF	255 / FF
whitesmoke	245 / F5	245 / F5	245 / F5
yellow	255 / FF	255 / FF	0 / 00
yellowgreen	154 / 9A	20 / 14	50 / 32

APPENDIX H

Navigator's Internal GIF images

This appendix documents Navigator's internal GIF images. These images are internal and cannot be rescaled using the `width` or `height` attributes of the `<img src>` tag. Internal GIFs load faster because there is no overhead in loading them from the network. They can be used as bullets, etc., within applications, or can be written out dynamically by a JavaScript application.

Gopher Icons

The gopher icons shown below are used by Netscape Navigator when you visit a `gopher://` based resource. Some of the best internal icons are found here, and are prefixed with the words "internal-gopher-".

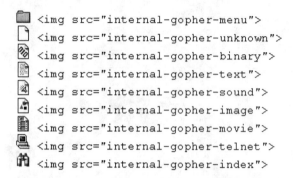

```
<img src="internal-gopher-menu">
<img src="internal-gopher-unknown">
<img src="internal-gopher-binary">
<img src="internal-gopher-text">
<img src="internal-gopher-sound">
<img src="internal-gopher-image">
<img src="internal-gopher-movie">
<img src="internal-gopher-telnet">
<img src="internal-gopher-index">
```

News Icons and Buttons

Navigator's internal news icons are used with the news-reading interface. These icons have been carried on from earlier Navigator versions, and are shown here:

```
<img src="internal-news-catchup-thread">
<img src="internal-news-rtn-to-group">
<img src="internal-news-go-to-newsrc">
<img src="internal-news-followup">
<img src="internal-news-followup-and-reply>
<img src="internal-news-post">
<img src="internal-news-catchup-group">
<img src="internal-news-subscribe">
<img src="internal-news-unsubscribe">
<img src="internal-news-reply">
<img src="internal-news-show-unread-articles">
<img src="internal-news-newsgroup">
<img src="internal-news-newsgroups">
```

Miscellaneous Icons

A number of other icons and images are supported by Navigator, a selection of which is shown here:

```
<img src="internal-icon-insecure">

<img src="internal-icon-notfound">

<img src="internal-icon-delayed">

<img src="internal-icon-baddata">

<img src="internal-icon-embed">
```

H

APPENDIX I

JavaScript Error Messages

This appendix lists each JavaScript error message and discusses possible reasons for the error. The error messages shown will appear in an alert box by Navigator when the error is encountered. Be aware that multiple errors can sometimes occur, in which case multiple alert boxes will appear. It may be best to click on the first alert box in order to focus on it so that you can see the very first error (and then work your way through each successive message).

Common Error Messages

A list of common JavaScript error messages is now given, along with an explanation for the likely cause of the error, and possible remedies.

◆ **break used outside a loop**

A for, for..in, or while loop can contain only a break statement. It may seem that you are using such a statement *outside* the body of a loop. Check to see if you have placed the break statement in the correct location. You may also want to check your loop body's "{" and "}" bracketing.

◆ **continue used outside a loop**

A continue statement can only exist within the scope of a for, for..in, or while loop. It seems that you are using such a statement *outside* the body (scope) of a loop. Check to see if you have placed the continue statement in the correct location. You may also want to check your loop body's "{" and "}" bracketing.

◆ **function defined inside a function**

Nested function definitions are not allowed in JavaScript; for example, you cannot have

```
function myFunc() {
    ...
    function anotherFunc() {
        ...
    }
}
```

◆ **function does not always return a value**

When a function returns a value it must do so upon *all* exit conditions. Ensure that you have a return statement for all exit points in the function; for example:

```
function myFunc(val) {
    if (val > 10) {
        gtTen = val;
        return(true);
    }
    else
        ltTen = val;
}
```

only returns a value when the argument val is greater than 10. Add a return statement for the else condition in such cases, because as the error

message states, the function does not *always* return a value otherwise—
"always" being the key term here.

◆ **identifier is a reserved word**
You have used a variable name that is a reserved word in the JavaScript
language; for example:

```
var null = 10;
```

would not be allowed because 'null' is a reserved word in JavaScript. All of
JavaScript's language verbs are reserved words and cannot be used for
variable or function names, etc.

◆ **illegal character**
A spurious character has crept into your application. Check the line in
question to see that you are using only normal ASCII characters and no
control characters, etc.

◆ **illegal variable initialization**
You are trying to initialize a variable with a value that is not valid, perhaps
with a misspelled function-call or method name, etc.

◆ **integer literal too large**
The numeric value specified within the statement is too large. Perhaps you
are passing a value to a standard JavaScript method that is just too big.
Check and alter accordingly.

◆ **? is not defined**
This is a common error that occurs when you are referring to a variable that
does not yet exist, for example:

```
var myVar = 100;
alert(yourVar);
```

The error will also occur with malformed numeric values—for example, with
the JavaScript statement:

```
var myVar = 10.94544Z6554;
```

because the character 'Z' has been placed within a numeric value. Navigator
assumes that 'Z' is a variable, hence the error. Beware when using the
open() and close() methods after defining variables, since if you refresh
the *current* document all variable references will be lost. Use

frameset-documents instead (see Chapter 9), and refresh specific frames only—keeping variables that you require to be persistent defined in the parent document only.

◆ **malformed floating point literal**
A floating-point number is a number with a fractional part. The floating-point value you are referring to has been malformed—check the value to see that no spurious characters have been inserted.

◆ **missing (after for**
A JavaScript `for` statement must specify a list of arguments contained within a bracketed format, for example:

```
for (var i=0; i < 100; i++) {
    ...
}
```

It looks like the first "(" has been accidentally omitted.

◆ **missing (before condition**
Check the bracketing of the `if` statement to see that a "(" bracket starts the expression.

◆ **missing (before formal parameters**
Check the bracketing of function-calls and around groups of function-parameters. A "(" bracket is probably missing.

◆ **missing) after formal parameters**
Check the bracketing of function-calls and around groups of function-parameters. A ")" bracket is probably missing.

◆ **missing) after argument list**
Check the bracketing of function-calls and around groups of function-parameters. A ")" bracket is probably missing.

◆ **missing) after condition**
Check the bracketing of the `if` statement to see that a ")" bracket ends the expression.

◆ **missing) after constructor argument list**
Check all object-constructors and object-prototypes (see Chapter 6) such as
`Array()`, etc., to ensure that they all have equal numbers of matching
brackets.

◆ **missing) after for-loop control**
Check the syntax of all `for` statements. A bracket is missing, probably after
the loop update-expression part.

◆ **missing : in conditional expression**
JavaScript supports a conditional statement of the form:

```
(condition) ? true : false
```

Ensure that the ":" exists, and that a statement is mentioned afterwards.
Nested ? statements often cause this error. Check the entire statement to see
that a true and false part is specified.

◆ **missing ; after for-loop condition**
A `for` statement must have two ";" characters: the loop assignment variable
from the loop condition, and the loop condition from the loop-update
expression, for example:

```
for (var val=0; val < 10; val++) {
    ...
}
```

It seems that the ";" character after the "val < 10" in this example (the
loop condition) is missing. Check the syntax again and ensure all semicolons
are present.

◆ **missing ; after for-loop initializer**
A `for` statement must have two ";" characters: the loop assignment variable
from the loop condition, and the loop condition from the loop-update
expression, for example:

```
for (var val=0; val < 10; val++) {
    ...
}
```

It seems that the ";" character after the "var val = 0" in this example (the
loop initializer) is missing. Check the syntax again and ensure all semicolons
are present.

◆ **missing] in index expression**
Array objects use an index variable to reference a particular array element;
for example, `parent.frames[0]` is the first frame within a
frameset-document. If the "`[`" character is omitted, or is malformed, this
error will occur, e.g. "`[0`" or "`[0[`".

◆ **missing { before function body**
A "`{`" character must start a function-body, and a "`}`" must denote the end of
the function (or the *scope* of the function). You have probably omitted the
"`{`" character by accident. Check all bracketing to see if there are equal
amounts of each bracket.

◆ **missing } after function body**
A "`{`" character must start a function-body, and a "`}`" must denote the end of
the function (or the *scope* of the function). You have probably omitted the
"`}`" character by accident. Check all bracketing to see if there are equal
amounts of each bracket.

◆ **missing } in compound statement**
This error message commonly occurs when an `if` statement invokes more
than one statement and those statements are not bracketed properly. Ensure
that the statements start with a "`{`" bracket, and end with a "`}`" bracket
accordingly.

◆ **missing formal parameter**
Check all functions to see that the parameters they accept match those in
the invoking function-call. You have omitted a parameter when the function
expects such a value.

◆ **missing function name**
It looks as if you have left out the name of a function after using the
`function` statement, for example, using an erroneous statement such as:

```
function {
  // statements...
}
```

where the name of the function has been omitted.

◆ **missing operand in expression**
An *operand* is a value such as a JavaScript variable or the result of an
expression. The expression you have formed is missing an operand. Carefully

check the syntax to see that a single value is produced by the expression that you have specified.

◆ **missing operator in expression**
This error occurs when you leave out the quotes in a string (when assigning the string to a variable, for example), or when a JavaScript operator (+, +=, etc.) has been omitted accidentally from within a statement, for example:

```
var myString = Hello" // Should be "Hello"
```

would cause this error (although perhaps this should be a syntax error), as would the following program:

```
var x = y = 10;
alert(x _ y);
```

because an underscore character ("_") has been placed in the second statement, rather than a minus (subtraction) sign ("-")—the user must have pressed the SHIFT key when typing in this character, hence the error. Since the underscore is not a valid JavaScript operator, the error is issued.

◆ **missing ; before statement**
Individual JavaScript statements can be optionally terminated by a semicolon, but only in the case where a statement occupies a single line. Some event-handler functions require semicolons to be used, for example:

```
<a href="#"
   onClick="bookMark()"
   onMouseOver="window.status='Bookmarks'; return true">
<img src="button1.gif">
</a>
```

makes the image `button1.gif` into a clickable hyperlink that when clicked invokes the user-defined function named `bookMark()`. The `onMouseOver` event-attribute has also been specified and in this case changes the Navigator status bar to the string "Bookmarks" whenever the user is hovering over the link with the mouse cursor. Because there are two statements in the `onMouseOver` attribute, a semicolon must separate the two parts of the statement. You can also join individual statement lines together by using semicolons, for example:

```
var x=100; var y=300
```

although omission of the semicolon in the line above will cause an error because two individual `var` statements have been specified.

◆ nested comment

Program comments cannot be nested within each other in JavaScript programs. A comment that can span multiple lines starts with "/*" and ends with "*/".

◆ return used outside a function

The `return` statement is used to return a value from a JavaScript function and cannot be used outside of the scope of a function, which is what you have done in this case, hence the error.

◆ syntax error

Errors in syntax account for just about every other error that has not been covered elsewhere in this appendix. A typical syntax error could occur when an operand is omitted from a statement, for example:

```
var result = 45 *;   // Should be 45 * 10 etc
```

◆ test for equality (==) mistyped as assignment (=)?

This is a common error that occurs when you use the '=' as the equality operator, when it should be "==". For example:

```
function myFunc(val) {
  if (val = 100)
     alert("Value equals 100");
}
```

would cause this error since `val` is being assigned to the value `100`, rather than being tested for equivalence. The "=" character is the assignment operator in JavaScript.

◆ unterminated comment

Comments that span multiple lines need to have a start and endpoint. This error is displayed when a comment such as "`<!--`" does not match an ending "`-->`", or vice versa, of course. Simply add an appropriate comment tag to solve this error, and make sure they match. JavaScript program comments take the form "`/* comment */`". The former are HTML comments, although both are still scanned for validity since they may both be part of the script.

◆ `unterminated string literal`

A *string literal* is a string value such as `"hello"`, where 'hello' is the literal value of that string object. If you pass a string object to a JavaScript function and leave out a quote, this error message will be displayed; for example:

```
alert("hello);
```

will cause this error. In fact, *two* errors will be generated in this case. A *"missing) after argument list"* error message will also appear since the incorrectly formatted `"hello` argument has now made Navigator think that the statement has no ending bracket. To solve the error in this statement, simply place a double quote before the last bracket. The mismatching of quotes also causes the previous errors to occur, for example, as shown in this erroneous JavaScript statement:

```
alert("hello');
```

APPENDIX J

About the Accompanying Disk

The disk that accompanies *JavaScript Essentials* contains each of the 171 JavaScript programs that are contained within the book. Each example program, described in the table below, is numbered using a code of the form `C-X`.htm, where `C` is the chapter number and `X` is an example number. For example, the file `5-1`.htm is example 1 from Chapter 5. Each of the GIF images and other supporting files can also be found on the accompanying disk.

To identify each program against the examples in the book, each JavaScript program also has a number which is the same as that explained above. This takes the form:

```
<!--
  Program 7-6
-->
```

which in this case refers to the sixth program in Chapter 7. You can match this number against the files on this disk in order to extract the required program(s), i.e. `7-6.htm`. All of the example files are stored as ASCII text and can be edited using the Windows Notepad program or another plain-text editor. The code examples from Appendix D (ready-to-use programs) can be found in the files beginning with the prefix "D-" (`D-6.htm` is example 6 from Appendix D).

Many of the source code examples are full-fledged applications in their own right, and can be loaded into Netscape Navigator 3.0 immediately. Some examples, particulary those in Appendix D, are structured as JavaScript functions, and need to be integrated into an existing application before they can be used; for example, `D-1.htm` (from Appendix D) contains the function `makeArray()` that creates a one-dimensional array structure, and resembles the following:

```
<!--
  Program D-1
-->
<script>
function makeArray(n) {
   this.length = n;
   for (var x=0; x <= n; x++) {
      this[x] = 0;
   }
   return(this);
}
</script>
```

In order to use this JavaScript function you would cut and paste the example from `D-1.htm` into your own JavaScript application. Needless to say, there are many, many JavaScript examples that will show you how to use arrays, and Appendix D explains each function in more detail. In fact, just about every source code example has a line-by-line explanation.

Many of the examples in Appendix D are "generic" functions that have been extracted from elsewhere in the book so that they can be used in their own right, i.e. they do not depend on any particular single application, and can be integrated into a range of JavaScript programs. Remember that functions, when read into Navigator, will not perform any visible operation if there is no code that actually uses the function. For example, the function in example D-1 (above) is only read into memory by Navigator and does not actually get "invoked."

Source Code Index

Chapter 1	
`1-1.htm`	Demonstration of JavaScript comments and `alert()` method
`1-2.htm`	The `<script>` tag's `src` attribute demonstrated
`1-3.htm`	Embedding scripts within comments example
`1-4.htm`	Demonstration of inline evaluation using `&{};`
`1-5.htm`	Using the `<noframes>` container for non-Navigator 2.0/3.0 users
`1-6.htm`	Example of a JavaScript error and alert box
Chapter 2	
`2-1.htm`	Example showing all of the links within the current document
`2-2.htm`	Validating a `<a name>` anchor using JavaScript
`2-3.htm`	Creating a hyperlink dynamically using `link()`
`2-4.htm`	Creating a hyperlink dynamically according to the weekday
`2-5.htm`	Invoking a JavaScript function using the `javascript:` URL and the `<a href>` tag
`2-6.htm`	Loading a frameset-document using a URL and a JavaScript variable

J

2-7.htm	Loading a frameset document using a JavaScript variable and the `javascript:` URL with the "parent" window synonym
2-8.htm	Changing link colors using the `linkColor` property
2-9.htm	Using a client-side imagemap with the `javascript:` URL to invoke an appropriate JavaScript function
Chapter 3	
3-1.htm	Dynamically generating an `<hr>` tag of increasing width
3-2.htm	Displaying objects and their properties using a dynamically created `<table>` structure
3-3.htm	Displaying a simple times-table using JavaScript
3-4.htm	Demonstration of the `break` statement to exit a `while()` loop
3-5.htm	Defining a JavaScript function to draw a horizontal rule
3-6.htm	Changing colors dynamically using `if()` statements
3-7.htm	Using the `arguments` array to display function arguments
3-8.htm	Dynamically altering document colors
3-9.htm	Dynamically altering document colors
3-10.htm	Changing background colors according to the number of seconds
3-11.htm	Using the `?` statement to change background colors dynamically
3-12.htm	Demonstration of variable scope using the `this` statement

3-13.htm	Demonstration of local variable scope within a JavaScript function
3-14.htm	Using onChange to detect when a text-field has been changed
3-15.htm	Displaying all of the elements within a form using the JavaScript elements array
Chapter 4	
4-1.htm	Displaying the date and time dynamically in a table
4-2.htm	Altering background bitmaps dynamically
4-3.htm	Example checkbox
4-4.htm	Displaying form elements using a JavaScript function
4-5.htm	Changing an images location using the src property of an image via the images array
4-6.htm	Animation of two images using the images array
4-7.htm	Extracting options from a <select> list
4-8.htm	Deteting when a textarea field has changed
Chapter 5	
5-1.htm	Validating a numeric field (range check)
5-2.htm	Example to allow field movement after entry of a specific string
5-3.htm	Selection list and onChange event handler
5-4.htm	onClick events and buttons
5-5.htm	onClick events and checkboxes
5-6.htm	Ascertaining when a checkbox is enabled (i.e. checked)

5-7.htm	Updating a text-area field when moving over a hyperlink
5-8.htm	Image animation example
5-9.htm	Validating a form and allowing/disallowing form-submission
5-10.htm	An e-mail/JavaScript form-based interface (with validation)
5-11.htm	Detecting image frames within a GIF89a animated file
5-12.htm	Example that allocates an `onClick` event to a button dynamically
Chapter 6	
6-1.htm	Adding new elements to arrays created with `Array()`
6-2.htm	Using arrays to display object and property information
6-3.htm	Using arrays to design a hexadecimal-to-decimal conversion table application
6.4.htm	A client-side database implemented using JavaScript arrays
6-5.htm	A times-table program
6-6.htm	Manipulating JavaScript objects using array structures
6-7.htm	Testing for null object values using the `typeof()` operator
6-8.htm	Creating object prototypes (a string character count program)
Chapter 7	
7-1.htm	A sample HTML form
7-2.htm	A sample text-field value display application
7-3.htm	Example of the `this` statement to pass values to a function

7-4.htm	Displaying checkbox values, v1
7-5.htm	Displaying checkbox values, v2
7-6.htm	Diaplaying radio button values
7-7.htm	Loading a URL into a frame of a frameset-document using dynamic HTML to populate a frame
7-8.htm	A sample (single) selection list
7-9.htm	A sample (single) selection list with default selection
7-10.htm	Viewing selection list items (single list)
7-11.htm	Viewing selection list items (multiple list)
7-12.htm	A sample multiple selection list
7-13.htm	Seeing which items are selected in a multiple list
7-14.htm	Dynamic movement in a selection
7-15.htm	Updating a selection list dynamically according to the day, v1
7-16.htm	Updating a selection list dynamically according to the day, v2
7-17.htm	Updating selection list option text dynamically
7-18.htm	A sample text-area field
7-19.htm	A sample button an onClick event to show the current date/time
7-20.htm	Calling a JavaScript function from a button
7-21.htm	Validating a text-field to see that all input is numeric
7-22.htm	Validating a text-field to see that no numbers are present
7-23.htm	Validating a text-field to see that it is not empty

J

7-24.htm	Allowing entry to a second field only after the first is populated with data by the user
7-25.htm	Validating a text-field to see that it is not empty, and does not contain all spaces
7-26.htm	Converting a text-field to uppercase
7-27.htm	Validating a text-field to see that it is all uppercase
Chapter 8	
8-1.htm	Opening a window and loading a URL from a JavaScript variable
8-2.htm	Creating a window by pressing a form button
8-3.htm	Manipulating form values in different windows
8-4.htm	Using multiple windows to show product information
8-5.htm	Focusing child and parent windows
8-6.htm	Toggling the focus/open function on a window
8-7.htm	Closing a window
8-8.htm	Example window-opening function for use in later examples
8-9.htm	Toggle open/close function on a window using a single button
8-10.htm	Creating and validating a window (seeing if the window exists)
Chapter 9	
9-1.htm	Example frameset-document
9-2.htm	Row- and column-based nested frame example
9-3.htm	Two-columned frameset example
9-4.htm	Keeping a persistent function within a parent frameset-document

9-5.htm	Loading frames with data from JavaScript variables using the `javascript:` URL
9-6.htm	Generating a frameset-document from a nonframed HTML document
9-7.htm	Using the `<noframes>` container tag to warn users that they need a frame-compatible browser to read frameset-based pages
9-8.htm	Checking browser versions using the navigator object
9-9.htm	Invoking a search-engine using JavaScript and frame documents
9-10.htm	Creating a frame within a frame (nested frames)
9-11.htm	Nested frames and URL loading example
9-12.htm	Two-rowed frameset example
9-13.htm	Two-rowed frameset example
9-14.htm	An example USENET group interface using frames
9-15.htm	Page navigation using frames
Chapter 10	
10-1.htm	Alarm-call timeout program example
10-2.htm	A real-time clock displayed within a text-field
10-3.htm	A real-time clock displayed using GIF digits (frameset)
10-4.htm	Updating messages periodically within a frameset-document
10-5.htm	Example of a scrolling status bar messages using a time-out
10-6.htm	Example of a scrolling status bar message in a text field

J

10-7.htm	Animation of a GIF graphic using a timeout event
10-8.htm	Animation during document loading
Chapter 11	
JavaToJs2.htm	Sending Java variables to JavaScript
JsToJava.htm	Sending JavaScript variables to Java
Chapter 12	
12-1.htm	Displaying plug-in names
12-2.htm	Displaying plug-in names, sufixes, and MIME details in a table
12-3.htm	Showing Navigator's MIME details via the mimeTypes property
12-4.htm	Detecting a specific plug-in using JavaScript
12-5.htm	Detecting a plug-in and generating an <embed> tag
Chapter 13	
13-1.htm	A cookie-based hit-counter program implemented in JavaScript

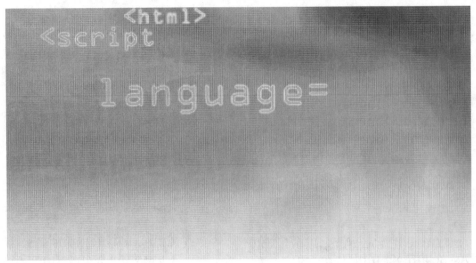

Index

E

F

O

P

Q

R

S

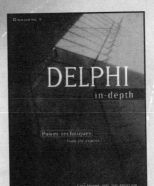

FUTURE CLASSICS FROM

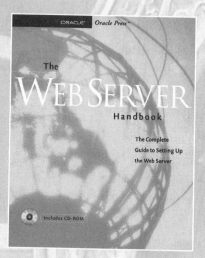

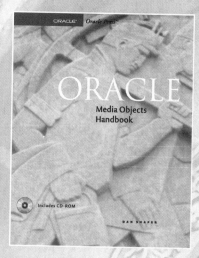

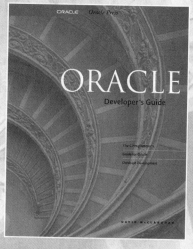

THE WEB SERVER HANDBOOK

by Cynthia Chin-Lee and Comet

Learn how to set up and maintain a dynamic and effective Web site with this comprehensive guide that focuses on Oracle's new Web solutions.

ISBN: 0-07-882215-7
Price: $39.95 U.S.A.
Includes One CD-ROM

ORACLE MEDIA OBJECTS HANDBOOK

by Dan Shafer

The power, flexibility, and ease of Oracle Media Objects (the cross-platform multimedia authoring tools) are within your reach with this definitive handbook.

ISBN: 0-07-882214-9
Price: $39.95 U.S.A.
Includes One CD-ROM

ORACLE DEVELOPER'S GUIDE

by David McClanahan

Loaded with code for common tasks, developers will find all the information they need to create applications and build a fast, powerful, and secure Oracle database.

ISBN: 0-07-882087-1
Price: $34.95 U.S.A.

ORACLE: THE COMPLETE REFERENCE

Third Edition

by George Koch and Kevin Loney

ISBN: 0-07-882097-9
Price: $34.95 U.S.A.

ORACLE DBA HANDBOOK

by Kevin Loney

ISBN: 0-07-881182-1
Price: $34.95 U.S.A.

ORACLE: A BEGINNER'S GUIDE

by Michael Abbey and Michael J. Corey

ISBN: 0-07-882122-3
Price: $29.95 U.S.A.

TUNING ORACLE

by Michael J. Corey, Michael Abbey, and Daniel J. Dechichio, Jr.

ISBN: 0-07-881181-3
Price: $29.95 U.S.A.

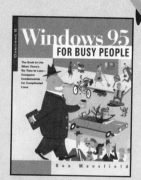

DIGITAL DESIGN
FOR THE
21ST CENTURY

You can count on Osborne/McGraw-Hill and its expert authors to bring you the inside scoop on digital design, production, and the best-selling graphics software.

Digital Images: A Practical Guide
by Adele Droblas Greenberg
and Seth Greenberg
$26.95 U.S.A.
ISBN 0-07-882113-4

Scanning the Professional Way
by Sybil Ihrig and Emil Ihrig
$21.95 U.S.A.
ISBN 0-07-882145-2

Preparing Digital Images for Print
by Sybil Ihrig and Emil Ihrig
$21.95 U.S.A.
ISBN 0-07-882146-0

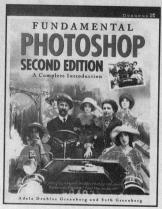

**Fundamental Photoshop:
A Complete Introduction,
Second Edition**
by Adele Droblas Greenberg
and Seth Greenberg
$29.95 U.S.A.
ISBN 0-07-882093-6

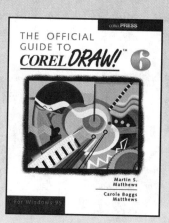

**The Official Guide to
CorelDRAW!™6 for Windows 95**
by Martin S. Matthews and Carole Boggs Matthews
$34.95 U.S.A.
ISBN 0-07-882168-1

**The Official Guide to Corel
PHOTO-PAINT 6**
by David Huss
$34.95 U.S.A.
ISBN 0-07-882207-6

ORDER BOOKS DIRECTLY FROM OSBORNE/McGRAW-HILL

For a complete catalog of Osborne's books, call 510-549-6600 or write to us at 2600 Tenth Street, Berkeley, CA 94710

Call Toll-Free, *24 hours a day, 7 days a week, in the U.S.A.*
U.S.A.: 1-800-262-4729   *Canada:* **1-800-565-5758**

Mail *in the U.S.A. to:*
McGraw-Hill, Inc.
Customer Service Dept.
P.O. Box 182607
Columbus, OH 43218-2607

Canada
McGraw-Hill Ryerson
Customer Service
300 Water Street
Whitby, Ontario L1N 9B6

Fax *in the U.S.A. to:*
1-614-759-3644

Canada
1-800-463-5885
Canada
orders@mcgrawhill.ca

SHIP TO:

Name _____

Company _____

Address _____

City / State / Zip _____

Daytime Telephone *(We'll contact you if there's a question about your order.)*

ISBN #	BOOK TITLE	Quantity	Price	Total
0-07-88				
0-07-88				
0-07-88				
0-07-88				
0-07-88				
0-07088				
0-07-88				
0-07-88				
0-07-88				
0-07-88				
0-07-88				
0-07-88				
0-07-88				
0-07-88				

Shipping & Handling Charge from Chart Below

Subtotal

Please Add Applicable State & Local Sales Tax

TOTAL

Shipping & Handling Charges

Order Amount	U.S.	Outside U.S.
$15.00 - $24.99	$4.00	$6.00
$25.00 - $49.99	$5.00	$7.00
$50.00 - $74.99	$6.00	$8.00
$75.00 - and up	$7.00	$9.00
$100.00 - and up	$8.00	$10.00

Occasionally we allow other selected companies to use our mailing list. If you would prefer that we not include you in these extra mailings, please check here: ❑

METHOD OF PAYMENT

❑ Check or money order enclosed (payable to Osborne/McGraw-Hill)

❑ AMERICAN EXPRESS   ❑ DISCOVER   ❑ MasterCard   ❑ VISA

Account No. ⬚⬚⬚⬚⬚⬚⬚⬚⬚⬚⬚⬚⬚⬚⬚⬚

Expiration Date _____

Signature _____

In a hurry? Call with your order anytime, day or night, or visit your local bookstore.

Thank you for your order

Code BC640SL

Copyright Statement

This software is protected by both United States copyright law and international copyright treaty provision. Except as noted in the contents of the disk, you must treat this software just like a book. However, you may copy it into a computer to be used and you may make archival copies of the software for the sole purpose of backing up the software and protecting your investment from loss. By saying, "just like a book," Osborne/McGraw-Hill means, for example, that this software may be used by any number of people and may be freely moved from one computer location to another, so long as there is no possibility of its being used at one location or on one computer while it is being used at another. Just as a book cannot be read by two different people in two different places at the same time, neither can the software be used by two different people in two different places at the same time.

WARNING: BEFORE OPENING THE DISK PACKAGE, CAREFULLY READ THE TERMS AND CONDITIONS OF THE FOLLOWING LIMITED DISK WARRANTY.

Limited Warranty

Osborne/McGraw-Hill warrants the physical disk enclosed herein to be free of defects in materials and workmanship for a period of sixty days from the purchase date. If the disk included in your book has defects in materials or workmanship, please call McGraw-Hill at 1-800-217-0059, 9am to 5pm, Monday through Friday, Eastern Standard Time, and McGraw-Hill will replace the defective disk.

The entire and exclusive liability and remedy for breach of this Limited Warranty shall be limited to replacement of the defective disk, and shall not include or extend to any claim for or right to cover any other damages, including but not limited to, loss of profit, data, or use of the software, or special incidental, or consequential damages or other similar claims, even if Osborne/McGraw-Hill has been specifically advised of the possibility of such damages. In no event will Osborne/McGraw-Hill's liability for any damages to you or any other person ever exceed the lower of the suggested list price or actual price paid for the license to use the software, regardless of any form of the claim.

OSBORNE, A DIVISION OF THE McGRAW-HILL COMPANIES, INC., SPECIFICALLY DISCLAIMS ALL OTHER WARRANTIES, EXPRESS OR IMPLIED, INCLUDING BUT NOT LIMITED TO, ANY IMPLIED WARRANTY OF MERCHANTABILITY OR FITNESS FOR A PARTICULAR PURPOSE. Specifically, Osborne/McGraw-Hill makes no representation or warranty that the software is fit for any particular purpose, and any implied warranty of merchantability is limited to the sixty-day duration of the Limited Warranty covering the physical disk only (and not the software), and is otherwise expressly and specifically disclaimed.

This limited warranty gives you specific legal rights; you may have others which may vary from state to state. Some states do not allow the exclusion of incidental or consequential damages, or the limitation on how long an implied warranty lasts, so some of the above may not apply to you.

This agreement constitutes the entire agreement between the parties relating to use of the Product. The terms of any purchase order shall have no effect on the terms of this Agreement. Failure of Osborne/McGraw-Hill to insist at any time on strict compliance with this Agreement shall not constitute a waiver of any rights under this Agreement. This Agreement shall be construed and governed in accordance with the laws of New York. If any provision of this Agreement is held to be contrary to law, that provision will be enforced to the maximum extent permissible, and the remaining provisions will remain in force and effect.

NO TECHNICAL SUPPORT IS PROVIDED WITH THIS DISK BY OSBORNE/MCGRAW-HILL. PLEASE FOLLOW THE DIRECTIONS IN THE README FILE ON THE DISK AND IN APPENDIX J.

Source Code for *JavaScript Essentials*

The source code examples for *JavaScript Essentials* can be found on this disk. Each example is numbered using a code of the form,

```
C-X.htm
```

where *C* is the chapter number and *X* is an example number. For instance, `5-1.htm` is Example 1 from Chapter 5. All of the GIF images and other examples can also be found on the accompanying disk. Each program in the book has a unique number, and you can match this number against the files on this disk in order to extract the required program(s). All files are stored as ASCII, and can be edited using Windows Notepad, etc.

- ♦ The code examples from Appendix D (ready-to-use programs) can be found in the files beginning with the prefix "D-" (`D-6.htm` is Example 6 from Appendix D).

- ♦ See Appendix J for more information on the contents of the disk, and to review an index to the source code.

Technical Support

If you have a JavaScript-related question or other query, please e-mail it to:

question@spuddy.mew.co.uk

For JavaScript and HTML information, drop by "The Essential Internet Home Page" located at the following URLs:

```
http://www.mcgraw-hill.co.uk/JJM/index.html
```

```
http://www.gold.net/users/ag17/index.html
```

Details of other Osborne titles can be found at

```
http://www.osborne.com
```

Happy scripting,

Jason Manger